Executing the Rosenbergs

Executing
the Rosenbergs

Death and Diplomacy in a Cold War World

LORI CLUNE

OXFORD
UNIVERSITY PRESS

OXFORD
UNIVERSITY PRESS

Oxford University Press is a department of the University of Oxford. It furthers
the University's objective of excellence in research, scholarship, and education
by publishing worldwide. Oxford is a registered trade mark of Oxford University
Press in the UK and certain other countries.

Published in the United States of America by Oxford University Press
198 Madison Avenue, New York, NY 10016, United States of America.

Library of Congress Cataloging-in-Publication Data
Names: Clune, Lori, author.
Title: Executing the Rosenbergs : death and diplomacy in a Cold War world / Lori Clune.
Description: New York : Oxford University Press, 2016. | Includes
bibliographical references and index.
Identifiers: LCCN 2015040550 | ISBN 978–0–19–026588–5 (hardback)
Subjects: LCSH: Rosenberg, Julius, 1918–1953—Trials, litigation, etc. |
Rosenberg, Ethel, 1915–1953—Trials, litigation, etc. | Trials
(Espionage)—New York (State)—New York. | Trials (Conspiracy)—New York
(State)—New York. | United States—History—1945-1953. | BISAC: HISTORY /
United States / 20th Century.
Classification: LCC KF224.R6 C58 2016 | DDC 345.73/0231—dc23 LC record available at
http://lccn.loc.gov/2015040550

Portions of Chapters 3 and 4 have appeared in a previously published form in
"Great Importance World-Wide: Presidential Decision-Making and the Executions of
Julius and Ethel Rosenberg," *American Communist History* 10, no. 3 (2011): 263–284,
http://www.tandfonline.com/doi/abs/10.1080/14743892.2011.631822.

1 3 5 7 9 8 6 4 2
Printed by Sheridan, USA

To the memory of Anthony Salvatore Scimeca

CONTENTS

PREFACE

My research into the case of Julius and Ethel Rosenberg began as a minor detour. I was writing—or thought I was writing—a book about international perception of various high-profile Cold War security cases. Singer Paul Robeson, actor Charlie Chaplin, Senator Joseph McCarthy, atomic scientist J. Robert Oppenheimer: they were the main subjects of my investigations. It was their cases that led me to the State Department archives when I discovered the perplexing case of the missing Name Cards.

Whenever an American diplomat abroad reports back to Washington, D.C., the State Department keeps a record of the communication. In the 1950s, when a Foreign Service officer stationed overseas wrote to the State Department in Washington, officials labeled and catalogued the correspondence and created a Name Card for anyone referenced in the message. Though sometimes problematic in terms of objectivity and translation accuracy, these diplomatic communications included foreign policy considerations and sensitivities that were carefully considered back in Washington.[1]

Diplomats sent dispatches from their posts to alert Washington of issues and controversies, often asking for clarification or guidance, and occasionally offering policy suggestions. The resulting Name Card Index consists of hundreds of boxes packed with thousands of tissue-thin pieces of three-by-five paper. Each of these "cards" contains cross-referenced document numbers and is alphabetized under the last name of everyone mentioned in the communication. This index is indispensable for researchers delving into State Department Cold War documents.

For example, in the State Department Name Card Index for 1950–1954, located in National Archives II in College Park, Maryland, there are more than fifty Name Cards for Senator Joseph McCarthy.[2] That means that diplomats sent at least fifty telegrams or memos to Washington, each documenting international reaction to the senator and his anti-Communist tactics. The immigration case of Charlie Chaplin garnered international attention, prompting a handful of Name Cards. When the State Department rescinded J. Robert Oppenheimer's security clearance, a half a dozen Name Cards resulted. Paul Robeson and his suspended passport generated about twenty Name Cards.

The case of Julius and Ethel Rosenberg had attracted even more international attention than those of Chaplin and Robeson. FBI agents arrested thirty-two-year-old Julius Rosenberg in New York City in 1950 and officially charged him with conspiracy under the Espionage Act of 1917. Specifically, officials accused Julius of using his military spy ring to pass the secret of the atomic bomb to the Soviet Union. A few weeks later, agents arrested his wife, Ethel. The Communist Party members claimed their innocence and refused to name names; they were convicted and sentenced to death. Appeals and protests lasted more than two years before their grisly executions in 1953 made orphans of their two young sons. In 2008, Rosenberg codefendant Morton Sobell (who had served eighteen years in prison) admitted that he and Julius had indeed passed military secrets to the Soviet Union.[3] FBI Director J. Edgar Hoover went so far as to claim the Julius and Ethel Rosenberg affair was the "crime of the century."[4]

As I continued my research, I decided to look at the State Department documents on the international response to the Rosenberg case. Historians had told small pieces of the overseas reaction, but I was hoping there was more.[5] I was confident that diplomatic officials stationed overseas wrote at least a handful of telegrams concerning the Rosenberg case. So I looked for Julius and Ethel's Name Cards. There were none.

As I thumbed through the Name Card Index for 1950–1954, I discovered it jumped from "Rosenberg, Bertha" to "Rosenberg, Ludwig."[6] I pulled the box for 1955–1959, thinking interest remained in the years following the executions. Still there was nothing. Surprised, I asked College Park archivist Edward Barnes what he thought had happened. He was perplexed, saying he had never seen anything like this before. If the Cards existed, he explained, the State Department could have removed them before the boxes were shipped to the archive or after being housed with the National Archives. But he believed neither of these possibilities likely. State Department archivist David Pfeiffer, also stumped, agreed to keep looking.[7]

Historians frequently cite one particular document describing foreign protest over the executions: Ambassador to France C. Douglas Dillon's May 1953 telegram to Secretary of State John Foster Dulles. Since Secretary Dulles forwarded this cable to the White House, a copy can be found in the Eisenhower Library in Abilene, Kansas.[8] Ambassador Dillon wrote of the "long term damage" he believed the "execution of the Rosenbergs would do to foreign opinion of the U.S. and of our whole democratic process."[9] Yet the State Department Name Card Index shows the government did not receive any evidence of international

Map 1 World Protest Map—Embassies, Consulates, and Legations that Documented Rosenberg Case Protest to the State Department, 1952–1954. Courtesy of Ben Emerzian.

protest, not even this Dillon telegram. How could this be? And if more diplomatic cables did exist, how could they be found without Name Cards? It was like trying to find buried treasure without a map.[10]

A few weeks after my visit to the National Archives in College Park, archivist David Pfeiffer wrote to say that after conducting additional searches in areas where the documents could have been, he had located two boxes. He thought it looked "like very good material," but the boxes had not been referenced in the Name Card Index and had never been seen before.[11] I was excited but cautious; I knew that two boxes could mean just a few files and only a handful of documents. Stuck in California at the start of a semester of teaching, I asked my Maryland-based sister if she would consider spending an hour or so taking digital photos of the documents in College Park. She graciously agreed. An hour turned into fifteen, and as the deluge of digital documents flooded my inbox, I knew David Pfeiffer had found the treasure chest full of gold. More than nine hundred gold pieces, actually.

These boxes contain newly unearthed documents from more than eighty cities in forty-eight countries around the world: newspaper clippings, editorial comments, petitions, and placards, all attached to detailed correspondence from embassies, consulates, and legations, spanning 1952 to 1954. They show that protests extended from Argentina to Australia, from Iceland to India, and from Switzerland to South Africa (Map 1). These documents prove that the May 1953 Dillon memo was far from unique; on nearly a dozen separate occasions the American ambassador to France himself wrote to complain about the government's handling of the Rosenberg case.

We may never know why the State Department hid these sources. A handful of officials declassified most of the documents in late 1973.[12] Did these individuals know that the Name Cards were missing, or did they even remove them themselves? Whoever was responsible decided in this case that the need for secrecy trumped any desire for government transparency. In pulling the Name Cards they buried the documents, making them all but impossible for archivists to find and historians to use.

This gift—a cache of unseen and unused documents—prompted a wholesale rethinking of my research. This is the resulting project. I am confident future historians will further mine these sources and find gems. They fuel the narrative of the Rosenberg case as a pivotal and transnational Cold War event. Telling the story without including global protest is akin to solving just one face of a Rubik's Cube. It only looks complete from one angle.

ACKNOWLEDGMENTS

This project came to fruition due to the support and wisdom of many kind individuals. I owe a great deal to David Pfeiffer at the National Archives in College Park, Maryland for using his "very educated guess" on an indefatigable hunt to track the untrackable Rosenberg State Department documents. I am indebted to wonderful and knowledgeable people at the Eisenhower Library in Abilene, Kansas (particularly Valoise Armstrong); the Truman Library in Independence, Missouri (Sam Rushay and the late Liz Safly); Jan Adamczyk of the Slavic Reference Service at the University of Illinois at Urbana-Champaign; the Reference Department at the Jagiellonian Library in Krakow, Poland; the scholars at the State Department Office of the Historians; Andrew David at Boston University; and fabulous Fresno State librarians Carol Doyle and Chris Langer. I am grateful to anonymous readers for their insightful and thought-provoking comments on the manuscript, and to Mike Meeropol for his generosity in both time and insights. Oxford University Press provided the perfect home for this work and the remarkable Susan Ferber, with her sure hand and enthusiastic support, significantly improved the manuscript. Thanks also to Maya Bringe, Anne Sanow, Alana Podolsky, and Bob Schwarz.

I am thankful for Fresno-based students and teachers who shared their enthusiasm for this project, particularly the folks at Literatures, Arts, and Cultures of the Americas (LACA); the Jewish Studies Association; TAH teachers; and Smittcamp Honors College, HIST 100W, and graduate students, especially Edward Machain II, Jeff Moosios, Michael Owens, Samantha Peel, and Khou Vang. Many thanks to Stephen Muir Bohigian, Olen Budke, Kim Davidson, Luke Fleeman Martinez, Alicia Wolfe, and Emily Wolfe for research assistance; Angelique Duvet-Tovar for careful translations; and Vernon Creviston, Ben Emerzian, Zac Emerzian, Tony Petersen, and Dalton Runberg for terrific editing advice.

I am fortunate to be at California State University, Fresno, where Dean Luz Gonzalez and the College of Social Sciences provided me with course releases, research funding, a sabbatical, and much encouragement. Interim dean and former department chair Michelle DenBeste provided unfailing guidance and support, and former chair William Skuban encouraged me from the beginning and remained consistently enthusiastic. I am indebted to wonderful colleagues, gifted scholars, talented writers, and dear friends who graciously took special interest in this project, particularly: Kimberly and Mark Arvanigian, Kyle Behen, Lisa Cady Bennett, Dan Cady, Honora Chapman, Karen Clark, Sara Conboy, Kevin Emerzian, Annabella España-Nájera, Alex Espinoza, Jayne Fanelli, John Farrell, Jill Fields, David Goldhill, Cristina Herrera, Sandra, Kurt, Kassandra, and Shoji Hishida, Tom Holyoke, Brad Jones, Flo Cheung Jones, Callie Johnston, Melissa Jordine, Sue "Bubbe" Kaufman, Ethan Kytle, Karen Lentz, Maria-Aparecida Lopes, Maritere López, Mike Lukens, Gemma McLintock, Bernadette Muscat, Janice Peterson, DeAnna Reese, Blain Roberts, Malik Simba, Robin Sischo, Beth Slutsky, Anna Vallis, and Fred Vermote.

At SHAFR conferences I found the generous support of amazing historians, particularly Andrew David, Mary Dudziak, Brandon Gauthier, Andy Johns, Kimber Quinney, Katie Sibley, and Kathryn Statler. Thanks to Phillip Deery who reached out from Melbourne to generously share his research on Australia. This work also benefitted greatly from the New Narratives of the Cold War conference in 2014, where, nestled in Switzerland at the University of Lausanne, I explored the Cold War with scholars including Andreas Agocs, Rachel Applebaum, Ruramisai Charumbira, K. A. Cuordileone, Barbara Falk, Maureen Fielding, Isabella Ginor, Grace Huxford, David Johnson, Iona Luca, Alan Nadel, Christopher O'Brien, Anca Parvulescu, Gideon Remez, and our gracious host, Agnieszka Soltysik.

At the University of California, Davis I am grateful to the History Department for research funding through the Marchand Research Grant and the Reed-Smith Research Grant; to Alan Taylor for providing support and wisdom, and forgiving me for being a Mets fan; to my Davis cohort for kindly enduring the early dissertation phase of this research; to Sally McKee for patiently nurturing this project in its infancy; to Lorena Oropeza for offering enthusiastic criticism; and to Ari Kelman for providing indispensable guidance and remaining intrigued by the "fetching forest" as it grew from dissertation to manuscript. Kathryn Olmsted embodies all that a great adviser should be, and remains encouraging and spot-on brilliant. Kathy understood this work from its embryonic stage and provided the ideal support to bring it to completion. While errors are mine alone, any possible contribution is due largely to her.

I am thankful for my supportive and loving family, particularly my mother Monica, late father Leonard, Aunt Terry, and cousins Rita, Val, and Dave. My sister Kathy became an unpaid emergency research assistant and eagerly devoted dozens of hours to deliver hundreds of documents to her little sister. I can never repay her for her love and support. Link and Nessy—loving, crazy, felines— provided delightful distraction. Zoe was the best writing buddy ever and we still miss our joyful little pug.

My extraordinary sons, Ben and Zac, helped me stay grounded and relatively sane, and showed remarkable patience when I had just one more Rosenberg story to share. As they developed into gifted writers, they graciously proofed and edited. They grew up with this case, and I accept full responsibility for any psychological damage that has caused. I continue to learn so much from them (well beyond video games, comic books, and Pokémon) and am bursting with pride at the young men they have become.

I dedicate this work to the memory of my grandfather, Anthony Salvatore Scimeca, who dreamed of watching his grandchildren be the first in the family to go to college. Grandpa Tony worked as an organizer for the United Shoe Workers of America, and ran for assemblyman from Brooklyn in 1944 on the American Labor Party ticket. According to the FBI, he was an active member of the East New York Club of the Communist Party as of March 1944, but his "last known subversive activity occurred in 1950," and he was openly anti-Communist by 1952.[1] His opinion on the Rosenberg case is the one I wish I had.

Executing the Rosenbergs

Introduction

Friday, June 19, 1953
Sing Sing Prison, Ossining, New York

The room smelled faintly of ammonia, and the dark oak seat was still warm. A little after eight o'clock on a muggy summer night, prison officials carefully strapped the woman into the electric chair. The prison rabbi had stated that her husband was dead, killed by the same chair just minutes before. If she offered the name of any spy, the rabbi urged, she could save her life for her children. "No, I have no names to give," the woman calmly replied. "I'm innocent. I'm prepared to die."[1]

The woman could not have known that at that moment, in London, protesters were begging Prime Minister Winston Churchill to call the American president and demand clemency for the condemned couple; that tens of thousands of Parisians were demonstrating in the Place de la Concorde and one had already been shot; that protesters throughout Europe, Asia, Africa, and the Americas—in more than eighty cities around the world—were demonstrating on her behalf. And she never knew that her eldest son, Michael, had been watching a baseball game on television when a news bulletin interrupted the broadcast and announced his parents would die that night.

The thirty-seven-year-old mother sat silently as guards attached electrodes and dropped a leather mask over her face. The chair designed for larger frames dwarfed the petite woman.[2] After the electricity surged through her body—the same voltage and duration used to kill her husband—prison doctors placed the stethoscope on the thin green fabric covering her chest. They looked at each other, dumbfounded. Her heart was still beating.

Prison officials tightened the leather straps and applied additional electricity, conjuring "a ghastly plume of smoke" that sprang from her masked head.[3] A guard in the tower above the prison's front gate crossed his arms before the waiting crowd, then "spread them out like an umpire signaling a player safe at home."[4] More than two years after being convicted of conspiracy to commit espionage, Julius and Ethel Rosenberg were dead.

Before the Rosenberg execution, the U.S. government had tried to win a pro-paganda victory by crafting a narrative of this Cold War case. The definitive guilt or innocence of the couple was not the issue for administration officials. As in any good advertising campaign, it was not the truth, but the perception of reality that was important. The federal government was selling the guilt of two atomic spies and the superiority of the American judicial system. As protests broke out around the world, it became clear that the battle had been lost.

The far-reaching conflict between the United States and the Soviet Union known as the Cold War dominated American domestic and foreign policy during the second half of the twentieth century.[5] Communist countries were determined to spread their philosophy throughout the world. Nations that embraced democracy, or at least anti-Communism, were equally committed to slowing, stopping, or pushing back the encroachment of Communism in this zero-sum game. To many Americans, Communism was a threat to democracy, capitalism, religious freedom, and "the American way of life."

With the world war still a vivid memory Americans continued to feel vulnerable. Architects of U.S. foreign policy—both Democrat and Republican—understood this and made national security their primary responsibility. They assured Americans they would protect U.S. values, "deter aggression and eventually secure peace."[6]

During the Cold War, Americans believed that the primary threat was world domination at the hands of the Communists.[7] Politicians, even liberals, would reinvent themselves as tough, manly, aggressive Cold Warriors to stand up to the threat of Stalinism.[8] Both Democratic President Harry S. Truman and Republican President Dwight D. Eisenhower pledged to keep the United States strong and tough against the Communist menace. They were convinced that timidity and weakness directly threatened national security. Truman and Eisenhower also emphasized the importance of religious faith, America's democratic government, and the country's struggle against atheistic Communism.

Representatives such as Senator Joseph McCarthy criticized foreign policy that was "weak" and "soft" because it left Americans vulnerable overseas.[9] Aggressive anti-Communist rhetoric grew to also include accusations of Communist infiltration within the United States, as the Cold War came to influence domestic politics.[10] Critics labeled liberals who were sympathetic to Red Communists as "pink" and increasingly accused them of being soft on Communism and effeminate New Dealers.[11] Domestic pressures and the alleged moral decline of the United States in the postwar years prompted many Americans to fear the country was ripe for a Communist revolution.[12] A weak stand on the Communist threat quickly became a political liability for any early Cold War politician. Democrats were particularly vulnerable to the pink attack, as being soft on Communism became an effective political weapon. Truman made decisions about intervention in Korea and development of increasingly deadly atomic weapons based on pressure to shed the image of weak New Deal liberalism and assert himself as a masculine Cold Warrior. Even Republican Eisenhower was vulnerable, and the intense political climate formed the foundation for much of his presidential decision-making.[13] Topping the list of threats to U.S. national security were American citizens who switched sides and spied to aid the enemy.

Much more is now known about Soviet espionage in the United States than in the 1950s. More than five hundred Americans—most from the Communist Party of the United States (CPUSA), along with a smattering of fellow travelers who supported much of the Communist platform—spied for the Soviet Union in the 1930s and 1940s. They were part of a network that infiltrated the U.S. government and the industrial companies with whom the federal agencies partnered.[14] And indeed, the spies forwarded sensitive military, technical, political, and counterintelligence information to Moscow.[15]

Three different sources provide this information: high-level defectors or spies who turned against the Soviets, Venona transcripts, and KGB files.[16] The defectors included Whittaker Chambers, an American writer, Soviet spy, and Alger Hiss informant; Elizabeth Bentley, a former American spy handler for the Soviets; and Igor Gouzenko, a Soviet cipher clerk and defector.[17] These informants provided the FBI with information that linked spies to codenames and reconstituted numerous spy rings.

Fearing the Soviets might seek a separate peace with the Nazis, in early 1943 U.S. government officials ordered the Signal Intelligence Service (predecessor of the National Security Agency) to break the Soviet diplomatic code.[18] Codenamed Venona, the top-secret effort achieved success three years later and cryptographers could examine fragments of diplomatic cables dating back to 1939.[19] By 1948, intelligence officers had compiled proof of Soviet spies dating back to 1942, and J. Edgar Hoover assigned an agent as FBI liaison for Venona.[20] Within a year, Soviet agents Kim Philby (British Secret Intelligence Service officer and KGB spy) and William Weisband (a linguist with Army Signal Intelligence) had likely informed the KGB that U.S. officials could read Soviet cables.[21] The program was so secret that even President Truman was unaware of its existence, and the CIA was kept in the dark until 1952.[22] After the breakup of the Soviet Union, Senator Daniel Patrick Moynihan and others pressured federal officials to expose the program. The first of nearly three thousand Venona decryptions were released to the public in July 1995. Documents from the former Soviet Union confirmed the existence of Soviet espionage.[23]

Why did hundreds of Americans spy for the Soviets? The FBI used the acronym MICE (Money, Ideology, Compromise [blackmail], Ego) to explain why someone might turn against their own country. Julius Rosenberg never admitted he engaged in espionage, so other spies provide possible explanations. For some it was about reducing danger by eliminating a nuclear bomb monopoly. Manhattan Project physicist Theodore Hall sincerely thought he was helping point the way to a "pathway to a better, more harmonious world."[24] Others felt loyalty to the Soviet Union as it fought fascism during World War II. Engineer Joel Barr justified passing along secrets because he and his friends trusted that the Soviet Union was a great Communist experiment and an ally against fascism.[25] Decades later, Rosenberg codefendant Morton Sobell admitted that he continued spying even after the defeat of fascism and in the wake of damaging disclosures of Soviet political repression, purges, show trials, and public executions.[26] Still idealistic, Sobell later claimed, "I did it for the Soviet Union."[27]

The discovery of a vast Soviet espionage network in the United States made the Soviet Union seem more of an enemy and a risk to national security through the final years of World War II.[28] Public disclosures of CPUSA-sponsored espionage triggered fear and a nationwide Red Scare.[29] A more nuanced picture is necessary to comprehend the understandable fright that Soviet espionage inspired.[30]

One of the five hundred panic-provoking spies went by the cover names Antenna, Liberal, and King. Publicly he was known as Julius Rosenberg. Beginning in 1942, Julius gathered whatever intelligence he could for the Soviets, but his greatest contribution was the recruitment and management of spies. His military spy ring consisted of nearly a dozen friends and engineers and was, according to historian Steven Usdin, "one of the most effective industrial espionage operations in history."[31] From 1944 to 1950 they forwarded radio, sonar, military electronics, and jet engine technology that helped the Soviets keep up with the Americans. By early 1945, Julius's spy network included Joel Barr, David Greenglass, Ruth Greenglass, Russell McNutt, William Perl, Alfred Sarant, Michael Sidorovich, Morton Sobell, and Nathan Sussman.[32]

Though Rosenberg's spy ring was extensive, prosecutors focused on the atomic bomb. The military intelligence Julius forwarded to the Soviets was significant, but unwilling and unable to risk disclosure of secret sources, federal prosecutors stuck to the atomic espionage they could prove. KGB spies had infiltrated the Manhattan Project, which they codenamed Enormous, allowing the Soviets to test an atomic bomb an estimated one to five years earlier than they otherwise would have done.[33] Enormous had been hugely successful for the Communists, and the Americans responded by targeting Julius in order to expose Soviet treachery.[34]

Julius Rosenberg recruited two individuals working on the atomic bomb. Russell W. McNutt was an engineer at the uranium processing plant in Oak Ridge, Tennessee.[35] The recruitment of a high-level engineer, confirmed in 2009, indicates Julius's importance to the Soviets.[36] The other recruit, David Greenglass, worked in Los Alamos, New Mexico, on the development of the atomic bomb. David was an army mechanic, a Communist sympathizer, and Julius's brother-in-law. While the significance of atomic bomb information from Greenglass was negligible—he largely corroborated material already forwarded by physicist spies—prosecutors saw him as the key to bringing down the Rosenberg spy ring.[37] To justify the prosecution and sentencing of the Rosenbergs, Justice Department officials stated that Greenglass gave "the secret" of the bomb to the Soviets.[38] There was, of course, no one "secret of the bomb," but rather multiple and indispensable pieces of information about its mechanics and physics, most significantly material provided by physicist Klaus Fuchs. Neither was it a simple, linear process. Some espionage information may have led the Soviets down a dead end that delayed their development of the bomb rather than accelerating it.[39]

Ethel Rosenberg was aware of her husband's espionage activities and shared his ideals.[40] Far less clear is the extent of her support. Some claim she never engaged in espionage herself.[41] Others say she provided some assistance—particularly as a messenger for Julius and by stowing money and documents—but she was not a full-fledged spy and had no codename.[42] Some state that she knew members of her husband's spy ring and had met two Soviet handlers.[43] Others interpret the Venona transcripts as indicting Ethel as an accessory and a coconspirator for the conspiracy charge. Nearly all believe the evidence does not justify her execution.[44]

The Rosenbergs remain the only married couple executed for a federal crime in the United States, and the only civilians put to death for conspiracy to commit espionage. No American civilian has ever been killed for espionage or treason, let alone conspiracy to commit these crimes. Even during World War II, soldiers who deserted and fought with the Nazis, and individuals convicted of treason, such as Iva Toguri D'Aquino (aka Tokyo Rose) and Mildred Gillars (aka Axis Sally), only received sentences of life in prison, or less.[45] None were executed. Ethel Rosenberg remains only the second female killed for a capital offense in the United States, following Mary Surratt, a conspirator in the assassination of Abraham Lincoln.

The Justice Department demanded the extreme sentences to crack Julius Rosenberg and get him to talk. This intimidation, seen by many as psychological torture, was used to scare other spies straight and prove the strength and superiority of American democracy.[46]

Propaganda has been a consistent force in U.S. foreign policy since the colonists first courted French favor in the late eighteenth century.[47] During the mid-twentieth century propaganda consisted of implementing psychological warfare to impress both ally and enemy nations, as well as to woo nonaligned nations in Africa, Asia, and Latin America—then referred to as the Third World.[48]

America's national security, according to historian Andrew Preston, depended on "a world order in which the interests of as many countries as possible were aligned" with the United States.[49] The devastating potential of nuclear conflict and mutually assured destruction necessitated using "soft power" to wage the Cold War.[50] Administration agencies controlled the spin by aggressively packaging and managing the government's official version of events. The United States, officials argued, stood on the side of law and order and human rights, while Soviet Communists governed through depravity and terror. In this zero-sum game any news story that did not conform to this worldview was a propaganda victory for the Communists, a defeat for Americans, and subject to government censorship.[51] Government officials saw appealing to hearts and minds as fundamental to winning the Cold War.[52]

In this context, federal government agencies created images to package and sell the American side of the Cold War, as one would craft an advertising campaign to sell a product, and officials assumed that the Soviets were doing the same thing. Emulating 1950s admen who used psychology, early Cold War presidents sold fear and insecurity on the home front.[53] Politicians warned Americans to be afraid of Communists, and generally they were. Officials instructed citizens to fall in line with Cold War policy, and largely they did. Then Truman and Eisenhower assured these anxious Americans that the United States could wield the weapons of democracy and justice to save the country from the threat of Communism.

Much that transpired within the United States, however, also was swept up in this global battle of images.[54] As "salesmen in chief," Truman and Eisenhower needed to convince friends and allies of the righteousness of America's cause.[55] Projecting a positive image of the United States overseas, regardless of any domestic challenges, was so important it required several agencies and millions of dollars. Democracy was the product, American democracy the brand. Officials always insisted that the United States supported democracy even in cases where it did not (as in Iran in 1953 and Guatemala in 1954).

Both the Truman and Eisenhower administrations succeeded in convincing America's closest allies, and the United Nations, to support numerous ventures. Government officials were quite successful in exporting homophobic guidelines when they persuaded others to purge homosexuals from their government agencies.[56] In 1950, administration officials were also able to sway more than a dozen nations to join the United States and the United Nations in halting the spread of Communism in Korea. When Eisenhower failed to lead in the area of civil rights, he did finally react when blatant racism threatened America's image abroad.[57] He responded to the concerns documented by embassies overseas and sent troops into Little Rock, Arkansas in 1957 to help integrate its public schools. In doing so, Eisenhower provided a boost, albeit a limited one, to the civil rights movement and, as he put it, limited the damage "done to the prestige and influ-ence" of the country due to the actions of Southern segregationists.[58]

The Rosenberg case, however, provided unique challenges. When the Truman and Eisenhower administrations responded to conditions they them-selves created—arrest, trial, clemency denial, and death—they were surprisingly ill prepared to package and present an effective message for global consumption. While some consider Truman competent at global propaganda, and Eisenhower the master, this case shows there is reason to question that characterization.[59]

Troubling aspects of the government's handling of the trial cast doubt on the integrity of the process and, by extension, the verdict.[60] Evidence clearly shows that officials applied the death penalty to Julius and Ethel to pressure one or both of them to talk, but both refused to name other spies and went to their deaths. They did not sit in prison, crack under the strain, and name members of their spy ring. They did not provide intelligence that exposed other espionage networks. If the primary goal was to get them to talk, then following through on the death penalty was a blunder. Insufficient evidence against Ethel provoked particular criticism, causing many to label it a moral error and, as historian Kathy Olmsted put it, a "tactical mistake."[61]

Unprecedented as it was, the Rosenberg case tested the limits of the federal government's new Cold War propaganda apparatus. New evidence sheds light on the global campaign to package and sell America's message and undermines the image of propaganda effectiveness. Both the Truman and Eisenhower administrations struggled to manage the narrative of the case and use it to export the ideas of democracy and freedom overseas. *Executing the Rosenbergs* reveals that both administrations were unprepared to deal with the global reaction to the conviction and execution of these two Communists. Officials viewed this case largely as a domestic problem and were caught flat-footed when they realized the foreign implications, in the process diminishing the standing of the United States in the eyes of many around the world at a very sensitive time.

After the death of Stalin, the figurehead of global Communism, Eisenhower appealed to the international community more than ever. But to Rosenberg protesters and others, he looked cruel, callous, and unjust. The death penalty appeals process took more than two years, giving a small protest movement the opportunity to gather steam and become a force in more than forty-five coun-tries. The death sentences inspired some to protest the executions even though they believed the Rosenbergs were guilty.

Once executed, Julius and Ethel Rosenberg were transformed from accused spies into martyrs. The case captured—and still demands—attention precisely because they were killed. Their deaths prompted allies to question America's leadership in waging the Cold War. Allies, and potential allies in Third World countries, remained unconvinced that American democracy would prevail in the global struggle against Communism.

Chapter 1 begins with the end of World War II and the start of the Cold War since the arrest, trial, and sentencing of Julius and Ethel Rosenberg can only be understood in the context of this global conflict. Of particular importance are the events in Korea. The Truman administration crafted policy assuming that the Rosenbergs gave the atomic bomb to the Soviets, and, thus empowered, Stalin ordered his subordinates in North Korea to invade South Korea. Truman chose to support the South Korean government and contain the spread of Communism because he feared the impact of inaction on global peace and on the political future of the Democratic Party. The judge in the Rosenberg case agreed the couple caused the Korean War and sentenced them to death. The facts are not that simple, however.

In Chapter 2 the international spotlight on the case brightened as the Truman administration slowly learned of the global significance of the Rosenberg case. During the final two months of Truman's presidency, officials attempted to manage the propaganda spin as opposition spread from Communists to anti-Communists, from Jews to Protestants and Catholics. Just as Secretary of State Dean Acheson began to recognize the importance of the case to America's image abroad, the administration's term was over and a new president moved into the White House.

Chapter 3 starts with the Eisenhower administration inheriting both the Korean War and the Rosenberg case in January 1953. From day one the administration focused on propaganda as an essential weapon in the Cold War. Eisenhower found it easier to disengage the United States from Korea, however, than to win hearts and minds through the impending execution of the two famous spies. In the Rosenberg case the new president faced numerous challenges that plagued efforts to spin the story and control the message: the transfer of power from competing administrations, interagency rivalries, an unclear message, the spreading impact of the pope's opposition, and increasing discontent throughout the world. Eisenhower enjoyed the support of the majority of the American people who viewed him as likable, wise, and grandfatherly. His handling of the Rosenberg case created an overseas image of a cruel and callous leader hell-bent on defeating Communism whatever the cost.

The increasingly frenzied global reaction to the execution of the Rosenbergs in the couple's final two weeks is the subject of Chapter 4. Eisenhower administration officials continued to attempt to manage an acceptable narrative for global consumption, but the machinations of the Supreme Court and increasingly vocal protest, especially among friends and allies, complicated the challenge. The pro-clemency sentiment continued to take many forms but coalesced around whether Eisenhower should deny the Soviet Union two martyrs and, more broadly, if the death penalty had any place in a free and civilized nation like the United States. The chapter ends with the couple's execution by electrocution on June 19, 1953.

The controversy surrounding the case did not die with the couple, however. Chapter 5 explores the aftermath of the executions, contentions over the final interment of the Rosenbergs, and the saga of the surviving sons, Michael and Robert. Eisenhower endeavored to dispense the problems inherited from Truman—such as Korea and the Rosenbergs—and navigate his own path as both an advocate for peace and an aggressive Cold Warrior. Administration officials continued to manage the Rosenbergs' story as it evolved even after their deaths, but activists, artists, musicians, filmmakers, and historians soon took over the task of telling the disparate and disputed tales, processing new information along the way. All contributors claim to represent the truth, and confirm that the Rosenberg case still commands attention to this day.

Surely after more than sixty years there are some aspects of the Rosenberg case and its meaning that can be agreed upon. In an attempt to transcend the landscape of contested narrative, this book moves beyond questions of guilt and returns the Rosenberg case to its rightful place as a central event of the early Cold War.

1

Truman

You will believe that this undertaking has not been without its misgivings. They are heavy on us today, when the future, which has so many elements of high promise, is yet only a stone's throw from despair.
—J. Robert Oppenheimer, *1945*

In the predawn hours on June 25, 1950, North Korean troops charged across the 38th parallel into South Korea. More than 100,000 Koreans had already died in the bloody civil war that engulfed the small peninsular nation, a country still reeling from Japanese assault during World War II. This particular assault on that Sunday morning, however, caught the attention of Secretary of State Dean Acheson and President Harry Truman. Within days American troops intervened in a "police action" in Korea under the cloak of the United Nations that militarized a "cold" war into a surprisingly warm bloodbath. As a string of victories shifted over time toward stalemate and defeat, Americans wondered how they were drawn into this disastrous conflict thousands of miles from home, and who they could blame. Julius and Ethel Rosenberg would soon provide an answer.

Truman administration officials believed the following chain of events: (1) the Rosenbergs gave "the secret" to the atomic bomb to the Soviet Union; (2) the bomb then inspired Stalin to be more aggressive in Korea; (3) Kim Il Sung and the other North Korean Communist leaders were subordinate to Stalin and obeyed the Soviet leader's order to invade South Korea; and (4) as the leader of the free world the United States intended to contain the spread of Communism and militarily support Republic of Korea President Syngman Rhee in pushing the Communists out of South Korea. Exposing Communism at home took on a fanatical approach referred to as McCarthyism, and to prove his tough anti-Communism Truman led Americans into a massive war that would kill millions, including more than 36,000 Americans whose families were left questioning why.[1]

Rankled, the Truman administration blamed the Rosenbergs for empowering the Soviets, and by extension the North Koreans, and causing the bloody stalemate in Korea. Truman instructed the Justice Department to prosecute the couple to the full extent of the law. When the international community began to disapprove of the persecution of the Rosenbergs, administration officials were shocked and confused. Propaganda was essential to winning hearts and minds in the Cold War, but the administration ultimately failed to persuade the global population, largely because rival federal agencies had conflicting approaches and officials assumed the protesters were all Communists sympathetic to the Soviet cause. Ambassadors and other American diplomats serving overseas were on the front lines of global dissent, but left with little clear direction they responded in a disorganized and counterproductive manner. Individuals protesting the Rosenberg case, both Communists and anti-Communists, emphasized issues of morality, martyrdom, justice, anti-Semitism, and the death penalty. Caught off-balance, the Truman administration was forced to play catch-up, struggling to get a handle on the propaganda concerning the case and adequately address the adversarial response of the global community.

The United States and the Soviet Union had been cautious allies since Germany invaded the U.S.S.R in June 1941, but the final months of World War II brought increased tension. By 1944 mistrust plagued the tentative alliance, exacerbated by spies who confirmed fears of traitors living among the American people.[2] Anxieties mounted when their common enemy, Germany, surrendered in May 1945, and again when Americans dropped two atomic bombs on Japan that August. As word spread of the devastation and radiation that Little Boy and Fat Man unleashed on Hiroshima and on Nagasaki, the shocked world entered a new atomic age. Americans had a bifurcated response of optimism and fear.

A few weeks after the bombs were dropped, polls showed that nearly 70 percent of Americans believed that construction of the atomic bomb has been a positive thing.[3] J. Robert Oppenheimer, who oversaw the construction and testing of the bomb at Los Alamos, New Mexico, explained why they had built it.[4] Initially motivated by the fear that the Nazis would build one first, and the hope that their work would shorten the war, the physicist admitted a certain amount of curiosity and "sense of adventure." A scientist, Oppenheimer explained, believes "it is good to find out how the world works."[5] A year later, however, readers were stunned when John Hersey described the lives of six Hiroshima citizens in the moments after the explosion, a piece that filled the entire issue of the *New Yorker*.[6] "I had never thought of the people in the bombed cities as individuals," one reader admitted.[7] A reviewer summarized that this account "most shudderingly brings home to the reader the utter horror of the atom bomb."[8]

Some Americans had another frightening thought: if U.S. officials could keep such a huge project secret, what else could they conceal?

As Eastern Europe reeled from the aftermath of world war and the spread of Communist rule—and Winston Churchill declared an "Iron Curtain" had descended across Europe—American policymakers struggled to craft a strategy in the midst of increasing fear. In February 1946 George Kennan, State Department official and Moscow expert, produced a long telegram that detailed the policy of containment. As the self-proclaimed leader of the free world, the United States prioritized its foreign policy toward containing the spread of Communism. A few months later, the Soviets replied with their own telegram emphasizing their efforts to counter U.S.-sponsored capitalism, militarism, and imperialism. Just two months after the bombings of Hiroshima and Nagasaki, George Orwell labeled this U.S.-U.S.S.R conflict a "cold war" with "a peace that is no peace."[9] With Communism seemingly advancing everywhere, many Americans blamed the anemic foreign policy of Franklin Roosevelt and Harry Truman and their Democratic administrations.[10] The November 1946 election reflected this rejection of Democrats; Americans voted in the first Republican majority in both houses of Congress since 1928.

The American people viewed each Communist advance as a threat to U.S. national security. Weak and timid policy seemed the breeding ground for this threat; the solution necessitated leaders able to stand strong.[11] Americans looked for politicians who would exert robust, masculine power to protect U.S. core values of liberty and democracy from the threat of encroaching Communism.

As the sides of the Cold War lined up, actions at home and abroad prompted a refinement of U.S. containment policy. When Great Britain complained it could no longer support anti-Communists in Greece and Turkey, Harry Truman replied with what marked the start of the Cold War: the Truman Doctrine. The president went before a special session of Congress, and, employing the terms of a religious crusade against atheistic Communists, asked for military and economic aid to save the two countries from certain Soviet domination.[12] He received it, and more.

Truman—a religiously tolerant and devout Christian—reached out to religious leaders of all faiths to secure "the morals of the world on our side" in the fight against godless Communism.[13] To help shore up Judeo-Christian support, the president recognized Israel and reached out to Pope Pius XII to arrange diplomatic discussions with the Vatican.[14] The pope agreed with Truman: "A lasting peace among nations can be secured only if they rest on bedrock faith in the One, True God, the Creator of all men."[15] Since the atomic bomb had raised the stakes by putting the very survival of the human race at risk, the United States would lead the "free world" in a defensive war against Soviet Communism for the continued existence of humanity. The world was at risk, and they needed God on their side in the religious crusade that was the Cold War.

Global events triggered immediate American response. In the aftermath of the Soviet-crafted coup in Prague in early 1948, Truman announced the creation of a recovery program to provide assistance to nations vulnerable to the spread of Communism. Truman called it the Marshall Plan after its creator George C. Marshall, who would be awarded a Nobel Peace Prize in 1953 for his efforts. When Communist Yugoslavian leader Marshal Tito publicly broke with Stalin in 1949, Secretary of State Dean Acheson (Figure 1.1) hoped to exploit this crack in global Communism by embracing Tito, claiming he was now "our son of a bitch."[16] To combat increasing threats, the United States joined its allies to create the North Atlantic Treaty Organization (NATO); Moscow replied in turn with the Warsaw Pact. In June 1948, when Stalin ordered a blockade of Berlin, nestled deep within Soviet-controlled East Germany, Truman countered with a fifteen-month airlift of supplies to keep Berlin open to the West. The Soviets ultimately lifted the blockade, but construction of the Berlin Wall, the symbol of the Cold War, would follow. As the Cold War became more complex and demanding, Congress approved the creation of the National Security Council (NSC) to help the White House coordinate foreign policy and reconfigured intelligence gathering under the new Central Intelligence Agency (CIA).

Figure 1.1 President Harry Truman and Secretary of State Dean Acheson at Acheson's Swearing-in Ceremony, January 21, 1949. Abbie Rowe, National Park Service. Courtesy of Harry S. Truman Library.

Truman waged the Cold War at home as well. When critics accused the Truman administration of being soft on Communism the president issued Executive Order 9835 in March 1947, creating Loyalty Boards to weed out Communists and other suspected subversives from the federal government. When fear of Communist indoctrination swept across the country, the House Committee on Un-American Activities (HUAC) interrogated Hollywood writers and directors, universities fired radical professors, and states required loyalty oaths.[17] When George Orwell released his dystopian novel *1984* in 1949, many saw it reflective of the pervasive and escalating paranoia of the day.

In the summer of 1949, Truman stunned Americans when he announced that the Soviets had tested their first atomic bomb. The Soviet government had been funding research into the bomb since 1940, when, as an American physicist later recalled, they were tipped off that the Americans were working on the bomb when there was no U.S. response to a Soviet paper detailing "rare spontaneous fissioning in uranium."[18] At any other time that paper would have prompted a vigorous response. "Russia," the physicist remembered, "was as mysterious and remote as the other side of the moon and not much more productive when it came to really new ideas or inventions." A common joke among scientists at the time reflected this underestimation of the Soviets: "Russians could not surreptitiously introduce nuclear bombs in suitcases into the United States because they had not yet been able to perfect a suitcase."[19] In 1946 Truman had asked Berkeley physicist and Manhattan Project director J. Robert Oppenheimer if the professor knew when the Soviets would be able to build their own atomic bomb. Oppenheimer responded he did not know, but the president insisted he himself did. "When?" Oppenheimer asked. "Never," Truman confidently replied.[20]

In his radio address announcing the bombing of Hiroshima in 1945, Truman had thanked God for giving the knowledge "to us instead of to our enemies" and prayed that God would "guide us to use it in his ways and for his purposes."[21] Many Americans wondered how it was possible that a mere four years later the atheistic Communists now had the knowledge. Democratic Senator Brian McMahon, a devout Catholic and member of the Joint Committee on Atomic Energy, claimed that the bombing of Hiroshima was "the greatest event in world history since the birth of Jesus Christ."[22] How could the enemy now enjoy this power?

There were two reasons Americans should not have underestimated Soviet atomic efforts: one was the Smyth Report, the second was espionage. Princeton physicist Henry D. Smyth crafted a report of the atomic information publicly available on the Manhattan Project, while omitting the most classified material.[23] For example, it included how to purify uranium and chemically separate plutonium, but left out implosion. The White House and War Department published the Smyth Report days after bombing Hiroshima and Nagasaki.[24] Many scientists supported international control and cooperation concerning the atomic bomb, including Albert Einstein and J. Robert Oppenheimer, who joined others in establishing the *Bulletin of the Atomic Scientists* in December 1945.[25] Yet nearly 75 percent of Americans wanted the United States to keep control of the newfound technology to itself, and most government officials and military leaders agreed.[26] The Smyth Report represented a final attempt at openness. The subsequent, short-lived United Nations Atomic Energy Commission failed to create international regulation, which led to a dangerous free-for-all in the development and stockpiling of nuclear bombs.[27]

The Soviets translated the Smyth Report into Russian in early 1946 and distributed it to all scientists and engineers working on the U.S.S.R bomb project. But the Soviets had another source of information on the Manhattan Project that corroborated and filled in the holes of the Smyth report.[28] That source, which assigned the codename Enormous to the U.S. bomb project, was Soviet Communist spies.

Initially, Americans were too panicked that the Soviets had developed a working atomic bomb to worry about how they did it. Front pages around the country shouted: "RUSSIA HAS ATOMIC BOMB!"[29] In spite of articles that explained there was no reason to think war was imminent, Americans were filled with terror.[30] Teachers instructed schoolchildren to "duck and cover," and officials required students in Los Angeles and New York City to wear dog tags to school in order to help identify bodies after an attack. Families began to build bomb shelters, stocking them with canned goods and tranquilizers.[31] A symbol of that fear was the *Bulletin of the Atomic Scientists'* Doomsday Clock, constructed to give a graphic representation of the changing threat of nuclear war. In June 1947 it began at seven minutes before midnight, or doomsday; in the fall of 1949 it jumped to a mere three minutes before.[32] The resulting paranoia was palpable, leading some to describe the early Cold War years as the opposite of the age of reason.[33]

Fear of Communists prompted articles like *Look* magazine's "How to Spot a Communist."[34] The author advised that by understanding that Communists "think differently from other kinds of Americans," one could avoid being "a sucker for a left hook." If someone labeled critics as "Fascists" and criticized capitalism and democracy as "decadent," one could assume they were Communists.[35] Federal officials took more direct action and charged American Communist Party (CPUSA) leaders with inciting revolution under the Smith Act. The evidence, officials claimed, was not what the Communists did, but what they read and discussed. The Supreme Court upheld the Smith Act convictions in *Dennis v. U.S.* (1950), and eleven of America's top Communists went to prison for up to five years. Some were not content to simply imprison Communists; one Hearst columnist claimed the only way to deal with them was to kill them all.[36]

Events in Asia caused an increase in fear in autumn 1949. Little more than a week after the Soviets confirmed their nuclear explosion, Mao Zedong announced the creation of the People's Republic of China. America's great ally from World War II had become the most populated Communist country on the planet. Mao's two-month-long visit to Moscow that December resulted in a Sino-Soviet Treaty, which solidified in the minds of government officials the menace of one all-encompassing, global Communist movement. Reeling from this one-two punch, the Truman administration was more intent than ever to contain the threat while combatting accusations that all Democrats were weak, Communist coddlers.

When high-level diplomat and accused spy Alger Hiss was convicted of perjury in 1950, Americans feared that Communists were undermining the strength of the United States from within.[37] Secretary of State Acheson's public statement of support for his former Harvard classmate—"I do not intend to turn my back on Alger Hiss"—proved disastrous for an administration already facing accusations of being soft on Communism.[38] Right-wing Republicans vilified Acheson for his loyalty to Hiss.[39] The Hiss case, and other Communist spies, permitted conservatives to take the high ground and put Democrats on the defensive.[40] *Newsweek* magazine declared that Alger Hiss's trial "uncovered Russian pipelines into the State Department."[41] Hiss accuser Whittaker Chambers's memoir, *Witness*, soon landed on the bestseller list, and Hiss's name became synonymous with traitor. Senator McCarthy likely intentionally slipped when he twice mistakenly referred to the 1952 Democratic presidential nominee Adlai Stevenson as "Alger."[42]

Evidence of spies mounted when Great Britain announced the arrest of Klaus Emil Fuchs (codename: Charles) in early February 1950. A German theoretical physicist and devout Communist, Fuchs had played a key role on the Manhattan Project in Los Alamos, New Mexico.[43] From 1942 to 1948 he told all he knew— which was considerable—to the Soviets, and was undoubtedly the most important spy within the Manhattan Project.[44] The Soviet diplomatic cables decrypted under the Venona project helped track Fuchs, which quickly led to his courier, American chemist Harry Gold (Goose, Arno, Mad). Gold's other informant was David Greenglass (Bumblebee, Caliber, Zinger), the man who named his brother-in-law Julius Rosenberg (Antenna, Liberal, King) and later his sister Ethel Greenglass Rosenberg.[45] Klaus Fuchs was Great Britain's problem. They found him guilty and sentenced him to fourteen years in prison; he served nine before they shipped him off to East Germany.[46] In the United States, Harry Gold was convicted and served less than half of his thirty-year sentence. David

Greenglass served ten of his fifteen-year sentence. The Rosenbergs would not be so lucky.

Disclosures of espionage, piled on top of events in China, put Truman on the defensive. Eager to demonstrate strength against the growing threat of Communism, the president made a "historic decision" and announced on February 1, 1950 that he had ordered scientists to develop the hydrogen bomb.[47] Insisting "he must defend [the] nation against a possible aggressor," and keep an atomic edge over the Communists, Truman took the advice of the National Security Council and approved speeding up production of the more power-ful hydrogen bomb.[48] This thermonuclear weapon promised to deliver previ-ously unattainable and unfathomable levels of destruction. The decision to pursue such a weapon was so controversial that J. Robert Oppenheimer urged Truman to reconsider.[49] Truman promptly rejected the physicist's recommen-dation and questioned his loyalty. Government officials would soon investigate Oppenheimer, accuse him of Communist affiliations, and ultimately revoke his security clearance.

While most Communist spies had long been drummed out of the federal gov-ernment, Senator Joseph McCarthy found a cause he could latch on to and rode it to popularity. He struck a chord with many Americans when in his February 1950 Wheeling, West Virginia, speech he revealed that an undisclosed number of State Department officials were card-carrying members of the Communist Party.[50] That number would fluctuate in the days and weeks ahead, and the sena-tor would fail to expose any Communist spies in his career, but he would suc-ceed in exacerbating American fears. Communist spies had infiltrated the federal government under Secretary Acheson's watch, McCarthy argued. Acheson was a "pompous diplomat in striped pants, with a phony British accent," the senator charged, who "endorsed Communism" and "high treason," causing the United States to lose its atomic edge.[51] If he, a self-made man from America's heartland, did not expose these Communists, U.S. national security, already in a "position of impotency," would surely suffer defeat.[52]

Truman charged the National Security Council (NSC) to keep pace with these dramatic changes and review the entire U.S. national security apparatus. The advisers responded with NSC-68, a document that became the blueprint for fighting the Cold War. Declaring the conflict to be "in fact a real war in which the survival of the free world is at stake," the NSC saw that the "greatest threat to the security of the United States" was the Soviet Union's "hostile designs and formidable power."[53] Council officials warned that "within the next four or five years the Soviet Union will possess the military capability of delivering a sur-prise atomic attack."[54] The United States, they urged, "must have substantially increased general air, ground, and sea strength, atomic capabilities, and air and civilian defenses to deter war."[55] This would require a massive increase in military spending to combat Soviet efforts to dominate the free world. "Budgetary considerations," officials rationalized, "will need to be subordinated to the stark fact that our very independence as a nation may be at stake."[56] But Americans would not have to go it completely alone. By using effective propaganda to "strengthen the orientation toward the United States of the non-Soviet nations," advisers explained, Americans would inspire their allies to join the cause and defeat global Communism.[57]

NSC-68 represented a dramatic, new approach to national security and Truman was hesitant to approve its implementation.[58] Events in Korea, however, soon compelled him to act.

On the rainy Sunday of June 25, 1950, North Korea invaded South Korea.[59] The Truman administration originally had no intention of intervening in a large conflict in Korea, but when troops crossed into South Korea debate over NSC-68 shifted from theoretical to pragmatic.[60] Truman eagerly embraced the new national security dictates, supporting a more dramatic increase in military spending than the document had originally called for.

Since Japan's defeat in 1945, the Soviets had occupied Korea north of the 38th parallel and American troops south. The parallel line was an arbitrary plan to temporarily divide the country, and most Koreans refused to recognize this artificial separation of their homeland. Soviets set up the Communist government of Kim Il Sung in the north, while Americans supported the regime of Christian anti-Communist, Syngman Rhee, in the south. Koreans tried to reunite their country under one government, resulting in violent clashes that produced more than 100,000 casualties. Both Soviets and Americans, however, wanted to avoid all-out civil war in Korea.[61] American officials refused to ship heavy-duty infantry equipment to allies in the South and declined to approve provocative actions along the 38th parallel. Similarly, Stalin was hesitant to support Kim's military aggression.[62] Available Soviet documents indicate a message of restraint on the part of Moscow parallel to the message coming out of Washington.[63]

In spite of mutual attempts at control, increasingly larger raids continued along the 38th parallel through 1949, as Koreans hoped to take advantage of perceived weaknesses and grab land across the fortified border. Historians continue to debate what likely prompted North Korea to launch a sizeable offensive into South Korea in June 1950. According to Kathryn Weathersby, evidence indicates that the invasion "was not the result of Soviet determination to expand the territory under its control, and it was certainly not the opening salvo in a broader Soviet attack on the American sphere of influence."[64] Stalin had repeatedly rejected Kim's plan for invasion, even when he was asked just after the Soviet's first successful atomic bomb test in August 1949, presumably when Stalin was feeling strong and confident.[65] But Kim kept pressing and Stalin finally relented, stating on January 30, 1950 that he was "ready to help him [Kim] in this matter."[66]

Why had Stalin finally agreed to support Kim Il Sung? First, Stalin credited the importance of the Communist victory in China, since Mao and his troops could now provide support. When Stalin and Mao signed the Sino-Soviet Treaty of Friendship in February 1950, they formally solidified the alliance and the Soviets would no longer have to accept sole responsibility in Korea. Second, Stalin feared U.S. intervention if North Korea attacked and made it clear to Kim that if he got into trouble, the Soviet Union would not help. The Soviet leader demanded that Kim get Mao's approval before any attack: "If you should get kicked in the teeth, I shall not lift a finger. You have to ask Mao for all the help."[67] Kim assured Stalin that they would enjoy a quick victory before the Americans could become involved.[68] After Secretary Acheson gave a speech that appeared to exclude Korea from the U.S. "defense perimeter," American involvement seemed even less plausible.[69]

Chinese support was likely the key. By early 1950 large numbers of experienced troops, fresh from fighting in the Chinese civil war, were heading back into North Korea. While Stalin appeared to be very hesitant to support North Korean aggression, Mao seemed more inclined to endorse Kim's plan of attack. The evidence does not indicate that Stalin ordered the invasion because he was emboldened by possession of atomic weaponry. Yet that is exactly what U.S. government officials believed.

Truman and his advisers were convinced that Stalin's acquisition of atomic bomb technology was not only connected to North Korea's invasion of South Korea, but gave the Soviet leader the strength to order it in June 1950.[70] Many prominent Americans believed Truman's anemic foreign policy triggered the Communist aggression. Billy Graham, the famous evangelical minister, blamed Truman for a weak anti-Communist policy in China, saying his "blunder" in "losing" China caused North Korea to invade the South.[71] Senator McCarthy accused Secretary of State Acheson of giving the Soviet Union "a green light to grab whatever it could" in Korea.[72] One week before the invasion John Foster Dulles, the likely Republican choice for Secretary of State, visited Seoul. Some feared Dulles had negotiated an agreement with Rhee while in Korea and that this understanding prompted North Korea to invade.[73] Less than twenty-four hours after the invasion, Truman pointed to Iran on a globe in the oval office. "Here is where they will start trouble if we aren't careful," he explained. "Korea is the Greece of the Far East. If we are tough enough now," he continued, "they won't take any next steps. But if we just stand by, they'll move into Iran and they'll take over the whole Middle East. There's no telling what they'll do if we don't put up a fight now," he concluded.[74] Under terrific pressure and fear, the president determined he had to respond.

Truman called the American military into action, under the guise of United Nations Security Council Resolutions.[75] The Soviet representative to the

Security Council could not veto either measure; he was boycotting the United Nations because the officials had not allowed the Communists to be seated to represent China. Less than five years after World War II, Americans were once again fighting and dying in a far off land, but they did not go it alone. Troops from Great Britain, Canada, Australia, and several other smaller nations joined them.[76] By wrapping the fight in Korea in the United Nations flag, Americans could confront Soviet aggression and protect their national security.[77] But working under UN cover did not diminish the fact that Americans had become the policeman of the world.[78] In the final six months of 1950 U.S. defense spending, which included increased aid to the French in Indochina, would nearly quadruple.[79]

At a press conference on June 29, Truman explained his actions. South Korea had been "unlawfully attacked by a bunch of bandits" and the United Nations Security Council approved "going to the relief of the Korean Republic" to counter the aggression. The U.S. military was part of that effort. A reporter asked Truman if "it would be correct, against your explanation, to call this a police action under the United Nations." The president replied, "Yes. That is exactly what it amounts to."[80]

Three weeks later Truman spoke directly to the American people in a nostalgic fireside chat to remind them why they were fighting in Korea. Americans, he explained, were using their military might to protect their national security and stop Soviet aggression. The Korean territory was the site of a Communist invasion and, while distant, the war directly impacted U.S. security. The president called for an economic as well as military commitment, which was "an important step in the direction of NSC-68" and paying for the increasing defense budget.[81]

The undeclared police action in Korea cast a shadow over the entire Rosenberg case. Julius and Ethel's arrest coincided with the start of war, and their executions took place a few weeks prior to armistice in 1953. The overlap of the war and the case prompted one scholar to later wonder whether the government took "advantage of a patriotic, less probing press."[82] Truman administration officials endeavored to sell the necessity of the Korean War at home and abroad, while eager for a victory in Korea that would contain Communism and give Americans a psychological boost.[83] They simultaneously struggled with the two Communist spies accused of emboldening Stalin by passing atomic secrets to the Soviet Union.

Prior to becoming the focus of the "crime of the century," Julius and Ethel Rosenberg and their two young sons lived on the Lower East Side of New York City in an apartment complex called Knickerbocker Village.[84] Born into Jewish immigrant families, both Julius and Ethel were true Communist believers, joining the CPUSA in the 1930s.[85] Ethel graduated high school and worked several jobs, including clerking for the U.S. Census Bureau in Washington, D.C., in 1940, before having children and becoming a stay-at-home mother.[86]

Julius earned a Bachelor of Science degree in electrical engineering from City College of New York in 1939, and he gained access to classified military information while working with Emerson Radio Corporation and the Signal Corps. Through his work with the Communist Party Julius made connections. When he offered to spy for the Soviet Union, the KGB codenamed him Antenna, which was changed to Liberal in 1944, and assigned him to Alexander Feklisov, a Soviet spy handler. Feklisov later described Julius as intelligent if "perhaps something of a dreamer," who viewed his espionage work "as a kind of religious calling."[87] Julius primarily recruited others to the cause, ultimately managing a spy ring of a dozen engineers. He did occasionally spy himself, however, as when he gave a prototype proximity fuse to Feklisov as a Christmas present in December 1944. A sophisticated trigger mechanism used to get closer to a speedy aircraft to take it down, a version of this proximity fuse was used by the Soviets to shoot down Francis Gary Powers and his U2 reconnaissance plane over the Soviet Union in May 1960.[88]

In addition to his engineer friends, Julius also recruited Army sergeant David Greenglass, Ethel's younger brother, to spy for the Soviets. The KGB gave David the codename Bumblebee and later Caliber; Julius also enlisted David's wife Ruth Greenglass in December 1944 to serve as an intermediary under the codename Wasp.[89] According to Feklisov, Ethel was not an active participant in espionage, and thus did not warrant a codename.[90] In September 1944 Julius was pleased to learn that his brother-in-law would soon have access to very valuable information. David had been tapped to work in Special Engineer Detachment at Los Alamos, New Mexico, as a machinist constructing the precision molds for high-explosive lenses for the Manhattan Project.[91]

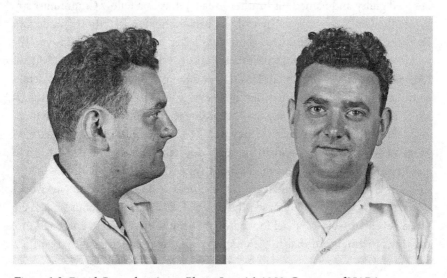

Figure 1.2 David Greenglass Arrest Photo, June 16, 1950. Courtesy of NARA.

At Los Alamos, coworkers described David Greenglass as "a loudmouth" who did not hide being "pro-Russian and liberal minded."[92] He was overly curious about every item that came through the shop and questioned all scientists and engineers he worked with, committing the information to memory. No one ever put his outspoken politics and his inquisitive nature together to equal espionage. David often relayed information to Ruth, which included notes on how to obtain uranium-235, "a 22-page description of the nuclear bomb," and a 33-page description of "calculations and information regarding a structural solution to the problem of a uranium bomb."[93] Alternately, David passed information to a courier who identified himself by providing a matching half of a cut-up Jell-O box. Greenglass gathered information, and at least one souvenir uranium ashtray, until he was discharged from the army in February 1946.[94]

Rosenberg's spy ring began to unravel in late August 1945, when KGB courier Elizabeth Bentley walked into the FBI field office in New Haven, Connecticut. Agents initially assumed she was pretending to be a spy and set her information aside for weeks, but gradually the bureau recognized Bentley's value as a turncoat.[95] Bentley named several Americans who spied for the Soviet Union, helping the FBI down a path that would eventually lead to fellow courier Harry Gold and Manhattan Project physicist Klaus Fuchs.[96] Shortly after the Soviets tested their first atomic bomb, Fuchs confessed he had helped make it possible. As the espionage trail grew hot in the spring of 1950, David Greenglass assured Julius Rosenberg that "under no circumstances . . . would he ever become an informer."[97]

A week later FBI agents brought Greenglass in for questioning. It took David just eight hours with the FBI to forgo his promise to Julius and confess.[98] On the morning of June 16, 1950, FBI agents arrested David for stealing atomic secrets. He pled guilty and named his brother-in-law Julius as a fellow Communist spy. When the U.S. Attorney set Greenglass's bail at one hundred thousand dollars, David reached out to Julius for money to cover "everything, bail, lawyer, the whole works."[99] The Justice Department indicated they would not arrest Ruth as long as Greenglass cooperated; David kept talking.[100] He later disclosed details to the grand jury, but insisted that he "never spoke to my sister about this at all."[101] FBI agents were unaware that, according to Ruth, her husband sometimes "would say things were so even if they were not."[102] The FBI prepared to go after Julius a few weeks later, confident he would not "take a powder" and skip town.[103]

On Monday, July 17—less than a month after the invasion of South Korea—FBI agents barged into the Rosenbergs' one-bedroom apartment on New York's Lower East Side. Seven G-men swiftly handcuffed and arrested Julius Rosenberg while seven-year-old Michael looked on.[104] Another five agents crammed into the tiny apartment on that hot, muggy evening to conduct a nearly two-hour search for incriminating evidence. The FBI agents complained that Ethel "made a typical Communist remonstrance" when she demanded a "warrant and the right to call an attorney."[105]

Julius's wife Ethel initially faced no charges, since Greenglass had denied that his sister was involved with Julius's espionage ring.[106] The morning after Julius's arrest, however, Ethel took the initiative to call the press to the Rosenbergs' apartment for a photo shoot. Ethel posed drying dishes in her modest kitchen, replicating a common advertising layout that depicted her role as a typical 1950s American housewife (Figure 1.3). When questioned Ethel claimed to be completely unaware of Julius's activities, protesting that FBI agents had rifled through everything looking for damning evidence, even her "stack of three *Parent* magazines."[107] Ethel used the dishes and the magazines to project the image of an innocent mother, one who could not possibly be the wife of a Communist spy. Regardless, the FBI would later condemn her for being a master espionage agent who disguised herself as a simple housewife, and use her as a key to breaking Julius.[108]

Hoping to persuade Julius to name the members of his espionage ring, FBI agents considered "every possible means to pressure Rosenberg and make him talk," including "a careful study of the involvement of Ethel Rosenberg," so charges might be filed against her.[109] A handwritten note, presumably composed by an assistant to FBI Director J. Edgar Hoover, concurred: "Yes by all means. If Criminal Division procrastinates too long let me know."[110] Not all federal officials agreed, however. In a Justice Department memo the same day an official warned there might be insufficient admissible evidence to charge Ethel Rosenberg.[111] Hoover rejected this argument and advised the attorney general to force Julius to talk, explaining that the FBI was "proceeding against his wife" so she "might serve as a lever in this matter."[112]

Pressure mounted on the FBI as events seemed to be spinning out of control. While General Douglas MacArthur continued to project optimism, emphasizing the thousands of North Korean troops killed and the large number of enemy tanks destroyed, Truman announced he would draft yet another 100,000 men to serve in Korea.[113] The threat posed by the Communists was reflected in the latest issue of the weekly investigative magazine *Collier's*; the ominous cover illustration of an atom bomb devastating New York City terrified readers.[114] Someone needed to be held responsible for handing the Soviets the bomb and Julius Rosenberg fit the bill. The federal government responded with decisive action.

FBI agents arrested Ethel directly after she testified before the grand jury on the afternoon of August 11, 1950. Prosecutor Myles J. Lane, in emphasizing the seriousness of her crime, stated it "is one of the worst that could be committed, because it jeopardizes the lives of every man, woman, and child in this

Figure 1.3 Espionage Suspect Ethel Rosenberg in Her Kitchen the Morning After Her Husband Julius's Arrest, July 18, 1950. Courtesy of Bettmann/CORBIS.

country."[115] He also linked Ethel to the war Americans were waging halfway around the world: "If the crime with which she is charged had not occurred perhaps we would not have the present situation in Korea."[116] The prosecutor imposed a one hundred thousand dollar bail, rejecting a plea for parole that would have given Ethel a chance to make arrangements for her young children. Considered a national menace, she posed for her mug shot in a polka dot dress and white gloves.

Figure 1.4 Julius Rosenberg Arrest Photo, July 17, 1950. Courtesy of NARA.

Hoover defended using Ethel to pressure her husband because the FBI direc-tor needed Julius to testify against the others to prove his industrial spy ring had forwarded radar, electronics, and jet engine technology to the Soviets from 1944 to 1950.[117] Greenglass would testify against Rosenberg, but since the prosecu-tion could not expose Venona (the top-secret program that deciphered Soviet diplomatic cables) in the courtroom, it needed Julius's testimony to go after the others. The FBI arrested Julius's wife, and the mother of his children, to use her as a "lever" to get him to talk. Prosecutor Lane agreed, writing to the attorney general that the arrest "could lead to others who may be presently engaged in

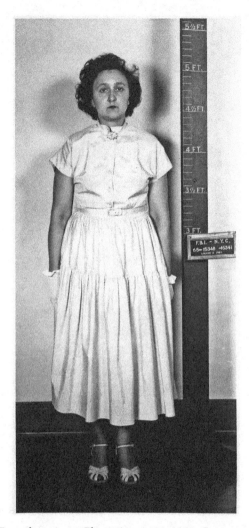

Figure 1.5 Ethel Rosenberg Arrest Photo, August 11, 1950. Courtesy of NARA.

espionage activities."[118] The weak evidence against Ethel, however, would prove to be problematic for government officials long after the trial concluded.

The Justice Department charged both Julius and Ethel Rosenberg with conspiracy to commit espionage during wartime, citing the period June 6, 1944 through June 16, 1950.[119] The Espionage Act made it unlawful to disclose information affecting national defense to any foreign nation.[120] The Americans and the Soviets were allies during World War II, and in the Cold War years the Soviet Union was an undeclared enemy. However, none of this made any difference under the Espionage Act. As the judge in the case later clarified, "Espionage . . . means spying on the United States to aid a foreign power"—any foreign power.[121]

Signed into law by President Woodrow Wilson in 1917, Congress had drafted the Espionage Act to address spying and dissent during World War I. Conspiring to spy was a crime punishable by death, or imprisonment of not more than thirty years; a sentence of life in prison was not an option.[122] The charge of conspiracy to commit espionage against the Rosenbergs centered on delivering atomic bomb secrets to the Soviets because that was the evidence Greenglass could provide. While the atomic information Greenglass provided was of debatable value, that did not matter. The quality was not relevant, merely its existence. Intelligence that assisted any foreign nation was espionage. In order to justify conviction and harsh sentencing—and to use the Rosenbergs as an example of what happens when Americans are caught spying—Justice Department officials stated that David gave the secret of the bomb to the Soviets.[123] The questionable impact of this espionage material on national security would continue to be troublesome for government officials defending the persecution of the Rosenbergs.[124]

The Truman administration chose the conspiracy to commit espionage charge over a straight espionage case because conspiracy—two or more people making an agreement to spy—was far easier to prove. As the judge later explained, "A conspiracy is a partnership in criminal purposes."[125] While evidence indicates Ethel was not an active spy herself, it does, however, reveal she was aware of her husband's activities and was thus cognizant of the conspiracy. The Rosenbergs pled not guilty, refusing to cooperate with the prosecution and name names.

When Ethel's arrest failed to get Julius to talk, government officials increased the pressure by threatening to apply the death penalty. The Justice Department issued a statement declaring Julius's actions to be a capital offense and simultaneously encouraged the Atomic Energy Commission (AEC) and the Joint Congressional Committee on Atomic Energy to support the sentence.[126] The chairman of the AEC testified before the congressional committee, stating that Julius Rosenberg was "the king pin of a very large ring" and that "if there is any way of breaking him by having the shadow of a death penalty over him, we want to do it."[127] The committee agreed and chose to secure a judge willing to impose the death penalty on Julius.

Irving R. Kaufman, a prickly, demanding adjudicator, was just that judge. If Roy Cohn is to be believed, Kaufman even lobbied for the job.[128] Cohn— a twenty-four-year-old Assistant to the U.S. Attorney—later claimed he "was instrumental in getting Irving Kaufman assigned to the Rosenberg case."[129] According to Cohn, Kaufman was intent on sentencing Julius to death even before the trial started.[130] At the time, no one considered the possibility of applying the death penalty to Ethel as well.[131] During the trial Kaufman engaged in improper *ex parte* consultations with U.S. Attorney and chief prosecutor Irving Saypol and Cohn to ensure the opportunity to issue the death penalty.[132] The sentence, which some called extreme, would prove controversial even for those who accepted the couple's guilt.

As the Rosenbergs sat in Manhattan's House of Detention awaiting their trial, news from Korea devastated Americans and the Truman administration. North Korean troops had pushed southward, forcing a retreat that left American and UN forces clinging to the southeastern edge of the Korean peninsula by September 1950. The casualty figures for American troops that final week of August rose to nearly 2,000, with 8,863 casualties since the start of the conflict.[133] UN Commander General Douglas MacArthur—who had declared "I can handle it [North Korea] with one arm tied behind my back"—scrambled to reclaim the southern territory.[134] MacArthur implemented an amphibious landing and in a stunning victory recaptured Seoul, forcing North Korean troops north of the 38th parallel by October. The United States had taken a stand and halted the spread of Communism.

The speed of MacArthur's success tempted Truman to not just contain Communism, but to forcefully push it back.[135] Diplomat W. Averell Harriman later recalled that "it would have taken a superhuman effort to say no" and not cross the 38th parallel and push the Communists back to unify Korea.[136] Assuming China would not send troops into the Korean conflict, Truman ordered MacArthur to surge the UN troops past the 38th parallel, venturing well into North Korea. However, Mao had long ago decided to assist the North Koreans should they need it.[137] On October 19, even before UN forces reached the border with China, "thick columns of four Chinese armies" numbering 120,000, crossed the Yalu River into Korea.[138] Undeterred, UN troops continued north, stretching supply lines as winter approached.

Chinese troops changed everything. American soldiers, enjoying Thanksgiving dinner on the Yalu River and thoughts of victory by Christmas, were devastated by the late November Sino-Korean attack. UN forces quickly withdrew and in little more than two weeks they were forced back south of the 38th parallel. Bombing, napalm, counterassaults, and even threats of atomic weapons failed to push back the Chinese and North Koreans. What in August 1950 had promised to be a quick and easy victory had turned into a drawn-out and deadly conflict.

With a definitive win proving elusive, the Truman administration adjusted how to sell the Korean War to the American people. According to historian Steven Casey, officials chose to "abandon the soothing tones and low-key actions of July and August" and replaced them with "a series of calls for vigilance."[139] Truman needed a united home front to secure a clear victory in Korea and ramped up the Cold War rhetoric aligned with his administration's more aggressive stance. As victory in Korea became an increasingly complex feat, the administration saw a way to strike at Communism through the Rosenbergs. The trial and conviction of Communist spies would be an example, in Truman's mind, of the vigilance he had called for.

To help improve morale, *Time* magazine announced the American Fighting-Man as the Man of the Year for 1950. That same fighting-man, however, was writing increasingly critical and uncensored letters from the war zone, complaining about dreadful conditions and graphically describing the hell of war.[140] As word spread about the inept handling of this unpopular war, legislators responded.

American politics shifted to the right in the fall of 1950. Congress passed the repressive Internal Security (McCarran) Act, which required Communist Party members to register and face likely prosecution. One of the House members to vote against the McCarran Act was Helen Gahagan Douglas. A California congresswoman, Douglas suffered defeat in her 1950 run for the Senate at the hands of fellow congressmember Richard M. Nixon. Known through his anti-Communist activities with HUAC, Nixon labeled Douglas the "Pink Lady"— pink even "down to her underwear"—and claimed that her election would stand as a victory for Joseph Stalin and the Communist Party.[141] In embracing Joseph McCarthy's anti-Communist crusade, Republicans picked up twenty-eight seats in the House and added five new senators.[142]

The spies blamed for causing the military debacle in Korea prepared for their day in court. While awaiting his trial, Julius Rosenberg entertained himself with a daily chess game with convicted thief Jerome Eugene Tartakow.[143] From all accounts the two became friends and confidantes until Julius was shipped to Sing Sing Prison in Ossining, New York in December 1950. Upon release, Tartakow would work for the Rosenbergs' attorney, driving him to Sing Sing and keeping in contact with Julius. What Julius did not know was that Tartakow was also an FBI informant. The entire time he knew Julius he relayed information to the Bureau, including pivotal information to locate an important witness.[144] But nothing Tartakow relayed to the FBI would prove as damaging to the Rosenbergs as David Greenglass's "revised" testimony.

In February 1951, just eight days prior to the trial and more than five months after his sister's arrest, the FBI reinterviewed David Greenglass and threatened to arrest Greenglass's wife. Ruth Greenglass had been the messenger between Julius and David, which included memorizing David's details about the size and layout of the facility at Los Alamos and relaying them to Julius.[145] Terrified that his wife and the mother of his children would be indicted, Greenglass changed his statement. David instead corroborated Ruth's revised story and said that his sister Ethel not only knew about Julius's espionage activities, but also that she typed reports for him.[146] With David Greenglass's false testimony, the FBI could prosecute Ethel effectively. A federal prosecutor later admitted that there would have been no case without David's testimony.[147] Though far more involved than Ethel, Ruth Greenglass was never indicted.

In an interview with *New York Times* reporter Sam Roberts in 2001, Greenglass admitted embellishing his story about Ethel to save his wife.[148] In 2008, the federal government released Ruth's grand jury testimony from August 1950, where Ruth explained she wrote out David's notes longhand. David's grand jury testimony, released in July 2015, confirmed that Ethel played no role.[149] At the trial, however, Ruth altered her story and testified that Ethel typed the reports because David's handwriting was "very difficult to under-stand."[150] In his trial testimony David agreed with her. "I told them the story and left her [Ethel] out of it, right? But my wife put her in it," David later explained. "So what am I gonna do, call my wife a liar? My wife is my wife. I mean, I don't sleep with my sister, you know. There's more to it than sex, you understand. You make a life with somebody. In my generation, that's the way I would go. My wife is more important to me than my sister."[151] This crucial, damning evidence led to Ethel's conviction and death. The prosecution would contend that as she had "on countless other occasions," Ethel "sat at that typewriter and struck the keys, blow by blow, against her own country in the interests of the Soviets."[152] Facts known even at the time caused many observers to question the government's case against Ethel, though some wondered the opposite. Could a brother send "his sister to her doom" if she had not "involved him in a real conspiracy" to pass secrets to the Soviets?[153]

Eight months after their arrest, on Tuesday, March 6, 1951, the Rosenberg trial began in New York City's Foley Square Courthouse.[154] Manny Bloch and his father Alexander, both attorneys for left-wing causes, represented the Rosenbergs.[155] Morton Sobell, a Rosenberg friend and fellow Communist, was tried along with the Rosenbergs. Sobell had fled to Mexico upon hearing of Julius's arrest and the Mexican police had turned him over to U.S. authorities.

During the three-week trial, David Greenglass took the role as primary wit-ness against his sister and brother-in-law.[156] While the trial focused on atomic information—Greenglass admitted to passing along sketches of high-explosive lens molds to the U.S.S.R—prosecutors were not free to discuss other scientific data. The AEC imposed strict limits on what its witnesses could disclose during the trial, relying on a limited scope of atomic information.[157] These restrictions would prompt scientists to later question the significance of the bomb informa-tion Greenglass provided. For example, in November 1952—more than a year after the trial ended—four British and French scientists attested that Greenglass "could not possibly have remembered the details about which he testified" and that "the information Greenglass testified to was not secret and had been in pub-lications and periodicals."[158]

Rosenberg representative Manny Bloch inadvertently aided the government's case when he asked the court to impound David's sketch of the atomic bomb. Bloch had hoped this would make his clients appear patriotic—by not divulging information that might put national security at risk—but this backfired. It made the drawing appear to have value after all.[159]

Instances during the trial served as reminders to the jury of the continuous Communist threat the nation faced and likely helped the prosecution's case. Just a day into the trial jurors read newspaper reports detailing the continued blood-letting in Korea. South Korea had already suffered 169,000 casualties in the war, while American casualties topped more than fifty thousand.[160] During week two of the trial another Communist spy, Alger Hiss, arrived at the same courthouse to begin his five-year prison sentence for perjury. When the Rosenbergs chose to use the Fifth Amendment—"I decline to answer on the ground that this might tend to incriminate me"—they did so in response to questions about Communist Party membership or when asked if they knew a particular Soviet agent.[161] This testimony left doubts in juror's minds about the couple's innocence. Just sixteen days into the trial lawyers delivered closing remarks. While the prosecution had called eleven witnesses to the stand, the defense rested after just four.[162] Defense attorney Bloch also helped the prosecution in his summation when he thanked Kaufman for a fair and dignified trial; it would be difficult for Bloch to later claim otherwise.[163] With this assistance, the prosecution presented a strong case, arguing that the defendants were dangerous Communist spies who had given nuclear secrets to the Soviets.

In turning the case over to the jury, Judge Kaufman reminded the twelve jurors that the prosecution only needed to demonstrate that the defendants conspired to commit an act and that the indictment referred only to assisting a foreign country, not necessarily an enemy nation. He also reiterated that the charge concerned "not only atomic bomb information, but other secret and classified information" intended to help any foreign government.[164] He ordered the jury not to discuss the case outside of the jury room and dismissed them with "God bless you all."[165]

After deliberating for nearly eight hours, the jury found the accused guilty of conspiracy to commit espionage (Figure 1.6).[166] Kaufman dismissed the jury, admitting he would "miss seeing" their "faces here morning after morning."[167] The judge prepared for sentencing.

Prosecuting attorney Roy Cohn initially recommended that Judge Kaufman give the death penalty to Sobell and the Rosenbergs, or death for Sobell and Julius, with thirty years for Ethel in the hope she might someday name members of her husband's spy ring and they could be prosecuted.[168] Kaufman decided on a lighter sentence of fifteen years for David Greenglass as reward for his cooperation with the prosecution; he served ten years before his release in 1960.[169] The judge chose thirty years for Sobell since the prosecution could not prove Sobell's connection to atomic espionage, but he also recommended denying early parole. Kaufman's suggestion was later ignored and Sobell served eighteen years before

Figure 1.6 Ethel and Julius Rosenberg as they leave the U.S. courthouse after being found guilty by the jury, March 29, 1951. Roger Higgins, *New York World-Telegram & the Sun* Newspaper Photograph Collection. Courtesy of Library of Congress.

his release in 1969.[170] In September 2008, after a lifetime of denials, Morton Sobell finally admitted he had been a Soviet spy.[171] On April 4, Judge Kaufman thanked the FBI for "a fabulous job" and, gushing, commended the agents in his courtroom for being "as gentlemanly and delightful as anyone could be."[172] The next day Kaufman sentenced Julius and Ethel Rosenberg to death.

In his lengthy justification for imposing the death penalty, Judge Kaufman took the courtroom on a journey of his reasoning. He began with a lie, claiming to have "refrained from asking the Government for a recommendation" and concealing the many government officials he consulted for sentencing advice.[173] He clarified that espionage—"sordid, dirty work" which included "the betrayal of one's country"—deserved the maximum sentence.[174] He explained the penalty for espionage was up to thirty years in prison or death if committed during wartime, and since the prosecution proved the conspiracy "commenced on or about June 6, 1944 at which time the country was at war," the death sentence was justified.[175]

While the espionage began during World War II, it was the Cold War that Kaufman focused on. "This country is engaged in a life and death struggle," he explained, and the "punishment to be meted out in this case must therefore serve the maximum interest for the preservation of our society against these traitors in our midst."[176] Seemingly quoting from NSC-68, Kaufman argued that "never at any time in our history" did we ever face "such a challenge to our very existence" as the threat of Soviet Communism.[177] With national security at risk the judge intended the severe sentence to stop all of those engaged in military espionage, "whether promoted by slavish devotion to a foreign ideology or by a desire for monetary gains."[178] Leniency toward the Rosenbergs "would violate the solemn and sacred trust that the people of this land have placed in my hands" and be "an indication of weakness."[179]

Kaufman understood that sentencing a young mother to death required further explanation. While Julius "was the prime mover in this conspiracy," the judge explained,

> let no mistake be made about the role which his wife, Ethel Rosenberg, played in this conspircy [*sic*]. Instead of deterring him from pursuing his ignoble cause, she encouraged and assisted the cause. She was a mature woman,—almost three years older than her husband and almost seven years older than her younger brother. She was a full fledged partner in this crime.[180]

In addition to the she-should-have-known-better argument, Kaufman accused her of loving Communism more than she loved her children.

Kaufman ended with the final nail in the Rosenbergs' coffin: Korea. In justifying his decision, he reiterated the Truman administration and blamed the "arch criminals in this nefarious scheme" for instigating the invasion of South Korea.[181]

> I consider your crime worse than murder . . . I believe your conduct in putting into the hands of the Russians the A-bomb years before our best scientists predicted Russia would perfect the bomb has already caused, in my opinion, the Communist aggression in Korea, with the resultant casualties exceeding 50,000 and who knows but that millions more of innocent people may pay the price of your treason . . . It is not in my power, Julius and Ethel Rosenberg, to forgive you. Only the Lord can find mercy for what you have done.[182]

The same day Kaufman condemned the Rosenbergs to death, the Defense Department confirmed American casualties surpassed 50,000 and combat deaths reached nearly 10,000.[183]

It was not altogether surprising that Judge Kaufman echoed Truman and blamed the Rosenbergs for the debacle in Korea. The president's "Free World vs. Communist world" rhetoric had failed to make Korea a popular war.[184] Battlefield defeats had crushed the belief that rich, technologically advanced forces always won.[185] Several times a week newspapers across the country reported figures of American servicemen killed, wounded, or missing in action. Americans saw they were suffering a bloody stalemate in Korea, and wanted someone to take the blame for the death of the dream of U.S. military superiority. For many observers the Rosenbergs were responsible. When Kaufman claimed millions "may pay the price of your treason," he led many to mistakenly conclude that the Rosenbergs had been convicted of treason and not conspiracy to commit espionage. Months later, Supreme Court Justice Felix Frankfurter would contend that the couple had been "tried for conspiracy and sentenced for treason."[186] Years later, jurors would mistakenly recall they had declared the Rosenbergs guilty of treason.[187] Many history textbooks continue to get this wrong.

Hoping to thwart accusations of anti-Semitism—an emotional issue in the shadow of the Holocaust—Kaufman emphasized his own reliance on Judaism. He claimed he had "prayed at his synagogue for guidance the night before he sentenced the Rosenbergs to death."[188] Not all viewed the judge's reliance on faith in a positive light. Justice Frankfurter disagreed with "a judge who feels God told him to impose a death sentence," and later called the action "unjudicial conduct."[189] For Irving Kaufman, however, the sentence merely represented justice served.

Before the trial began the judge was determined to sentence Julius to death, yet he had wavered on whether to give the same penalty to his wife.[190] Pondering Ethel's sentence, Kaufman took to a phone booth next to the Park Avenue Synagogue to ask Roy Cohn for his advice.[191] "The way I see it is that she's worse than Julius," Cohn later recalled telling the judge.

> She's the older one, she's the one with the brains, she recruited her younger brother into the Young Communist League and into the spy ring, she's the one who typed the atomic bomb documents, she engineered this whole thing, she was the mastermind of this conspiracy. So unless you're willing to say that a woman is immune from the death penalty, I don't see how you can justify sparing her.

Cohn concluded: "Irving, it's your baby."[192] Kaufman had to agree. The next day the front page of the *New York Daily News* blared: "A-SPY COUPLE DOOMED TO DIE."

Less than a week after the Rosenberg sentencing claimed newspaper front pages around the country and the world, shocking news from Korea became the big story. On April 11, 1951, President Truman fired the popular seventy-one-year-old UN Commander, General Douglas MacArthur. Truman had determined that MacArthur, and his insubordination in publicly threatening to extend the war into China, needed to be silenced to ensure civilian control over the military.[193] In replacing MacArthur with General Matthew Ridgway, Truman suffered politically, but likely kept the Korean War from expanding into a global conflict.[194] While MacArthur enjoyed a farewell speech before Congress and a ticker-tape parade with seven million New Yorkers, Truman's approval ratings plummeted and never recovered.[195] Baseball fans booed the president when he threw out the first pitch at the Senators home opener against the Yankees, and, more importantly, he lost any influence he had in Congress, becoming more of a "caretaker president."[196]

Determined to prove he could win in Korea, Truman considered nuclear weapons. In April 1951, the president signed an order passing control of nine Mark IV nuclear capsules to the U.S. Air Force in Guam.[197] In the confusion following General Douglas MacArthur's removal the order apparently was not sent.[198] By late spring 1951 troops were back to the 38th parallel, bogged down in bloody trench warfare. This police action would last for two more years, making the conflict less newsworthy but no less deadly; the press coverage could only cover ever-increasing casualty figures.[199]

The Rosenberg executions scheduled for May 1951 were immediately stayed, or temporarily suspended, pending appeals. Officials transported Ethel from the Women's House of Detention in Manhattan to Sing Sing Prison, twenty-nine miles north in Ossining, in Westchester County. In operation since 1825, Sing Sing was the site of all New York state executions from 1914 to 1963.[200] Julius joined Ethel at the prison a few weeks later. The couple occupied separate cells, but visited each other once a week, separated by wire mesh. At Sing Sing they waited out the lengthy course of their appeals.[201]

The Truman administration's goal for the case was not just to prove American strength and the superiority of its judicial system, but also to use the death sentence to deter future spies.[202] Believing the prosecution had achieved just that, Attorney General J. Howard McGrath praised Roy Cohn for his part "during this extremely important trial."[203] FBI Director J. Edgar Hoover concurred, stating, "this case is truly a sterling example of our democratic processes in action and a distinctive achievement to be enrolled in the annals of our courts' history."[204] Expressions of appreciation indicated the importance of the case and the gratitude the Truman administration felt toward those who had succeeded in securing convictions. As the FBI waited for Julius to feel the pressure of the death sentence and name names, the administration turned to what they saw as the simple task of convincing the global community of the necessity of prosecuting these Communist spies to the full extent of the law.

Truman turned to the newly created Psychological Strategy Board (PSB) to manage the government's spin of the case.[205] Organized to coordinate Cold War psychological warfare and propaganda, the PSB consisted of representatives from the CIA, the Joint Chiefs, and the Departments of State and Defense. The fledgling agency struggled to navigate the divide between the diplomatic corps and the White House, while staying apprised of CIA efforts, and stumbled more often than not. While the PSB tried to craft a tightly woven official account of the Rosenbergs' crimes and justify their punishment, individuals and organizations at home and abroad began to poke holes in the board's flimsy narrative. Dissenting voices demanded more information about the evidence against the couple, the role of Ethel in the spy ring, and particularly the severity of the sentence.

As questions emerged without a clear government response, other voices filled the void. Two developments—one journalistic, one organizational—moved a vocal minority of Americans to question the case and had an even greater impact on global opinion. The New York–based, progressive weekly paper the *National Guardian* was eager to keep the plight of the Rosenbergs fresh in readers' minds.[206] In August 1951, James Aronson and William Reuben published the first in a series of essays criticizing the death sentences that would orphan two children, highlighted discrepancies concerning the guilt of the defendants, and raised the question of a possible miscarriage of justice.[207] Aronson in particular won the trust of Julius and Ethel, who named him as a possible guardian to their sons.[208] The paper also printed several letters Julius and Ethel Rosenberg wrote to each other while in prison; their death house correspondence reminded readers of the small family at the center of the case.[209]

The *National Guardian*'s embrace of the Rosenberg cause prompted a small group of concerned Americans to organize. New Yorkers David and Emily Alman formed the National Committee to Secure Justice in the Rosenberg Case (NCSJRC) in October 1951. For years the NCSJRC planned petitions, protests, and press releases supporting the Rosenbergs.[210] They also produced a "16-mm black and white film and a 78 rpm vinyl record" to be used at "open-air sound-truck meetings."[211] In March 1952 more than a thousand interested New Yorkers attended the first meeting, and by the following month there were more than a dozen local chapters throughout the United States, with an additional sixty local committees in New York City.[212] As appeals continued over the following months and years, the small and inexperienced committee had a chance to grow in size and influence. Both the NCSJRC and the *National Guardian* used press and protest efforts to highlight the plight of the young boys and their parents.

With no competing or coherent story emerging from the White House, administration officials discredited the growing protest movement as Communist shenanigans. J. Edgar Hoover ordered FBI agents to find evidence that the CPUSA, under the direction of the Soviet Union, coordinated the pro-clemency campaign. Hoover went to herculean lengths to prove this connection, including recruiting the babysitter of NCSJRC organizers David and Emily Alman as an informer.[213] The NCSJRC was probably not a front for the Communist Party.[214] The CPUSA initially tried to limit the committee's activities, fearing Julius might break down and confess and bring the party down with him. This distance could have helped preserve the Rosenbergs' claim of innocence. Also, it is unlikely the CPUSA would have been a very effective propaganda manager since the party was still reeling from the removal of its top leaders by Smith Act court cases. Consistently bad news from Korea, however, continued to remind Americans of the dangerous position Communists had put them in.

In the summer and fall of 1951, failure in Korea prompted Truman's approval ratings to plummet to 23 percent. The Defense Department reluctantly admitted that 73,604 Americans were casualties of the Korean War, of which 12,202 were combat fatalities.[215] In October, *U.S. News and World Report* somberly observed that the Korean "police action" had caused more casualties than the first fifteen months of World War II.[216] Claiming to see no way "to win a clear military victory" and "no end to the conflict in sight," reporters began to refer to the struggle as the "forgotten" war.[217] "Korea is so embarrassing," one writer observed, that nearly two years before it would end "officials are trying to forget it."[218] Even Secretary of State Acheson called Korea "a sour little war," unwinnable and best forgotten.[219]

Many Americans believed the atomic bomb had forced them into Korea in the first place, and a desperate Truman again considered unleashing its power on the Korean battlefield.[220] To test the feasibility of its use, the president authorized Operation Hudson Harbor. American pilots flew B-29 bombers, testing bomb runs and dropping "dummy" atomic bombs over numerous targets in North Korea.[221] A mere six years after the bombing of Hiroshima and Nagasaki in neighboring Japan, these B-29s triggered panic in the already terrified Korean population.[222] Fearing escalation, representatives from all parties met in Kaesong, the ancient Korean capital, to discuss a cease-fire. Negotiations stumbled over repatriation of the large number of prisoners of war and talks dragged on through 1952.[223] By October 1952, more than 20,000 Americans had been killed in Korea.[224]

Meanwhile, the legal options open to the Rosenbergs hit a major roadblock when the U.S. Supreme Court rejected their appeal in October 1952. Shortly after Ethel observed her thirty-seventh birthday, she and Julius heard the news over the Sing Sing Prison radio. They promptly issued a statement promising to continue pleading their case "before the bar of public opinion" since their "pleas to the Supreme Court" had been "restricted by legal protocol."[225] In voting against *certiorari*, or review, the Supreme Court indicated insufficient reason to rehear the case.[226] "Washington is silent over the horrible decision to execute Julius and Ethel Rosenberg," the CPUSA newspaper the *Daily Worker* lamented.[227] The court action triggered immediate protest from the NCSJRC, at the time boasting branches in more than twenty-five cities across the United States. It would be months before the Supreme Court would again weigh in on the case.

The *Daily Worker* reported the emergence of global protest with front-page coverage in Communist papers "from Scotland to China."[228] American embassy officials began acknowledging the protests and bringing them to Washington's attention. The State Department cited a piece in the October 1952 *Vorwaerts*, the Communist daily paper in Bern, Switzerland, the first foreign press report.[229] The article set a precedent for Communist protest journalism in that it questioned the couple's guilt and the American judicial system; emphasized the fate of the Rosenberg children; and issued a call to action, as modeled by the *National Guardian* and the NCSJRC. "The 'Rosenberg atomic affair' was arranged by the American Gestapo," the Swiss paper argued. "The mother of two children and her husband are waiting in the condemned cell at Sing-Sing," and their lives "depend on a protest by the public throughout the world. Demand a commutation of the death sentence from President Truman. Prevent this from being another Sacco and Vanzetti case."[230]

The Swiss Communists chose to link the Rosenbergs to the infamous 1920s Italian anarchists to highlight what they saw as a pattern of American injustice. Immigrants and radicals, Nicola Sacco and Bartolomeo Vanzetti were convicted of a robbery and murder in Massachusetts in 1921 and executed in 1927 after a lengthy legal and political battle. This cause célèbre captured international attention.[231] Questions of guilt, innocence, and irregularities in the trial continue to envelope the case, and opponents of the Rosenberg verdict would reference Sacco and Vanzetti as shorthand for American injustice.[232]

Evidence from Soviet archives indicates that Soviet Communists did not direct the Swiss press piece. Available KGB documents and transcribed Venona transcripts allow a glimpse of the Soviet propaganda campaign for the Rosenbergs.[233] KGB officials grappled with a propaganda dilemma in an April 1951 document: how to help Communist spy Julius Rosenberg without acknowledging his value to their espionage program.[234] The Soviets admitted placing a few articles in their own press, but emphasized initiating a "vigorous" campaign that would target "first and foremost" the non-Communist foreign press.[235] The KGB stressed using non-Communist newspapers to avoid Soviet fingerprints on the propaganda operation.[236] Soviet agents ordered that these articles focus on several key propaganda points: (1) the general "spy-mania" atmosphere surrounding the trial, which threatened to turn the United States "completely fascist"; (2) prejudicial aspects of the trial and the questionable value of the secrets supposedly delivered; (3) the harsh punishment of a mother of two, especially in comparison to sentences for Japanese spy Tokyo Rose and German spy Axis Sally; (4) the immorality of the death sentence as an example of American injustice; and (5) the effort by the U.S. government to "shift the blame for war in Korea off of themselves and onto Jews and Communists."[237] While the talking points of this April 1951 memo would often remain consistent, these pieces appeared only in Communist newspapers for a few months, indicating the Soviets had either failed, or had little to do with the protest.[238]

As pro-Rosenberg articles continued to appear in the international Communist press, U.S. Foreign Service officials assumed that they were Soviet-directed. This misinterpretation overemphasized the strength of the Soviet propaganda apparatus, while simultaneously belittling what amounted to a growing global protest movement. Even if the KGB tried to direct Rosenberg propaganda, evidence indicates that Soviet officials were unable to craft and manage an unwieldy, emotional, and lengthy global propaganda effort.[239] U.S. government officials, specifically the Psychological Strategy Board (PSB), would have the same problem.

Dramatic events in Czechoslovakia briefly took center stage. The Slansky treason and sabotage trial began in Prague in 1952 with the torture of the defendants and concluded quickly with the hanging of Rudolph Slansky, the former Marxist secretary general of Czechoslovakia, and Vlado Clementis, the Czech foreign minister. Nine other Communist Party members were also executed. Eleven of the original defendants were Jews accused of Zionist crimes against the state.

Many Communists became interested in the plight of the Rosenbergs to take attention away from the accusations of anti-Semitism surrounding the Slansky trial.[240] One Communist Party leader in France claimed that the conviction of the Rosenbergs "was an example of anti-Semitism but the execution of eight Jews in Czechoslovakia last week was not."[241] CIA officials concluded that the Soviets were trying—unsuccessfully in their view—to charge anti-Semitism in the Rosenberg case to counter the negative publicity surrounding the Slansky trials.[242] Western European Communists distinguished Slansky's conviction as one confirmed by a confession, though few could see it as anything but coerced. In contrast, the Rosenbergs continued to declare their innocence.

The Slansky trial seemed to provide a propaganda opportunity. The American ambassador to London proposed that the State Department could directly compare the Rosenberg case to the "recent Czech Commie trial" as example of the superiority of American justice over the Soviet style. There were "certain obvious comparisons and contrasts" that could be made, he explained, to highlight the justice given to the Rosenbergs and the kind of anti-Semitic justice available under Soviet Communism.[243] The CIA urged the president, whether he decided to commute the death sentences or not, to "avoid presidential propaganda activity," especially if it merely followed the pattern set by the Communists, in comparison to the Slansky case.[244] State Department officials agreed with CIA agents and quickly rejected the ambassador's request, at least for the time being.

Untethered from Soviet propaganda, the Swiss Communist Party's public embrace of the Rosenbergs opened the floodgates. Communist Party writings spread throughout Western Europe, emphasizing the extreme sentence, the injustice of the trial, and judicial irregularities that seemed to point to the innocence of the couple.[245] For example, in late October, U.S. embassy officials in Rome and The Hague reported their first cases of "Commie" press coverage criticizing the pending executions.[246] Both embassies also described the non-Communist news coverage as "brief and factual" with no editorial comment, despite the KGB propaganda effort to place inflammatory pro-Rosenberg reporting in mainstream newspaper outlets.[247]

By the end of October 1952, the American Embassy in London received hundreds of letters and telegrams asking for leniency for the Rosenbergs. Within a month, that number doubled. Walter Gifford, American ambassador to London and former AT&T executive, reported increased coverage of the case in the Communist Party press, citing front-page stories in the British *Daily Worker*.[248] Protest letters continued to stream in from Communists, British lawyers, and trade unionists, and in November activists in London opened a British branch of the Committee to Secure Justice in the Rosenberg Case (CSJRC).[249] Gifford claimed that the coverage on the case was limited to the Communist press, but conceded that a large number of British citizens believed American justice was "wayward and inferior" to that of the United Kingdom, and many were "inclined to regard with horror any death sentence," especially for espionage during peace time.[250] Gifford suggested that Secretary Acheson either provide a fact sheet for the press, or avoid publicity about the case altogether. In response to mounting pressure, Acheson agreed with the ambassador and instructed State Department officials to produce an information memo that contrasted the Rosenberg case with the Slansky trial.[251] When the embassy endured several cases of picketing, Gifford complained to Acheson: "From [a] public relations point of view here, the sooner [the] *final outcome* [in the] Rosenberg case is reached the better."[252]

In the fall of 1952, the first Communist protests from Canada constituted the start of a "strong movement" emphasizing American injustice.[253] Activists in Montreal created an emergency Committee to Save the Rosenbergs (CSR) and promptly embarked on crafting petitions and picketing the American Embassy in Ottawa. Foreign service officials saw that half of the protesters were women, and assumed they were "motherly types who had been enlisted as fronts."[254] In Quebec, Communists distributed postcards to mail to the White House with the inscription: "The American tradition for humanity and justice would be seriously undermined in the eyes of the world should the Rosenbergs be electrocuted."[255] One Vancouver woman wrote her own letter to Truman: "In the interests of civil liberties, democracy, and human justice, I demand that the Rosenbergs live!!!"[256] Three Canadian Jewish newspapers—the *Toronto Daily Hebrew Journal*, *Winnipeg Jewish Post*, and *Vancouver Jewish Western Bulletin*—pleaded with President Truman to intervene on the Rosenbergs' behalf.[257] The White House never dignified such protests with a response. Nevertheless, the outcry signaled the beginning of a consistent flow of angry communications from America's neighbor to the north.

That autumn the French Communist Party launched a full-scale campaign that would soon dwarf all other efforts. James Clement Dunn, the "experienced, level-headed and earnest" American ambassador to France, warned Secretary of State Dean Acheson that the "local Commie protest machinery" would soon go "promptly into motion."[258] The Communist Party called for Parisians to appeal directly to President Truman to free the Rosenbergs. The left-wing paper *L'Humanité* claimed the Rosenbergs were "ordinary young American non-Communists persecuted solely for their progressive ideas," and the charges were "trumped up" by Democrats "anxious" to prove they were "as good as Republicans at massacring 'reds.' "[259] Ambassador Dunn's concerns hardly set off alarms or received prompt action; officials did not forward his telegram to the Assistant Secretary for Public Affairs for two months.[260] State Department staff were not worried about what they again assumed was Soviet propaganda.

The FBI, in contrast, had been concerned about anti-American protests in Paris for months. When Judge Kaufman informed the Bureau of his intent to visit Paris in the summer of 1952, J. Edgar Hoover had advised him not to go. French sources had informed Hoover that the Communist Party in Paris might not limit itself to "passive anti-American action, such as painting signs on automobiles," but possibly could "engage in acts of violence or sabotage."[261] Hoover warned Kaufman that the French Communists were "pretty rabid in their demonstrations against Americans at the present time" and the Bureau could not guarantee the judge a safe visit to Paris.[262] The FBI soon became so worried about the judge's safety that they assigned him police protection even within the United States.[263]

The ramping up of protests in France was a foreboding sign of things to come. An election rapidly approached, bringing with it a new occupant of the White House, but Truman would still be in charge for two more months. He had inherited a world torn apart by global war and oversaw the transition to a different kind of conflict against global Communism. In his administration's final months he would struggle to bring the deadly catastrophe in Korea to an end and strengthen U.S. security by gathering allies and potential allies closer. But those same nations increasingly questioned America's commitment to justice and democracy, particularly as seen through the lens of the Rosenberg atomic spy case. And the fate of those convicted spies became increasingly uncertain.

2

Transition

I am extremely sorry that you have allowed a bunch of screwballs to come between us. You have made a big mistake, and I'm hoping it won't injure this great Republic.

—Truman to Eisenhower, *August 16, 1952*

On the first day of November 1952, the United States tested its first hydrogen bomb. The H-bomb—equipped with 10.4 megatons of thermonuclear energy and adorned with a photograph of Hollywood sex symbol Rita Hayworth—obliterated Elugelab, part of the Enewetak atoll in the Marshall Islands.[1] Referred to as the Super, it left a crater one-half mile deep and two miles wide and was a thousand times more destructive than the bomb dropped on Hiroshima. Truman had ordered the development of the deadly bomb in an effort to stay ahead of the Soviets in the nuclear bomb race, but not all agreed with that decision. Numerous physicists, including J. Robert Oppenheimer, had objected, and even America's close ally Winston Churchill voiced concern.[2] "There is an immense gulf between the atomic and hydrogen bomb," the British prime minister argued. "The atomic bomb, with all its terrors, did not carry us outside the scope of human control," but the H-Bomb revolutionized the "entire foundation of human affairs" and mankind is now "placed in a situation both measureless and laden with doom."[3]

Determined to reassure anxious Americans, the chair of the Atomic Energy Commission (AEC) issued a statement. Gordon Dean admitted that the detonation of "many, many thermonuclear weapons" could "conceivably" pollute the planet "with elements which are inconsistent with human life." However, he explained that that possibility was unlikely and "something that I wouldn't worry about at the moment."[4] He urged Americans to do the same.

Alarmed by humanity's ability to obliterate itself with relative ease, and unending war in Korea, Americans headed to the voting booth. They turned to a new leader, a man they felt they knew and could trust. Instantaneous change, however, was not possible, and strained relations between Truman and the president-elect only exacerbated the often-difficult presidential transition period.

For the Rosenbergs, a leadership vacuum in Washington from November 1952 to January 1953 could not have come at a worse time. The State Department— caught off balance—played catch-up for the remainder of Truman's term, trying to control the propaganda on the death sentence and adequately address the global community's concerns.

On November 4, 1952, Americans elected representatives who they hoped would stay strong against Communism.[5] The residents of Wisconsin approved aggressive anti-Communist tactics and re-elected Senator Joseph McCarthy. Since his Wheeling, West Virginia, speech in February 1950, McCarthy had continued to accuse government officials of being soft on Communism, claiming that even one Communist was one too many.[6] He once told a group of reporters that if anyone did not support him, they must be either "a Communist or a cocksucker."[7] While some dared to criticize McCarthy—one reporter claimed, "Joe didn't know Karl Marx from Groucho"—as a senator he commanded attention and wielded tremendous power in Washington.[8]

McCarthy extended his influence when he gave a speech on the senate floor criticizing George C. Marshall. The senator accused the former secretary of state of being the central figure of a Soviet Communist plot, "a conspiracy so immense and an infamy so black as to dwarf any previous venture in the history of man."[9] While Senate Democrats boycotted McCarthy's lengthy speech, Republican presidential candidate Dwight D. Eisenhower did not have that luxury. The candidate bowed to McCarthy's political strength during a campaign speech in McCarthy's home state of Wisconsin. Eisenhower did not defend Marshall, his friend and mentor, choosing instead to cut the section of his speech where he praised the five-star general and condemned the senator. McCarthy would soon chair the Senate Permanent Subcommittee on Investigations, where he continued spreading blame and fear.[10]

Eisenhower, himself a popular former general, also prevailed when voters supported him in a landslide victory. For the first time since the election of Herbert Hoover, Americans were sending a Republican to the White House. He defeated Adlai Stevenson, who Eisenhower's running mate Richard Nixon claimed held a "PhD from Dean Acheson's cowardly college of Communist containment." Nixon had warned that if Stevenson were elected, he would "bring more atomic spies" and "more crisis."[11] Running on a campaign against "Korea, Communism, Corruption," Eisenhower had projected the image of a plainspoken man from Kansas.[12] He promised to end the bloody stalemate in Korea—where more than 21,000 Americans had been killed—and stand firm against Communism at home and abroad.[13] Just a few weeks after the election, the president-elect validated the significance of Korea when he headed there on a fact-finding tour.[14] This action did not please the sitting president.

When President Truman welcomed the president-elect to the White House a fortnight after the election, all was not well. The *New York Times* called the meeting "coolly formal" and detected "evidence of tension between Mr. Truman and his successor."[15] While the relationship had once been cordial, the election season brought with it a series of misunderstandings that left a rift. Truman believed that Eisenhower had abandoned a great man when the candidate had not supported General George Marshall as he endured Senator Joseph McCarthy's attacks.[16] The president was also infuriated when Eisenhower declined the president's offer to attend foreign policy briefings with the CIA.[17] When Eisenhower followed through on a campaign promise and went to Korea to assess the war first-hand, Truman belittled the trip as "a piece of demagoguery."[18]

The president and the president-elect rarely spoke during the two-month transition period. The two would never discuss the Rosenbergs. They would never consider the irregularities of the case. And they would never confer on how to manage the unwieldy propaganda campaign to convince the world of the virtue of executing the couple.

In late December 1952, Judge Kaufman complained he had been "hounded and pounded" when he rejected the Rosenbergs' motion for a reduced sentence.[19] "Their traitorous acts were of the highest degree," Kaufman explained.[20] They gave "our deepest military secrets . . . to a foreign power," and then continued "to traffic in our military secrets when this allegedly friendly country became hostile to us and engages in a cold war with America."[21] The judge included a special reference to Ethel, highlighting that she was not only "older in years" but also "wise in Communist doctrine."[22]

Kaufman also took an unusual stance in a domestic legal case—he publicly suggested that the president intervene. The judge admitted that he had "not considered the international consequences of the Soviet propaganda" concerning the death sentences, but feared that these "false characterizations of this trial" might poison "the minds of the people of the world." He explained that as a judge he was not able to evaluate the "effectiveness" of the American propaganda campaign "upon our foreign relations," but he advised the president to do so. Kaufman explained that Truman was "vested with power to grant reprieves and pardons for offenses against the United States," and that perhaps in this case he should consider doing so. The "public welfare," including the "international as well as national situations," might "be better served by inflicting less than the judgment fixed."[23] The judge understood that his hands were tied, but he saw the government's propaganda efforts failing and pressed the president to act.

The judge agreed to stay the executions until January 1953 to give the Rosenbergs the chance to submit their formal clemency appeal to the president. Meanwhile, Kaufman felt vulnerable as the process continued and requested police protection.[24] The Supreme Court had announced their denial of *certiorari* earlier that fall, so as the January 12 date approached the deaths seemed far more imminent, sparking a new wave of global protest.[25]

Soviet propagandists were pleased, and U.S. government officials surprised, when European protest began to spread beyond Communists to Socialists and other liberals. The recently discovered State Department documents indicate a rapid spread in the pro-Rosenberg campaign. Many of these activists accepted the possibility of the Rosenbergs' guilt, but advocated clemency for the couple based on opposition to capital punishment. The death penalty issue continued to lure supporters over the course of the Rosenbergs' appeal process since many European countries had either eliminated it or would halt executions within twenty years.[26]

CIA agents reported that Communist press coverage had sparked activity in France, Italy, Norway, England, and Israel.[27] In Italy, for example, Pietro Nenni, the leader of that country's Socialist party, wrote to Truman on behalf of the Rosenbergs. Italian Socialists had been allied with Americans against Mussolini during World War II and continued to be valuable as a counter to the Communist majority threatening to take over the Italian Parliament. The Cold War, however, eliminated political nuance, and the Truman administration did not distinguish Communists from others on the political left. When Nenni publicly urged action to save the Rosenbergs, the embassy in Rome conveyed the message to Secretary of State Acheson. Floundering with little direction from Washington, a diplomat in Rome suggested that if the president denied clemency, the State Department would need to publicly refute Nenni's pro-Rosenberg statements and argue that his appeal constituted "flagrant interference in the internal affairs of another country."[28] Diplomats typically ignored Rosenberg protests, but they admitted that "given the considerable influence" Nenni would exert in the 1953 elections, it might help "to demonstrate that he talks out of both sides of his mouth."[29]

It took more than a month for Secretary of State Acheson to respond to the embassy's concerns regarding Pietro Nenni. In a telegram to the embassy in Rome, Acheson halted the discussion: "When [a] decision [is] reached regarding Executive clemency for Rosenbergs, [the] embassy will be informed and will be instructed."[30] The secretary of state's top-down approach discouraged much input from the field; as demonstrations escalated around the world Acheson continued to ignore or belittle protests as Communist propaganda, even when they came from friendly sources like Pietro Nenni.[31]

Meanwhile, embassy officials offered advice. The U.S. ambassador to Rome, Ellsworth Bunker, requested a "detailed story" of the Rosenberg trial that "should describe every move" the defense attorneys made to save their clients' lives.[32] Diplomats in Warsaw complained that the Polish press simply followed the "worldwide Commie propaganda theme" and suggested the Polish Voice of America (VOA) should give a factual account of the Rosenbergs' activities and the trial procedures, contrasting this story with the particulars of the Slansky trial in Prague.[33] The embassy in Bonn also recommended a VOA radio show to distinguish the Rosenberg case from trials behind the iron curtain, like those in Prague.[34] Under the purview of the State Department since 1945, the VOA broadcast American anti-Communist propaganda around the world to counter Communist misinformation. If the VOA intended to persuade global listeners of the U.S. commitment to democracy and freedom, they missed this propaganda opportunity, instead remaining back on their heels as protests grew in Europe.[35]

A few State Department officials in Washington began to voice alarm about the portrayal of the case in the European press, particularly "the fact that even some of the liberal, though non-Communist, papers were handling the case" in a manner that "indicated either a definite bias or a woeful ignorance of the real facts in the case."[36] One official questioned how far this could possibly spread to non-Communists since he assumed that the only organization behind all these protests, the Committee to Secure Justice in the Rosenberg Case (CSJRC), was Communist inspired if not Communist directed.[37] Their concerns prompted the State Department, apparently with little input from the Psychological Strategy Board (PSB), to begin a campaign to refute what they saw as Communist propaganda. Several State and Justice Department officials produced a memo to correct inaccuracies about the Rosenberg case they saw as "already proving harmful to the United States."[38] The dispatch emphasized key points: (1) Ethel's brother David Greenglass's testimony was given and corroborated in an open court; (2) life in prison was not an option under the Espionage Act; (3) Greenglass's reduced sentence was common in international law for those who confess; (4) Greenglass "was no simple mechanic," but a skilled Manhattan Project worker; (5) the judge and jury were not biased; (6) charges of anti-Semitism were "preposterous"; and (7) the sentence was not overly severe for the crime since the Rosenbergs' espionage activities were not "sporadic," but rather "deliberate, long continued, and unrepentant."[39] The State Department sent the memo to Paris, with copies to the other major European embassies in Moscow, London, Rome, Bonn, and Brussels.[40] The information, while certainly better than nothing, lacked analysis, and only whetted officials' appetites.

Increasingly concerned, Secretary of State Acheson ordered his subordinates to send even more materials to embassies in Europe. Officials forwarded to Paris and London eighty-five additional pages on the case, including the Joint Congressional Committee on Atomic Energy report, a bulletin of the American Civil Liberties Union, and a series of articles from the *New York Post*.[41] Acheson would soon also forward documents on the Court of Appeals and Supreme Court decisions, and the Justice Department's summary.

In France, protest escalated as Parisian activists opened their own branch of the CSJRC. American officials complained that information on the case came primarily from two sources: inadequate U.S. Information Service (USIS) briefings and Communist propaganda pieces. Novelist Howard Fast's article in the French left-wing paper *L'Humanité*, for example, highlighted judicial irregularities and argued for the couple's innocence.[42] Press attaché Ben Bradlee had seen enough.

In charge of press relations for the American Embassy in Paris, Bradlee hunted for better information on the case, claiming he was tired of not "knowing my ass from my elbow."[43] He feared "executing the Rosenbergs would surely worsen an already bad diplomatic crisis," referencing policy disputes between the United States and France.[44] He also believed that the case had become a "symbolic rallying point for everyone who had a bone to pick" with the U.S. government.[45] By the close of 1952, Bradlee complained to any American official who would listen that a majority of the French press was against the United States.

Ambassador James Dunn in Paris confirmed Bradlee's concerns when he declared that non-Communists had joined the French Rosenberg clemency campaign. Telegrams by the hundreds continued to flood the embassy from Communist and front groups, but were now joined by correspondence from individuals and organizations that, according to Dunn, had "no axe to grind."[46] The French Communist press also continued its campaign unabated, but the non-Communist press now added its voice. The mainstream paper *Le Monde* gave the Rosenbergs prominent front-page coverage, echoing the Communist theme that they "were scapegoats for American anti-Semitism."[47] The paper also compared Washington to Prague, in a reference to the Slansky trial. When the other mainstream paper, *Le Figaro*, interviewed fourteen prominent French intellectuals, many went beyond protesting the death sentence and made impassioned pleas declaring the couple's complete innocence. Ambassador Dunn regretted this "confused thinking" and reluctantly credited the "Commie campaign" with some success.[48] He implored Washington to strengthen the government's position on the case, explaining that the facts "have never been satisfactorily presented to French public and even our friends often are at [a] loss [to] know what to believe."[49] Dunn recommended that the State Department provide the French press—"preferably through French correspondents in U.S."—with a solid review of the Rosenberg case at the earliest opportunity.[50] Convincing documentation of espionage was necessary, he argued, to "correct Commie propaganda distortions and restore case to its true perspective here."[51]

In spite of Dunn's close working relationship with Acheson, France's position as an important ally, and Dunn's compelling argument, the State Department ignored the ambassador's telegram, an official scrawling across it "no action, file."[52] While the spread of criticism to the non-Communist press cannot be determined as a Soviet propaganda achievement, it was clear that diplomats on the ground had a different perspective than officials in Washington. There was a distinct, if inexplicable, time lag for concern and a missed opportunity to effectively sell America's version of the story to the French people.

French journalists continued to press for answers. They questioned the validity and reliability of Greenglass's testimony, the lack of corroborating witnesses, the unprecedented utilization of the death penalty in a civil court for espionage, and the severity of the sentence as compared to the fourteen years given to British scientist and convicted spy Klaus Fuchs.[53] Exasperated by the lack of government response, the Paris press attaché took matters into his own hands.[54]

Bradlee traveled to New York to review the Rosenberg trial record at the Foley Square library.[55] The Justice Department, however, did not appreciate the press attaché's efforts and denied him access to confidential files on the case.[56] Limited to only trial transcripts, Bradlee headed back to Paris in late December to produce an eighteen-page paper addressing the issues of the case he believed the French press got wrong. He later claimed the lack of State Department direction left him, "in effect, the Rosenberg attaché."[57]

Ambassador Dunn welcomed Bradlee's analysis and immediately ordered it translated and forwarded to the French press. He also sent copies to Secretary Acheson "for such use as may be deemed appropriate."[58] Dunn suggested Acheson might want to distribute it to other embassies, and took the initiative himself to send copies to a dozen Western European cities and several French colonial capitals with pro-Rosenberg movements.[59]

Bradlee's position paper consisted of a detailed summary of the case, with descriptions of witness testimony, a characterization of the jury and their selection process, and an explanation of the court appeals to date.[60] The final two pages, in question-and-answer format, addressed what Bradlee saw as the most significant issues troubling Parisians:

Why wasn't Ruth Greenglass indicted?

A husband cannot be compelled to testify against his wife.

How could Greenglass, a mechanic, know anything about atomic energy?

The drawing Greenglass provided was of the high explosive lens and a schematic of the principles of the bomb dropped on Nagasaki.

Was the information transmitted by Greenglass and Rosenberg as valuable and important as claimed by the government?

Defense attorney admitted it was a pretty good description of the atomic bomb.

Why didn't the government call the atomic scientists Urey and Oppenheimer, or General Groves as witnesses after their names were given to the defense on a list of government witnesses?

Not necessary for prosecution's case, the defense could have called them if they had wanted to. [Groves, in closed testimony, stated that Greenglass/Rosenberg atomic espionage did not help the Soviet Union. Urey and Oppenheimer made similar statements in 1953.]

Didn't anti-Semitism play an indirect role in the Rosenberg case, and especially in the sentence?

Judge and prosecutor were Jewish, no way of knowing if jurors were.

[None actually were, though nearly one in three New Yorkers at the time were Jewish.][61]

While the answers to these questions were clear, Bradlee ignored significant issues that plagued many Europeans, particularly the severity of the sentences, the apparent cruelty of executing young parents, and the flimsy evidence against Ethel. More importantly, his limited report highlighted Washington's uncoordinated global propaganda effort to address key Rosenberg case concerns.

Bradlee also dismissed the issue of anti-Semitism. As early as August 1952, the CIA had raised concerns about vulnerability to charges of discrimination against Jews.[62] But Bradlee brushed these concerns aside, claiming that it was "difficult to see how anti-Semitism can be attributed to a Jewish judge and a Jewish prosecutor."[63] This conclusion ignored the difficult position Judge Kaufman was in as a Jewish judge sentencing a Jewish couple; many contend he had to bend over backward to prove he was not overly sympathetic to the Rosenbergs as fellow Jews.[64] Jewish organizations convinced Truman administration officials to head off criticism by including Jews among the prosecutors.[65] The Rosenberg case provided American Jews with an opportunity to display their loyalty and patriotism, correct the claim that most Jews were Communists, and distance themselves publicly from radicals, Communists, and spies.[66]

In this way the case divided the American Jewish community, as seen in the American Jewish Committee's (AJC) decision to dissociate from convicted spies like the Rosenbergs.[67] Once the CPUSA claimed that anti-Semitism had tainted the trial, the AJC and other Jewish organizations were compelled to adopt the opposite argument.[68] Ben Bradlee's explanation ignored the fact that the virulent anti-Communism sweeping America made it necessary for Jews to distinguish themselves from Communists. Julius and Ethel Rosenberg were but two of the nearly five million Jews living in the United States in 1950, but as graffiti on a New York to Washington express train declared—"Keep Traitor Jews Out of the Country Remember Traitor Jews Rosenbergs"—they were the ones that mattered.[69]

By embracing the Rosenbergs' guilt, the AJC hoped to head off an increase in anti-Semitism should Americans link all Jews with Communism.[70] The fact was that a large number of American Communists were Jewish.[71] However, when the board of the American Civil Liberties Union (ACLU) overwhelmingly passed a resolution denying that the case raised any valid civil liberty issues, it effectively affirmed the fairness of the trial and for many took the issue of anti-Semitism off the table.[72]

The jury foreman confirmed the judge's position when he later explained, "Any other judge would have been more lenient than Kaufman ... the Jews hated the Rosenbergs for the disgrace they had brought upon their race."[73] The foreman concluded: "I felt good that this was strictly a Jewish show. It was Jew against Jew. It wasn't the Christians hanging the Jews."[74] However, regardless of how much government officials refuted charges of anti-Semitism, the view persisted, particularly among protesters overseas.

In direct contrast to many American Jews, the international Jewish community openly supported the Rosenbergs. In Toronto, twenty-two Israeli rabbis appealed to President Truman, pleading for commutation and imploring "all liberal and progressive people in Canada" to do the same.[75] The American legation at Tripoli, Libya, forwarded a letter from the president of the Jewish Community of Tripolitania, who said he represented the Jewish community and urged Truman to revoke the Rosenbergs' death sentence.[76] He feared that the executions would damage "the nobility of the American traditions" and concluded optimistically, "We trust that the magnanimity of the President of the USA, his humanity and that of the great American people will not be pitiless for the two Rosenbergs."[77] In Israel, the American Embassy in Tel Aviv reported that press coverage—especially editorials in *Haboler* and the *Jerusalem Post*—argued that clemency would emphasize the difference between humane justice in America and authoritarian justice in countries such as Prague. The papers accepted the Rosenbergs' guilt, but complained that the executions were "cruel and unusual punishment." Chief Rabbi Herzog of Israel wrote to Truman, requesting he order the couple's release to spare their two sons from becoming orphans and having their lives "ruined forever."[78] In addition, a delegation of women representing the Democratic Women's Organization of Israel asked the president for a new trial based on a "miscarriage of justice" and "in the name of human rights and for the sake of the two little children."[79] The American Consul in Haifa accepted the letter but ignored the women, assuming they were blindly following Communist directives.[80] American diplomats consistently dismissed protests, particularly Jewish opposition, as Soviet-directed and Communist, and were slow to recognize the growing global protest movement that accusations of anti-Semitism propelled forward.

Diplomats at the American Embassy at Bonn, the de facto capital of West Germany, begged Washington for help.[81] Bradlee's analysis had not yet arrived, and they suggested the State Department consider providing material to refute numerous claims about the case, including that the jury was "under [the] spell of U.S. hate psychosis" and that the trial had exposed the "'pogrom spirit' in Fascist USA."[82] Acheson suggested that while waiting for Bradlee's analysis, Bonn officials should contact Bradlee in Paris since he "is fully briefed and has complete documentation."[83] Acheson implied that he had handpicked Bradlee, brought him up to speed on the Rosenberg case, and put trust in him, when it was Bradlee himself who initiated the fact-finding trip with little or no assistance from Washington.

Soon diplomats in France were again expressing concern. In Paris, Ambassador Dunn repeated his complaint about the "basic factual errors" in the USIS Daily Radio Bulletin concerning the Rosenberg case, which "seriously complicate efforts to present [the] truth."[84] The radio story stated incorrectly that Morton Sobell was convicted to death along with the Rosenbergs (he received a thirty-year sentence) and that all were charged with transmitting atomic secrets (the crime was conspiracy to commit espionage). A subsequent USIS article inflated the number of government witnesses to more than one hundred. This error was "particularly serious," Dunn explained, "since one of main themes of Communist propaganda is that government said they would produce more than 100 witnesses and in fact produced only twenty-three."[85] Dunn again took matters into his own hands and gave Bradlee's analysis to select members of the press with general distribution to follow.

The next day Acheson thanked Dunn for "catching errors," which the department "deeply regretted."[86] While Acheson assured him preventative steps were being taken to avoid such problems in the future, it would not be the last time factual errors marred propaganda efforts to control the spin of the case. Still concerned, Dunn again took it upon himself to pouch to Washington a French translation of Bradlee's analysis with carbon copies to capitals around the globe, including Beirut, Berne, Brussels, Cairo, and Tangiers, and resent it to Algiers, Casablanca, and Saigon.[87]

Days later, Secretary Acheson instructed Ambassador Dunn to send the Bradlee analysis to an expanded list of twenty-three embassies and consulates, including Ankara, Athens, Buenos Aires, Capetown, Caracas, Colombo, Havana, Hong Kong, Istanbul, Karachi, New Delhi, Panama, Rangoon, Rio de Janeiro, São Paulo, Santiago, Sydney, Taipei, Tel Aviv, Tehran, and Wellington.[88] It is likely that the State Department had received reports of protests in these cities or saw them as vulnerable to the pro-Rosenberg propaganda campaign. The next day Acheson requested twelve "additional English copies" of the Rosenberg analysis.[89] It is difficult to imagine a situation in which the most efficient way for Washington to get copies of the report was for officials to ship them across the ocean from Paris. The rushed reproduction of Bradlee's paper indicates that Acheson belatedly placed some importance on the analysis and its propaganda benefits.

Soon embassy officials in Paris were reporting that their "efforts to counteract Communist propaganda about Rosenbergs" had produced some results.[90] Portions of Bradlee's analysis could be seen in several papers, including editorials in the three largest morning dailies, *Figaro*, *Parisien-Libéré*, and *L'Aurore*, along with *Franc-Tireur*, the largest evening paper. Even *Evidences*, a monthly published by the French branch of the American Jewish Committee, highlighted Bradlee's analysis. Yet the embassy emphasized that while these articles noted that the Rosenbergs had been "fairly convicted and guilty as charged . . . *all these stories have also expressed strongly [the] belief that execution is too severe a punishment.*"[91] Although the second page of this telegram is missing, the embassy likely continued to express concern that while American propaganda had succeeded to the extent that many Parisians believed the couple guilty, public relations efforts had not convinced the majority of Parisians of the necessity of executing the Rosenbergs.[92]

Paris embassy officials took to writing Secretary Acheson every few days in January 1953, fearing that the executions would produce a "barrage of Commie anti-American propaganda to which non-Commie elements may be receptive."[93] The embassy was receiving about fifty telegrams, letters, and petitions a day and the press coverage of the case had reached a "new high" in the Communist press and continued to spread into the non-Communist papers.[94] A front-page article in the mainstream paper *Le Figaro* endorsed clemency and placed a new emphasis on martyrdom. Arguing that "militant Communists" would continue to spy regardless of the threat of a death sentence, the "execution would be welcomed and used by Communists with cold satisfaction. Because Communism needs martyrs."[95] The paper implored, "Don't play their game. Don't give them these martyrs."[96] The front-page piece concluded referencing the Slansky trial in Prague: "It would be a wonderful victory over Communism if hangings of Prague were answered by clemency of Washington."[97] This reasoned plea from the mainstream press in France imploring the United States to seize the propaganda advantage failed to capture the attention of State Department officials in Washington, even when forwarded by embassy staff in Paris.

Diplomats, in falsely assuming all European protests were Communist-directed, underestimated the growing liberal, anti-Communist movement. Embassy officials at The Hague reported that more than a thousand people had signed petitions or sent telegrams protesting the Rosenberg case. Press coverage in The Hague spread from Communist to liberal papers, with a focus not on the guilt or innocence of the couple, but on the severity of the sentence and its assumed connection to McCarthyism. Both the liberal newspaper *Nieuwe Rotterdamchse Courant* and the workers' paper *Het Parool* emphasized that the Kremlin would benefit from the executions, because the Rosenbergs' "halos as martyrs" would "serve to attract others."[98]

Protests also spread in Germany. The American Consul in Duesseldorf received several missives from concerned citizens, while in Hamburg the Communist press distributed printed postcards, with drawings of the Rosenbergs on the front, to an estimated 30,000 people and pressed them to return the postcards to the American Consulate.[99] The Consul General explained that "this office intends to make a careful count of the postcards received and the signatures thereon, and hopes that the total will possibly indicate the number of hard core Communists in this consular district."[100] In this way, many embassies and consulates used the Rosenberg protests to uncover and track suspected Communists.

In the Netherlands, forty "well-behaved, young persons" petitioned at the American Consulate in Amsterdam and attached posters to the building that read, "The Rosenbergs must not die!"[101] According to the consulate there was "no outward sign that they were communists," but the petition they presented carried 540 signatures and focused on the talking points of the CSJRC—the possible innocence of the couple and the "barbarous sentence" they faced.[102] The consulate received 650 additional petitions for clemency in early January. Most of the correspondence emphasized the fate of the Rosenberg children, the possibility of the couple's innocence, and the role of American anti-Semitism, all Communist talking points.[103] Communist protest continued in Oslo, Norway, and in Budapest, Hungary.[104]

In Brussels, the Belgian Socialist press joined the Communists in criticizing the case. Socialist Senator Henry Rolin called for signatures on a telegram to Truman requesting a pardon for the Rosenbergs. Embassy officials called Rolin an "argumentative crank" and mocked his "meddling," which they claimed only produced eighteen Socialist MP signatures, or just 13 percent of parliament members.[105] Days later, when protest in Brussels spread to the non-Communist liberal paper, *Le Matin*, the embassy took notice. The newspaper affirmed the guilt of the couple and yet argued that the case would be a Communist victory because "either the Rosenbergs are executed and Communist propaganda will make out of them legendary martyrs for the cause," or their sentence will be reduced and "Communist propaganda will be triumphant in claiming the power of the 'Partisans of Peace.' "[106] The editorial urged Belgians, with their "alert conscience," to protest the impending executions on humanitarian grounds, regardless of the stance of the worldwide Communist movement.[107]

Ambassador to Belgium Myron M. Cowen—emboldened by an increase in pro-Rosenberg support in the Socialist, Christian Democratic, and non-Communist press—offered his own solution. Cowen explained that while the embassy did "not recommend commutation, we feel it is important to take into account reaction abroad if commutation is decided upon."[108] The ambassador—unsolicited—proposed a draft of what Truman should say if the president chose to commute the couple's sentence.

> I commuted the Rosenbergs sentence not because I believe for one moment that they are innocent, but because I know that the Soviet Government wishes them executed. During their lifetime the Rosenbergs have served the Soviet Government well as spies, and now that they are no longer of use alive, the Soviet Government wishes to make good use of them as martyrs. I have no desire to give that government satisfaction in the matter.[109]

Cowen boldly suggested the president's statement, but two days later, Secretary of State Acheson shot him down. "Your statement will be taken into consideration in drafting final release," Acheson explained, but "[I] suggest you consider what local Communist reaction would be to denial of clemency and suggest means" of countering this response.[110] Acheson implied that clemency was unlikely, and as the Truman administration wound down the secretary was more concerned with mitigating the damage he assumed would follow the Rosenberg executions. Acheson, of course, would have no way of ensuring that the incoming Eisenhower administration would take this statement into consideration, or that the incoming secretary of state would share Acheson's concern for countering Communist propaganda. The strained and noncommunicative presidential transition period had all but assured a diplomatic disconnect between administrations.

Non-Communist protest continued to spread in Italy. In Rome, the Italian Social Democratic Party sent an appeal for clemency to the American embassy, hoping that mercy "would further underline before universal conscience the difference between humanity of democratic justice and fanaticism of tribunals of totalitarian states."[111] Alarmed, Ambassador Ellsworth Bunker explained that this "appeal by responsible leadership of one of Democratic parties is in [a] different category from mass of Communist-inspired 'protests' alleging Rosenberg innocence."[112] Bunker requested instructions from the State Department on how to respond to this appeal, but he was left waiting until the new administration was in place.[113] The American Consulate in Milan received more than 180 postcards from women protesting the Rosenbergs' death sentences and emphasizing concern for the couple's children. Attributing the cards to a Communist-inspired propaganda campaign, the consulate noted the unprecedented number of communications concerning the case: "While isolated letters of protest are received from time to time," protest letters against the Rosenberg sentence "have reached unusually high levels."[114] The American Consul General, apparently a handwriting expert, determined that the communications concerning the case had signatures that "without exception" were the "characteristically cramped scrawls of persons who have had little education."[115] The consulate officials attributed the lack of public demonstrations to what they perceived as a customary practice of Communist propaganda efforts to avoid "active demonstrations," in spite of a large amount of evidence to the contrary.[116]

The State Department also received non-Communist protests from America's closest ally, Great Britain. Three members of the Labor Party and the non-Communist left wing called on the American Embassy in London and requested clemency, explaining that the executions "would give ammunition to Commies who could portray Rosenbergs as martyrs, and that it would be useful to those interested in promoting anti-American sentiment and disrupting Anglo-American accord."[117] They agreed that the conduct of the trial was fair, but believed that the majority of Labor Party members and a substantial minority of Conservative members of Parliament were against a death sentence.[118] To that point, London had received one thousand petitions and protests with several thousand signatures, and the embassy fully expected that number to increase. The Psychological Strategy Board had no propaganda plan, and the State Department declined to respond to these impassioned pleas even when they came from close allies.

President Truman's final weeks in office saw a marked rise in Canadian protest, though it became increasingly impossible to pinpoint the level of Communist involvement. Seventy-five members of the Toronto CSCEJR gathered at the Toronto Consulate General and presented an appeal for Truman that emphasized the "cruel, harsh, and unprecedented" death penalty that would "cause harm to the good name of the United States."[119] Days later they conducted a rally at Toronto's Massey Hall where more than two thousand attendees approved a resolution pleading for clemency (Figure 2.1). Members also contributed funds to sponsor some one hundred Torontonians to participate in round-the-clock picketing of the Canadian National Committee to Save the Rosenbergs (NCSR) at the Ottawa Embassy, the focal point of Canadian protest.[120] A consulate observer at the meeting could only identify one Communist—"a midget woman of about forty who has been described to me as an important local Communist"—and was forced to acknowledge that the clemency campaign had spread well beyond Communist Party supporters.[121] One group visited the embassy, claimed they were not influenced by any Communists, and presented a petition which emphasized the wide range of protests around the world, called the sentence excessive, and stressed that commutation would prove the United States was "strong enough to temper justice with mercy."[122] Truman administration officials failed to convince these protesters that the Rosenberg case was an example of American strength; many around the world instead interpreted it as reactionary, anti-Communist fear.

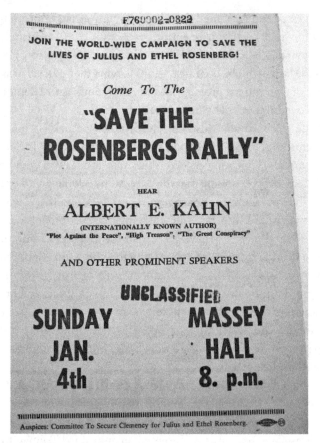

Figure 2.1 Flier for Pro-Rosenberg Rally, Toronto, Canada, January 4, 1953, RG 59. Courtesy of NARA.

Alarmed by the increased activity, the Second Secretary of the American Embassy in Ottawa forwarded two telegrams to Acheson. In a handwritten note the official requested help: "There is a whole pile of Rosenberg stuff. Please let me know to whom we send it."[123] No reply is indicated. The State Department did not know how to proactively control the propaganda war, how to respond to the worldwide Rosenberg clemency campaign, or even where to file the mounting paperwork.

By the end of 1952, pro-Rosenberg committees operating in Austria, Belgium, Denmark, Italy, Sweden, Switzerland, Germany, Ireland, Israel, and Eastern Europe confounded the PSB and the State Department.[124] American journalists confirmed what State Department telegrams revealed: "Picketing in front of American consulates and embassies overseas [had become] commonplace."[125] The *New York World-Telegram & Sun* agreed that the Rosenberg movement "here and abroad, in capitals of Europe, Africa, Asia" had "reached a white heat."[126] According to *U.S. News & World Report*, the Save the Rosenbergs campaign had become "a case study of how Communists can turn on the heat."[127] *Time* magazine complained that the "shrill" Communist protesters consistently "shrieked" about anti-Semitism.[128] While the State Department relied on Bradlee's analysis, the Justice Department was sufficiently concerned about European protest to rush a forty-page paper explaining the Rosenberg case to "countries on the continent."[129] Despite these attempts, clemency protests persisted.[130]

As international pressure to commute the Rosenberg sentences mounted, the Christmas holiday season arrived. Ethel Rosenberg sent a "Yuletide note" to their lawyer, complaining that "justice" prevented her from doing any holiday shopping.[131] Julius reminded his wife that it was sixteen years ago that week that they had met and assured her that they would "see many more Christmas days" together.[132] Members of the Civil Rights Congress (CRC), in collaboration with the NCSJRC, organized a rainy day holiday protest at the gates of Sing Sing, where they left a wreath, which read "Greetings to Julius and Ethel Rosenberg from the People."[133] The NCSJRC also led the first of many pro-Rosenberg picket lines along the east side of the White House grounds.[134]

Several well-known and respected individuals added their voices to the protest. Reverend Charles E. Raven, chaplain to Queen Elizabeth II and former vice-chancellor of Cambridge University, stated: "This savage verdict underlines the conviction that America, instead of leading the world to a more righteous and liberal way of life, is becoming so hysterical in its dread of communism, as to betray the very principles upon which the Constitution is founded."[135] Dr. Harold C. Urey, the Nobel Prize–winning chemist, declared he was "amazed and completely outraged" by the way the Rosenbergs were treated. While convinced that the couple held Communist opinions, Urey did not "believe in punishing people unless they commit crimes."[136] Artist Pablo Picasso and playwright Bertold Brecht protested the pending executions through their work and wrote to friends pleading for their support.[137] Jean-Paul Sartre, the French existentialist philosopher and writer, spurred protest in France and beyond when he stated: "We must save the Rosenbergs because they have continuously pleaded their innocence and the judges concerned have never been able to prove their guilt."[138] He spoke for many protesters when he emphasized the universality of the case: "We must save them for their own sake and because of ourselves. In protesting this unfair trial, we do it for the sake of the Democracy of the U.S.A. and for the sake of the Democracy of France."[139] The *Daily Worker* ran a multiple-page list of writers, artists, actors, musicians, scientists, and academics from the United States, Mexico, England, and France who all "raised their voices against the death penalty for the innocent pair."[140] By early 1953 the campaign supporting the Rosenbergs had grown into a global movement.

Meanwhile, in Washington, D.C., ten representatives from the NCSJRC requested a meeting with the Secretary of State.[141] A State Department representative, Vincent P. Wilber, took the meeting in Acheson's place. Committee members urged Wilber to appeal directly to the president for clemency, stressing the global propaganda context of the case and focusing on the negative reaction the case had garnered around the world. America's "moral prestige" was at risk, NCSJRC representatives argued, and individuals around the world were comparing the Rosenberg case to the execution of Sacco and Vanzetti and yet "another time of hysteria."[142] They feared that carrying out of the death sentence of "two American-born citizens accused of having aided an ally" would make "cooperation between ourselves and our allies" that much more difficult.[143] "Clemency," they concluded, "would be welcomed as a reaffirmation of our traditional reputation for fair play, compassion and mercy."[144] Wilber claimed to be bureaucratically stymied when he justified his inaction. He explained to the committee representatives that the Rosenberg case was the "responsibility of the Department of Justice," and as such there was "little" the State Department could do.[145] NCSJRC representatives left the meeting disappointed and baffled by Wilber's logic.

On January 7, White House officials were preoccupied with preparations for Truman's final State of the Union address when they received word about a papal announcement: Pope Pius XII would publicly condemn the scheduled executions. The staunch anti-Communist issued a statement explaining that the death sentence for the young couple was "so pitiful" that even "those not animated by any ignoble partisan interest" (i.e., anti-Communists) wanted "to save their lives."[146] The Vatican announcement concluded with a humanitarian plea:

> In particular, that a woman should wait in a "death chamber" for the moment of execution is in itself an event as tragic as it is rare and is such as to arouse instinctively a sense of horror. When, then, two children, Michael nine years old and Robert five, are involved in this tearful fate, many hearts can be melted, before two little innocents on whose soul and destiny the death of their parents would forever leave sinister scars.[147]

According to the Pope Pius XII, abhorrence of the death penalty trumped aversion to Communism. Truman was flabbergasted. After years of collaboration with the pope to bring "the morals of the world" together to fight "godless" Communists—and after the pontiff cracked down on any Catholics who supported the Communist cause—it was unbelievable that he would now support two convicted Communist spies.[148] As State Department officials worked on how to respond, they chose to ignore the pope's proclamation. Meanwhile, the pope's powerful words reverberated throughout the world, particularly in strongly Catholic countries.[149]

While Communist protest had emanated from such Latin American countries as Cuba, Guatemala, and Chile, the pope's statement opened the floodgates of Catholic, anti-death-penalty dissent.[150] For example, non-Communist protest voices dramatically increased in Brazil. American embassy officials in Rio de Janeiro had received fifty communications containing more than four hundred signatures, the Porto Alegre consulate acknowledged a petition with 127 signatures, and the consulate general in São Paulo received a petition with several thousand signatures.[151] Protesters focused on the Rosenbergs as victims of prejudice and injustice and pressed President Truman to issue clemency and remove the "shadow on the glorious U.S. flag."[152] Diplomats concluded that the protests resulted from Brazilian antipathy to the death penalty and the influence of the pope's support of clemency. They were not sure how to respond.

In predominantly Catholic France, the American consul general in Marseilles described an increase in demonstrations with some five thousand attending a meeting in Paris.[153] "People of shabby appearance" dominated the protestors, the official noted dismissively, but he admitted, "one delegation was led by a young priest."[154] A member of the clergy in leadership positions spoke to the pope's pro-clemency stance and confirmed the spread of protest well beyond Communist circles. Even the non-Communist press *La France* stated the couple was guilty, but recommended they be imprisoned in lieu of execution to avoid gifting Moscow with two martyrs.[155]

Five days after the pope's statement, Albert Einstein wrote to President Truman, explaining that his "conscience" compelled him to seek clemency for the Rosenbergs.[156] The theoretical physicist agreed with his colleague, chemist Harold C. Urey, when he insisted on "a careful reconsideration of this sentence" since it seemed based on "contradictory and inconclusive" evidence.[157] While Einstein's statement fell on deaf ears in the White House, his opinion was heard around the world. For example, on January 13, France celebrated "Save the Rosenbergs Day" and used quotes from Einstein's letter in posters and press reports. The Paris embassy received 150 petitions with an average of twenty-five signatures on each; they would continue to receive petitions, letters, and telegrams on a daily basis.[158]

Anti-Communist protest spread throughout France. For example, a front-page editorial in Lyon's largest paper, *Le Progrès*—under the headline "The Execution of the Rosenbergs Would be a Moral Defeat for the Free World"—described the nearly two years already served on death row as cruel and the executions as a possible propaganda victory for the Communists.[159] American consulate officials complained to the State Department that the misunderstanding concerning the prison time—"to give them every opportunity to exhaust all means of appeal"—was odd in "a country such as France whose legal system is not greatly dissimilar to ours."[160] This issue was not adequately addressed in Bradlee's analysis, or any other American propaganda effort, and would remain confusing.

In Italy, officials in Rome received a thousand protests that they assumed were Communist-inspired, but had to admit they likely also reflected Italian Catholic support for their pope. The Communists were gaining support by "getting some cooperation from some organizations (culture groups and war veterans) not generally considered Communist."[161] In both East and West Germany, accusations of injustice and fascism dominated protests. In Duesseldorf, the American Consulate General received a "flood" of thousands of postcards, letters, and telegrams, all emphasizing the innocence of the couple and protesting the death sentence.[162] Diplomats in Bonn also reported that based on communication with other Foreign Service posts, "This propaganda campaign on behalf of the Rosenbergs is of interest because it departs from the usual practice of the Communists which is to disavow compromised agents and to label them police provocateurs."[163] Bonn acknowledged continued protests, including more than three thousand postcards and several dozen letters and telegrams. One letter, from the German-Soviet Friendship Society in East Berlin, highlighted the Rosenberg's "effort to maintain peace" by sharing atomic technology and the unjust persecution they faced as a result of American "fascism."[164] A telegram sent from the Association of Nazi Persecutees of Kreis Parchim in East Berlin also emphasized concern over the apparent re-emergence of fascism.[165] At a mass meeting in East Berlin attendees charged United States with anti-Semitism mixed with "war hysteria" led by "Wall Street hangmen."[166] German press coverage increased in frequency and often included descriptions of demonstrations at the gates of Sing Sing Prison.[167]

Protests continued unabated in Canada, and Secretary Acheson requested that Paris forward copies of Bradlee's analysis to twelve consulates throughout Canada.[168] Acheson's concerns about Canada were warranted. In Winnipeg, the Committee to Secure Clemency for Ethel and Julius Rosenberg (CSCEJR) held regular meetings and rallies, which hundreds of protestors attended, and presented a petition signed by local citizens urging clemency on humanitarian grounds.[169] A diplomat in Montreal noted the increasing protests and blamed them on what he saw as a gaping hole in the American propaganda regarding the Rosenberg case. "In all the material on the Rosenbergs which has come to us from Paris" and the State Department, he explained, "there was no reference to" the assertion that one of the witnesses for the prosecution gave perjured testimony.[170] The official requested that if State had "anything on this point" they forward it "air mail special delivery" so they could "swat down promptly" what appeared to be "just one more lie."[171] Acheson's response was to resend Bradlee's analysis, which failed to adequately address the issue.[172]

In Ontario, both the consulates in Toronto and Windsor reported an increase in demonstrations in front of their buildings.[173] When the Canadian National Committee to Save the Rosenbergs (NCSR) demonstrated in Windsor, an editorial in the *Windsor Daily Star* suggested that any non-Canadian-born picketers should be deported. However, a second editorial in the *Star* failed when it made an awkward attempt to link Julius and Ethel Rosenberg to Nazi Party official Alfred Rosenberg, accusing demonstrators of not knowing "which Rosenberg" they were "really trying to eulogize in their shuffling little turnout Saturday."[174] Linking Julius and Ethel with a deceased Nazi with the same surname likely did not further the American propaganda campaign in Canada.

The largest Canadian protests continued in the capital of Ottawa.[175] The Canadian National Committee to Save the Rosenbergs (NCSR) mounted an effort on January 10 when some three hundred individuals from Montreal, Toronto, and Welland staged a quiet morning vigil in front of the embassy and left a petition signed by more than five hundred Canadians from nine cities protesting the death sentences.[176] In the afternoon another rally took place at a local dance hall, where speeches emphasized the severity of the sentence, the war hysteria that clouded the trial, the potential innocence of the couple, and the fear that "hysteria justice" might spread like a disease north into Canada.[177] The attendees listened to the San Francisco Labor Theatre's "soap-opera style" radio production, "They Shall Not Die."[178] An embassy official noted the predominantly Communist (*The Canadian Tribune*) and liberal (*Ottawa Citizen*) coverage in the Canadian press, which emphasized the couple's guilt but remained supportive of clemency.[179] The sentiment of the embassy was that the NCSR had "misfired," but the official had to admit that some "highly influential" officials in the government were taking a different position.[180] The diplomat concluded by admitting, "especially from the point of view of countering any charges of anti-Semitic prejudice in the U.S., perhaps it might be well to commute the sentence."[181] Following three single-spaced pages refuting the significance of the Communist Party campaign to save the Rosenbergs, the official admitted that it might be worthwhile to decide in favor of clemency after all. No State Department response exists.

Protest spread around the globe. In India, protest telegrams, letters, and petitions streamed into the embassy in New Delhi from as far away as Calcutta and Madras.[182] Officials concluded that the "geographical concentration" of the protests pointed to "Commie inspiration" as a way to limit the spread of such a campaign.[183] Days later embassy officials reported the continuation of protests, choosing to describe the correspondence from the Bengal, Assam, Pepsu, and Bihar regions of India as a baseball "box score: 125 telegrams, 20 circulars with 1,131 signatures, and twenty-six letters, cards."[184] Diplomats provided no analysis or explanation. In the African country of Tunisia, consulate officials in Tunis reported the persuasive efforts of the Tunisian Communist Party, which emphasized the innocence of the "devoted patriots," the bias of the judge and jury, and the climate of America's "beastly anti-Communism."[185] In Sydney, Australia, hundreds of people demonstrated on two separate occasions outside the consulate and presented petitions for President Truman, pleading for clemency (Figure 2.2).[186]

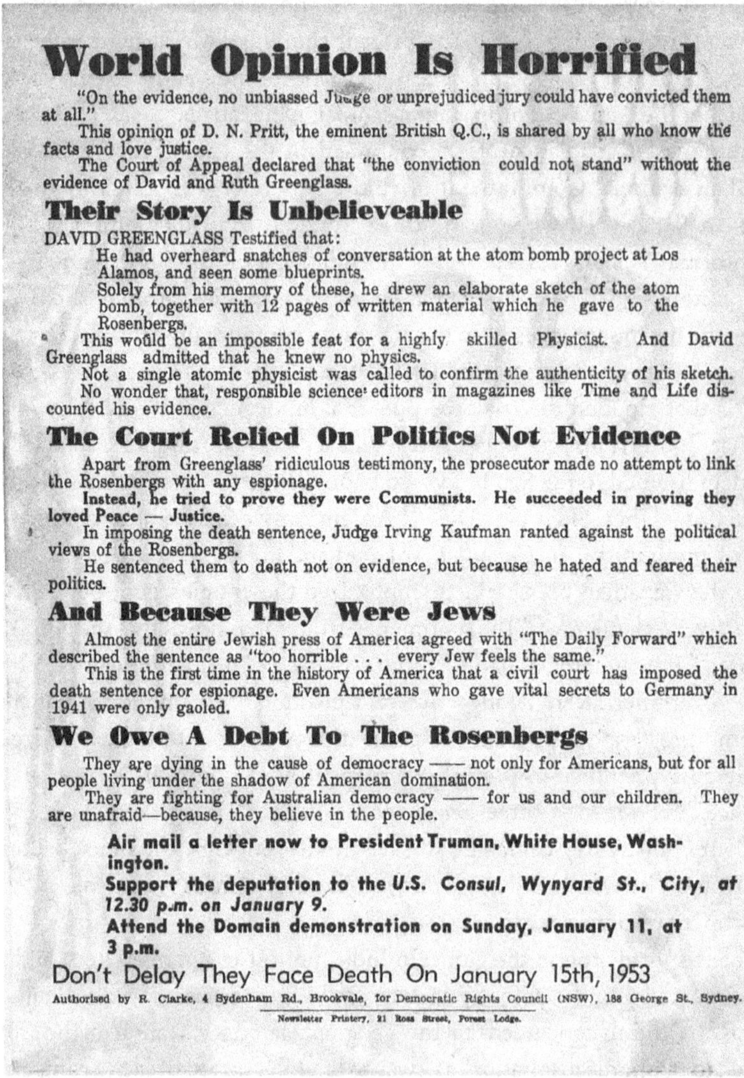

World Opinion Is Horrified

"On the evidence, no unbiassed Judge or unprejudiced jury could have convicted them at all."

This opinion of D. N. Pritt, the eminent British Q.C., is shared by all who know the facts and love justice.

The Court of Appeal declared that "the conviction could not stand" without the evidence of David and Ruth Greenglass.

Their Story Is Unbelieveable

DAVID GREENGLASS Testified that:

He had overheard snatches of conversation at the atom bomb project at Los Alamos, and seen some blueprints.

Solely from his memory of these, he drew an elaborate sketch of the atom bomb, together with 12 pages of written material which he gave to the Rosenbergs.

This would be an impossible feat for a highly skilled Physicist. And David Greenglass admitted that he knew no physics.

Not a single atomic physicist was called to confirm the authenticity of his sketch.

No wonder that, responsible science editors in magazines like Time and Life discounted his evidence.

The Court Relied On Politics Not Evidence

Apart from Greenglass' ridiculous testimony, the prosecutor made no attempt to link the Rosenbergs with any espionage.

Instead, he tried to prove they were Communists. He succeeded in proving they loved Peace — Justice.

In imposing the death sentence, Judge Irving Kaufman ranted against the political views of the Rosenbergs.

He sentenced them to death not on evidence, but because he hated and feared their politics.

And Because They Were Jews

Almost the entire Jewish press of America agreed with "The Daily Forward" which described the sentence as "too horrible . . . every Jew feels the same."

This is the first time in the history of America that a civil court has imposed the death sentence for espionage. Even Americans who gave vital secrets to Germany in 1941 were only gaoled.

We Owe A Debt To The Rosenbergs

They are dying in the cause of democracy —— not only for Americans, but for all people living under the shadow of American domination.

They are fighting for Australian democracy —— for us and our children. They are unafraid—because, they believe in the people.

Air mail a letter now to President Truman, White House, Washington.

Support the deputation to the U.S. Consul, Wynyard St., City, at 12.30 p.m. on January 9.

Attend the Domain demonstration on Sunday, January 11, at 3 p.m.

Don't Delay They Face Death On January 15th, 1953

Authorised by R. Clarke, 4 Sydenham Rd., Brookvale, for Democratic Rights Council (NSW), 188 George St., Sydney.

Newsletter Printery, 11 Ross Street, Forest Lodge.

Figure 2.2 Sydney, Australia, Save the Rosenbergs Flier, January 11, 1953. Original flier courtesy of Phillip Deery, Melbourne, Australia.

Back in New York, on January 9 Julius and Ethel Rosenberg also requested clemency. The couple filed their thirty-seven-page petition for executive clemency with the Justice Department, prompting Truman administration officials to explore their three options.[187] The president could pardon the Rosenbergs and set them free, commute their sentences—which for this federal crime meant a maximum of thirty years—or he could allow the judge's execution ruling to stand. Keeping the threat of death over the Rosenbergs kept the pressure on them to talk, so issuing a pardon or commutation was not a likely option. But White House officials scrambled to take the global temperature of the case before crafting an official response. Soon it became clear that government agencies disagreed over how the Rosenberg case was understood around the world, and what Truman's official response to presidential clemency should be.

The State Department weighed in through F. Bowen Evans, the Coordinator for Psychological Intelligence in the Office of Intelligence Research. In charge of "coordinating the execution of U.S. foreign information programs," Evans declared the case "received no mention" in the Russian media and described the lack of Soviet attention as "consistent with past practice," citing that the Soviet Union "always ignored such cases of espionage and spying brought before the courts of other countries."[188] According to Evans, the Soviets refrained from making propaganda points in hopes of sparing the Rosenbergs' lives. This conflicted with administration officials who interpreted the Soviet lack of support as favoring execution, with an eye toward converting the Rosenbergs into Communist martyrs. Even two years into the case, officials had not reached a consensus on the Soviet Union's role in crafting the pro-Rosenberg argument, which was odd given the administration's penchant for interpreting all protests as part of a monolithic Communist propaganda machine.

Evans believed that only two Eastern European satellite countries—Romania and Hungary—allowed their press to express opposition to the sentence in the case. Reporters in both Romania and Hungary argued that the Rosenbergs were "victims of an anti-Semitic policy," the evidence against them was "without substance and on the basis of entirely unsubstantiated slanders," and their sentence represented "persecution of progressive peace-loving" individuals "by Wall Street war mongers."[189] Evans speculated that other satellite countries ignored the Rosenbergs because they were a low priority and could not be "fit" into their "local propaganda commitments."[190] By drawing this conclusion, he ignored the "worldwide Commie propaganda" campaign in Warsaw, Poland, that American embassy officials had detected and reported on.[191] Even within the State Department, diplomats had trouble agreeing.

Evans described the increased propaganda campaign on behalf of the couple in Western Europe and attributed it to Communists and Communist-front organizations. He argued that "much of the non-Communist press in Western Europe still opposes clemency, and this is particularly true in England and Scandinavia."[192] However, Evans voiced concern for protests of the case that had expanded to the non-Communist, and in some cases conservative, elements within Western Europe and admitted that evidence "indicates a trend toward increasing sentiment" in favor of clemency.[193] Concerned, the State Department requested "a quick roundup of overseas reaction" from the PSB to use as a basis for discussion and policy formulation.[194]

PSB Director Admiral Alan G. Kirk, as leader of the organization charged with coordinating Cold War propaganda, had already been considering how to counter the growing global pro-Rosenberg movement. Just before Christmas the White House had asked him to provide "the view of your Board as to whether such a statement [supporting the sentence] should be issued and . . . to have your help in preparing it."[195] Emboldened by administration attention, Admiral Kirk had immediately made a personal visit to the White House and set up a committee consisting of representatives from State, Defense, the CIA, and the PSB to consider the president's possible actions.

Meanwhile, the PSB met to discuss the case and reached consensus on four points. All board members agreed that the "Communist apparatus run by the USSR" had launched a "major campaign on behalf of the Rosenbergs." Second, they agreed that foreign interest in the case did "not represent any significant doubt on the part of the non-Communist public regarding the integrity" of the United States.[196] The Soviets had coordinated the global propaganda campaign, and they had failed. This assertion that the pro-Rosenberg overseas campaign consisted solely of Communists and that the case did not damage the reputation of the United States contradicted much of what diplomats around the world had been reporting on for months. Third, they believed that whatever statement was made, "it should be an 'eleventh hour' proposition" because "no one can antici-pate all the last minute maneuvers that may develop in this case," therefore they needed to withhold "any statement or comment until the very last minute."[197] Finally, all PSB members advised that Truman deny clemency to the Rosenbergs.

The PSB then drafted a presidential statement refusing clemency that focused on the seriousness of a crime that involved "the deliberate betrayal of the entire nation."[198] It reiterated Judge Kaufman's false accusation that the crime prompted the conflict in Korea, still stalemated. The statement also emphasized that the Rosenbergs had benefitted from the "time-honored tradition of American jus-tice" in getting multiple appeals.[199]

One week later, on January 7, PSB officials began to express concern about the timing of the announcement. They feared the possibility of Truman being forced to announce his clemency decision just before Eisenhower's inaugura-tion "or on inauguration day itself."[200] Alternately, they wondered if the decision would be carried over into the new administration. The PSB argued that "the Communist campaign" on this case had "left no stone unturned to keep the issue confused. It would be typical of them to try and make its climax coincide with the Inaugural period."[201] The PSB still seemed reactive, struggling to control the official government story.

Inexplicably, on January 15, the PSB reversed its position and unequivocally advocated clemency for the Rosenbergs.

Negative global reaction prompted a conversion among PSB members who now voiced their grave concerns about the execution itself. A reduced sentence statement, they argued, would emphasize that the "death sentence is not lightly passed down in the United States," and that while the Rosenbergs were "unquestionably guilty of the gravest sort of crime against humanity," the United States would not provide the Soviets with a propaganda victory by handing them two martyrs and "play to the tune of Kremlin leaders."[202] "Serious thought," the board explained, "should be given to providing key members of the White House staff, whether Harry's or Ike's, with the thought that a commutation of the Rosenbergs' sentence could be used very effectively."[203]

The memo's closing sentence, however, highlights the PSB's serious limitations. "If the Director agreed to this line of thought, Bill could probably get it placed before the President on an informal basis through his friend Roger Tubby, who is now the President's Press Secretary."[204] The PSB may have been charged with coordinating Cold War propaganda but it had limited access to the president and thus had little hope to affect policy.[205] The board had changed its position on the case, but by January 1953 few were listening.

Many government officials disagreed with the PSB and drowned out their pro-clemency stance. For example, Myles Lane, the U.S. Attorney for the Department of Justice and one of the team of lawyers who prosecuted the Rosenbergs, defended his reasoning in a five-page letter to the pardon attorney.[206] "It is my considered judgment" that Truman "should not alter or in any way commute the sentence," the attorney explained, because "the most important purpose of a death penalty" was "as a deterrent to keep others from committing the same crime."[207] Using distorted fragments of logic, Lane concluded: "Any commutation in the sentences of these defendants would more permanently seal their lips than the execution of the judgments which have been imposed."[208] According to Myles Lane, dead spies were more likely to talk than living ones sitting in prison.

The judge in the Rosenberg case also rejected clemency. When Judge Irving Kaufman read of the pope's pro-clemency stance he was concerned that it would persuade Catholics around the world to oppose the death sentences. Kaufman tried to convince New York Cardinal Francis Spellman to come out publicly in opposition to the pope. As an aggressive anti-Communist and defender of Senator McCarthy, Spellman likely supported the death sentence for the

Rosenbergs. However, the cardinal had been appointed by Pope Pius XII and was hesitant to lose favor with the pontiff, so he refused to speak out against the pope.[209]

The majority of Americans also opposed a reduced sentence for the Rosenbergs. Public opinion indicated an overwhelming concern for ongoing violence in Korea and skewed in favor of executing the spies they held responsible for starting the war.[210] The public remained supportive of the government's handling of the Rosenberg case and was not swayed by what they saw as Communist-sponsored propaganda.[211]

Not all Americans, however, approved execution. On Truman's final day in office, a woman from Frankfort, Indiana, telegrammed the president: "Sir wake up. This is not Ike's baby. You started your administration with death; finish with Rosenbergs' life. They may be confused concerning their democracy but making and dropping atomic bombs is our doings. The Lord is the judge."[212] There was no time for a reply.

At his final presidential press conference Truman admitted he had not reached a decision in the case, claiming he could not do so until the case was placed on his desk.[213] Due to Judge Kaufman's stay to allow for an executive clemency plea, Truman did not have to make that decision. The Rosenbergs' clemency request would be waiting for the new president when he arrived. It would become Ike's baby.

On the cloudy morning of Tuesday, January 20, Harry Truman left the White House—and the fate of Julius and Ethel Rosenberg—to his successor. Truman had assumed that allies would blindly follow America's lead.[214] When this did not happen, administration officials ignored some countries and gave perfunctory case summaries to others. Without a comprehensive, point-by-point response to the protests spreading around the globe, questions remained unanswered. Just as Washington was beginning to grasp the global ramifications of the Rosenberg case, a new president brought in a new administration. Thanks to stunted communication during the transition period, however, Eisenhower's staff would have to reinvent the wheel. The incoming president would have his hands full with a stalemated war and two atomic spies sitting on death row.

The Eisenhower campaign had stumbled when critics accused vice presidential candidate Richard Nixon of campaign fund irregularities, but a stellar performance in his so-called Checkers speech on live television proved that the California Republican could craft and sell an image of himself to the American people. In January 1953, Eisenhower and Nixon would take their turn crafting an image of the United States as the leader of the free world combating Communism and selling it to the global community. Even under the likable Eisenhower, however, world opinion continued to spin out of U.S. control as the Rosenbergs sat in prison awaiting their fate.

3

Eisenhower

Political language . . . is designed to make lies truthful and murder
respectable, and to give an appearance of solidity to pure wind.
—George Orwell, *"Politics and the English Language," 1946*

At 9 p.m. on Monday, January 19, 1953, 44 million American tuned in to CBS
to watch the Ricardos on *I Love Lucy* welcome their firstborn son, Little Ricky.[1]
Lucy did all the work off-screen, mimicking real-life Lucille Ball who had delivered a son via a scheduled caesarean section that morning. Ball and her infant
son soon graced the cover of the first issue of *TV Guide*, reflecting her status as
the First Lady of Television Comedy on the most-watched television program
of the 1950s.[2] The immense popularity of Lucille Ball and her television antics
would help her overcome accusations of Communist Party membership. Later
that September, the House Committee on Un-American Activities (HUAC)
confronted her with evidence she had registered to vote as a Communist in the
1930s. Ball pled ignorance, claiming never to be "politically minded," and HUAC
let her go, announcing there was no proof of party membership.[3] Americans
never wavered in their support of the entertainer; as *The New Republic* admitted,
"everyone still loves Lucy."[4]

Americans also liked Ike. Dwight D. Eisenhower's approval ratings hovered
near 78 percent when, the day after Little Ricky's birth, he took the oath of office
as the thirty-fourth president of the United States.[5] Reflecting a poly-religious
emphasis, the inauguration began with a rabbi's prayer and included a bishop's
benediction. Most surprising, Eisenhower broke with presidential tradition and
began his address by "uttering a little private prayer," asking God for the "power
to discern clearly right from wrong" and for help in fighting the "forces of evil."[6]
From day one, Ike built on Truman's efforts and set a tone of religious inclusivity,
emphasizing the Cold War as a religious crusade.[7]

It is understandable that Eisenhower appealed to a higher power for assistance.
He moved into the White House as the leader of the free world, facing nuclear-
charged danger across the globe. As a new president Eisenhower inherited a full

plate, including extracting American troops from the bloodletting in Korea, where more than 22,700 Americans had already perished.[8] Ike would soon discover that while Americans enjoyed his lovable, grandfatherly personality, international opinion of him was more suspect. Critics from around the world openly questioned his leadership ability when they saw him bow to Senator Joseph McCarthy's aggressive anti-Communism.[9] While the president understood the significance of projecting a positive image in fighting the Cold War, interagency rivalries, incompetence, and buffoonery plagued propaganda efforts in the early days of his administration. Eisenhower did not want to lose the support of allies—particularly Great Britain, Canada, Australia, and Belgium, who were supplying fighting units for the war in Korea. Though the peaceful transition of power between rival parties was the hallmark of American democracy, the shift from Truman's Democratic administration to Eisenhower's Republican one caused complications in government propaganda efforts, with implications for the Rosenberg case. The government's inept management of the case's narrative resulted in increased criticism of the persecution, prosecution, and impending execution of Julius and Ethel Rosenberg. In the eyes of the world in the first months of 1953, the United States seemed more arbitrary and erratic than reasoned and democratic.

As Eisenhower swept in a fresh slate of Foreign Service officers, from ambassadors to consul generals, the Truman administration's accumulated knowledge on the global reaction to the Rosenberg case was lost. The novice diplomatic corps scrambled to get up to speed on a wide range of global Cold War issues, but was unlikely to consult with outgoing Democratic officials. In the case of the Rosenbergs, as the newly discovered State Department documents detail, the timing could not have been worse. On January 9, Truman's Justice Department received Julius and Ethel Rosenberg's petitions for executive clemency and chose to delay action.[10] It was Eisenhower who would decide—twice during his first five months in office—whether the Rosenbergs would live or die. To some, the case represented his first significant domestic challenge.[11]

Eisenhower had enthusiastically supported psychological warfare during his days as a general in World War II, and brought many like-minded individuals into his administration in 1953.[12] As they waged the Cold War, the Eisenhower administration expanded its arsenal to include subversion and propaganda to deny gains to Communist nations and to maintain America's favorable image abroad.[13] Eisenhower understood the conflict was not a "shooting war," but one they needed to win on the "political warfare front."[14] As president he appeared to do whatever was necessary to keep countries on the side of the United States.[15] After seeing a flawed military strategy in Korea, Eisenhower renewed his commitment to improve and centralize America's psychological efforts. According to Ike, success in the Cold War necessitated an all-encompassing global psychological battle "for the minds and wills of men."[16]

Eisenhower knew about appealing to the minds of men. As a presidential candidate in 1952, he understood the importance of image and agreed to alter his to get elected.[17] He used Batten, Barton, Durstine, and Osborne (BBDO), a Madison Avenue advertising agency, to package and sell Dwight D. Eisenhower to the American people. In turn his administration used Cold War incidents, such as the Rosenberg case, to sell the world on the supremacy of American democracy in the conflict against global atheistic Communism that many saw as a religious crusade.

First, building on the spiritual overtones of Truman, Eisenhower needed to convince the American people of the sincerity of his religious convictions. As such, he joined a Presbyterian church and, less than two weeks after taking the oath, became the only president to be baptized while in office.[18] Eisenhower attended the first National Prayer Breakfast. After he offered a short prayer at the start of the first cabinet meeting, members asked to continue the practice.[19] In 1954, he declared September 22 a National Day of Prayer.[20]

Congress endorsed this renewed religious fervor, approving the adoption of "In God We Trust" as the U.S. motto and placing it prominently on currency. The legislature also took Eisenhower's suggestion and added "under God" to the Pledge of Allegiance through a joint resolution of Congress in 1954.[21] These acts, which allowed for government-endorsed open profession of faith, were directly linked to waging the Cold War.

Eisenhower believed that devotion to God separated the free world from that of the Soviet bloc, which embraced atheism and opposed all religious beliefs.[22] The president was not the only public figure invoking religious rhetoric. Ronald Reagan gave a 1952 commencement address in which he combined divine intervention and American exceptionalism.[23] "I believe that God," Reagan preached, "in shedding his grace on this country has always in his divine scheme of things kept an eye on our land and guided it as a promised land for these people."[24] Reverend Billy Graham, the celebrity evangelical preacher who would serve as a spiritual adviser to many presidents including Ike, explained that Communism was "intrinsically wicked" and "master-minded by Satan himself."[25] Senator Edward Martin, a Republican from Pennsylvania, called on his fellow Americans to confront Communism "with the atomic bomb in one hand and the cross in the other."[26] One Washington clergyman claimed that in the struggle against Communism an American atheist was "a contradiction in terms."[27]

Once the Soviets developed the atomic bomb—which Eisenhower agreed with Truman was due to the Rosenbergs—they more aggressively asserted their Communism.[28] In response, Americans eagerly embraced whatever faith they had.[29] According to historian William Inboden, to wage the Cold War "Protestants, Catholics, Jews, and Mormons were asked to leave their ideological distinctions at home and embrace a common public faith based on basic tenets such as prayer, God, the divine origins of human rights and freedom, and the unique blessings and responsibilities bestowed on America."[30] Eisenhower used his public relations skill to create accord among Americans of all religious persuasions and undermine global Communism. In building this consensus the president would reach out to all religious leaders, and in particular mend fences with the pope following the pontiff's criticism of the Rosenberg executions.[31] He would also need to improve America's ability to wage an effective propaganda war, and his new secretary of state agreed.

John Foster Dulles, a lawyer and Washington, D.C., native, was the grandson of one secretary of state and the nephew of another.[32] A young Dulles had attended the 1919 Paris Peace Conference, and he served briefly in the Senate before Eisenhower appointed him to head the State Department.[33] During his tenure Dulles enjoyed a close working relationship with the Central Intelligence Agency, primarily because his younger brother Allen served as its director. The elder Dulles soon became Eisenhower's closest adviser, working directly with the president to formulate foreign policy until illness prompted Dulles to resign in April 1959 (Figure 3.1).[34] As concerned about public opinion as Ike was, Dulles became the first secretary of state to hold regular department press conferences.

Figure 3.1 Dwight Eisenhower and John Foster Dulles, New York City, ca. 1952. Courtesy of Bettmann/CORBIS.

The secretary also shared his boss's views on religion. Dulles agreed with Eisenhower that the United States was "God's chosen instrument," and also viewed the Cold War as a moral conflict and spoke of it in theological terms.[35] At his confirmation hearings, Dulles explained that Soviet Communism was "the gravest threat" to "Western civilization, or indeed any civilization . . . dominated by a spiritual faith."[36] Both men attended the same church in Washington, yet while Ike came to his public religious convictions relatively late in life, Dulles had embraced a spiritual worldview much earlier on. With a missionary grandfather and a prominent Presbyterian minister father, Dulles's religious lineage matched the prestige of his political ancestry. The new secretary of state read the Bible regularly and kept one on his desk at the State Department. It was likely this view of the Cold War as a religious crusade that prompted Dulles to react with frustration when America's allies could not see the righteousness of the actions of God's chosen country.

During the administration's first week, the secretary of state discovered the growing global movement protesting the inherited high-profile spy case. Dulles was so disturbed by the response to the Rosenberg case overseas that forty-eight hours after the inauguration he pouched an update to twenty-five major embassies and consulates around the world.[37] In that dispatch, Dulles explained that the Justice Department was formulating their recommendation regarding the Rosenberg petition for executive clemency and that the Foreign Service officers would be advised as soon as they reached a decision. In their first days in office, Eisenhower's men showed they were more determined than previous Secretary of State Acheson and the rest of the Truman administration had been to control propaganda on the case.[38]

While the Eisenhower administration mulled the Rosenbergs' fate protests intended to influence the decision mounted, and diplomats, some new with the administration, struggled to respond. Pope Pius XII's recent statement in support of the couple resonated in Latin America, prompting protests throughout Argentina, Brazil, Colombia, Guatemala, and Uruguay.[39] For example, Argentina's first pro-Rosenberg editorial, in the English-language paper the *Buenos Aires Herald*, complained that it was "inconceivable and inconsistent with the high office of the President, that the life or death of two human beings could be the subject of political maneuverings," and argued that the two years the couple had spent in prison waiting for the death sentence bordered "dangerously on the sadistic."[40] The administration of President Juan Domingo Perón controlled the majority of the Argentinean press including the *Herald*. Perón's support of social justice issues and economic independence alarmed both Truman and Eisenhower administration officials, who equated his views to Communism. This was particularly true in those Latin American nations controlled by politicians U.S. officials viewed as so left-wing that they could not rationally argue with them. As under the Truman administration, the State Department chose not to respond to dissent and scribbled on the diplomatic cable: "Protests in the Rosenberg case are not been [*sic*] dignified by a reply" (Figure 3.2).[41]

It was not just the pope's stance that generated protest throughout Latin America. Many who opposed the execution of the Rosenbergs saw the persecution of the couple as proof of a flawed justice system and a disturbing example of what they labeled U.S. imperialism. By questioning democratic institutions and then linking the case to "imperialism"—a term certainly laden with historical meaning in Latin America—a growing protest movement struck the opposite chord than the Eisenhower administration had intended. In both the words of the pope and the unflattering depiction of the United

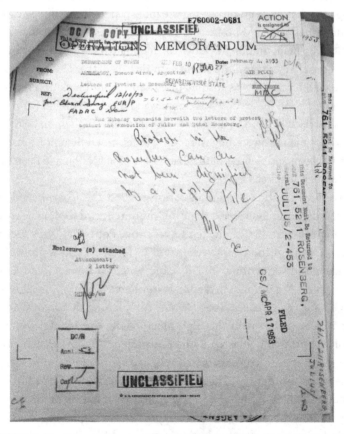

Figure 3.2 State Department Memorandum from American Embassy, Buenos Aires, Argentina, February 4, 1953, RG 59. Courtesy of NARA.

States, government officials were woefully unprepared for the challenging propaganda battles they faced.

Some Latin American protests were easier to deal with because they were tempered by concern over a reaction by its powerful neighbor to the north. In the Dominican Republic, the editor of *El Caribe* apologized to U.S. diplomats for the "anti-American material" in a recent article on the case.[42] While denying the article's author was a Communist, the editor regretted the anti-death-penalty stance and promised to "scan the columns more closely in the future."[43] The editor also offered space to the State Department to run a rebuttal refuting the author's claims.[44] Rafael Trujillo, the right-wing dictator of the Dominican Republic, depended on the United States for sugar markets and military support.[45] Not wanting to jeopardize this special partnership, Trujillo silenced the protests.[46]

Protest continued to bubble over into anti-Communist, Christian communities, which was particularly disconcerting to an administration striving to build religious coalitions to fight the Cold War.[47] Prominent Methodist Bishop G. Bromley Oxnam—"one of the leading mainline voices in the country" who feared working too closely with the Vatican—surprisingly sided with the pope in favor of clemency.[48] Oxnam sent a petition to Secretary Dulles signed by 2,258 individuals opposed to the death penalty.[49] The secretary thanked him, writing, it is "useful for me and for the Department to be kept informed of such items."[50] Eisenhower and Secretary of State Dulles both received letters from the Fellowship of Reconciliation in New York City, with more than five hundred signatures from individuals representing churches in France and the United States.[51] The self-proclaimed "Christians and non-Communists," argued that while they deplored the actions of the Rosenbergs and supported the fairness of the trial, they opposed the "extreme penalty" and supported clemency, believing it would

> provide multitudes in all countries, including totalitarian lands, a striking demonstration that the spirit and behavior of a democratic people can be more objective, restrained, and humane. It will help to assure our friends in many countries—and some are in need of such assurance—that the government and people of the United States are not victims of panic, fear, and hysteria.[52]

A State Department official scrawled on the letter, "It has been decided that there would be no replies to petitions for clemency in the Rosenberg case which have been referred to State by the White House. It would seem that the same treatment might be followed and this letter filed without reply."[53] Even respected, anti-Communist American and French religious leaders—integral to the spiritual coalition waging the Cold War—could not be heard.

Propelled by the pope's pro-clemency statement, protest spread from France to her colonies. Madagascar was gradually moving out from under French control in the early 1950s, though after sixty years of rule there was still significant French influence. The Malagasy anti-death-penalty organization, *Comité de Solidarité de Madagascar*, asked the American consulate in the island capital of Tananarive, to stand with "those of simple people around the entire world" and urge "your country, the country of Abraham Lincoln" to commute the Rosenberg sentence.[54] Diplomats dismissed the letter, insisting it did not reflect the will of the people of Madagascar who had "never heard of Julius and Ethel Rosenberg" and had likely come from the French Communist Party.[55]

The proliferation of non-Communist protest shocked Truman ambassadors in their final days of service, as they overlapped time with their Eisenhower administration counterparts. For example, the Italian Social Democratic Party sent an appeal for clemency to the American embassy in Rome, hoping that mercy "would further underline before universal conscience the difference between humanity of democratic justice and fanaticism of tribunals of totalitarian states."[56] Alarmed, outgoing Ambassador Ellsworth Bunker in Rome explained to the State Department that this "appeal by responsible leadership of one of [the] Democratic parties is in [a] different category from mass of Communist-inspired 'protests' alleging Rosenberg innocence."[57] Ambassador Bunker requested instruction on how to respond, but received no reply; Eisenhower appointee Clare Booth Luce would soon take his place.

Controversies surrounding the case—the pope's anti-death-penalty statement, a growing number of Christian leaders joining the pope in his opposition, and the planned execution of two Jews in the shadow of the Holocaust—pointed to perceived flaws in the nation's democratic process. Heading down the path initially charted by the Truman administration, Eisenhower aides struggled to make the most of the situation. They wondered if the Rosenberg case could be crafted into a propaganda victory for the United States.

One CIA agent in the psychological warfare division proposed a novel way the Rosenbergs could be used to benefit the United States. The agent suggested that the FBI offer to reduce the sentence of Julius and Ethel Rosenberg if the couple agreed to "appeal to Jews in all countries to get out of the Communist movement and seek to destroy it."[58] Communist parties worldwide had "built up the Rosenbergs as heroes and martyrs to 'American anti-Semitism,'" the agent explained.[59] If the famous couple turned on the party, the government's international campaign against Communism would benefit by splitting "world Communism on the Jewish issue."[60] A "highly intelligent rabbi" with a "radical background" might be a persuasive emissary, the agent proposed.[61] Julius and

Ethel understood their sentences would be reduced if they admitted guilt and named other spies, as David Greenglass had done. However, by pulling Ethel into the case, the federal government had forced her into a position of turning on her husband and detailing his espionage activities, or accepting her fate. If Ethel had turned on Julius, she might have been executed anyway. It remains unclear whether the FBI ever located the requisite rabbi to convey this offer to the Rosenbergs.

As American Jews remained divided on the case, Jews throughout Europe were similarly conflicted. Jewish leaders in Communist Hungary supported the Rosenbergs, writing to Eisenhower: "In the name of Hungarian Jewry which escaped from the death camps of the fascist anti-Semitic murderers, we join with hundreds of millions who have reached the point of indignation at the wickedness of the death sentences."[62] However, according to the CIA, other European Jews were increasingly hostile to the Soviet Union and Communism in general when, after a diplomatic incident on February 9, the Soviets broke off diplomatic relations with Israel.[63] CIA agents noted that Jews throughout Europe increasingly believed that the Soviet Union was an openly anti-Semitic state and that "Jews who previously supported the request for clemency for the Rosenbergs" believed that the couple "should be punished as enemies."[64] The policies of the Soviet Union would continue to impact European Jews and their view of the Rosenberg case.

Conversely, many Australian Jews—joined by Communists, social democrats, and liberals—campaigned aggressively to save the Rosenbergs from the harsh sentence as Eisenhower approached his impending clemency decision deadline.[65] The American Embassy at Canberra received a delegation with a petition from Sydney and Melbourne, but they had "not thought it worthwhile to report" previous communications they had received demanding Eisenhower grant clemency for the Rosenbergs.[66] However, since embassy diplomats sent the protest via air pouch, taking two to five days to arrive, White House officials were unable to take this into account—even if they had wanted to—before Eisenhower made his clemency decision.[67]

Emerging protests took many forms. Eisenhower was in office just a few days when Arthur Miller's *The Crucible* opened on Broadway. Set in Massachusetts Bay, the Tony Award–winning play dramatized the Salem witch trials of the seventeenth century.[68] Even at the time many saw the work as an allegory for McCarthyism, a critique of HUAC, and a dramatization of mass hysteria.[69] Others saw it as an example of art imitating life with the central couple in the play, John and Elizabeth Proctor, as stand-ins for Julius and Ethel Rosenberg. During the witch trials—as during the hunt for Communists—naming names was rewarded with a lesser punishment because it expanded the web of accused individuals.[70] Critics contended it was difficult to watch the final scene of John

Proctor's confession and recantation without thinking of the Rosenbergs.[71] The judge's speech in *The Crucible*—"A person is either with this court or he must be counted against it; there be no road between"—was suggestive of Judge Irving Kaufman's unforgiving sentencing of the Rosenbergs.[72]

Just as the president weighed clemency for the Rosenbergs, the judge in the play decided he would "not receive a single plea for pardon or postponement," arguing that those who "will not confess will hang."[73] Arthur Miller would deny connections to the Rosenberg case, but did admit he was inspired by current events when choosing to write about the witch trials he had learned about in a college history class. He recalled crafting the play in 1949 and 1950 when he "heard actual lines being spoken by American prosecutors which I vaguely remembered from reading about the witchcraft in 1692."[74]

On the eve of Eisenhower's February 1953 clemency decision, the CIA got their hands on Bradlee's analysis of the case and recycled it. Agents sent the report to all CIA area and division chiefs, calling it "Refutation of Complaint Charges in Connection with the Rosenberg Case."[75] They took the occasion to remind agents: "Insomuch as Communist-inspired agitation in regard to the Rosenbergs will doubtless continue over a long period of time regardless of the outcome of their appeal for clemency, it is believed that the material will prove of continuing value to the field stations."[76] Bradlee's analysis, however, continued to fail to address the increasingly pointed questions surrounding the trial and growing anti-death-penalty sentiment.

In a last-ditch effort to influence the clemency decision, Rosenberg attorney Emanuel H. Bloch requested a meeting with Under Secretary of State General Walter Bedell Smith. Having been Eisenhower's Chief of Staff during World War II and the former director of the CIA, Smith had a very close working relationship with the president.[77] Bloch probably knew this and pressed Smith to meet with him, arguing that the Rosenberg case had become a "cause célèbre" with "repercussions throughout the entire world."[78] Two days later, writing on behalf of Smith, a State Department legal adviser rejected Bloch's request. "I do not feel that an appointment would be appropriate at this time," he explained. "If it should later develop that a meeting with you would be appropriate and desirable, we will be glad to advise you."[79] Bloch would never meet with any representative from the State Department, or anyone in the Eisenhower White House, concerning his clients' case.

Also concerned about global ramifications, former first lady Eleanor Roosevelt weighed in. "We might say that we would like to substitute the life sentence on humanitarian grounds," Roosevelt urged Eisenhower, "I think there is a great deal of hope that this will be done."[80] She likely viewed the Rosenberg case through the lens of the Universal Declaration of Human Rights, which she had stewarded through the United Nations a few years earlier.[81] A bill of rights for the world, it included articles denouncing torture as "cruel, inhuman or degrading treatment or punishment," which was how many protesters saw the death threat hanging over the Rosenbergs.[82] President Eisenhower, however, was not swayed. He did not enjoy a particularly good relationship with Mrs. Roosevelt, especially since she had campaigned against him in 1952, and he disagreed with her liberal politics.[83] Eisenhower likely disregarded her letter.

Some Americans offered creative solutions to get the Rosenbergs to confess and save themselves. A publishing executive contacted the FBI with a self-described "screwball idea."[84] He wanted to make a "substantial cash offer" to the Rosenbergs in exchange for exclusive rights to publish their confession.[85] He hoped it would prompt the couple "to want to confess in order to have a means of financially assisting their children."[86] A New York City agent turned down the offer, replying that any Rosenberg confession would be "highly confidential," and that the FBI "could in no way participate in such a plan."[87] Many were considering ways to get the Rosenbergs to talk, and the Eisenhower administration thought denying clemency would do just that. Diplomats prepared for the expected onslaught of protest.

In the final week of the Truman administration, outgoing Secretary of State Acheson had made an unusual request of the Brussels Embassy: please supply "suggestions in the event that the President should not grant clemency."[88] The response provides a tantalizing glimpse into the preparation of Cold War propaganda. The Brussels embassy staff—delighted to have been asked after being so consistently ignored—quickly pulled together a three-page list of suggestions. Focusing on countering "probable Communist methods," diplomats suggested preparing a response to the use of terms such as "martyrs," "orphans," "the new Sacco and Vanzetti case," and symbols of American atrocity.[89] As a countermeasure, the embassy wondered "whether the Department might . . . be able to obtain enough material to make a story" out of the "Czech student who, after recommending that his father be given the full treatment at the Prague trial, later committed suicide because his schoolmates scorned him."[90] Embassy officials believed that such a story "might make the Rosenberg 'orphans' less interesting to European muddle-heads."[91] They suggested a writer should be hired, "or at least sign his name to it so that it can be treated as a commercial story," and placed with a "cooperative press syndicate."[92] Diplomats recommended the piece include pictures, to "develop the 'human interest' theme."[93]

Brussels embassy officials also suggested the State Department refute Nobel Laureate Urey's opinion that the material passed to the Soviets through the Rosenbergs was inconsequential. They suggested the secretary of state get a "well-known atomic scientist or physicist" to write a letter explaining the science, since they believed this was "the most damaging single element" in the Rosenberg case propaganda.[94] If the executions did proceed, the diplomats explained, there would be "considerable interest in their children" and if they were later adopted by a couple who "would assure them a proper American upbringing—particularly if they should be adopted by well-known people—this might be of sufficient importance to warrant rather heavy press treatment, again indirectly."[95] Finally, embassy officials reiterated using a presidential statement on the case that a staff member had proposed earlier in the month. By late January 1953, however, Secretary Acheson, who made the initial request, was no longer reading Brussels's recommendations. Eisenhower's staff received the answer, and, as expected, Truman diplomats prompted little response from John Foster Dulles's State Department; they likely ignored the Brussels correspondence. A note scribbled more than two weeks after Washington received the correspondence spoke volumes: "White House refused clemency. File."[96]

The Psychological Strategy Board (PSB), fulfilling its mission to coordinate propaganda on the case, also weighed in. PSB officials initially reported that foreign interest in the case did "not represent any significant doubt on the part of the non-Communist public regarding the integrity" of the United States and prepared a statement denying clemency to the Rosenbergs.[97] During the transition period from the Truman to the Eisenhower administration these same officials had shocked all who bothered to listen when they changed their minds. After receiving additional information regarding a growing protest movement they reversed their position and supported clemency.[98] Their words fell on mostly deaf ears, as the PSB no longer garnered support.

In the first days of the Eisenhower administration, Ike detected bureaucratic ineffectiveness in the PSB and sought to replace it.[99] He indicated his priorities when he created the President's Committee on International Information Activities, and ordered its members to make recommendations for strengthening psychological warfare efforts. Referred to as the Jackson Committee after its chair, investment banker and intelligence service veteran William H. Jackson, the group determined that the "Cold War cannot be won by words alone. What we do will continue to be vastly more important than what we say."[100] Psychological warfare was an integral part of U.S. foreign policy, they argued, and should be integrated into the policymaking process.[101] Eisenhower agreed and psychological strategy under the guise of the Operations Coordinating Board (OCB) became a key component of his "New Look" Cold War agenda. Unfortunately, for the Rosenbergs, these changes were not presented to Eisenhower until June 30, 1953, eleven days after the couples' execution. Meanwhile the president appointed C. D. Jackson (Charles Douglas, no relation to William H.) his Special Assistant for International Affairs and Cold War Planning. C. D. Jackson tried to coordinate an effective propaganda campaign to handle the issue of Rosenberg clemency, but his efforts were seriously hampered without a fully functioning and integrated psychological warfare structure. Eisenhower, for his part, embraced the PSB's initial anti-clemency report and disregarded the subsequent pro-clemency memo.

On February 11, the president issued a direct statement denying clemency to the Rosenbergs.[102] He used the original PSB statement verbatim, which reiterated the perceived link between the couple and the ongoing war in Korea:

> The nature of the crime for which they have been found guilty and sentenced far exceeds that of the taking of the life of another citizen; it involves the deliberate betrayal of the entire nation and could very well result in the death of many, many thousands of innocent citizens. By their act these two individuals have in fact betrayed the cause of freedom for which free men are fighting and dying at this very hour [in Korea].[103]

Nearly 23,000 American servicemen had died in Korea, and Eisenhower made sure that some of that blood was on the Rosenbergs' hands.[104]

Eisenhower overruled clemency and repeated the prosecution's trial summation: "Leniency would be merely an invitation to increased activity by those dedicated to the concept that compassion is decadent and mercy an indication of weakness."[105] According to administration officials, religious leaders were wrong and clemency did not indicate compassion; it equaled weakness. Based on the PSB's initial recommendations and the advice of his attorney general, Eisenhower declined to intervene in the judge's death sentence ruling.[106] In turn, Judge Irving Kaufman rescheduled the executions for the week of March 9, but the Second Court of Appeals immediately stayed the executions so the Supreme Court could consider the case.[107]

Eisenhower's rejection of clemency heightened the immediacy of the case. Judge Kaufman called the FBI, stating that he was afraid the Supreme Court might not decide on the petition for *certiorari*, or review, before spring adjournment in late April or early May.[108] Kaufman overstepped his bounds and insisted the FBI get the Justice Department to "push the matter vigorously."[109] After nearly two years the judge yearned to put this case behind him. Indeed, the Supreme Court would repeat its October 1952 vote against *certiorari* in April, indicating once again that there was insufficient justification to rehear the case.[110]

In the United States the president's clemency rejection prompted increasing vocal protest. Within twenty-four hours of the announcement, the White House received 436 telegrams in opposition and fifty-seven in support. Eisenhower aides dismissed the majority of the protest messages because they "came from population centers on the east and west coasts," implying they were Communist directed or inspired.[111] Ultimately the White House would

receive thousands of telegrams and letters from Americans concerning the
president's decision, many stressing the foreign appearance of the case.[112] CBS
News reported that White House mail the week before the announcement of
the denial was up from the usual 25,000 pieces to some 35,000, with "nearly
half of messages urging Eisenhower to commute death sentence," and thousands
coming from overseas.[113] The State Department sent the mail to the Justice
Department because, according to the reporter, "the government wants to organize a propaganda backfire."[114] At this late date, the Eisenhower administration
was still constructing an effective response.

Spurred on by the clemency rejection, the NCSJRC ramped up protests,
holding rallies and vigils in February in Chicago, Washington, D.C., and Los
Angeles.[115] Protesters carried signs emphasizing the Rosenbergs' innocence and
the negative impact their executions would have on America's image abroad.[116]
The NCSJRC sold copies of the trial transcript to raise much-needed funds and
to inform the American people about the case. Some newspapers refused to
accept ads from the NCSJRC but protests continued.[117]

African American organizations came out in favor of clemency for the
Rosenbergs. An American Labor Party official recalled sending a "sound truck
all over New York to gather signatures" to petition against the executions.[118] "We
were in every neighborhood, and people were terrified," the official explained.
"Even in the Jewish neighborhoods on the Lower East Side, people would say,
'Well, where there's smoke, there's fire. There must be something to it.' . . . But in
Harlem we didn't have to argue or prove that it was a frame-up."[119] Famous African
American actors and singers, such as Paul Robeson and Harry Belafonte, also
spoke out for the Rosenbergs.[120] The Civil Rights Congress (CRC) led crowds
picketing the national headquarters of the Republican Party in New York City in
February, and in March protesters held a large rally to support the Rosenbergs at
New York City's Carnegie Hall.[121]

One night in March 1953, thousands of Americans watched Walter Cronkite's
popular history-based program *You Are There*; the episode investigated the Salem
witch trials.[122] Inspired by *The Crucible*, the program included simulated reports
and interviews with historical characters.[123] Many viewers likely noted the parallels to the present day when Cronkite reported, "The Salem hysteria spread. No
one was safe."[124] A few days after the broadcast, nearly two dozen pastors from
New Jersey joined the protests, sending a letter to Eisenhower imploring him
to reconsider clemency.[125] A month later, some 10,000 raincoat-clad protesters
would oppose the Rosenbergs' death sentence and rally at Triborough Stadium
on Randall's Island in New York City.[126]

Even David Greenglass, serving time at Lewisburg Federal Penitentiary in
Pennsylvania for his role in the Rosenberg espionage ring, felt compelled to
plead for leniency for his sister and brother-in-law. "Guilty as they are," he wrote

to Eisenhower, "the sentence is still one that puts a stain on the record of these United States."[127] Greenglass explained that their executions would not be the deterrent the government hoped, because "how can you deter a fanatical communist?"[128] Any espionage information they have would die with them. "May God in his mercy," Greenglass concluded, "change that awful sentence."[129]

Michael Rosenberg also wrote to Eisenhower asking for his parents' release.[130] Under the direction of the NCSJRC, Julius and Ethel's older son attempted to tug at the president's heartstrings when he wrote: "My mommy and daddy are in prison in New York. My brother is six years old his name is Robby. He misses them very much and I miss them too."[131] The young boy never received a reply from the president, but he did receive a birthday letter from his father. Julius took the opportunity to remind Michael that "people all over the world" were joining the cause to prove their innocence.[132]

Despite the outliers, the majority of Americans supported the president's decision to allow the Rosenbergs to die. During the first weeks of Eisenhower's administration, just prior to his announcing his decision to allow the Rosenbergs to die, 68 percent of Americans approved his handling of the presidency; after the announcement it remained a statistically consistent 67 percent.[133] Most Americans still liked Ike. The president also enjoyed the editorial support of the majority of the American press, which included widespread opposition to clemency for the couple.[134] This support reflected a cooperative relationship between print and broadcast news and the State Department.[135] Journalists and government officials created a consensus, agreeing that the Cold War was indeed a war, and as such all information was vital to national security and needed to be handled with care.[136] It is also likely that journalists were hesitant to openly criticize the Truman and Eisenhower administrations during the course of the Korean War, and that in turn, the government took advantage of a less questioning press.[137] Indeed, the *Chicago Daily News* was the only major American newspaper that winter to advocate for a lighter prison sentence, hopeful the couple would provide valuable information while in jail.[138] Overall the Eisenhower administration managed the Rosenberg case narrative within the United States far more successfully than it did around the globe.

Eisenhower's closest official advisers—the members of his cabinet—swallowed any reservations they may have had about executing the Rosenbergs. When the cabinet met the day after he denied the Rosenbergs' clemency, Eisenhower asked if any members disagreed with his decision on the "record of the trial," or if there appeared "any advantage to this country to remit the death penalty."[139] None replied. The president said he believed there was sufficient "substance to the crime" to warrant death, and no one disagreed.[140] When he asked what "psychological effect" would result if "the Executive were to reverse a decision of the Judiciary," he answered his own question, insisting there would be an "adverse reaction" if "our democracy was unable to take a definite action" in such a "clear-cut case."[141] Eisenhower ended by saying he would reconsider the case if prior to the execution any cabinet members "believed that by doing so the best interests of the country would be served."[142] Although members of the cabinet, particularly UN Ambassador Henry Cabot Lodge and Secretary of State Dulles, would privately convey concerns over the next three months, there is no evidence they informed Eisenhower, even though he had specifically asked them to do so.[143] This may reflect the inability of the president to manage his administration so early in his term, or a fear of openly supporting a decision that would be politically unpopular at home. Whatever the reason, to Eisenhower the silence indicated agreement, and the executions would proceed.

Press secretary James Hagerty prepared to face journalists in the first press conference following the clemency denial. Assuming he would be barraged with Rosenberg questions, he asked Secretary Dulles for advice. How should he reply if Eisenhower's denial of clemency or Pope Pius XII's anti-death-penalty stance came up in questioning?[144] Dulles "suggested that he say that neither the White House nor the State Department had any knowledge" of the pope's statement "except for the press report," and reiterate that the pontiff made his appeal "some time before the president announced his decision," and thus one did not impact the other.[145] In the end, the press asked whether the White House had prior knowledge of the pope's statement, and Hagerty simply replied that it did not. A reporter followed up by asking if Eisenhower's clemency decision would be the final word and the press secretary answered that the statement spoke for itself.[146] The reporters were satisfied and saw no need to ask further questions.

The following day, Valentine's Day, Eisenhower enjoyed his first round of golf as president.[147] When in Washington he often played at Burning Tree Golf Club, a private, all-male country club in Maryland that was a thirty-minute drive from the White House. Ike believed golf to be "the best game of them all" and used it to relieve the pressures of the office more than any other sitting president.[148] He later had a putting green installed on the White House South Lawn for when he could not squeeze eighteen holes into his busy schedule.[149] More than 70 percent of Americans polled approved of the time he spent playing.[150]

Young Michael and Robert spent their Valentine's Day at Sing Sing Prison bringing valentines to their parents.[151] The boys met with each parent separately, providing a much-needed morale boost after the president reaffirmed their death sentence. Newspapers around the globe ran pictures of the Rosenbergs' young sons at Sing Sing holding valentines. Embassy officials in Cuba complained that the photos tugged at heart strings and suggested that American news and photo services "may fail to realize their propaganda value for the Communists."[152] They encouraged the State Department to limit the distribution of these inflammatory pictures, but it remains unclear if officials were ever able to do so.

Julius took the opportunity to send a loving card to Ethel and to write an angry letter to their lawyer. The decision to deny clemency, Julius argued, "is based on a one-sided prejudicial evaluation and not founded on the facts in the case."[153] He condemned the speed with which Eisenhower made the decision, blaming Ike's "military career" for replacing his "natural instincts" with a "cynical . . . contempt for the people."[154] Julius concluded that "this monstrous miscarriage of Justice against two innocent Americans" was now "exposed for all to see."[155]

Ethel also wrote a card to Julius on Valentine's Day, hoping they would soon "know of happier days."[156] Julius and Ethel had met when they were young, fallen in love, and by all accounts were deeply devoted to each other. When children came along Ethel left the workforce, choosing to focus her energies on keeping their family home and raising their children. In many ways the Rosenbergs were like any other loving married couple with children.

Of course the Rosenbergs were anything but an ordinary family. While they shared "common interests and common ideals"—a characteristic Mrs. Dale Carnegie attributed to a healthy marriage in her 1953 guide *How to Help Your Husband Get Ahead in His Social and Business Life*—those interests included Communism and espionage.[157] While many in their generation "were striking out on their own, going after their share of the American dream by moving to the suburbs," the Rosenbergs were likely too poor to afford a suburban home.[158] Many Americans criticized the couple and the life they chose to lead as Communist Party members.

Ethel herself was particularly vilified as a wife, mother, and spy. Eisenhower's disdain for Ethel echoed the FBI's views as crafted by ACLU attorney Morris Ernst.[159] While Ernst had never met the Rosenbergs, that did not stop him from creating a psychological profile of the couple for the FBI based on stereotypes of Communists. Ernst explained that "in Communist marriages the wife is the more dominant partner" and in this case "Julius is the slave and his wife, Ethel, the master."[160] Ernst employed an outdated psychological method, not used for more than half a century, instead of approaches that viewed behavior as a product of environment.[161] Administration officials, including the attorney general and the president, embraced this study, using it to justify the pending execution of the Rosenbergs.[162]

Indeed, in executing the couple, the federal government would be involved in destroying a nuclear family and orphaning two young boys. One of the key aspects of modern childhood assumed that children needed adult care and parental authority to thrive.[163] In the view of the administration, Communists and spies did not have the kind of families society should protect. Likely, some Americans believed Michael and Robert would be better off raised by parents who were not involved in Soviet espionage.

The American press took their cue from government officials and demonized Communist women, particularly wives.[164] This depiction was largely the result of inaccurate ideas about female activism in the Communist Party and fears about changing gender relations during the early Cold War years.[165] Journalists labeled Ethel Rosenberg alternately a "deceptively soft-looking, dumpy little woman" and a deadly "red spider" who unnaturally dominated her younger, weaker husband.[166] They even falsely depicted her as taller than her five-foot-nine-inch husband.[167]

Upon her arrest the FBI saw Ethel only as an accomplice to the conspiracy and useful as a "lever" to get her husband to talk. After she refused to work with prosecutors, however, they viewed her as the domineering leader of a spy couple who put the needs of the party above those of her children.[168] Using circular logic, FBI agents argued that Ethel was a "bad mother" and thus she had to be guilty, because why else would she abandon her children? The president concurred and further disdained what he saw as Ethel's defiance of her traditional role as a woman, her neglect of her responsibilities as a mother, and her apparent disregard for the well-being of her children.[169] Historian Kathryn Olmsted claims: "Ethel received a disproportionate punishment because she had overstepped traditional female boundaries."[170]

Before the judge's sentencing, FBI Director J. Edgar Hoover had privately expressed concerns about Ethel. Hoover understood that her participation "consisted only in assisting in the activation of David Greenglass," and he was worried that her execution might cause a "psychological reaction" that would reflect negatively on the U.S. government.[171] Hoover may have been one of the few government officials uncertain about the wisdom of executing parents.[172] After the sentencing, however, the director's reluctance only reflected a practical desire to keep the Rosenbergs alive. Sitting in prison they could be of value to the United States by supplying the names of other spies; dead they became two martyrs for the Soviet Union.[173]

Hoover pressed the issue with Secretary Dulles in late February. Hoover wrote to Dulles that, based on FBI information from Sing Sing, "the Rosenbergs feel the report made by you to the President on your return from your recent trip abroad has caused the President to deny them clemency, and they are blaming you for this denial."[174] Unwilling to play this blame game, Dulles replied: "I have never discussed the Rosenberg case with the President."[175] While Dulles and Eisenhower probably did confer about the case, Dulles refused to divulge those conversations to Hoover. Rebuffed but not budging, Hoover continued to press Dulles, vowing to keep the secretary informed if he heard any more about the Rosenbergs' "previously expressed belief that you were responsible for the denial of clemency to them."[176] Dulles apparently remained unfazed.

Initially, few advisers advocated clemency as a means of pressuring the couple into confessing. C. D. Jackson was one of them. As Special Assistant for International Affairs and Cold War Planning, Jackson was Eisenhower's point man for psychological warfare. A public relations guru, Jackson had left work as a Time-Life executive to be Deputy Director of the Office of War Information with General Eisenhower during World War II. As Jackson ran the psychological warfare program against the Axis Powers, he and Eisenhower became friends. That relationship carried over into their Cold War collaboration as president and adviser.

In late February 1953, Jackson suggested that Attorney General Brownell "get a really skillful Jewish psychiatrist" to "try to crack at least one of the Rosenbergs."[177] Reiterating Hoover's plan for pressuring the Rosenbergs to name other spies, Jackson explained, "they deserve to fry a hundred times for what they have done to this country. But—if they can be cracked, what they can tell us may save the lives of hundreds of thousands of Americans later."[178] Ethel had seen a psychiatrist since 1949 who continued to visit her at Sing Sing, and a psychologist to address parenting concerns mostly prior to her arrest. It remains uncertain—and unlikely—that officials ever asked either of them to interrogate Ethel or her husband.[179]

Immediately following the announcement of Eisenhower's clemency denial, Secretary of State Dulles anticipated the inevitable fallout overseas. Hoping to pre-empt it, he forwarded a lengthy telegram to seventy-eight diplomatic posts around the world.[180] Dulles advised "matter-of-fact treatment" when clarifying or commenting on the president's action and ordered all officials to indicate both "in tone and content" that Eisenhower's decision was an "ordinary exercise of Presidential power based on [a] scrupulously fair process of law."[181] Avoid an "apologetic, defensive tone," he instructed, and focus on a "serious, factual presentation of facts."[182] He recommended that diplomats emphasize the legal history of the case and the "soundness" of the court's decision, and explain that the sentence, "however severe," was "well in proportion" to the "enormity" of the Rosenbergs' "deliberate and premeditated crime."[183] Dulles also suggested avoiding comparisons between the Rosenbergs ("convicted spies") and the Communist/Prague trials ("victims of Communist purges").[184] If accusations of anti-Semitism arose, Dulles urged restraint and suggested referring to a statement by the National Community Relations Advisory Council that condemned Communist efforts to imply "the religious ancestry of the defendants was a factor in the case."[185] With this telegram, the secretary confirmed the importance he placed on the case. In contrast to the previous secretary, Dean Acheson, Dulles explained how the State Department should prepare to deal with the onslaught of protest the denial of clemency would surely unleash.

Dulles was right to give instructions to department officials, because some diplomats were out of the loop and confused. For example, in January the pope had issued his public statement condemning the scheduled executions, sentiments he reiterated in a Papal Message in late February.[186] A few days later Texas Senator Lyndon B. Johnson asked the State Department for clarification regarding the Vatican's pro-Rosenberg stance.[187] In a draft to the senator, the perplexed Assistant Secretary of State for Congressional Relations replied: "There is nothing in the record of the Rosenberg case to indicate that Julius and Ethel Rosenberg are Catholics . . . it is consequently not likely that the religious persuasion of the Rosenbergs had anything to do with the interest of the Vatican in the Rosenberg case."[188] While this statement was ultimately deleted from the final letter, its inclusion in the draft reflects confusion about the pope's stance and the religious convictions of the couple among top-level State Department officials well into the spring of 1953.[189]

As anticipated, Eisenhower's clemency denial prompted reinvigorated protests from America's allies. Protest letters from London numbered nearly two thousand to that point, with several hundred more arriving immediately following the president's announcement.[190] In March the State Department denied a Labor Member of Parliament an entrance visa, because he was traveling to the United States to speak at a Rosenberg Clemency Committee function; officials were so concerned about the damage he might cause that they did all they could to prevent him from speaking.[191] Protests continued and by April more than two hundred British scientists requested the president reconsider clemency.[192]

In France, nearly all of the Parisian press opposed Eisenhower's clemency rejection. The pro-Atlantic paper *Franc-Tireur* claimed that Eisenhower had played into the hands of the very "enemy he wants to overcome."[193] The centrist *Le Monde* responded with an insult for the United States: "Americans appear much less interested in [the] Rosenbergs than are Europeans . . . Americans seem to have [an] excellent conscience: [the] president played golf and diplomatic parties continue."[194] Even the moderate *Figaro* wondered whether the "cause of freedom" would have "been better defended by more generosity?"[195] Demonstrations continued throughout France, resulting in more than a thousand communications sent to the Paris Embassy following Eisenhower's clemency denial, in addition to the several thousand received prior to the announcement.[196] The concerned embassy noted that the number of "protests considerably exceeds" that of any former Communist campaign.[197] The *New York Times* admitted that the Rosenberg case was the "top issue" in France, reflecting the success of "anti-American propaganda" even among staunch anti-Communists.[198] The FBI confirmed these large French demonstrations, describing a February 19 rally of 12,000 Parisians protesting Eisenhower's action.[199] These rallies used Louis Mittelberg's poster, *His Famous Smile*, to represent their critique; the Polish-born French artist depicted Eisenhower smiling, with electric chairs for teeth (Figure 3.3).[200]

Protest spread into French colonies as well. For example, the Saigon Embassy in Vietnam reported the first editorial about the Rosenberg case in a local newspaper, *Tieng Doi*. The author of the piece drew in part from his own participation in the Sacco and Vanzetti demonstrations in Paris back in 1927.[201] Embassy officials responded by forwarding Dulles's information sheet to the author.

In Canada, dissent continued unabated, as embassy officials struggled to respond. The Edmonton Committee for Clemency for the Rosenbergs (CCR) picketed the Alberta Consulate, insisting Eisenhower extend forgiveness to the

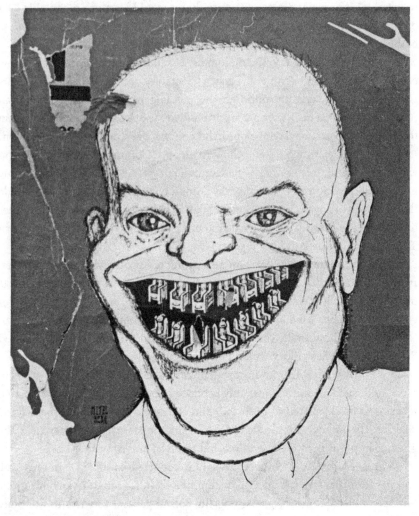

Figure 3.3 Louis Mittelberg, *His Famous Smile*, 1952, pencil on paper. Courtesy of Wisconsin Historical Society, WHS-3504.

Rosenbergs "as your first deed as President," and increased demonstrations in Winnipeg and Hamilton.[202] In Toronto a radio station broadcast a "pernicious . . . soap opera type" San Francisco Theater Guild production, which impugned the evidence used in the trial and its procedures, portrayed FBI agents as bullies, and emphasized the role anti-Communism and anti-Semitism played in the case.[203] The Toronto Consulate first tried to take "steps to bring pressure to bear for a cancellation of the broadcast" while not exposing American involvement.[204] Unable to prevent the show, consulate officials proceeded to "discreetly" expose the "Communist nature of the broadcast."[205] Officials planted the critique in the *Toronto Telegram* and accused the program of being "slanted," and "tawdry nonsense."[206] While admitting that the electrocution of two parents was "extremely regrettable," American diplomats wrote that it would be more regrettable "if a day dawned when many more kiddies were maimed as well as orphaned because of the actions of the Rosenbergs."[207]

Of even more concern to the diplomats, dissent had reached the highest levels of the Canadian government. Canada's Secretary of State for External Affairs Lester Pearson adamantly opposed the pending executions.[208] Alarmed, an American diplomat in Ottawa promptly phoned the State Department to explain that Secretary Pearson was not alone in his concern over the case and that dissent "extends to circles which have nothing to do with Communist propaganda and which are not subject to fellow-traveler influences."[209] While the future prime minister understood that "world-wide Communist propaganda no doubt made the extension of any clemency more difficult," he wanted Eisenhower and Dulles to know of the formidable and growing pro-clemency sentiment in Canada.[210] The State Department did not reply.

Eisenhower's clemency decision also prompted protest among other allies. In Italy, Ambassador Bunker reiterated his alarm that not just Communists but Democratic leaders were joining the protests in Rome.[211] The Naples progovernment paper *Mattino* editorialized that anti-Communists, and not proCommunists, should take the lead to convince those in power in the United States that "America's glory would be served better with clemency than inexorability."[212] They knew Communist statements would not move the U.S. government, and "such an attitude can only produce opposite effects, so much so that it seems to be calculated to push the unfortunate Rosenbergs into the electric chair."[213] The ambassador pleaded with Washington for advice on answering the growing opposition to the executions but received no response.[214]

Consulate officials in Antwerp, Belgium, reported an increase in picketing and petitions, which they assumed stemmed from Communist organizations but still aroused concern, prompting the consul general to write to the State Department four times in less then two weeks.[215] When protests continued in the Netherlands, the American embassy at The Hague took the opportunity to compile a list of the names of Communist cause supporters.[216] If embassy officials could do nothing about the protests, at least they could seize the opportunity to track presumed Communists.

Eisenhower's clemency denial also prompted spreading protests in West Germany. In Berlin, trade union sources predicted that when the Rosenbergs were finally executed, protest strikes would threaten to wreak havoc on the city.[217] Picketing and pro-clemency editorials from Communists and anti-Communists increased in Bonn, Frankfurt, Munich, Nuremberg, and Stuttgart.[218] In an effort to counter the dissent in Hamburg, consulate officials offered protesters copies of Bradlee's original analysis until the diplomats realized they had none on hand; one protester had to return three times before officials were able to secure a copy from Paris.[219] The anti-Communist press in Hamburg joined in urging clemency. The chief editor of the *Hamburger Anzeiger* emphasized that mercy for the Rosenbergs would indicate that the United States had "freedom of fear through superior strength."[220] An editor with the *Hamburger Echo* wrote that he remained unconvinced that the couple deserved death, calling the case "legal murder" and a possible repetition of the 1920s Sacco and Vanzetti "tragedy."[221]

Scandinavian protest also spread, a development that diplomats attributed to their geographic proximity to the Soviet Union.[222] Embassy officials in Stockholm reported protests by delegations of individuals whom they described as "mostly unkempt and un-Swedish looking" and probably Communist.[223] An editorial in Stockholm's *Sydsvenska Dagbladet* wondered whether "the Communist campaign will probably make it more difficult to the American authorities to stop the executions, an action that would immediately be proclaimed by world Communism as a Communist victory."[224] In Göteborg, hundreds of shipbuilding and textile workers presented letters appealing for clemency, and the consul general promptly declared them all Communists. Anti-Communist protest stemmed from two newspapers that emphasized the "traditional Scandinavian dislike of the death penalty."[225] The Helsinki legation continued to receive protests from Communist organizations, women's groups, worker's unions, and youth leagues.[226] One Helsinkian—a "chronic crank"—offered "himself as a candidate for the electric chair" in order to save the lives of the Rosenbergs.[227] Diplomats ignored the proposal.

The pope's statement and Eisenhower's denial of clemency also prompted reactions among far-off allies. In Australia, diplomats in Perth and Canberra received hundreds of protests, while in Sydney a Save the Rosenbergs Committee (SRC) held an "overflow public meeting" and cabled a clemency request to Eisenhower.[228] In New Zealand, the American Embassy in Wellington reported receipt of protest letters, ranging "the gamut from bombastic and violent accusations to a mild request that the death penalty be commuted."[229] "Undoubtedly," the embassy admitted, "some of them may be written by non-Communists genuinely concerned over what they consider to be an infringement of civil liberties," including a large number of signatures of clergy.[230] Some expressed deep disillusionment and resentment for the United States: "This case has thoroughly exposed so-called American democracy and leadership of free world in its most vile form," and "Your government has departed a long way from life, liberty and the pursuit of happiness."[231] One letter again linked the case to that of Sacco and Vanzetti and declared that if the couple was executed "world opinion will put [the] U.S. Government on [the same] level of a Southern State lynch mob."[232] Washington again offered no response.

Protest also surged in Egypt. Long a British protectorate, Egypt was struggling with political upheaval and a coup that removed the king in 1952. In the months before the establishment of a president-run republic, the American Embassy in Cairo kept a close eye on the political disruption and reported sizable protests, press comments, letters, and telegrams.[233] The weekly *Al Midan* published a coupon for readers to fill out and send to the embassy. The embassy received more than one hundred signatures on such coupons, and an additional petition with hundreds of additional signatures from Ibrahim University.

In Iceland numerous editorials emphasized anti-death-penalty sentiment, the use of questionable evidence in the trial, comparisons to Sacco and Vanzetti, and further protests in Western Europe.[234] Diplomats in Reykjavik were so concerned with the possible propaganda significance of these pro-Rosenberg editorials that they financed one Icelandic editor's "fact-finding trip" to the United States.[235] This was one of only a handful of instances in which American officials helped locals reiterate the U.S. government's version of the Rosenberg story.

Predictably, an elaborate dance of political theater evolved within the Soviet sphere of influence. Communist officials condemned Eisenhower's rejection of clemency while American officials occasionally tried to defend it. A committee to free the Rosenbergs operated in East Germany for much of 1953.[236] In Czechoslovakia, CIA agents tried to score propaganda points by emphasizing the differences between American and Soviet justice: "Had the Rosenbergs been tried within the Soviet orbit their punishment would have been so swift and merciless that even if someone dared ask for clemency the execution would have taken place before the ink was dry on such a petition."[237] American diplomats in Warsaw ignored most press criticism, which called the pending executions a "crime appalling [to the] human conscience and revolting in its vileness is being committed in view [of the] entire world" and labeled the Eisenhower administration murderers.[238] U.S. officials did not bother to respond to these editorials, but in Budapest they tried a different approach. When the president of the Hungarian Academy of Sciences telegrammed advising clemency, an American diplomat in Budapest replied that "the contents of that message lead me to believe that you . . . are not informed of the facts of the case," and offered to provide several *New York Times* articles on the case that explained Judge Kaufman's ruling.[239] The academy president wrote back that he was in possession of the newspaper articles referenced and they did not convince him. "On the contrary," he contended, "the view and tone of the document precisely reflects the spirit of instigation against which we have repeatedly protested and which was so clearly manifested in the sentence" of the Rosenbergs.[240] In the Soviet sphere, any American attempts to shift the narrative of the Rosenberg case seemed to backfire. The game changed in March.

Early on March 4, 1953, CIA Director Allen Dulles reported to Eisenhower that Soviet Premier Joseph Stalin had suffered a stroke and was likely dying. "The news from Moscow of the illness of Stalin quickly excited, and soon obsessed, official Washington," a White House aide later recalled.[241] At dinner the following evening Eisenhower learned of Stalin's death. Special assistant for psychological warfare C. D. Jackson was elated and pushed to "overload the enemy at the precise moment" the Soviets were "least capable of bearing even . . . [their] normal load."[242] Jackson suggested offering a peace proposal, in the hopes that it would spark deep divisions within the Soviet Union. In the days that followed, however, Eisenhower complained that the State Department lacked a strategy to maximize American advantage during this period of uncertain Soviet succession.[243] "We have no plan," he grumbled to his cabinet. "We are not even sure what difference his death makes."[244] Precious days slipped by as the State Department, the CIA, and the PSB debated a process that would take advantage of the situation.[245]

On March 16, new Soviet premier Georgi Malenkov seized the opportunity to act first and deliver his own major speech for peace, triggering a laundry list of foreign policy initiatives. In the following months the Soviets would relinquish territorial claims in Turkey, re-establish diplomatic relations with Israel, help end the Korean War, endeavor to improve relations with Yugoslavia and Greece, and emphasize "peaceful coexistence" with the West.[246] In addition to the good will generated by these actions, global Communism could improve its appeal once it was liberated from the image of Stalin's evil repression. "With Stalin's successors publicly clamoring for negotiations," historian Kenneth Osgood explains, "the rigid anti-communism of Eisenhower and Dulles—not to mention Joseph McCarthy—led many international observers to see the United States as the greater threat to international peace and stability."[247] As protesters around the globe decried the Rosenberg case as an example of rigid anti-Communism in the face of less rigid Communism, the global stakes were never higher.

Nearly six weeks after Stalin's death and four after Malenkov's speech, Eisenhower responded to the Soviets. Sandwiched between rounds of golf at Augusta National Golf Club in Atlanta, the president flew back to Washington on April 16 to deliver "The Chance for Peace" disarmament speech.[248] In one of the most effective addresses of his career, Eisenhower explained that a "nation's hope of lasting peace cannot be firmly based upon any race in armaments," and that the United States was currently losing this battle between guns and butter.[249] He proposed weapons reduction as a solution, with dramatic yet accessible reasoning:

> The cost of one modern heavy bomber is this: a modern brick school in more than 30 cities . . . We pay for a single fighter plane with a half million bushels of wheat. We pay for a single destroyer with new homes that could have housed more than 8,000 people . . . Under the cloud of threatening war, it is humanity hanging from a cross of iron.[250]

In what one White House aid referred to as a "rip-snorting" speech, Ike called for "a declared total war, not upon any human enemy but upon the brute forces of poverty and need," predating Lyndon Johnson's War on Poverty by more than a decade.[251] Eisenhower pledged to focus American leadership on peace: "We are ready, in short, to dedicate our strength to serving the needs, rather than the fears, of the world."[252] According to the *New York Times*, the speech "received approval from both parties in Congress" with "many noting that the President had 'seized the initiative' from the Soviet Union."[253]

Yet it was not a sincere peace proposal. In snatching the goodwill advantage away from the Soviets, Eisenhower laid out a plan that would force them to demonstrate through "deeds" their commitment to the "honest act of peace" before the global community could venture down "the highway of peace."[254] The Soviet proposal, the president argued, would prove to be "mere rhetoric" and insincere if not accompanied by "genuine evidence of peaceful purpose" that "would carry a power of persuasion not to be matched by any amount of oratory."[255] Actions—like peace in Korea with free elections uniting the peninsula, free elections throughout Eastern Europe including a united Germany, and military withdrawal from Indochina and Malaya—that Eisenhower knew full well were politically impossible even in the post-Stalin Soviet Union. The Eisenhower administration would continue to wage war to ensure peace.

C. D. Jackson and the PSB publicized the speech to continue the propaganda momentum. However, State Department officials soon noted that divergent perspectives on the impact of Stalin's death caused divisions not in the Soviet sphere, but between America and her allies.[256] At that precise moment, new information about the Rosenberg case propelled the couple back to newspaper front pages around the world and threatened to drive the free world even farther apart.

The *National Guardian* disclosed the first piece of controversial new evidence in mid-April. The prosecution's case had relied, in part, on a missing console table that had allegedly been a gift from the Soviets to the Rosenbergs for photographing documents.[257] Reporters for the *National Guardian* found the small table in Julius's mother's apartment and discovered its actual origin: Macy's Department Store. This raised issues of false prosecutorial evidence, prompting NCSJRC members to launch a nationwide campaign to expose perjury in the case and clamber for a new trial.[258]

Five days later the Paris Communist paper *Le Combat* released a second piece of new evidence—memoranda attributed to David Greenglass. In them Greenglass admitted that the information he passed along to Harry Gold (the spy courier) "may not be at all what I said in the [FBI] statement."[259] Greenglass's attorney confirmed these notes were "filched" from his office and it appeared to be legitimate exculpatory evidence.[260] According to the *New York Times*, the memos contained "points that were the absolute opposite of what Greenglass testified [to] in court."[261] When a handwriting expert verified that Greenglass had written one of the documents, New York Assistant U.S. Attorney Kilsheimer admitted that "complications" had arisen, and he needed clearance from the Department of Justice before he could speak any further on the matter.[262] Proof of the console table's origin and Greenglass's memos sparked a vigorous response among protesters, but this was not the only damaging propaganda the United States had to contend with in the spring of 1953.

In April, Senator Joseph McCarthy sent two aides on what became a disastrous seven-nation romp through Western Europe. Roy Cohn and David Schine began their quest in Paris removing more than 30,000 books by purported Communist authors from USIS libraries; their travels would include Berlin, Frankfurt, Munich, Bonn, Vienna, Belgrade, Athens, and Rome, before concluding in London. The world would now be safe for democracy with Herman Melville's *Moby Dick* and Dashiell Hammett's *The Maltese Falcon* off the shelves.[263] A public affairs officer in Bonn called Cohn and Schine "junketeering gumshoes"; in Paris Ambassador Dillon observed that Europeans had a "highly unfavorable reaction" to their "mission," which Ben Bradlee later labeled a "ludicrous, destructive crusade."[264] Skipping out on their hotel bill in Paris certainly did not help. Years later Roy Cohn admitted, "Yes, there are things I wouldn't do over again: the trip to Europe, I would never do that over again, because I didn't understand at the time . . . we just walked into a lion's den."[265] The European press also reacted with dismay, which prompted many Europeans, particularly allies, to doubt the efficacy of America's Cold War mission. *Time* magazine linked the fiasco to McCarthyism, claiming it had "cost the U.S. billions spent to promote international cooperation and trust and to advance U.S. leadership."[266] Even the nonpartisan Council on Foreign Relations, which avoided endorsing any position concerning U.S. foreign policy, had to admit that aggressive anti-Communism was damaging America's image. "Abroad, especially in Europe," the Council explained, "the effect of this campaign was to strengthen an already widespread impression that civil liberties in the United States had been seriously undermined and the country subjected to a minor reign of terror."[267]

To make matters worse, many Europeans connected the Cohn/Schine debacle to the Rosenberg case. Trying to demonstrate his maturity and experience, Cohn had proudly claimed that he personally prosecuted the atomic bomb spies. According to a diplomat in Paris, this only proved to "convince waverers" that if executed that June the Rosenbergs would not have benefitted from America's superior judicial system, but instead be victims of McCarthyism.[268]

Secretary of State Dulles reacted swiftly to the new evidence and the propaganda trouble he was certain it would cause. Indeed *Time* magazine soon observed that "the European alliance creaks with strain."[269] Concerned with his inability to "counteract the Communist intentions to cast doubt on the credibility" of Greenglass's testimony, Dulles wrote to eight American embassies in Europe on the evening of May 6.[270] He explained that the Paris Communist press had caused this crisis of confidence, and they alone bore responsibility for reviving interest in the case. The secretary addressed any doubts about the Greenglass testimony, explaining that "in any investigation more subjects are covered as the case develops."[271] He promised to forward the results of the FBI's authentication of the memo when they were ready. Meanwhile, he advised embassy officials to publicize that the Communist introduction of "allegedly new evidence" fit into a pattern of "attacking minor points," never questioning other key testimony, and ignoring legal channels in favor of "spinning the case out to obtain a maximum anti-American propaganda effect."[272] Dulles asked these diplomats to alert him to "any local use of this 'new evidence,'" because he feared the Greenglass documents would prompt renewed interest in the case.[273]

Dulles's suspicions were correct. The new evidence prompted reactions in many countries, some previously silent on the Rosenberg case. Dozens of groups in Oslo openly questioned the fairness of the trial, and a three-page list of protesting organizations included labor unions, Communist Party groups, the Norwegian Democratic Women's Association, and the Norwegian Housewives Association.[274] In an unprecedented move more than thirty doctors, lawyers, and labor union organizers in Lebanon wrote to the American embassy in Beirut insisting on clemency due to the weak evidence and extreme sentences; the shocked American ambassador stated this was the first expression of sympathy for the Rosenbergs in the country.[275] Public protests increased in The Hague, while an Argentinean composer wrote a song for the Rosenbergs, and a couple in Holland expressed their support by naming their newborn daughter Ethel Julia.[276]

The most passionate criticism came from France. Consulate officials at Strasbourg were shocked to read an editorial that openly criticized the

U.S. government in *Saarbruecker Zeitung*, "the most widely read daily paper in Saar."[277] Senator McCarthy's activities "have cost America very dear[ly] in recent months," the editorial stated, and "one can only hope that the American judicial process has not also been infected by the 'McCarthy bacillus.'"[278] A surprised consulate officer was compelled to take the unusual action of replying to the editorial without the State Department's prior approval. He clarified— incorrectly—that David Greenglass's testimony served only an "auxiliary" role in establishing the guilt of the defendants.[279] The official concluded with this obvious point: "The Rosenbergs have been sentenced to death. Effective intervention by the Executive can be made only before the sentence is carried out."[280]

Disagreements between the United States and France spread to the highest levels when Eisenhower met with French Prime Minister René Mayer that spring. The Americans wanted to discuss the situation in Southeast Asia and to convince the French that Soviet peace overtures were insincere rhetoric.[281] Eisenhower reminded Mayer that the Soviet Union was still a threat, and that the Premier Malenkov was merely trying to sabotage unity among the allies. However, the talks did not succeed, and divisions among the Western allies deepened.[282] Disagreements over the Rosenberg case only exacerbated these deteriorating relations.

C. Douglas Dillon, the new U.S. ambassador to France, was still acclimating to Paris when he reported to Washington in April that the new evidence had propelled protest back into the "non-Commie press."[283] Dillon, a lifelong Republican and former OSS worker, was known for "analyzing problems in a detached Wall Street style."[284] He struggled to remain detached as the Parisian press attacked the irregularities of the case. The mainstream *Le Monde* and moderate *Figaro* ran stories on the new evidence and continued to criticize the Rosenbergs' conviction. Dillon reported that several journalists "have asked us urgently for comment," and he suggested the State Department immediately forward "all possible material" to refute this evidence.[285] Nothing happened quickly. A Justice Department attorney requested the handwritten Greenglass memo, but he was not worried; he promised to "deny the authenticity" of the document even before he saw it because he was "confident" it was "fraudulent."[286] More than a week later Dillon was still waiting for solid refutation of the Greenglass memo.

According to Paris press attaché Ben Bradlee, by late April 1953 proving the Rosenbergs' guilt was not worth the time. "The real issue in France," he argued, "was clemency."[287] Whether guilty or not, the French opposed the executions.

Ambassador Dillon had seen enough. Following up on his four April telegrams, Dillon wrote another on May 16 that shifted the terms of the debate. He summarized his reactions after two months in France in an "Eyes Only" dispatch to Secretary Dulles, in which he explained why the president should reconsider clemency.[288] "I am deeply concerned with [the] long term effect of [the] possible execution of [the] Rosenbergs on French opinion," Dillon began.[289] Even among Europeans who accepted the Rosenbergs' guilt, there existed the belief that the death sentence was "unjustifiable punishment" especially when compared to other atomic spies.[290] A "substantial segment of [the] French opinion," he emphasized, distinguished between Julius's guilt "as the principal" spy and the guilt of "his wife as an accessory."[291] The ambassador employed his strongest words in an effort to educate Dulles on the role of Communist propaganda:

> We should not deceive ourselves by thinking that this sentiment is due principally to Communist propaganda or that people who take this position are unconscious dupes of Communists. [The] fact is that the great majority of French people of all political leanings feel that death sentence is completely unjustified from [a] moral standpoint and is due only to [a] political climate peculiar to [the] United States now . . . In view of the foregoing considerations, I feel bound to bring to your attention [the embassy's] strong conviction that if [the] death sentence is carried out, this will have a most harmful long term effect on the opinion and attitude of the French people towards the United States. We therefore urge that an appraisal of the Rosenberg sentence be made in terms of the higher national interest. I realize that the Communist Party will exploit any commutation as evidence that [the] trial was unfair, but I am convinced that any propaganda capital [the] Communist Party would and could make in [the] short run out of this obvious line would mean little compared with long term damage that execution of the Rosenbergs would do to foreign opinion of [the] U.S. and of our whole democratic processes.[292]

Dillon added that his views were "shared by other United States Mission Chiefs in Europe."[293]

Finally, a diplomatic correspondence made an impact. Dillon's cable triggered reverberations throughout Washington. State Department officials forwarded copies of the telegram to the PSB, the CIA, and Alexander Wiley, the senior Republican Senator from Wisconsin and chairman of the Senate Foreign Relations Committee.[294] Livingston T. Merchant, Assistant Secretary of State for European Affairs—building on Dillon's message—reiterated "reaction in other European countries has been reported to be similar to that in France."[295] Merchant suggested Under Secretary of State Walter B. Smith send a memo to Dillon, addressing the ambassador's fears.

Smith agreed and telegrammed Dillon, explaining that the ambassador's views on the case were "appreciated and carefully studied," but since the Supreme Court had not responded to the "latest appeal and since [the] appeal for clemency to

President has been rejected, I do not feel there is any further recommendation at this time, which I can make to the President."[296] While apparently thinking it futile—but wanting to keep Eisenhower in the loop—Smith passed Dillon's telegram to the president. "In view of the strength of the Ambassador's beliefs in the matter," Smith wrote to Eisenhower, "I believe that you would wish to see his telegram and my reply. I suggest that this exchange also be made available to Mr. C. D. Jackson in view of the propaganda implications involved."[297] Eisenhower never issued a reply.[298]

Dillon's telegram also caught the attention of FBI Director J. Edgar Hoover. Shocked and angered by Dillon's late-hour plea for commutation, Hoover demanded an investigation.[299] Hoover questioned Dillon's motives and ordered a background check on Dillon and his political advisers in Paris.[300] Despite a resulting report that confirmed the loyalty of Dillon and his fellow American diplomats in Paris, Hoover continued to raise the question of trustworthiness. The director complained about Dillon to the attorney general, claiming that the ambassador had allowed other more radical embassy officials to prepare the telegram.[301] It is unclear what Attorney General Brownell did, if anything, with this information, but Hoover's effort to impugn Dillon speaks to his effort to silence dissent on the case.[302]

Julius Rosenberg would spend his thirty-fifth birthday on May 12 writing to his children, visiting with his wife, and enjoying a "ride through the prison" to see evidence of spring in the "lush green lawn" and "rows of tulips."[303] Later that day the prison dentist yanked out a molar. "Imagine spoiling my birthday by pulling a tooth," he wrote to his son, "There just ain't no justice."[304] But justice had not yet issued its final word.

During the final week of May the Supreme Court took action in the case. While in April the Court had again rejected a petition to review the Rosenberg case, suddenly Supreme Court Justice William O. Douglas had a change of heart.[305] Douglas—who had been appointed by Roosevelt in 1939 and would ultimately serve nearly thirty-seven years, the longest term in the court's history—was known as the liberal voice on the court.[306] In a memo to his colleagues he explained that he had "done further work" on the case and concluded that "the conduct of the prosecutor" could not be "as easily disposed of as the Court of Appeals thinks."[307] Douglas referred to the allegation that the U.S. attorney exhibited prejudicial conduct during the trial. Justice Douglas "reluctantly concluded that *certiorari* should be granted," meaning the case would be heard before the high court to investigate these allegations.[308] Confusing negotiations ensued, and infighting erupted on the Vinson Court.[309] While acknowledging Douglas's late change of opinion, Justice Felix Frankfurter and a bedridden Justice Hugo Black tentatively agreed with him. Justice Robert Jackson disagreed, calling Douglas's memo "the dirtiest, most shameful, most cynical performance that I have ever heard of in matters pertaining to law," but agreed to review to keep Douglas's dissent from becoming public.[310] In discussions Douglas offered to withdraw his memo. Any support for review withered and on May 25 the Court announced its decision to deny *certiorari* to the Rosenbergs. Judge Kaufman set the executions for the week of June 15.

In the White House, C. D. Jackson still hoped to get the Rosenbergs to talk. He implored Attorney General Brownell on May 27 to consider a "temporary stay of execution" to "play [a] war of nerves with [the] Rosenbergs," explaining that "the warden, matron, prison doctor . . . should have impressed upon them . . . the game that was being played."[311] Brownell affirmed, "The matron had managed to ingratiate herself" with Ethel and he "had hopes in that direction."[312] While it is true that Ethel had grown close to a prison matron, apparently this relationship did not prove as easily manipulated as administration officials had hoped.

The *Washington Post* changed its stance and supported clemency in an editorial in the following day's paper.[313] The *Post* staff agreed with the Supreme Court's decision to decline hearing the Rosenberg case, calling the ruling "eminently sound and correct."[314] They argued, however, that while Judge Kaufman had the right to impose the death penalty, the sentence had taken on propaganda value the judge could not possibly have foreseen. As such, they called upon President Eisenhower to reconsider. They acknowledged that "Communist propaganda stands to benefit" whether the couple is executed or sent to prison for thirty years.[315] Surely the president "could hardly ignore the fact" that the case had "become a powerful instrument of anti-American agitation abroad," and the paper recommended he keep these considerations in mind as a "fresh campaign for executive clemency is launched" and determine which was the path of "political wisdom."[316] This editorial reflected a nuanced concern for global opinion not prevalent in the American press or the public as a whole. Its logical approach fell on deaf ears.

As May 1953 came to a close, fighting in Korea began to wind down. In the aftermath of Stalin's death his successors advocated an end to the war; Chinese leaders were beginning to agree. Mao had feared a U.S. military escalation under Eisenhower, and a series of nuclear tests in Nevada that spring may have intensified his dread.[317] A Chinese assault along Bukhan River in late May prompted negotiators on all sides to agree on the final points of an armistice. An official end to the conflict was finally in sight.

As a grim reminder of the human cost of that conflict, in the final week of May 1953 thirty-nine American were wounded in Korea, and seven more were killed in action.[318] To honor those soldiers and all Americans who had lost their lives in battle, Eisenhower laid a wreath at the Tomb of the Unknown Soldier on Memorial Day, and then played a round of golf.

On Sunday, May 31, thousands of Americans watched CBS's popular historical docudrama *You Are There*. That night's episode explored the 1895 Dreyfus case.[319] French Captain Alfred Dreyfus, a Jew, had endured public humiliation and brutal imprisonment on Devil's Island after being falsely accused of treason.[320] After Dreyfus supporters proved that a miscarriage of justice had occurred involving falsified evidence and rampant anti-Semitism, the captain was exonerated in 1906. The Dreyfus case became known around the world as an extreme example of trumped up charges and religious intolerance. The TV show prompted many to draw parallels to the Rosenberg case.[321] Descendants of Captain Dreyfus themselves would appeal to the White House for clemency for the couple.[322] Some viewed this broadcast as a form of protest, highlighting issues of anti-Semitism that dogged the government concerning the Rosenbergs.

As the case entered its final frenzied weeks, the Eisenhower administration continued to play catch up on the propaganda front. Prompted by the pope's statement against the death penalty, Eisenhower's denial of clemency, the questions raised by "new evidence," the complications of the Supreme Court, and the rapidly approaching execution date—protests were spreading like a virus throughout the world, and anti-Communists were no more immune than Communists. While Americans largely supported the administration, both America's enemies and allies were openly questioning the righteousness of the U.S. government's actions.[323] Within the White House, the PSB, and the State Department disagreement, miscommunication, and inaction ran rampant; no one agreed on a narrative even for the sake of appearances. Julius and Ethel Rosenberg continued to sit in Sing Sing Prison and hope for a reprieve. But time was running out.

4

Execution

I deny this reality.

—Tom Baker as the Doctor, *Doctor Who, 1976*

On Tuesday, June 2, 1953—just two weeks before the scheduled executions—James V. Bennett of the Bureau of Prisons met with the Rosenbergs to get them to confess. Bennett spoke with the couple for more than hour, explaining that if they were going to talk they needed to do so soon in order to give officials ample time to verify the reliability of their information.[1] Bennett described Julius as more "belligerent" and "excitable" than Ethel, and admitted that both refused to cooperate and took the opportunity to denounce the attorney general, Judge Kaufman, and David and Ruth Greenglass. Julius later described the meeting as "mental torture."[2] Bennett, not exactly sympathetic to the couple's grim fate, complained when Julius "launched in[to] a quite emotionally charged tirade."[3]

Ethel and Julius Rosenberg responded by publicizing the federal government's offer of a deal. In a statement the couple explained they were told if they cooperated with the government their "lives would be spared."[4] By making this offer, the Rosenbergs argued, "the Government admits that it has doubts concerning our guilt."[5] The couple declined the proposal, refusing to "repudiate the truth of our innocence," and asserted: "We solemnly declare, now and forever more, that we will not be coerced, even under pain of death, to bear false witness and to yield up to tyranny our rights as free Americans. If we are executed, it will be the murder of innocent people and the shame of it will be upon the Government of the United States."[6] Their statement dramatically closed with the following line: "History will record, whether we live or not, that we were victims of the most monstrous frame-up in the history of our country."[7]

Yet as Julius acknowledged to his increasingly despondent wife, events were "beginning to happen at an increasing tempo."[8]

In the final days global protesters kicked it into high gear. They moved away from efforts to depict the couple as innocent of the charges against them and moved to a two-prong attack. First, protesters argued that the death penalty had no place in a free and civilized nation like the United States. Second, they portrayed the couple as individuals being put to death because of a belief, and that as such, killing the couple would only benefit global Communism by handing the Soviets two martyrs to their cause. Pro-clemency demonstrators urged Eisenhower to use the powers of the presidency to save the reputation of the United States and deny the Soviet Union this victory. With a reinvigorated protest movement, Julius pressed Ethel to believe that "the truth will out," but as the final days sped by, that seemed less and less likely.[9]

Eisenhower showed a crack in his pro-execution resolve. The president authorized C. D. Jackson to meet with Attorney General Brownell and FBI Director Hoover to further explore the idea of commuting Mrs. Rosenberg's sentence.[10] It is unclear what prompted Eisenhower to have second thoughts about Ethel's execution, but regardless, the president's request failed to produce significant results.[11]

A few days later, Eisenhower tried to express his hesitancy to a friend. "It is extremely difficult to reach a sound decision in such instances," he wrote to a former colleague at Columbia University. "Not all arguments are on either side."[12] However, Ike continued to defend his anti-clemency stance through the course of the letter. His resolve would soon return and the president hit his stride when he acknowledged the importance of America's image abroad. "As to any intervention based on considerations of America's reputation," he explained, "Communist leaders" believe "that free governments—and especially the American government—are notoriously weak and fearful."[13] He was convinced that weakness would be exploited in the Cold War climate and put Americans at risk. Eisenhower insisted that the Soviets believed they could spy against the United States "with no real fear of dire punishment on the part of the perpetrator."[14] The president would often return to this argument of the appearance of weakness, one that resonated with his fellow citizens, but not with advocates for clemency in the Rosenberg case, whether Communists or not.

As Eisenhower continued this line of thinking in the letter, he seemed to be convincing himself as well as his friend. Ike explained that he was confident that "one of these criminals—indeed the more strong-minded and the apparent leader of the two—is a woman," and that giving clemency would simply encourage "the Communists to use only women in their spying process."[15] In reiterating this gendered and stereotype-laden analysis of Communists—based on the profoundly defective psychological profile of ACLU attorney Morris Ernst— the president embraced the flawed arguments that would lead to Ethel's death.[16]

Others in the White House were more concerned about the American people's opinion of the Korean War, then entering its third year. In early June propaganda assistant C. D. Jackson gathered data on the war. Polls showed an increasing number of Americans feared that the United States would not be able to "reach a satisfactory agreement with the Communists" in order to "stop the fighting in Korea." From October 1952 through April 1953, roughly half of Americans polled believed that the war was not worth fighting.[17] The violence in Korea continued. Communists launched costly and unproductive offensives into South Korea in June, and the U.S. Air Force inflicted damage to key dams, threatening the North Korean food supply.[18] As the conflict dragged on, it became increasingly difficult to sell the limited war to the American people.

With little more than two weeks until the scheduled executions, the Psychological Strategy Board (PSB) struggled to be heard. The government agency created specifically to manage Cold War propaganda had major concerns about the issue of martyrdom. Having expressed reservations in mid-January, the PSB now insisted on clemency, demanding that the president reconsider the case "on the basis of its psychological impact abroad."[19] Convinced that the Soviet Union intended to make martyrs out of the Rosenbergs, the board directly contradicted Eisenhower's belief that the executions would be a sign of America's strength: "The risk that a measure of clemency will be taken as a show of weakness is very farfetched at the present time."[20] By using a "power-fully-worded statement," board members were certain Eisenhower could present his case, "namely that we do not yield to Communist pressure but smoke out Communist strategy."[21] They pressed the president to consider this case "an opportunity for demonstrating vividly the contrast between a free society sure of itself, cool and discrete in wielding its power of punishment, and a slave society which can stand only on the corpses of its victims."[22] They pushed him to act quickly to avoid the appearance of bending to Communist Party pressure. Eisenhower—who did not trust the PSB and would soon replace it—likely never seriously considered the board's argument for clemency.[23] Meanwhile protesters overseas continued to clamor for the president's attention in the Rosenbergs' final days.

Protests surged in Canada. In Montreal, dozens of women picketed with placards in both French and English stating "Clemency for the Rosenbergs," and appealing to Eisenhower on behalf of "mothers, parents, and children."[24] According to diplomats the women were "speedily dispersed by police and anti-subversive squad officers," but not before thieves used the protest as cover for a bank robbery.[25] A few days later Emily Alman, a neighbor of the Rosenbergs, led a rally of nearly 400 protesters.[26] Consul officials complained that if they had been alerted that Alman intended to speak, they could have prevented her from entering Canada in the first place.[27] In Toronto the CSCEJR presented the local consulate with a petition begging Eisenhower to save the lives of the Rosenbergs "on behalf of tens of thousands of Toronto citizens" who "implore you to heed the voices in your own country and throughout the whole world," including "some of the outstanding leaders of science and religion of our times."[28] These Canadians were ignored.

In Latin America protesters continued to take the pope's lead and oppose the executions. For example, the Chamber of Deputies in both Uruguay and Brazil voted in favor of a Catholic Party motion supporting the Rosenberg children's request for clemency for their parents.[29] In Guatemala, nearly half of the members of Congress and more than one hundred union leaders, journalists, teachers, and photographers—"from varying social strata, holding different political and religious beliefs"—petitioned President Eisenhower to suspend the executions.[30] The normally pro-U.S. *La Hora* carried a front-page editorial titled "Why It Is Inappropriate to Execute the Rosenbergs."[31] The piece emphasized opposition to the death penalty, but also used the martyrdom argument, reasoning that Communists wanted the execution to proceed "to provide new martyrs for international Communism."[32] Guatemala City officials were alarmed that the Communist campaign was "more than usually successful in drawing in non-Communists."[33]

Some Latin Americans pushed opposition to the executions further, labeling the persecution of the couple as bullying and proof of U.S. imperialism. They chose the term imperialism consciously to provoke an immediate, negative response. Protesters accused the United States of returning to the police power of the Roosevelt Corollary and keeping Latin American states from siding with the Soviet Union.[34] Many protesters viewed the Rosenbergs as an innocent couple who provided information to a World War II ally and worked for world peace. They believed Julius and Ethel were prosecuted solely because they were Communists and saw the death sentence as extreme, unjust, and an example of the United States acting imperiously. By questioning democratic institutions and linking the case to imperialism, the mounting Latin American protest movement painted an unflattering picture of its hemispheric superpower that administration officials were ill equipped to contest.[35]

In Asia-Pacific the first protests erupted in Indonesia. Labor unions passed resolutions protesting the executions and presented their demands to the Djakarta Embassy and the Consulate in Surabaya.[36] While Communist papers ran critical and emotional editorials, pointing to a failure of the American propaganda campaign to disseminate the facts of the case, two passionate editorials in the non-Communist press proved more surprising. The neutralist paper *Pengharapan* condemned the death penalty as "a barbarous act" that "no civilized person" could support, while the independent *Nieuwsgier* pleaded for clemency because they feared the executions would cause "more anti-American agitation than numerous positive deeds could undo."[37] Protests continued in nearby Australia, where demonstrators frequently gathered at the American consulate in Sydney. Claiming to represent thousands of Australians, they blamed Senator

McCarthy-inspired "war hysteria among the American people," accusing aggressive anti-Communists of pushing for the "murder" of the Rosenbergs to hasten "their plans for a third world war."[38] Consulate officials dismissed the protest as a "Communist-dominated" failure (Figure 4.1).[39]

News of U.S. Ambassador to France C. Douglas Dillon's May 16 proclemency telegram continued to spread, stimulating interest in the European response to the case. For example, Senator Alexander Wiley, the ranking Republican Judiciary Committee member, asked to see all Paris and Rome

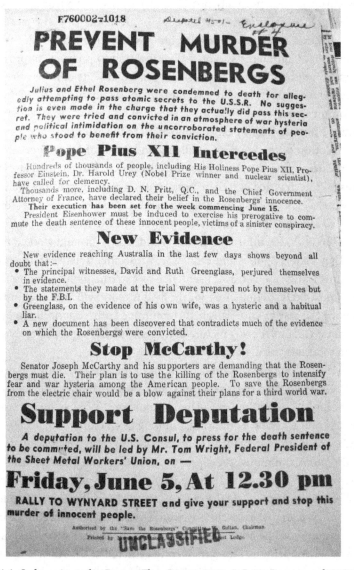

Figure 4.1 Sydney, Australia, Protest Flier, June 5, 1953, RG 59. Courtesy of NARA.

telegrams regarding the Rosenbergs from the last two weeks in May. State Department officials reluctantly agreed. The only correspondence that fit Wiley's parameters, however, was Dillon's May 15 cable. If the senator had asked for the previous seven months, he would have received more than twenty telegrams detailing ever-increasing Roman and Parisian protest about the case.[40]

On June 9, Ambassador Dillon wrote from Paris to elaborate on his May 16 telegram and detail increased dissent from French non-Communists. The left-wing (*L'Humanité, Droit et Liberté, Libération, Ce Soir*), mainstream (*Le Monde, Le Figaro*), and conservative (*L'Aurore*) newspapers all ran editorials opposing the death sentences.[41] French film star Simone Signoret and her husband, actor and singer Yves Montand, signed appeals to Eisenhower.[42] Dillon had personally met with several Parisian Socialist Party members who agreed that the Rosenbergs were guilty and had received a fair trial, but argued the "average Frenchman" could not understand America's judicial system.[43] The ambassador explained to Secretary of State Dulles that the executions "will cause a loss of confidence in U.S. and free world institutions" and "stir up considerable anti-American feeling in France."[44] Dillon—the conservative Republican businessman—stated that he and the other embassy officials agreed with the Socialist Party members and reiterated their stance that they "would be very pleased" if Eisenhower could commute the death sentences.[45] A State Department official scribbled "no action" on the telegram. It is unknown how Dillon reacted to being ignored, but, undeterred, he kept on writing.

Days later Dillon reported the increasing tempo of protests—including thousands of petitions and public appeals—and expanding press coverage.[46] The combination of an editorial in the Catholic paper *La Croix*, a lead editorial in the moderate *Paris-Presse*, another one in the centrist *Le Monde*, and the publication of the Rosenberg letters from prison in the moderate *Le Figaro* pointed to an alarming spread in French dissent.[47] Protest in France traveled beyond Paris to Lyon and Strasbourg, with scheduled mass meetings, and petitions inundating the consulates.[48] Diplomats in Lyon reported an unusual attack on an American Fulbright exchange professor who was "accused of being an agent of American imperialism."[49] In Strasbourg officials requested police protection after the consulate was vandalized, painted with tar reading "U.S. Go Home" and "Liberez les Rosenbergs."[50]

Protesters in London threatened to disrupt the coronation of Queen Elizabeth II. But when Londoners gathered in the drizzle on Tuesday, June 2 the American embassy officials reported no such instances.[51] Numerous French writers petitioned directly to the new British queen, believing she could use her sway with Eisenhower to prevent the Rosenberg executions; the next week 2,000 Australians signed a similar petition for the new queen.[52] Ten days later, in her first postcoronation excursion, Queen Elizabeth traveled through

London where she could not help but see a large banner on the two hundred and three foot tall monument to the 1666 Great Fire of London that read "SAVE THE ROSENBERGS."[53] The number of letters, telegrams, and petitions to the U.S. embassy in Britain arguing that the death penalty was "too severe" approached 300 in early June, prompting an official to complain they were beginning "to overwhelm" the London embassy.[54] Diplomats replied to these complaints— such as a petition from thirteen ministers of the Church of England—with a form letter that explained the trial, but officials reluctantly admitted that pro- testers remained "unconvinced."[55] The embassy accurately predicted they would receive many more protests as the execution date approached.

Opposition to the death penalty fueled protests in Belgium. Officials at the Brussels Embassy complained that local "opinion has again become seriously exercised over Rosenberg case," despite our "considerable efforts" and those of the embassy in Paris (presumably referring to Ben Bradlee's position paper).[56] Even after producing "circulars, releases and conversations," officials admit- ted that "widespread doubt" continued to exist concerning the Rosenbergs' guilt.[57] The death sentence, protesters argued, "represents the 'worst aspects [of] U.S. anti-Communist hysteria.'"[58] Both the "normally pro-American" liberal and conservative presses ran editorials calling the scheduled Rosenberg executions "political murder" and comparing the case to "Communist trials and execu- tions in Iron Curtain countries," and to Sacco and Vanzetti.[59] One opinion piece claimed the Rosenbergs were "condemned not by a court of justice," but "by the intolerance and the fears of men."[60] Speaking to the president's ability to alter their fate, the editorial implored: "An indulgence, perhaps unjustified, is better than an irreparable error." President Eisenhower, the author concluded, should

> know that a gesture of mercy would be also a political gesture. He would
> thus do more to tighten the western alliance than through his greatest
> oration. His stature would not be diminished but enlarged, because he
> would have put respect and charity vis-à-vis mankind above all else.[61]

Brussels also hosted the International Committee of Lawyers Established to Re-Examine the Rosenberg Case, a group of concerned attorneys.[62] Diplomats in Belgium lamented that these were reputable lawyers from Great Britain, France, Italy, the Netherlands, Switzerland, Luxembourg, Sweden, West Germany, Finland, and Belgium—and none were Communists.[63] The self-proclaimed International Tribunal intended to retry the case according to U.S. laws. Concerned and frustrated, embassy officials blamed the State Department, complaining that the material provided had been inadequate: "We trust" that department officials are "giving urgent consideration" to the "anticipated adverse European reactions," and hope that "even at this late date" we receive "more effective ammunition."[64] The level of consideration the State Department gave was indicated by the "no action, file" scrawled across the telegram.[65]

The Rosenbergs inched closer to death the second week in June. In New York City, Judge Irving Kaufman received motions for an evidentiary hearing to see if a new trial was warranted based on the new evidence concerning David Greenglass's testimony and the origins of the console table the Rosenbergs purportedly used to take pictures of documents.[66] Though Julius had hoped the possibility of a truce in Korea would prompt the world to see the execution "as an act of madness and a reversion to barbarism," the courts did not agree.[67] Kaufman heard oral arguments and, after fifteen minutes in chambers, ruled that the evidence did not justify a new trial. On June 10, the Court of Appeals affirmed Judge Kaufman's ruling without hearing arguments on the motion for a new trial, or on the stay of execution. Executions at Sing Sing normally took place on Thursday evenings. The Rosenberg electrocutions were set for Thursday, June 18, 1953, the couple's fourteenth wedding anniversary, and the third they would observe behind bars.

The new execution date spurred protest that reached the highest levels of government in Europe. In Belgium, Jean Rey—a former minister of reconstruction and pro-American liberal—spoke out against the scheduled Rosenberg executions in an article in *Le Soir*, the largest independent Belgian newspaper. Rey stated that he had no doubt the Rosenbergs were guilty and that the case was an American matter not a foreign one, yet he had grave concerns. "In recognition [of the] undeniable fact [that] European opinion is profoundly aroused," Rey wrote, "for purely pragmatic reasons" the president should grant clemency.[68] The two-year sentence already served is inhumane, he argued, and "Belgians would interpret clemency" as a "sign of strength—that U.S. does not fear enemies."[69] Embassy officials emphasized that the "Catholic press has *recently shown increasing concern over forthcoming execution* and has even exhorted readers to prayer."[70] As the execution date approached, diplomats predicted that the "intensity among Belgian political groups of sentiments favoring clemency" would increase.[71] In confirmation, three Belgian politicians visited the American embassy as "friends" of the United States and pressed the president to reconsider clemency.[72] American diplomats explained that Communist agitation was to be expected, but it was "an entirely different matter when words" of this type "come from circles friendly to the United States."[73] Officials assured Washington that there was a general sense that the executions would cause Europeans to "question [the] moral right of America to lead [the] Western community."[74] They concluded: "The Department will realize the significance which must be attached to opinions such as these when they emanate from America's friends and from supporters of the democratic way of life."[75] The consulate again received no response.[76]

Ambassador Dillon was shocked to learn that even top French government officials opposed the executions.[77] At lunch the French prime minister confided to the ambassador that he and many of his aides strongly favored clemency as an example of Christian mercy. Dillon implored that Secretary Dulles forward this message to Eisenhower: "Presidential clemency would be very popular and well-received, whereas execution would certainly create difficulties in French opinion."[78] With such high-level dissent, Ambassador Dillon took to updating Secretary Dulles several times a week.

Unprecedented protests emerged from Luxembourg. For example, an editorial in the Luxembourg popular daily paper *Luxemburger Wort* called the execution of the Rosenbergs "murder of justice" and argued that perhaps we should "follow the Catholics of France and other countries in recommending the review of the Rosenbergs' trial to the American courts."[79] While admitting that atomic espionage was "indeed one of the greatest crimes a citizen of the western hemisphere is able to commit," the execution "badly damages the cause of confidence, rights and freedom."[80] Protests, particularly concerning the fate of the two young Rosenberg sons, accelerated in nearby Germany.[81]

Communist efforts and press attention increased in Budapest as the date of the opening of the World Peace Council meeting approached. The Rosenberg case was placed "high on the agenda" of the June 15 meeting, and protesters claimed that "no effort will be spared to discredit the U.S. and its system of justice."[82] Officials lamented that the execution date coincided with this highly publicized meeting, which they feared would "provoke Communist propaganda field-day here."[83] The State Department provided no advice on how to manage the overlapping events. Discontent in Communist-controlled Hungary also spread to "many liberal but non-Communist Hungarians."[84] Opposition in the form of a steady stream of protest telegrams and letters, the diplomats argued, was not due to Communist propaganda, but to the "feeling that their execution would not quite fit in with" the model of "Anglo-Saxon justice."[85] Diplomats at the legation in Budapest were inundated with telegrams urging clemency for the Rosenbergs; they had sixty of them translated and forwarded to Washington. Officials also complained about the "frenzied and vicious press coverage" in *Magyar Nemzet*, the main Hungarian paper, which compared the Rosenberg case to the execution of Sacco and Vanzetti, and "in bloodthirsty inhumanity" and "brutal cannibalism it even surpasses the ill-famed Dreyfus case."[86]

A growing number of Canadians joined the groups protesting the case and picketed the American consulate in Montreal, passing out fliers that demanded, "WHAT HAVE *YOU* DONE *TODAY* TO HELP SAVE THE ROSENBERGS?"[87] When police intervened and took away the signs, the picketing turned violent. Authorities responded with nine police cars, 100 officers, and eleven arrests; a male protester bit one of the policemen's fingers "to the bone" while resisting arrest.[88] The Montreal Municipal Police predicted that "the Communists will cause serious trouble" in the next week, and consulate officials feared that the next protest would "seriously hamper police."[89]

Due to its proximity to the United States, friends of the Rosenbergs could easily join protests in Canada. Helen Sobell, the wife of defendant Morton Sobell, joined a Northwestern University Law professor and rallied a crowd of nearly 1,000 at a SRC meeting in Toronto. The group passed a resolution insisting both the queen and the Canadian governor general intercede, and they signed individual petitions to be delivered to President Eisenhower. About thirty protesters

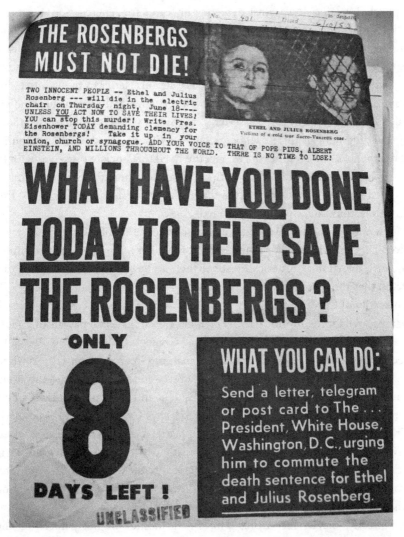

Figure 4.2 Montreal, Canada, Protest Flier, June 10, 1953, RG 59. Courtesy of NARA.

headed to the capital, Ottawa, that night to picket, while others stayed in Toronto and stage a "round-the-clock vigil."[90]

Some of Eisenhower's trusted advisers began to worry that the executions might be a mistake. Concerned about the increasing number and intensity of protests, on the afternoon of June 12 Secretary of State Dulles called Attorney General Brownell and explained his anxiety about global opinion, particularly in Europe. Dulles admitted that many trusted Europeans called the Rosenberg case the "most troublesome issue affecting relations between the United States and Europe."[91] The secretary claimed he did not want to change the course of action, but believed he should bring this issue to the attention of the attorney general.

UN Ambassador Henry Cabot Lodge Jr. agreed with Dulles. While Lodge supported the decision against clemency, he feared the repercussions if America did not make the "case clearer to our allies."[92] Eisenhower had originally offered the position of chief of staff to Lodge and encouraged him to keep track of domestic policies and their effects on America's prestige abroad.[93] In this capacity Lodge forwarded what he called a "very serious" letter to the White House from the archbishop of Lyon, a "most authoritative and responsible" individual.[94] The French archbishop asserted: "The entire world is rising up in concern for the judgment of the Rosenberg couple. Without any thoughts to political consequences," he continued, "we feel the need to associate ourselves with the numerous appeals that, in their entirety, demand a humanitarian decision . . . inspired by the common principles that make up Western Civilization."[95] Even this letter from Lodge went unanswered.

Eisenhower continued to receive correspondence about the case from several prominent individuals. For example, Harold C. Urey, the Nobel prize–winning chemist, questioned American justice when he telegrammed Eisenhower and stated that the "case against the Rosenbergs outrages logic and justice."[96] The University of Chicago chemistry professor—who had served as the director of war research for the Atomic Bomb Project at Columbia University during World War II—explained it was impossible that Greenglass "revealed to Russia the 'secret' of the atomic bomb," because "a man of Greenglass' capacity is wholly incapable of transmitting the physics, chemistry and mathematics of the atomic bomb."[97] Urey asked to meet with the president and explain his opinion in person. Instead of meeting with Eisenhower, Attorney General Brownell spoke with Urey briefly and then passed him off to a Justice Department attorney, who— perhaps in an attempt to discredit his scholarly perspective—labeled the chemist an "unstable person."[98] Though dismissed by the White House, protesters would take the professor's opinion to heart, using his words in their petitions when challenging the government's claims about the case.

Similarly, playwright Arthur Miller—the author of the parable of anti-Communist hysteria, *The Crucible*—warned the president of the negative impact the executions would have on America's standing in the world.[99] Fearing the death of the Rosenbergs would undermine what Miller argued was "America's most attractive ... point of superiority over ... all dictatorial systems—her humane justice," he concluded that the executions would "be a token of weakness in the eyes of both enemies and friends."[100] Eisenhower never replied.

During a contentious meeting on Saturday, June 13, the Supreme Court justices voted against a proposal to hear oral arguments on a stay of execution, and against a stay without an oral hearing.[101] The judges were in their last day of the term, but this would not be the final word from the Supreme Court.[102] The scheduled executions were now five days away.

The same day Secretary of State Dulles penned his longest and most widely distributed communication on the case.[103] Sent to more than forty posts throughout the world, Infoguide Bulletin 378 was a three-page list of what the State Department wanted emphasized in the final days. Writing in response to what Dulles labeled a Communist attempt to "portray U.S. as gripped by irresponsible political hysteria," the secretary explained that "widespread, intensive, non-Communist, emotional opposition" to the death penalty complicated the U.S. version of events.[104] Still believing that Communist propaganda represented the greatest concern, however, Dulles reaffirmed his earlier advice to emphasize the "scrupulous impartiality with which this trial [has] been conducted."[105] He suggested diplomats clarify that the trial was fair and that the couple was "found guilty of a crime which undermined U.S. and free world security," and recommended they avoid "being drawn into detailed public controversy which tends [to] obscure major issues."[106] Dulles recommended officials refer to court statements that the supposed new evidence did not justify a new trial and also to Eisenhower's announcement denying clemency. He promised to continue to "provide as much useful material as possible," and hoped this would silence protest.[107] His hopes were short lived.

On Sunday, June 14—in an indication of the size of demonstrations to come—the NCSJRC organized thousands of protesters to join a "clemency train" that stopped along the way from New Jersey to Washington, D.C., culminating in a march around the White House.[108] The subsequent vigil, which included 7,000 representatives from twenty different states, culminated with the Rosenbergs' older son, Michael, leaving a second letter for the president at the northwest gate of the White House. This letter asked for his parents' release on behalf of himself and his little brother, Robert.[109]

Action resumed at the Supreme Court on Monday, June 15, when the defense presented its final, desperate appeal. The justices were due to leave on summer holiday the next day. Rosenberg attorney Manny Bloch petitioned to bring the couple back into court for another hearing (a writ of habeas corpus) to address the accusation that the prosecution had used perjured testimony by David Greenglass to secure a conviction. Again, a majority of justices rejected the defense's argument.[110] However, in a private session Justice Douglas gave Bloch a glimmer of hope when he agreed to listen to new arguments up until noon the next day. The defense team scrambled to find just cause to halt the executions before the justices left for summer recess.[111]

Protests further intensified in familiar places that final week. In Canada, protesters begged Eisenhower to join with the "millions of ordinary people . . . in every part of the world" and heed the "conscience of mankind and have mercy."[112] Thousands of Belgians signed petitions, staged public debates, and endorsed "clemency for pragmatic reasons" and to show Christian compassion.[113] In the Netherlands, high-ranking Dutch politicians complained that the executions would have an "adverse psychological effect on European opinion," largely due to widespread European opposition to the death penalty.[114] Editorial support of the Rosenbergs had spread to the Dutch non-Communist press, and it was a "widely held Dutch view that death sentence in Rosenberg case should be commuted [to] life imprisonment."[115] American diplomats in Geneva turned away protesters, but not before accepting their petitions and sending the names listed to local Swiss authorities to be exposed as Communist sympathizers.[116]

New dissent also emerged. In Lisbon, hundreds of non-Communists who professed to be friendly to the United States wrote letters requested clemency on humanitarian grounds, primarily due to Portuguese opposition to the death penalty.[117] The government in Poland took an unusual step and officially offered the Rosenbergs political asylum.[118] Polish Foreign Minister Skrzeszewski himself handed the note to the U.S. ambassador in Warsaw, detailing the agreement of the government of the Polish People's Republic and the Central Board of the Polish Red Cross to provide refuge to the couple. Skrzeszewski requested that the ambassador inform the "appropriate U.S. authorities" immediately in case permission was granted for "the above-mentioned persons to leave the U.S."[119] The offer was made public two days later in the *Daily Worker*, stirring up further controversy.[120] Naturally the CIA interpreted this as a Soviet propaganda attempt, and ordered all posts to explain to every contact they could reach that this Polish offer of asylum was "designed by the Communists to place the U.S. Government in a position where it cannot easily grant them clemency."[121] The idea of sanctuary in Poland never gained traction.

As dissent exploded in France, an increasingly frantic Ambassador Dillon continued updating Secretary Dulles daily. Late on that Monday night, Dillon explained that the Paris Embassy had received a "mass of apparently unorganized non-Communist appeals" and he complained about the growing number of French lawyers, scientists, and religious leaders who also urged clemency. For example, Dillon forwarded a clemency appeal from the General Assembly of Reformed Presbyterian Church of France, which asked Eisenhower to "put [an] immediate end to [the] torture of twenty-six months under [the] death sentence."[122] The statement concluded that "there is [a] deep feeling in French religious circles that it would be most unfortunate for [the] Rosenbergs to be executed."[123] Developments at the Supreme Court would further complicate the story.

The next day several attorneys took a new approach. At 11 a.m. on Tuesday, June 16, Supreme Court Justice William O. Douglas sat in his chambers and listened as lawyers new to the case attempted to convince him that the Rosenbergs had been tried under the wrong law. In a ninth-inning effort, the lawyers argued that instead of the Espionage Act of 1917, the defendants should have been charged under the Atomic Energy Act of 1946.[124] Since the conspiracy charges applied to the Rosenbergs' activities from 1944 to 1950, they argued, the Atomic Energy Act superseded the Espionage Act for the atomic espionage committed after 1946. The atomic act would have resulted in the death penalty only if the prosecution had proven that the Rosenbergs' actions had assisted a foreign country and hurt the United States. In addition, under the 1946 act the jury had to recommend death; in the Rosenberg case the jury had found the defendants guilty, but it was the judge who had sentenced them to death. The attorneys questioned whether jury members—who took nine hours to deliberate guilt or innocent—would have been able to reach the required unanimous decision in favor of execution. They implored the justice to issue a stay, or temporary halt, of execution.[125]

Douglas later recalled being "deeply troubled" by this new argument and consulted with several justices to decide whether to suspend the executions.[126] Word leaked out that the justice was considering a stay, and he began receiving telegrams from citizens hoping to sway his opinion. One, from his hometown in Washington State, threatened, "If you grant the Rosenbergs a stay, there will be a lynching party waiting for you here."[127] Feisty and undaunted, Douglas wired back: "If there is to be a Yakima lynching party you'll have to furnish your own whiskey."[128] The justice would not issue his decision until the following morning.

Meanwhile, Secretary Dulles was so disturbed by growing international protests that he ordered a review compiled and sent it to the attorney general and the president.[129] The round-up included cables from Paris, Brussels, Strasbourg, Budapest, Rio de Janeiro, and Warsaw, and summarized that by the week of the scheduled executions the State Department had received nearly 95,000 letters from abroad protesting the case, the vast majority coming from Europe and nearly all recommending clemency.[130] Attorney General Brownell phoned Dulles, worried that Justice Douglas might succeed in reversing the actions of the entire Supreme Court.[131] Dulles agreed and explained that he feared the actions of the Supreme Court might impact the global view of the case, and, by extension, the U.S. government's standing in the world.[132] But the one man who could act on these concerns, Eisenhower, remained unconvinced that intervening and issuing clemency was in the country's best interest. Many, however, continued trying to persuade the president.

That afternoon, Ethel Rosenberg sent a two-page plea for compassion to President Eisenhower.[133] She begged him to take a "more personal consideration" of the case and "ponder" the wisdom of the death sentence since during the "protracted period of solitary confinement" both she and Julius had consistently denied their guilt.[134] She asked that since Eisenhower had been "liberator to millions" under Nazi rule in Europe, perhaps he could also free the couple so they could keep their "small, unoffending Jewish family" intact.[135] She concluded with a plea to the president, calling him an "affectionate grandfather," a "sensitive artist," and a "devoutly religious man."[136] She received no reply. Michael and Robert traveled to Sing Sing Prison that day for what would be their final visit with their parents. Michael later remembered wailing as they ushered him out, "one more day to live, one more day to live."[137] In response to the outburst, Ethel wrote to her son, directing him to "remain calm and free from panic so that we can do all we can to help one another to see this thing through!"[138]

Eisenhower, in a letter to his son John, acknowledged that the case "continues to cause a very considerable amount of furor," but he clung to the hope that the death sentence would discourage other spies.[139] Ike recalled a case from World War II when he made an example of two men convicted of rape and murder by ordering a semipublic execution in Normandy. President Eisenhower believed that he could deter espionage, as General Eisenhower had deterred violence. Concerning Ethel he admitted, "it goes against the grain to avoid interfering in the case where a woman is to receive capital punishment." Eisenhower repeated the FBI's psychological portrait of the couple, as he had days earlier in a letter to his friend from Columbia University. He argued that "in this instance it is the woman who is [the] strong and recalcitrant character, the man is the weak one. She has obviously been the leader in everything they did in the spy ring."[140] The president feared that if he commuted Ethel's sentence, "from here on the Soviets would simply recruit their spies from among women."[141] Eisenhower understood it was not just Communists who favored clemency, but also those who doubted the Rosenbergs' guilt, those who opposed the death penalty, and others who did not want to execute a couple with small children.[142] In his list of those who favored clemency, Eisenhower overlooked those who feared—as his university friend had written—"the name of America, instead of being associated with justice . . . would stand for just the opposite among tens of millions the world over."[143] Eisenhower held fast to his views of justice, the couple's guilt, and Ethel's role as a spy ringleader.

Sophie Rosenberg wrote on behalf of her son, Julius. She cabled Mamie Eisenhower at two that afternoon, desperate to save her son's life.[144] She pleaded with the First Lady to convince the president "to grant mercy" for the life of her son and daughter-in-law. "I beg of you," Mrs. Rosenberg wrote, "to think of two children for whom his holiness Pope Pius has expressed compassion."[145] The First Lady followed the president's lead and did not reply.

That afternoon a group of religious leaders met with President Eisenhower and challenged his views on the case. The rabbi and several reverends said they represented thousands of American clergymen and argued that martyrdom would only support the Communist cause. They feared the executions would be a sign of weakness rather than strength.[146] After thirty minutes the men left the White House and reluctantly told waiting reporters they had failed to convince the president.

Not all religious leaders, however, supported clemency. Reinhold Niebuhr, one of the most influential American Protestant theologians of the twentieth century, wrote at length on Communism as an "organized evil which spreads terror and cruelty throughout the world."[147] As proponents of such evil, Niebuhr argued against saving the lives of the Rosenbergs. In an essay titled "The Evil of the Communist Idea" he articulated these views, and State Department officials were pleased.[148] "We greatly appreciated such Niebuhrian flourishes," American diplomats effused, which "helped the government justify the Rosenbergs' fate."[149] The liberal realist would later regret his anti-clemency stance, but in the crucial days before the executions Niebuhr helped the government make its case.

With the executions scheduled for Thursday, protests in allied countries accelerated that Tuesday afternoon. In Canada, hundreds of protesters began round-the-clock picketing of the Toronto Consulate General; while they were "orderly and quiet," consulate officials feared violence and arranged for uniformed Toronto policemen to guard the building day and night.[150] In England the majority of the London papers admitted that the couple was guilty, but called for executive clemency as proof of American "mercy and political sagacity," arguing that two years in prison waiting on appeals constituted "moral ground for a reprieve."[151] Protesters from across England traveled to London to personally petition the American embassy.[152] In May and June, American diplomats accepted 7,360 telegrams, letters, and petitions supporting the Rosenbergs; during the same period they received just 22 communications protesting British losses in the Korean War.[153]

News of Latin American protests continued to flood into Washington. Argentinean newspapers ran editorials emphasizing the need to give the Rosenbergs the "benefit of doubt" since "world opinion sees justice clouded by political motives," and the Buenos Aires Embassy saw a sharp increase in mail with more than 1,000 letters pleading for clemency just that week.[154] In Porto

Alegre, Brazil, the City Council and Municipal Employee's Association appealed to Eisenhower for clemency, as did several unions in Caracas, Venezuela.[155] In Guatemala City, a group of female protesters demonstrated in front of the American embassy in the late afternoon.[156] Diplomats were shocked by an editorial in Mexico City's conservative newspaper *Excélsior* which pressed Eisenhower not to use the death penalty "as an instrument of revenge, no matter how great may have been the crime committed," but to "permit himself to be softened by the tears of the small children of the alleged 'atomic spies!'"[157]

Protests accelerated throughout Europe. Nearly one thousand Belgians protested in Brussels, and embassy diplomats argued they represented the "great numbers of perfectly respectable people, and perfectly friendly to the US, who have expressed their hopes for clemency."[158] Officials complained how laborious it was to respond to all reasonable protests, and that even at this late date they lacked a "really comprehensive 'hand-out'" to clear up confusions surrounding the case.[159] The American Embassy in Copenhagen received letters and petitions from hundreds of individuals and representatives of numerous Danish organizations, but the plea that received considerable press attention came from eight top lawyers in Copenhagen. "We are convinced that a pardon," the attorneys explained, "far from weakening respect for and confidence in the United States of America, will resound to the honor of the American people, who have so often shown the world proof of their sense of justice and noble forgiveness."[160] Embassy officials accepted the petition, but asked the State Department for clarification concerning the policy of refusing such petitions. Secretary Dulles replied that they needed to be careful since "the rejection of petitions such as those concerning the Rosenbergs would create adverse publicity."[161] Dulles's helpful response, however, would have been more relevant if he had sent it before the Rosenbergs were executed. That same afternoon, the Duchess of Bavaria in West Germany also begged the president for mercy for the parents of two small boys. "I do not want to interfere in your country," the duchess wrote, "but let me put my voice into the prayer on behalf of humanity to beg you dear president to save the life of the Rosenbergs."[162] Special assistant Sherman Adams forwarded the telegram to the State Department for "appropriate handling."[163] It was promptly filed, with no action taken.[164]

On Tuesday afternoon Clare Boothe Luce, the American ambassador to Rome, reported that for the first time all the newspapers in Italy were in favor of clemency. Luce—a devout Catholic, enthusiastic Cold Warrior, and wife of publishing mogul Henry Luce—was particularly troubled by the influence of the non-Communist Italian press.[165] The pro-American paper in Turin, *La Stampa*, for example, ran a front-page editorial advocating clemency and printed a list of movie stars in Italy who had signed appeals to President Eisenhower. The pro-government newspaper *Momento* editorialized: "There is nothing else to do now but send a plea for mercy to President Eisenhower."[166] In addition, prominent Italians, including the mayor of Rome, wrote directly to the White House and urged the president to intervene on behalf of the Rosenbergs.[167] While the ambassador in Rome was alarmed, the ambassador in Paris was in a virtual panic.

As protests flooded his office, Ambassador C. Douglas Dillon cabled Washington several times on Tuesday. At 1 p.m. he reported receipt of 1,500 petitions over the previous three days with numerous protesters lining up outside the embassy.[168] That afternoon, the French trade union leader and 1951 Nobel Peace Prize recipient Leon Jouhaux visited the ambassador and advocated clemency "as a friend of the U.S. who could not let this moment pass."[169] Fearing the great damage the executions "would do to us in France, and conversely the great impetus it would give to the Communist cause in France and throughout free Europe," Jouhaux argued, "the question was no longer one of justice but one of humanity."[170] Right-wing author Dominique Pado echoed this sentiment in an editorial: "It's no longer question of justice, but of pure humanity. Washington fears that commutation of Rosenberg sentence will appear to be [a] victory for Communist petitions. This fear is baseless."[171] If Eisenhower let the Rosenbergs live, he explained, "it will be honest men of all countries, opinions and religions who will approve."[172] Later that day two former French premiers, Edgar Faure and Jean Paul-Boncour, brought more than six separate clemency petitions to the embassy, explaining that "justice among men is fragile and fallible; it finds real grandeur only in generosity and clemency."[173] The petitions were from leading political and literary figures (including nine deputies, three senators, and seven former ministers); members of the League of Rights of Man; the staff of the largest newspaper in France (the moderate *France-Soir*); the staff of the leftist *Franc-Tireur*; the staff of *Populaire* (the Socialist daily); and representatives from National Radio, Radiodiffusion Française.[174]

Dillon's most surprising visitor came later that afternoon. In an unprecedented move, Georges Bidault, the French minister of foreign affairs, personally delivered a letter from the president of France. President Vincent Auriol advised clemency for the Rosenbergs, and Bidault agreed. The foreign minister insisted that Ambassador Dillon forward the letter directly to President Eisenhower. The highest-ranking member of the French regime had now weighed in against the executions, which required attention at the top level of the U.S. government. Dillon forwarded Bidault's message without comment to the State Department officials, who passed it on to White House Press Secretary James Hagerty the following day. The memo includes no marks to indicate where, if anywhere, it went after it landed on Hagerty's desk.[175] The concerns of the French president appeared to have no impact on the White House. The Supreme Court, however, still had time to act.

Late on Tuesday, Justice Robert H. Jackson arranged a meeting with Chief Justice Fred Vinson and Attorney General Brownell. Vinson—a Truman appointee and favorite poker partner of the former president—had just come from a meeting with Justice William Douglas, where Douglas asked the chief justice his opinion on issuing a stay of execution. While Vinson said he thought the Atomic Energy Act issue was "frivolous," he detected that Douglas was leaning toward delaying the executions to explore the issue. Agreeing with the attorney general, the chief justice stated that if a stay was granted he would "call the full Court into session on Thursday morning to vacate it." The court, and the world, awaited Douglas's decision.[176]

On the morning of Wednesday, June 17, Eisenhower looked forward to a round of golf. First, however, he needed to prepare for his regularly scheduled press conference. As was customary, his staff organized notes on topics the president would likely be asked about. The Rosenberg case appeared as number four on the list of a dozen possible topics. A possible armistice in Korea topped the list; 136 Americans were killed or wounded in Korea that week, with U.S. casualties topping 130,000 since the start of the conflict.[177] Second was the upcoming Big Three meeting of France, Great Britain, and the United States in Bermuda, and the third concerned the president's recent commencement address at Dartmouth College, where he denounced book burning.[178] At the press conference reporters focused on Korea and the destruction of controversial books. Just one day before the scheduled executions, no one raised questions about the case.[179] Justice William Douglas, however, did.

The case took a dramatic turn later that morning when Justice Douglas approved the stay of execution for the couple. "If we are not sure," he explained, "there will be lingering doubts to plague the conscience after the event."[180] Douglas ordered the case back to the district court and then hopped in his car for a road trip with his fiancé. At Sing Sing Prison, the warden announced the stay of execution over the loudspeaker system. With their deaths no longer imminent, the Rosenbergs were more hopeful than they had been in months (Figure 4.3).[181]

At 11:40 that morning Secretary John Foster Dulles called his brother, CIA Director Allen Dulles, to discuss the implications of Justice Douglas's actions. The CIA director lamented that the Rosenberg case would not be scheduled to come up for decision again until the Supreme Court was back in session in October 1953. This "put things in a hell of a mess," he bemoaned. Secretary Dulles agreed.[182] Neither welcomed the prospect of four more months of growing protest.

Meanwhile, demonstrators declared Wednesday a "day of action" in Europe. The French CDR had gone into "permanent session day and night," as outraged

Figure 4.3 Michael Rosenberg, age 10, reads about his parents as his brother Robert, age 6, looks on. Photo by Leonard Detrick/*New York Daily News*. Courtesy of Getty Images.

French citizens continued to plaster Paris with the Louis Mittelberg poster of Eisenhower with electric chairs in the place of his teeth.[183] Thousands picketed the U.S. Embassy in London, while in Ireland a delegation representing the Belfast branch of a national women's organization protested at the consulate on behalf of the Rosenbergs.[184] In Norway, the Rosenberg case remained on front pages; for example, in Oslo the labor press *Arbeiderbladet* editorialized its hope for a reprieve and argued that "spies have never been frightened by severe punitive measures . . . but people with democratic and humanitarian feelings can be dismayed by them," and the Christian People's paper, *Vaart Land*, argued Eisenhower could "afford to show clemency on behalf of his great nation."[185] In The Hague, the Catholic press *Catholic De Tijd* emphatically opposed the executions, explaining that Communist support for the couple should not inhibit the United States from granting clemency.[186] The Dutch conservative independent paper *De Telegraaf* declared that "this death sentence had done more harm than [any] act of the Rosenbergs could ever have done," while the pro–Labor Party independent paper *Haagsch Dagblad* argued that Eisenhower should have the "courage to speak [a] redeeming word: Clemency."[187] Embassy officials concluded that commuting the sentence "to life imprisonment on humanitarian grounds would receive overwhelmingly favorable spin in Netherlands."[188] In those final days, embassies and consulates throughout Europe were inundated with thousands of letters, petitions, and telegrams pleading for clemency.

Protests and around the clock vigils continued to spread throughout Canada, while dissent also accelerated in Latin America.[189] The press in Montevideo, Uruguay, even the pro-American papers such as *El Pais*, ran stories emphasizing dissent in Europe and the aggressive anti-Communist tactics at work in the United States.[190] Embassy officials bemoaned the "save-Rosenbergs, damn-the-United-States-as-fascists campaign" that was gaining traction in Uruguay.[191] In Costa Rica, an editorial by a former judge in the left-leaning paper *La Prensa Libre* turned the tables and criticized the government of the United States for its "negligence and unbelievable carelessness" in protecting "the secret of the atom bomb."[192] He also argued that since the Soviet Union was a vital ally in World War II and is "still allied to the United Nations," the Rosenbergs' crime did not constitute "treason meriting execution."[193]

In Israel, the American embassy in Tel Aviv described the intensification of activities and the increased rate and volume of letters and petitions on behalf of the Rosenbergs. The *Davar* paper reported that the "majority [of] Israelis hope for last minute 'act of mercy' not because they believe" in the Rosenbergs' innocence or support Communists, "nor primarily because of [the] Jewish factor 'although it does enter into calculations here,'" but because "they believe in democracy 'which is strong enough and, in face of the many gallows of totalitarianism, under obligation to refrain from executing a sentence against which there is no redress.'"[194] The mainstream newspaper, the *Jerusalem Post*, stated that the Rosenbergs deserved clemency because they were convicted on questionable evidence from a "self-confessed traitor," their punishment was "unusually severe for peacetime," in the sentence already served the Rosenbergs traveled through the "valley of death several times during last two years," and the Supreme Court was divided on the issue.[195] The *Post* concluded that the moral reputation of America rested in President Eisenhower's hands.

At 4 p.m. on Wednesday, Attorney General Brownell called Secretary Dulles, who was astonished that Justice Douglas had granted a stay.[196] Brownell assured Dulles that the administration had already asked Chief Justice Vinson to call the Supreme Court back. As planned, Vinson took the unusual move and declared a special session for noon the next day to address the stay of execution. Douglas's staff, having just raided his desk drawer for liquor and glasses to toast the Court's summer break, scrambled to find their boss and inform him of the special session. The justice was driving through Pennsylvania when a special report interrupted the classical music on the car radio and announced the Court's emergency meeting. Douglas immediately turned the car around and headed back to Washington.[197]

Unsure of the outcome of the stay, the FBI proceeded with preparations for the impending executions. Agents wrote a thirteen-page list of questions they would ask Julius if he chose to confess at the last minute. Among them, only one referred to Ethel: "Was your wife cognizant of your activities?"[198] Even at that late date, and as she sat on death row, the FBI remained uncertain what role, if any, Ethel had played in the espionage work of her husband.

Late on Wednesday, Eisenhower expressed concern in a letter to a friend. The president admitted that he had received a "large number of letters and petitions" urging clemency and claimed, "the Rosenberg case has disturbed me as much as it has anyone."[199] In no other written word does Eisenhower admit to this level of distress.

During that evening's broadcast of the popular CBS news program *See It Now*, Charles Collingwood updated viewers on the Rosenbergs' conviction, the Supreme Court stay, and the foreign protests. Filling in for the vacationing Edward R. Murrow, Collingwood concluded with an open-ended question: did viewers think "the quest for national security" would be "helped or hindered by the Rosenbergs' execution?"[200]

Time was running out. Thursday, June 18, was Julius and Ethel Rosenberg's fourteenth wedding anniversary. They spent the day at Sing Sing together, though separated by wire, while they waited for word from the Supreme Court.[201] The Court convened for the special session at noon on Thursday, but hearing arguments and writing opinions would take them late into the night. As the justices deliberated, more than 4,000 protesters gathered at a Washington, D.C., vigil.[202] The world, and the Rosenbergs, would have to wait until Friday at noon for the Court's final word. Newspapers struggled with how to meet deadlines for the next day's front page without definitive news. The *National Guardian* prepped two different headlines: "ROSENBERGS EXECUTED" and "ROSENBERGS SAVED."[203]

At Sing Sing Prison, FBI agents set up a command post to handle any last-minute confessions.[204] Prison officials provided the agents with a secret entrance to avoid the press stationed at the main gate, since the bureau did "not want it known that agents" were there.[205] Publicizing that FBI agents were stationed at the prison would have confirmed fears that the government was using the threat of execution to force a confession, though that is exactly what it was doing. The bureau insisted that only assigned agents be allowed to speak to the Rosenbergs, as only the FBI could "make a recommendation on reprieve or execution."[206] Two direct phone lines connected the prison to the FBI's New York office. The prison warden also provided a special interview room "on the second floor of the men's wing of the death house" for any last-minute confessions. No separate space was necessary for Ethel, as she was the sole resident of the women's section of death row.[207]

The news of Douglas's stay of execution sparked hope and increased protest. For example, in Central America, an editorial ran in that morning's Costa Rican paper, *La Nación*, criticizing the Eisenhower administration's "shameful" handling of the Rosenberg case and supporting Justice Douglas's reasoning that "it is important, before wiping out human life, that there be absolute certainty that such action is within the law."[208] Canadians continued picketing in Ottawa, with protesters carrying signs reading, "The People are Behind Justice Douglas."[209] Seven hundred protesters gathered outside the American consulate in Toronto, listening to a speaker fume about the Rosenbergs' impending death and Eisenhower's "Hitlerite military dictatorship." The demonstration teetered on the brink of violence.[210] Protests also took place in Montreal and at the Regina consulate in Saskatchewan.[211]

In India, the Calcutta press printed Douglas's stay of execution on the front page. Protests increased dramatically when a parade of 2,000 demonstrators marched to the American consulate, where speakers riled the crowd and called Americans "warmongers." The Indian government responded by stationing a squad of police. Protesters passed a resolution asking Prime Minister Jawaharlal Nehru to "come forward and save the lives of the Rosenbergs." Nehru refused.[212]

In France, Parisians continued to lead the world in the size and intensity of demonstrations. Seven thousand people attended a national day of action meeting, where they approved a telegram to send to the president. "This hour of choice, when [the] entire world turns towards you," it implored, "the people of Paris, united as never before since liberation, beg you not to make an irreparable gesture."[213] Ambassador Dillon admitted that the embassy received more than 2,000 petitions on Thursday, with the grand total of 12,000. At this late hour, all the State Department could write on Dillon's numerous telegrams was: "No action required. File."[214]

Early on Friday, June 19, Ambassador Dillon made one last, desperate effort from Paris. He sent an "Eyes Only" telegram with a top-secret cover sheet to Secretary Dulles. Responding to a widespread "lack of understanding of our legal processes," Dillon explained, "the most effective action we could take . . . would be a strong and relatively detailed statement by the President explaining our legal system and pointing out that our judges are not dominated by hysteria or McCarthyism."[215] "I feel," he concluded, "it is most important that [the] French get [the] impression that [the] President has given serious consideration to [the] case in recent days, particularly to the pleas of those who are friendly to us."[216] Believing he was past influencing action, on Friday morning Dillon had shifted to damage control mode. He was no longer suggesting a reprieve, but rather asking that it at least look like clemency had been considered. Once again, there is no indication that the Eisenhower administration responded to Dillon's concerns.[217]

The Supreme Court was due to issue its final word at noon on Friday. If the justices upheld Douglas's stay the Court of Appeals would rule, and then the Supreme Court would decide on the case when it came back into session in October.[218] Justice Douglas argued that "no harm would be done; the Rosenbergs were behind bars; they could be executed in October as well as June."[219] The Court heard arguments on the merits of the stay, which Douglas later recalled "lasted several hours before an audience more tense than any I had ever seen."[220] The majority of the justices were not persuaded by the Atomic Energy Act issue and ruled this question "not substantial" and without merit.[221] Only four justices supported shortening the stay to further explore the Atomic Energy Act issue. Douglas could not convince the necessary fifth judge.

Chief Justice Vinson—in what would be his final public appearance for the Court—announced they had voted to vacate or overturn the stay of execution, explaining, "we think further proceedings . . . are unwarranted."[222] Douglas, resigned to defeat, later acknowledged that the Rosenberg decision "was the product of the Cold War, not of reasoned law. I have no other way of explaining why they ran pell-mell with the mob . . . and felt it was important that this couple die that very week.[223] The majority of the Supreme Court sustained the government's actions and ended the controversy. The Rosenbergs would be executed that night. A Democratic representative from Kentucky barged onto the floor of the House and announced the impending executions, thanking "God, from whom all blessings flow" and the Supreme Court.[224]

At the regular Friday cabinet meeting the president asked Attorney General Brownell to update attendees on the Rosenberg case. A lengthy discussion ensued as Brownell explained the machinations of the Supreme Court, and Eisenhower complained that Justice Douglas had only added to the confusion by ordering a stay.[225] The president understood that he could only intervene when "statecraft" dictated, as in when the reputation of the U.S. government "in the eyes of the world" could be tarnished.[226] Eisenhower believed—despite plenty of evidence to the contrary—that this was not one of those times. With the executions scheduled for that evening, UN Ambassador Henry Cabot Lodge complained about the number of American diplomats who were having trouble publicizing their view of the case. Psychological warfare guru C. D. Jackson concurred: "The Rosenberg story is *not known*," and he advised they prepare a white paper to clarify the facts of the case as damage control, even at this late date.[227] Brownell agreed and explained that citizens "must take their lead from the Supreme Court and not from Communist propaganda." Lodge agreed: "We've got a good story to tell," and the facts of the case "can be easily explained." Eisenhower interjected,

"Not easily to me."[228] Cabinet members may not have known how to respond to his odd statement, for notes indicate that was the end of the discussion. As the clock ticked, the president seemed conflicted about clemency and aware of the weaknesses of the government's propaganda case against the Rosenbergs.

Eisenhower pushed aside any doubts he may have had on Friday morning and denied clemency for a second time. The attorney general had recommended rejecting leniency "since no facts warranted a reversal."[229] C. D. Jackson, Brownell, Lodge, and Dulles crafted a more extensive clemency denial than the one they had issued in February.[230] In it Eisenhower reiterated the Rosenbergs' guilt, blaming them for "immeasurably increasing the chances of atomic war." He explained:

> When democracy's enemies have been judged guilty of a crime as horrible as that of which the Rosenbergs were convicted;—when the legal processes of democracy have been marshaled to their maximum strength to protect the lives of convicted spies:—when in their most solemn judgment the tribunals of the United States have judged them guilty and the sentence just, I will not intervene in this matter.[231]

In addition to his concern about appearing weak, Eisenhower understood that clemency would be unpopular with his constituents.[232] The majority of Americans continued to support the president's decision to allow the executions to proceed. Through the second clemency denial and the executions, Eisenhower's popularity rating rose to over 70 percent.[233]

With the time of the executions at hand, however, government officials discovered a potentially disastrous public-relations problem. Mid-Friday afternoon, Judge Irving Kaufman complained to the FBI that he had received telegrams saying "he should be ashamed of himself" for "letting them go through with the executions on the Sabbath."[234] The judge, along with the FBI and the Justice Department, agreed that 11:00 p.m. that night (the standard time for electrocutions at Sing Sing) was unacceptable since it coincided with the Jewish Sabbath.[235] According to journalist Sam Roberts, the prison rabbi called Judge Kaufman from Sing Sing to argue for a delay until after the Sabbath. Rabbi Irving Koslowe suggested Saturday night and recalled the judge replying no, "the president wanted them to be executed—that was his decision."[236] The defense recommended that the executions be delayed for a day or two.

The prison warden—presumably in consultation with the FBI—chose instead to move up the time of the electrocutions, to that evening shortly before sunset.[237] This announcement caused a scramble at the prison, as officials frantically attempted to reach the electrician/executioner to ensure his prompt arrival.[238]

Defense attorney Emanuel Bloch crafted final clemency appeals to President Eisenhower and Judge Kaufman, but neither succeeded. Another member of the defense team frantically attempted to reach Justice Black, who had expressed opposition to the Rosenbergs' execution, hoping the justice could do something to secure more time. However, Black was unavailable, in the hospital undergoing elective surgery.[239]

As afternoon turned to evening, several of the president's closest advisors grew more concerned with their own image. At 5:50 p.m., Secretary John Foster Dulles met with his brother, CIA Director Allen Dulles, and then consulted with Attorney General Herbert Brownell. They had planned to attend the Washington Senators baseball game that evening. The officials determined that to attend on that particular night "would not only be dangerous, but would make for terrific propaganda," as the Communists would certainly make them look heartless. They opted instead for a late dinner at the White House.[240]

Protesters continued to picket outside the White House, but the majority of Americans "powerfully and broadly" supported the decision to go ahead with the executions.[241] Counterdemonstrators in Washington taunted protesters with signs that read, "Hang 'em and Ship Their Bodies to Russia," and "Two Fried Rosenbergs Coming Up."[242]

Around the world, demonstrations reached a fever pitch as the execution hour approached. More than 100 protestors gathered outside the consulate in Amsterdam in a silent vigil. Reflecting the Dutch opposition to capital punishment, the liberal independent *Nieuwe Rotterdamsche Courant* called the repeated execution postponements "torture."[243] A two-column front-page editorial ran in *Neue Zürcher Zeitung*, a highly regarded Swiss newspaper, which joined a number of Swiss papers in voicing objections to the imminent executions. In addition to Swiss opposition to the death penalty, the editorial argued: "However its complicated relationship to the present phase of the cold war may be, we should nevertheless say that a merciful action will seldom be regretted by those who have enough strength to reach such a decision."[244]

Members of the London Save the Rosenbergs Committee (SRC), having been rebuffed by the new queen, headed to 10 Downing Street. Protesters begged Prime Minister Winston Churchill to call President Eisenhower immediately and advise clemency for the condemned couple. Londoners were well aware of Churchill's close friendship with Eisenhower dating back to the latter's role as Supreme Allied Commander during WWII.[245] But this time Churchill did not try to sway his old friend. At midnight local time the group waiting outside received the prime minister's typewritten reply: "It is not within my duty or my power to intervene in this matter."[246]

Emotional protest turned violent when tens of thousands of Parisians poured into the Place de la Concorde hours before the executions. They carried signs that read: "It's Up to Us—The SS Shall Not March," "The Rosenbergs Shall Not Die," "We Demand Justice for the Rosenbergs," and "Rosenberg Case is US Legal Murder."[247] Police tried to restore order as pressure mounted and tempers flared. Officers shot into the crowd, wounding a French teenager. Authorities arrested four hundred protesters before the crowd finally dispersed.[248]

Julius and Ethel Rosenberg had no time for a formal last meal, dining instead on hard-boiled eggs, macaroni salad, and tea.[249] They spent their final hours together talking through a wire partition. Meanwhile, the FBI sent word to the Sing Sing warden, instructing him to stop the electrocutions if Julius or Ethel offered any information even after they were "strapped into the chair."[250] This contradicted the policy of strict silence in the execution chamber.

Ten-year-old Michael Rosenberg was watching the Philadelphia Athletics play the Chicago White Sox on television at the New Jersey home of his foster parents, a chicken-feed salesman and his wife.[251] Michael used baseball that summer as distraction from the horror unfolding around him. The boy was a Dodgers fan like his father, and would normally have been pleased their team had split a doubleheader with the Cubs that day.[252] However, a special news bulletin interrupted the broadcast, announcing that the president had denied clemency a second time and the executions would take place that night.[253] The young Rosenberg told the reporters camped out at his house: "You can quote me. The judges of the future will look back upon this case with great shame."[254]

At 7:20 p.m., the Rosenbergs were sent back to their separate cells. The prison barber visited Julius and Ethel and shaved patches of skin where officials would soon attach electrodes. Judge Kaufman rejected a final appeal from his Manhattan courtroom at 7:45 p.m. Ethel only had a few minutes to dash off some final notes, including one to the couple's lawyer, Manny Bloch: "You did everything that could be done—We are the first victims of American Fascism."[255]

But Bloch had one last fight in him. The attorney arrived at the White House minutes before the executions, desperate to see the president. Picketers with signs demanding that the Rosenbergs' lives be spared broke into cheers, but the White House police refused to let Bloch on the premises without an appointment. The lawyer begged to use the police telephone to call Sherman Adams or James Hagerty to ask to see Eisenhower. Police sent him to the pay telephone down the street.[256] It was too late.

Five minutes later Julius walked out of his cell. The FBI chose Julius to die first, hoping he would break down and confess.[257] The Sing Sing warden believed that Ethel was stronger and should die first, but FBI Director Hoover refused, claiming it would look bad if Julius confessed *after* they had killed the mother of two children.[258] Julius followed Rabbi Koslowe into the windowless execution chamber that housed the Sing Sing electric chair, referred to as "Old Sparkey" and operated by Joseph P. Francel.[259] The rabbi later recalled that Attorney General "Brownell said to me if they gave a name through me to him, or names, a stay of execution would be determined" even after they were strapped into the electric chair.[260] Julius obeyed the sign above the chamber door—"silence"—and never said a word.[261]

Bob Considine, one of the three wire service correspondents chosen to record the "grim spectacle," observed that "there didn't seem to be much life left in him" when thirty-five-year-old Julius entered the room. The *New York Times* reported that both Rosenbergs "went to their deaths with a composure that astonished the witnesses."[262] After being secured with five leather straps, a first shock of 2,000 volts, with ten amperes, surged through him at 8:04 p.m. His body temperature spiked to 130 degrees and a strand of smoke rose from the leather facemask. As author Sam Roberts explains, "The mask is not worn as a convenience to the condemned but as a palliative for the witnesses. It prevents the eyes from popping out of the head."[263] After two more jolts the doctor pronounced Julius dead at 8:06.[264]

Rabbi Koslowe informed Ethel that Julius was dead and pressed her to name any spies, to save her life. According to the rabbi, Ethel replied: "No, I have no names to give. I'm innocent. I'm prepared to die."[265] At 8:11 p.m., Ethel Rosenberg was strapped into the same electric chair that had killed her husband moments before.

With Julius gone Ethel was no longer the "lever" in the case against her husband, but there were no mechanisms in place to halt her execution. Moments later the thirty-seven-year-old mother met the same fate. At 8:16 p.m. on June 19, 1953, both Rosenbergs were dead.[266]

The two telephone lines the FBI set up to accommodate last-minute confessions remained idle. Similarly, an interview room, complete with two waiting stenographers, went unused. One of the six anguished FBI agents waiting at the prison later recalled, "We didn't want them to die. We wanted them to talk."[267] Along with the Rosenbergs died the hope of them naming other members of the Communist spy ring.[268] Deputy Attorney General William Rogers somberly concluded: "She called our bluff."[269]

Newly uncovered State Department documents describe protests occurring that night in Algiers, Buenos Aires, Brussels, Calcutta, London, Ottawa, Paris, Regina, Rome, Tel Aviv, The Hague, Toronto, Trieste, and New York.[270]

On that sweltering June evening as many as 20,000 protesters gathered for a vigil on Seventeenth Street near Union Square in New York City, just two miles from the Rosenbergs' old apartment in Knickerbocker Village.[271] With the temperature a muggy eighty-five degrees, one female protester fainted.[272] When the deaths were announced prematurely at eight o'clock, the "police ordered the loud speaker shut off" and the solemn crowd dispersed peacefully.[273]

Satisfied he could now finally put this case behind him after twenty-six months, Judge Irving Kaufman left the courthouse in New York City to celebrate his seventeenth wedding anniversary with his wife in Connecticut.[274]

On his walk from the prison to the train station, a *New York Post* reporter observed people laughing as they listened to the news on their car radios; he overheard one child say "she wished she could throw the switch."[275] In living rooms around the country that night most Americans were more concerned with the antics of a different famous couple. Viewers laughed as Harriet complained to Ozzie in an episode of *The Adventures of Ozzie and Harriet* that her husband never shared information about his work with her.[276]

At that evening's performance of *The Crucible*—as John Proctor's execution ended the play—Arthur Miller recalled that the audience "stood up and remained silent for a couple of minutes, with heads bowed" in an eerie act of solidarity.[277]

The deaths of Julius and Ethel Rosenberg, however, did not push them off of front pages or out of people's minds. In their final letter to Michael and Robert they reassured their sons, "you will not grieve alone."[278] They were right.

5

Reverberations

We're not talking about truth,
we're talking about something that seems like truth—
the truth we want to exist.
　　　　　　—Stephen Colbert, *New York Magazine, October 16, 2006*

Late on Friday, June 19, 1953—as word of the Rosenberg executions spread around the world—Eisenhower awaited Saturday on the golf course. The president had only been able to fit in four days of golf that June and he was eager to take advantage of the agreeable summer weather. Ike's public embrace of the game prompted golfing fever, which seized the country as Americans welcomed the distraction.[1] On this particular Friday, however, Sherman Adams consulted C. D. Jackson to see if Eisenhower should play. Jackson, worried how it would look to have the president enjoying eighteen holes so soon after the executions, replied "absolutely no."[2] It would be five more days before White House staffers permitted the president to tee off again.

It is not surprising that Eisenhower wanted to go back to playing golf. He understood that within the United States response to the executions would remain muted as most Americans embarked, as one Frenchman observed, on a "weekend with tranquil conscience."[3] While a vocal minority of Americans protested the outcome of the case, the majority went back to their lives, satisfied that the two Communist spies who prompted the Korean War got what they deserved and were going to, as reporter Bob Considine put it, "meet their maker."[4]

Author Sylvia Plath captured this subdued sentiment in her diary entry the morning of the executions. Living in New York as a guest editor for *Mademoiselle* she wrote,

> There is no yelling, no horror, no great rebellion. That's the appalling thing. The largest emotional reaction over the United States will be a rather large, democratic, infinitely bored and casual and complacent yawn.[5]

Americans were ready to move on. Eisenhower wanted to return to the golf course and forge ahead with his own correction to the course of the Cold War.

News of the Rosenberg executions, however, produced far more than a yawn outside of the United States. The couple was dead, but the global community continued to grapple with the meaning of their deaths. Eisenhower administration officials struggled to control their version of the case even after the deed was done. Now martyrs for the Communist cause, controversy and dispute over their legacy would not rest.

The bodies of Julius and Ethel Rosenberg lay in state until the funeral on the morning of Sunday, June 21. Perhaps ten thousand mourners gathered in the record heat at the chapel in Brooklyn. Due to the Greenglass family's disapproval of Ethel's silence, Julius's mother was the only immediate family member to openly attend.[6] Among the speakers was civil rights and peace activist W.E.B. DuBois, who had been horrified by the executions. In addressing the crowd DuBois built on themes he first explored in a poem he wrote for the couple earlier in the month: "Crucify us, Vengeance of God, As we crucify two more Jews."[7] After the viewing, the bodies were transported to a cemetery on Long Island, New York, where, in keeping with Jewish tradition, their tombstones would be unveiled one year later.

It was Manny Bloch's eulogy that dominated the press coverage. The Rosenbergs' lead defense attorney delivered a loving tribute and concluded with a passionate indictment: "I place the murder of the Rosenbergs at the door of President Eisenhower, Mr. Brownell and J. Edgar Hoover. They did not pull the switch, true, but they directed the one who did pull the switch."[8] Bloch's inflammatory speech prompted the New York City Bar Association to investigate his conduct and consider disciplinary disbarment. Senator Joseph McCarthy seized the opportunity and encouraged the investigation of all practicing Communist lawyers.[9]

Like Bloch, Supreme Court Justice William O. Douglas was also under increased scrutiny for his role in the Rosenberg case. Once Douglas issued a stay just days before the executions, he became a target of aggressive anti-Communists. Congressman W. M. Wheeler of Georgia initiated impeachment proceedings against the justice, claiming he "had committed treason by giving aid and comfort to the Communists."[10] Fellow House members initially applauded the impeachment effort, but it soon lost traction and died in committee.[11] Wheeler suffered politically and faced defeat in his re-election bid in 1954.[12] The *Washington Post* condemned the impeachment attempt:

> Whether Mr. Justice Douglas was right or wrong in granting a stay of execution to the Rosenbergs after the Supreme Court had recessed, he had indubitable authority to do so . . . Given the atmosphere of

excitement in which it was projected, it was an act of courage and moral stature. If judges were to be subject to impeachment every time some know-nothing Congressman disliked one of their decisions, the independence of the judiciary would become a fiction.[13]

Congressman Wheeler was not alone in denouncing the justice. Senator Lyndon Baines Johnson, whom Douglas called a "fair-weather friend," would not speak to Douglas in public for years after he issued the stay in the Rosenberg case.[14]

Justices of the Supreme Court did express themselves publicly, attempting to clarify the facts of the case and their actions even after the executions. In their dissenting opinions on the necessity of Justice Douglas's stay, Felix Frankfurter and Hugo Black argued that the Atomic Energy Act of 1946 had superseded the Espionage Act in this case. Frankfurter admitted that while it was too late to affect the outcome, it was necessary to state his views: "To be writing an opinion in a case affecting two lives after the curtain has been rung down upon them has the appearance of pathetic futility. But history also has its claims."[15] Justice Black feared there would always be lingering "questions as to whether these executions were legally and rightfully carried out," since the highest court in the land had not affirmed the "fairness of the trial."[16] History would show that the Court's prevalent sentiment was far less sympathetic to the Rosenbergs. Chief Justice William Rehnquist, serving as a law clerk to Justice Robert H. Jackson in 1953, explained his views on the death penalty in a memo to his boss. He referred to Julius and Ethel as "fitting candidates" for execution, adding, "It is too bad that drawing and quartering has been abolished."[17]

On the day of the executions, Secretary of State Dulles tried to silence dissent. In a bulletin he dictated that the "U.S.-based media should report" on the Rosenberg case in a "dignified" and "restrained fashion," focusing solely on the Supreme Court's decisions, the president's rejections of executive clemency, and the proceedings of the executions.[18] The secretary ordered journalists to observe "complete silence" on the case after filing their reports on the executions "unless otherwise instructed specifically."[19] Dulles overstepped his bounds as the top official overseeing U.S. foreign affairs, but reflected the Eisenhower administration's view on the case—the Rosenbergs were dead, there was nothing more to be learned, and it was best to move on.

The American press fell in line. The popular magazine *Life* typified the support of the government's narrative. They incorrectly inflated the Rosenbergs' crime to espionage and blamed the global protest movement to save the couple on "opportunistic Communists" who were part of "the worldwide web of Communist conspiracy."[20] The magazine also described the protesters marching around the White House as "noisy" individuals who carelessly discarded their signs in a trash heap upon hearing of the Rosenbergs' death.[21]

These protesters prompted one concerned reporter to act. Hoping that the *New York Times* could properly refute the "terrific barrage of propaganda," he asked the FBI to provide additional evidence that would definitively prove the guilt of the Rosenbergs.[22] An FBI agent refused to agree, explaining that further information was "superfluous" since "a jury and a competent United States Court had already found the Rosenbergs guilty, and there had been an execution of the sentence imposed."[23] The agent argued at length that it was both "impossible and completely impractical" for the FBI to comply.[24] While the reporter saw the need to further prove the case to an unconvinced segment of the population, the FBI believed their work was done.

Dulles was successful in controlling the American press, and the case promptly disappeared from the pages of U.S. newspapers.[25] The secretary took the bulletin he wrote to the U.S.-based media and forwarded it more than a dozen American embassies.[26] He was far less effective overseas.

Details about Julius and Ethel's deaths—often gruesome and compelling—sparked an increase in protest and outrage that reverberated around the globe. For example, in Toronto, seven hundred CSJJER protesters heard the announcement when relayed from a parked car radio and responded with loud wailing and cries of "shame" and "murder."[27] A speaker riled the crowd when he launched into an anti-American diatribe, claiming that Eisenhower himself "had pulled the switch," and was "responsible for the atrocities in Korea."[28] When the program ended, the group formed a procession behind two large pictures of the Rosenbergs and quietly dispersed. Yet not all protesters in Toronto chose to remain peaceful. Rage bubbled over in letters sent to the consulate that included inflammatory threats: "I am going to avenge the Rosenbergs!" "You too will die!" "You are murderers!" "You have defied God! Death to you!" "Get out of town you murdering pigs." "One of these nights you will get your throats cut." "Execution of Rosenbergs was murder! Eisenhower—Hitler Yankee go home!"[29] Diplomats turned to local police for increased protection.

Throughout Latin America the deaths further incited anger as protests and accusations of "Yankee imperialism" continued. At the embassy in Havana, demonstrators protested the "hysterical assassination" and held a vigil for "the first martyrs in the fight for peace."[30] Embassy officials admitted that "the Rosenberg case aroused much interest in Cuba."[31] CIA agents monitored protests in Uruguay, Panama, and Ecuador, which continued for months after the executions.[32] Demonstrators denounced the Eisenhower administration, argued that the United States executed the Rosenbergs "to tell the world that Russia is incapable of producing the atomic bomb without resorting to espionage,"

and attacked "imperialism, capitalism, and the Military [Rio] Pact," the controversial mutual security treaty.[33] Editorials filled newspapers in Argentina
and Paraguay, agreeing with the pope and denouncing the use of capital punishment.[34] Embassy officials in Buenos Aires received thousands of letters and
petitions after the deaths, and the police diverted several hundred people who
attempted to demonstrate in front of the USIS library. The American ambassador in Nicaragua attributed the smaller protests in Managua to the intimidat-
ing factor of President Anastasio Somoza's "strong anti-Red policies," though he
admitted "a few in the upper classes" called the death penalty "vindictive."[35]

In Africa, hundreds of protesters held public demonstrations in Algeria,
Tunisia, and South Africa. The *Alger Républicain* ran front-page headlines declaring the executions "assassinations" and included a political cartoon depicting
Eisenhower "wearily trudging forward with two electric chairs shackled to his
ankles."[36] The paper set up a makeshift chapel in the entrance hall of their building with pictures of the Rosenbergs, which Algerians filed by "in a reverent manner," placing flowers at the base of the portraits.[37] The French press coverage
spilled over into Tunisia, but diplomats reported coverage included "some original editorials" with most Tunisians being in opposition to the death penalty and
critical of the United States.[38] In South Africa, news of the executions received
full press coverage in both the English and Afrikaans papers.[39] Protesters at a
public meeting in Cape Town passed a resolution condemning the U.S. government and arguing that in ignoring the protests from "representatives of hundreds
of millions in all countries," the Eisenhower administration had "defied public
opinion in great areas of the world," made "the Rosenbergs victims of the Cold
War hysteria," and perhaps even "recorded the first blood drawn in a Third World
War."[40] The petition concluded with a pledge "to give whatever care, comfort and
support we can to Michael and Robby Rosenberg . . . and we convey to them
our lasting sympathy and grief."[41] Even an editorial supporting the executions
in the Port Elizabeth *Eastern Province Herald* conceded "that a large section of
[the] population feel otherwise" and that in leaving the couple on death row for
more than two years "one is left with the uneasy feeling that justice was inordi-
nately tardy."[42] In Tangier, then still under Spanish control, editorial comment
ran largely in opposition to the U.S. government and the executions.[43]

Reaction in the Middle East divided predominantly along religious lines. In
Israel, nearly three hundred protesters gathered at the embassy in Tel Aviv, where
the executions were announced at a little after 3 a.m. local time.[44] Editorial comment declared "Murder caused by hysteria" and "American democracy died with
Rosenbergs."[45] Some papers claimed Israeli Jews were now concerned over the
fate of Jews in America as a result of what happened to the couple.[46] Conversely,
in Baghdad, Iraqi newspapers argued that the Rosenbergs stole the secret of the
atomic bomb to forward it to the Soviets in exchange for the Soviet government's

recognition of Israel. Several Iraqi government officials were encouraged by Eisenhower's decision to allow the executions to proceed, claiming it confirmed that his administration was "not automatically a captive of pro-Jewish lobbies."[47]

In Calcutta, hundreds gathered for days of protests, with participants shouting, "Down with American imperialism!"[48] Numerous "critical and emotional editorials" came out of Djakarta.[49] The nationalist paper *Merdeka* deduced that "one clear-cut conclusion can be drawn from the Rosenberg trial; the U.S. lives in fear of an atomic war."[50] Even the "nationalist and neutralist" *Pengharapan* Indonesian language newspaper condemned the death penalty as "too heavy seen from the point of humanity."[51]

European protest continued. In Sweden, editorials from several important newspapers "thought that the United States had made a grievous political error in not commuting the sentences to life imprisonment."[52] *Se*, a major weekly, predicted: "Give them imprisonment and they will be forgotten; give them death and they will never die."[53] One of the pro-American papers, the liberal *Göteborgs Handelstidning*, went even further, stating that the executions may have "a detrimental effect on the position and reputation of the U.S. in the democratic world and render difficult that cooperation which alone could pave the way for a peaceful development in Europe."[54] Shipyard and factory workers in Göteborg presented a petition to the consulate to be forwarded to Eisenhower that emphasized their consternation over the case. A pardon, they explained, would have improved "America's stained reputation as a country of justice."[55] The workers abhorred the "medieval way" the U.S. government had of using the threat of the electric chair as a torture device.[56] They concluded: "America abandons justice and declares itself as an enemy to humanity. The gap between the people of Europe and the American government will be widened, and you, Mr. President, will be looked upon with distrust and bitterness. Similar to the majority of Sweden's people, we . . . demand redress of the Rosenberg couple."[57] Press coverage in Finland criticized the Eisenhower administration. *Sosialidemorkraatti*, a newspaper normally friendly to the United States, stated that when political executions take place in a democracy, especially "in a country that declares itself the guardian of western culture," then it "is both depressing and outrageous."[58] The executions, the editorial concluded, "were base, primitive, and shameful."[59]

Once the Rosenbergs were dead, Moscow could openly embrace them without endangering the couple's lives. The Soviets accused the American press of deliberately not reporting on the "wide-spread protests abroad."[60] Alexander Nesmeyanov, a chemist and president of the Soviet Academy of Science, criticized U.S. government officials, claiming they had set out to murder the Rosenbergs and that the executions, like actions of the Ku Klux Klan, revealed the true "American way of life."[61] Americans, Nesmeyanov argued, "again ignored the voices of millions of peace-loving people who protested this monstrous law-lessness and arbitrary rule," and "humanity will never forgive [these] murderers [for] their crime."[62] A CIA agent claimed that Soviet newspaper articles avoided mentioning that the Rosenbergs were Jewish, choosing instead to emphasize the question of American justice.[63] Similarly, Polish propaganda claimed that the Rosenbergs were "murdered" as the "latest victims" of the "American Gestapo—the FBI."[64] The Warsaw press—including the mainstream *Życie Warszawy* and *Szpilki*, a satirical weekly—printed vivid political cartoons to make its point. These cartoons included several depictions of the Statue of Liberty: strapped into an electric chair crying, being dragged out of court, and Eisenhower step-ping on her to light his cigar with her torch (Figure 5.1).[65]

Western Europeans generated the strongest reactions. Peaceful demon-strations took place in London, Geneva, Milan, Rome, Turin, Naples, Trieste, Florence, and The Hague, but others turned violent.[66] In Dublin, shortly after the executions, a demonstrator tossed two bottles of kerosene with slow-burning wicks through the window of the United States Information Service library.[67] In Lausanne, a protester threw a rock through a plate glass window of the American Express Company with "an inscription protesting the execution."[68] The embassy in Rome endured a bomb scare and demonstrations prompted the arrest of more than 140 protesters.[69]

Much of the European press content focused on opposition to the death penalty. Reaction in Portugal concerned the devastating effects of capital pun-ishment, especially on the young Rosenberg sons. Embassy officials attributed relative editorial restraint on the part of the Lisbon press to pressure from the Portuguese government not to anger their American allies.[70] Journalists in the Netherlands also emphasized Dutch opposition to capital punishment, with the liberal independent paper *Nieuwe Rotterdamsche Courant* labeling the repeated death sentence postponements as torture. The Dutch Communist press, *De Waarheid*, described the executions as "the most horrible crime in the history of this century."[71]

Moving beyond disagreement over capital punishment, anti-American edi-torial comment in the European press was widespread. An *Irish Times* opinion piece criticized Eisenhower for a "gross disregard of international sentiment" concerning the case, explaining that the "psychological conviction that there has been an act of barbarism has been planted in many minds—and may grow."[72] The editorial assumed that "the cause of anti-Americanism" had been helped considerably by the executions that "must seem to simple and non-political people everywhere to conflict strangely with the noble pronouncements of humanitarian principles with which official utterances from the U.S. are spiced so generously."[73]

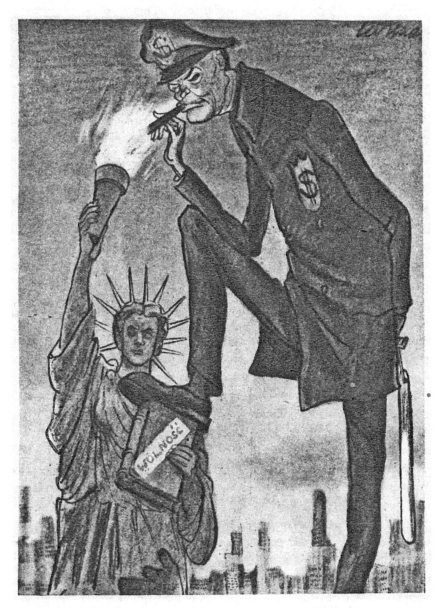

Figure 5.1 Political cartoon printed in *Szpilki*, a Polish satirical magazine, originally printed in *Dikobraz*, a Czechoslovak periodical, June 1953. Courtesy of Jan Adamczyk, Senior Library Specialist, Slavic Cataloging, University of Illinois at Urbana-Champaign and the Reference Department, Jagiellonian Library, Krakow, Poland.

Opposition to the executions was especially strong in Italy. Most newspapers—both Communist and non-Communist—argued that the killing of the Rosenbergs "raises horror and indignation in Italy and in all the world."[74] Turin's conservative newspaper, *Stampa*, proposed that while "seven minutes and fifty seconds were sufficient to remove them physically . . . much more time will be needed before America succeeds in dispelling [the] hateful effects [that Eisenhower's] refusal to grant a reprieve has left with [the] enormous majority of European people."[75] The neo-Fascist paper *Secolo* emphasized the mistake the Americans made: "If they had kept the Rosenbergs in jail, they . . . would have had the possibility of one day obtaining the confession the couple refused to make on [the] threshold of death."[76] The piece concluded, "A nation whose government so totally lacks human and political sensibility and psychology and comprehension of popular feelings has no right to pose as a guide of the free world."[77]

Days after the deaths, U.S. Ambassador to Italy Clare Boothe Luce wrote directly to the White House. Luce, who enjoyed a close relationship with Eisenhower, explained that officials of Italy's Christian Democratic national government—including the prime minister—dreaded political repercussions because of the executions. They feared the Italian people held such passionate sympathy for the Rosenbergs that the case would have a pro-Communist impact that could spill over into national elections. Eisenhower personally responded, chiding Luce: "I would have thought Italian leaders could have easily shown to their own people that the Rosenberg case was strictly an American domestic affair."[78] He was surprised "that the Italian people could have no knowledge of the enormity of the offense committed by the Rosenbergs" and reiterated "the dangers inherent in weak-kneed action with respect to the spy rings established by the Soviets throughout the world."[79] Eisenhower deemphasized global attention to the case and stressed the risk of an anemic response, brushing aside Luce's concerns and reiterating his public stance on the meaning of the case.

The French continued to be the most vociferous protesters (Figure 5.2). Large demonstrations left one Parisian dead and hundreds arrested, and the fate of the Rosenbergs had a significant and lingering impact on Franco-American relations. A CIA informant observed that the executions "caused quite an uproar" in France, and "not only from the Communists, but from everywhere."[80] Many French, even some of his own friends, misunderstood the American "official point of view" and were "deeply and sincerely hurt by [the] Rosenbergs' execution."[81] Press attaché Ben Bradlee agreed, later recalling, "I felt the State Department had treated it as an abstract incident with some diplomatic repercussions, rather then the vitally complicated drama it was."[82]

Ambassador Douglas Dillon summarized the Paris press reaction the morning after the executions. "From right to left, and with varying degrees of

Figure 5.2 Paris Memorial for Ethel and Julius Rosenberg, Tuileries Garden, June 23, 1953. Courtesy of Bettmann/CORBIS.

bitterness, Paris editors indicated disapproval of atom spies execution."[83] The pro-Gaulist *Parisien-Libéré* newspaper claimed the deaths would "only satisfy those who blindly support supremacy of the State" where "passion won out over reason."[84] The moderate newspaper *Paris-Presse* declared the executions the "biggest political error" the United States had "thus far committed" in the Cold War. It predicted that the "name of Rosenberg will live on, whether we like it or not and whether it is true or false, in the conscience of millions in free world."[85] The mainstream *Le Monde* claimed that the executions were a "serious defeat for [the] entire Atlantic coalition and a victory for its enemies," and they indicated the "profound ethical differences between Americans and Europeans."[86] In denying clemency Eisenhower did not display strength, the paper continued, but rather was "overexcited by witch-hunting."[87] French philosopher and playwright Jean-Paul Sartre wrote that the Rosenberg case was not just an American issue, but was "our business," because "whenever innocent people are killed it is the business of the whole world."[88] Killing the couple, Sartre argued, was "a legal lynching which smears with blood a whole nation," that confirmed "the bankruptcy of the Atlantic Pact" and America's "inability to lead the Western World."[89] "Be careful," he warned his fellow Europeans, "the United States has rabies. Let us sever our ties—or we may in turn be bitten and catch the disease."[90] Robert Barrat, a reporter for the independent lay Catholic journal *The Commonweal*, argued that "the loss of prestige the United States suffered in France through the Rosenberg execution is heavy."[91]

President Eisenhower was confused by this daunting overseas opposition. Days after the executions the president phoned Secretary of State Dulles and explained that the reports he had received from the State Department "indicated that it would be better to go ahead, and not let Commies brag that they had influenced our justice." Dulles agreed that "this had been his view" as well, in spite of the plentiful evidence to the contrary.[92] That Eisenhower wondered why dissenters were still protesting indicates his level of misinformation. Had the secretary "gone to the trouble of giving a resume of the Rosenberg case to the Ambassadors abroad?" the president asked.[93] Dulles admitted he was unsure "that the President's statement was sent."[94] Clearly, White House officials would have to engage in a postmortem propaganda effort to convince the world of the necessity of the Rosenbergs' executions.

Ambassador Dillon also continued to clamor for a way to make the facts of the Rosenberg case known and understood in France. Specifically, the ambassador insisted the administration clarify the issue of reduced sentences being offered in exchange for a confession, which was "one of the aspects of the case most widely misunderstood in France."[95] Many in France, he explained, thought that "a mere confession of guilt would have resulted in a commutation of sentence," and this was generally seen as reminiscent "of the Soviet trials where the accused even though innocent, are always forced to confess."[96] Dillon advised that the department make clear that "a mere confession by the Rosenbergs" would not have been enough; they would have had to fully cooperate and name other spies.[97] The ambassador also alerted the FBI that the International Association of Democratic Lawyers, believed to be a Communist-front organization, intended to conduct a re-trial of the Rosenbergs which could further "divide" the United States "from its European allies."[98]

Dillon pressed Washington not to underestimate the continuing anti-American propaganda campaign. He suggested that the Justice and State issue a white paper—a follow-up to Ben Bradlee's position paper—to explain the complexities of the case and refute continuing "Communist distortions."[99] Secretary Dulles agreed and forwarded Ambassador Dillon's recommendation to Attorney General Brownell. White House official C. D. Jackson, astonished by the "way the enormity of the crime was ignored or belittled, particularly abroad," brought up the issue at a July cabinet meeting.[100] Jackson persuaded other officials that to counter the misinformation a white paper would not suffice; they would need a larger piece of counterpropaganda to explain the case to foreign readers.[101] The

president was on board, and by autumn the position paper became a book written by Rabbi Solomon Andhil Fineberg.

The Eisenhower administration eagerly endorsed Fineberg's expose, *The Rosenberg Case: Fact and Fiction*, and made it part of their belated Rosenberg counterpropaganda campaign.[102] A member of the American Jewish Committee (AJC), Fineberg used the work to shower praise on the government, the jury, and the judge. He belittled any protests as Communist propaganda, and in doing so he further bifurcated "good" anti-Communist Jews from "bad" Communist ones. The United States Information Agency (USIA), the newly created public relations arm of the executive branch, distributed the book in French, Italian, and Israeli editions, aggressively marketing it overseas. USIA officials also asked C. D. Jackson if he could encourage the AJC to distribute copies of the book with their own cover letter. "This would get the facts into the hands of Jews overseas" through a nongovernmental organization that "would be far more convincing than USIA distribution."[103] When he finally replied after several months, Jackson claimed he was "terribly sorry to have taken so long about this, but I just devel-oped a psychic block about getting at it."[104]

C. D. Jackson was not the only government official who wanted to move on. Well into the summer, the Justice Department staff tried to physically put the case behind them by boxing up "literally hundreds of thousands" of letters, peti-tions, and telegrams into thirty large cartons.[105] Out of sight, they hoped, would lead to out of mind.

The CIA, for their part, was not quite done with the documents. Agents con-tinued to mine the material to compile lists of individuals from around the globe who had supported the Rosenbergs. The agency offered these names to local diplomats "for whatever use" they might "desire to make" of them.[106] Nearly a year after the deaths, the CIA decided to go beyond compiling names and inves-tigated the signatures on some 69,000 pieces of protest mail sent to the White House prior to the executions. Referring specifically to correspondence origi-nating from "Norway, Sweden, Denmark, Asia Minor with the exception of Iran, all Asiatic countries, Indonesia and the Philippines, all African countries, and all Latin American countries," agents targeted countries not strongly aligned with either the United States or the Soviet Union. The scope and results of this inves-tigation remain a mystery.[107] For the CIA the case might have been closed, but avenues to track suspected Communists were still open.

White House officials were not the only ones continuing to wage a propa-ganda battle. Having failed to save the Rosenbergs' lives, European activists, par-ticularly in France, shifted their attention to certifying the couple's martyrdom. The French Committee for the Defense of the Rosenbergs (CDR) transformed into the Committee for the Rehabilitation of the Rosenbergs (CRR).[108] The new CRR invited all to embrace a thirteen-point plan to resurrect the Rosenbergs' image in the face of their brave deaths. Committee members published a pamphlet detailing the facts of the case and using documents to assert the couple's innocence and "perpetuate their martyrdom in the memory of mankind."[109] They encouraged each municipality in France to name a street after the Rosenbergs and asked all to write thank you letters to the couple's lawyer, Manny Bloch. Eisenhower administration officials hoped the Fineberg book would discredit such martyrdom efforts. Meanwhile, the CRR also pledged to stay apprised of the "welfare of the Rosenberg children" and make that information available to the public.[110]

To the chagrin of the Eisenhower administration, in October 1953 the Rosenberg children returned to the front pages of newspapers around the world. Michael and Robert had been staying with a foster family in Toms River, New Jersey, but the superintendent of schools soon denied the boys access to public school since the foster parents were not their legal guardians and therefore the children were not legal residents of the town.[111] Authorities ordered the boys to return to New York City, and to their legal guardian Manny Bloch, for their education. Bloch publicly accused the federal government of "some kind of political plot" and questioned if the superintendent was "acting on his own or got orders from someone."[112] USIA officials, endeavoring to project a positive image of the country, complained to C. D. Jackson that this "could easily become a 'thing' unless nipped" quickly.[113] Jackson attempted to mitigate the public relations damage by appealing to Alex Smith, the Republican senator from New Jersey. Meanwhile the boys remained in the press as Bloch sought to find a permanent home for Michael and Robert, and the NCSJRC hosted a speaking tour for the attorney to raise money for a trust fund for the Rosenberg sons.

The fate of the Rosenberg children was again in question in early 1954 when Bloch suddenly died of a coronary occlusion. With the fifty-two-year-old lawyer gone, the Rosenberg sons had lost their guardian and their future was uncertain.[114] The overseas press called Michael and Robert "spy orphans," and gave front-page coverage to the resulting custody fight.[115] Telegrams, letters, and editorials from Australia, England, France, Germany, Hungary, Israel, and South Africa flooded the White House, expressing concern for the two grade-schoolage boys.[116] The judge for the custody case claimed that it seemed that "every worker in France was taking a personal interest in the resolution of the custody fight."[117] He ordered custody of the boys to their paternal grandmother, Sophie Rosenberg, and to the dean of the New York School of Social Work, Kenneth Johnson.[118] Both Rosenberg and Johnson agreed that Abel and Anne Meeropol, Jewish educators, writers, and "committed leftists," should adopt Michael and Robert.[119] Under the pseudonym Lewis Allan, Meeropol had composed numerous songs, including the anti-lynching song "Strange Fruit" made famous by

Billie Holiday in 1939.[120] As the courts finalized the adoption in 1957, the sons took the Meeropol name and slipped into anonymity.

Eisenhower administration officials, eager to keep the Rosenbergs and their orphaned sons off of the front page, were happy to replace the story with some good news: the conflict government officials blamed on the couple finally showed signs of ending. After devastating losses for the Communists in June 1953, the largest since 1952, solid steps were taken toward an armistice in Korea.[121] The president was ready for the forgotten war to truly be forgotten.

A last-minute hitch, however, threatened to derail the truce. Just before the armistice was to be signed, South Korean President Rhee allowed some 25,000 Korean nonrepatriated prisoners to escape. Voluntary repatriation, which gave war a moral imperative by allowing North Korean soldiers to stay in the south, had begun under Truman in late 1951, but a release so close to the truce put negotiations at risk.[122] Eisenhower was furious, and envoys scrambled to continue the talks.

The Korean War reached its tentative conclusion on July 26, 1953, just six weeks after the Rosenberg executions.[123] The ceremony was a solemn affair with the participants barely looking at each other, and the South Koreans refusing to attend.[124] That night Eisenhower recommended that the American people be cautious: "We have won an armistice on a single battleground, not peace in the world."[125] The cease-fire agreement only ended the fighting. It was not a peace treaty and it left Korea divided, with a 2.5-mile-wide "demilitarized zone" that remains in place more than sixty years later. Three long years of war cost 36,940 American lives. A staggering 415,000 South Koreans, 900,000 Chinese, and 2 million North Koreans perished.[126] Historian Steven Casey notes that in the United States the "armistice was greeted with relief rather than rejoicing."[127]

The Rosenbergs were dead and the Korean War—forgotten even while in progress—quickly faded further from memory. Unencumbered by Truman administration baggage, Eisenhower endeavored to chart his own course. Ike had learned from his predecessor's mistakes, and embraced a New Look to wage the Cold War. His national security strategy sought to keep the United States strong economically and militarily, while using psychological warfare, nuclear deterrence, and covert action to counter Soviet Communism over "the long haul."[128] In his version of fellow Republican Theodore Roosevelt's approach— walk softly and carry a big stick—Eisenhower would simultaneously embody the strong Cold Warrior and the peace crusader.

Eisenhower the warrior turned first to the CIA. On the day of the Rosenberg executions Kermit Roosevelt—Theodore Roosevelt's thirty-seven-year-old grandson—landed in Tehran. Eisenhower administration officials hoped regime change in Iran could provide a victory after Korea while simultaneously striking a blow against Communism.[129] The CIA operative in charge, Kermit Roosevelt was awaiting final authorization of Operation Ajax. The plan was to orchestrate a coup to overthrow Mohammed Mossadegh, the democratically elected prime minister of Iran who embraced progressive reforms, particularly nationalization of the oil industry. Mossadegh's lean toward Socialism alarmed Eisenhower and others; *Time* magazine had recognized him as Man of the Year for 1951 for the significant threat he posed in the Middle East.[130] The August coup in Iran took just a few days and the Shah the Americans put in place proved far more pro-American and anti-Socialist. Eisenhower was pleased he could orchestrate regime change so quickly and without a full military commitment. Less than a year later the CIA would assist with another coup, this time overthrowing a left-leaning president of Guatemala and replacing him with a pro-American military dictator.

Eisenhower turned to the CIA, flush from success in Iran and Guatemala, to take on more Cold War responsibilities. A little more than a year after the death of the Rosenbergs, Lt. Gen. James H. Doolittle charted a new course for the agency in a report that bore his name. Describing the destructive and threatening terms of the Cold War, the Doolittle Report reevaluated the role of CIA regarding U.S.-U.S.S.R relations. The Americans were pitted against a "police state," an "implacable enemy" whose goal was "world domination by whatever means and at whatever cost."[131] "There are no rules in such a game," the report continued, "hitherto acceptable norms of human conduct do not apply. If the United States is to survive, long-standing American concepts of 'fair play' must be reconsidered."[132] Eisenhower wholeheartedly endorsed this hardline report in September 1954 and abandoned "acceptable norms of human conduct" in places like Vietnam and Cuba, with debilitating long-term results.

In a public display of strength and nuclear readiness, Eisenhower ordered the testing of a hydrogen bomb in March 1954. The 15-megaton blast devastated Bikini Atoll in the Pacific Ocean and proved far more powerful than the hydrogen bomb test in 1952, and more than a thousand times more destructive than the bomb dropped on Hiroshima. Shifting winds caused radioactive ash to fall on the Marshall Islands, contaminating food and water. This public demonstration of American power was meant to counter the news that in the month after the executions the Soviets had tested their own hydrogen bomb. Using an original design, the Soviets had thwarted an American thermonuclear monopoly.[133] Eisenhower, determined to show strength in the face of losing the hydrogen bomb edge, publicly tested larger and more deadly weapons. The *Bulletin of the Atomic Scientists* moved its Doomsday Clock to two minutes before midnight, the most precarious setting in the sixty-five-year history of the atomic timepiece.[134]

The Soviet test effectively ended the White House's support of J. Robert Oppenheimer's "call for candor."[135] Administration officials had cleared Oppenheimer's article in *Foreign Affairs* that emphasized openness in U.S. nuclear policy and was published the day the Rosenbergs were executed. Eisenhower had initially supported the release of nuclear information—the rate of weapons production, size of stockpile, and U.S. government estimate of enemy capabilities—but the essay prompted debate within the administration about how much honesty concerning atomic bombs was really necessary.[136]

For some officials, Oppenheimer's embrace of openness indicated Communist sympathies; perhaps the father of the atomic bomb posed a confidence risk. Security hearings held over a four-week period in the spring of 1954 concluded there was no evidence that Oppenheimer ever passed any secrets. His allegiance to the political left and his support of openness concerning nuclear policy, however, prompted federal officials to revoke the physicist's security clearance in May 1954. As a result, dissenting voices influencing policy were silenced as acceptable public discussion narrowed in those early Cold War years.[137]

The Eisenhower administration, with the help of Congress, continued to stifle dissent. In order to prevent future espionage cases legislators cracked down on what they saw as the source of Soviet espionage, the Communist Party. Introduced by liberal Democratic Senator Hubert Humphrey and cosponsored by some twenty senators including John F. Kennedy, the Communist Control Act of 1954 went a long way toward making the CPUSA and its activities illegal. Sometimes referred to as the Rosenberg Act—a reminder of the damage seemingly innocuous Communists could cause—the legislation declared the Communist Party an instrument "of a conspiracy to overthrow the government" and rescinded any legal rights, privileges, and immunities the party previously had, thus subjecting its members to registration.[138] Though the CPUSA was largely impotent already thanks to significant FBI infiltration, the act further crushed the party and Ike eagerly signed the legislation.

While Eisenhower endeavored to display strength in the aftermath of the Rosenberg case, he simultaneously embarked on a public relations peace crusade that represented a mini-détente. In pursuing peace the president attempted to reclaim the moral high road, which much of the world believed he had veered away from when he allowed the Rosenbergs to be executed.

Eisenhower the peace crusader attended a meeting in Bermuda in early December 1953. The gathering of high-level representatives from Great Britain, France, and the United States signaled a common front in the face of the continued Soviet threat.[139] While in Bermuda, Eisenhower consulted with the prime ministers about an address he was preparing to give at the United Nations. He wanted to make a "serious proposal" about constructive use of nuclear energy to quell hysteria concerning the atomic bomb and to "demonstrate our will for peace."[140] The allies approved the speech, though Churchill was reluctantly supportive.

Upon his return from Bermuda, Eisenhower proceeded directly to the United Nations to deliver the dramatic "Atoms for Peace" speech. Recognizing that the newly tested hydrogen bomb had unleashed a global panic, the president tried to "solve the fearful atomic dilemma" and draw attention to a "more positive image of the atom."[141] Eisenhower emphasized the "peaceful power" that could be obtained from atomic energy and proposed an Atomic Energy Agency (AEA) to store and protect fissionable materials for peaceful uses.[142] "It is not enough just to take this weapon out of the hands of the soldiers," the president explained. "It must be put into the hands of those who will know how to strip its military casing and adapt it to the arts of peace."[143] Eisenhower hoped to convince the world that the United States was the only nation that could be trusted to be a conscientious steward of the advanced technology. This "peaceful counteroffensive" to Soviet post-Stalin overtures for peace was a larger gesture than Eisenhower's "Chance for Peace" speech from April 1953, and for his efforts the president received an enthusiastic response from UN delegates.[144] Eisenhower wanted to usher in a period of calmer, more rational discussions of nuclear issues and leave his warmonger image behind.

The Soviets countered two weeks later. They argued that Eisenhower's plan would do nothing to halt production of atomic weapons, but would instead spread dangerous nuclear material around the world. U.S. officials ignored these complaints and instead highlighted America's intent to share peaceful atomic technology by exporting nuclear power reactors to nations in need of inexpensive energy. Carefully placed news stories emphasized the peaceful atom and the response was enthusiastic.[145]

Stalin's successor Georgi Malenkov continued to challenge the Americans. He claimed in March 1954 that the Soviet government stood for "further weakening of international tensions" and "for a stable and durable peace."[146] Malenkov shocked the Politburo when he argued that the use of the hydrogen bomb in war "would mean the destruction of world civilization."[147] The Eisenhower administration had no comment. Ambassador to Moscow Charles Bohlen later wrote, "Washington's failure to engage Malenkov in meaningful negotiations over nuclear weapons and other issues was a missed opportunity."[148] In a speech six weeks later Malenkov returned to belligerent language, claiming that if attacked the Soviets would use atomic weapons to crush capitalist aggressors.[149] The moment for rational discussion was lost. By early 1955 Malenkov would be forced to resign, ultimately replaced by Nikita Khrushchev.

Some U.S. government officials took a different approach to return sanity to the discussion of nuclear weapons. Days after Malenkov's speech, Atomic Energy Commission (AEC) spokesman James Beckerley publicly stated that is was time to "stop 'kidding' ourselves about atomic 'secrets.' "[150] The Soviets, Beckerley explained, "have the skills and the plants to make fission materials and bombs," and Americans are not "just better than the USSR in technical matters."[151] Atomic bombs, he argued, "are not matters that can be stolen and transmitted in the form of information," and they "were not stolen from us by spies."[152] General Leslie Groves, the military liaison in charge of the Manhattan Project agreed, further clarifying: "I consider the information passed in the Rosenberg Case of minor value."[153] Due to its controversial nature Groves insisted that his statement be kept secret, and government officials would not release his words publicly until 1979.[154] These statements would fuel doubts held by those who questioned the necessity and wisdom of the Rosenbergs' executions.

Eisenhower, the crusader for peace, endeavored to reassert moral authority after the executions and keep God on his side.[155] Reaffirming the Cold War fight against Communism as a religious crusade, Ike signed a bill on June 14, 1954, adding "under God" to the Pledge of Allegiance. On that Flag Day, the president joined Congress and the majority of Americans in openly embracing their deity, hoping that under the blanket of divine protection, Americans could combat all fears, particularly atheistic Communism.[156]

In the months and years after the execution of Julius and Ethel Rosenberg the facts of the case, and clarity on their meaning, remained contested. By creating and recreating the story of the Rosenbergs, many have laid claim to their version of the truth. In his character on *The Colbert Report*, comedian and political satirist Stephen Colbert spun off of a definition of truth to embrace the more accommodating "truthiness"—not true, but what we want to believe is true.[157] While historians cannot ever reach "truth," they do spend much time grappling with issues of fact and historical memory. Now and then facts, as they emerge from new research, contradict long-held beliefs and faulty memories of the past.[158] The Rosenberg case remains one of those instances where Americans—and the global community—struggle with competing narratives inherent in the story of a nuclear family destroyed when the parents were executed for conspiracy to commit espionage.

One year after the Rosenbergs' funeral, emotions still ran high as supporters unveiled the couple's tombstones. The service was at one o'clock on the afternoon of Sunday, June 20, also Father's Day.[159] Unaware of the Rosenberg anniversary, hundreds of visitors headed to the cemetery to visit fathers' graves. Cemetery decorum evaporated as fights broke out when some 12,000 people congregated for the unveiling of the Rosenberg stones.[160] "There are plenty, like us who came out here for Father's Day," one man protested, and "are shocked to find our beloved ones must sleep in the same ground as these two."[161] In addition, administrators at the cemetery protested to the FBI that the NCSJRC had "no right to conduct *any* memorial or unveiling service" because the burial plots had been purchased "by fraudulent representations."[162] An unidentified man had claimed they were for his two sisters who had been killed in a car accident.

Memorials and protests beyond the gravesites also marked the first anniversary of executions. Indefatigable a year later, the NCSJRC hosted a meeting in San Francisco as part of a month-long memorial for Ethel and Julius Rosenberg.[163] Stage and screen actor Howard DaSilva read poems and writings from people around the world who expressed their disapproval over the handling of the case, including Jean-Paul Sartre's accusation that the execution was "a legal lynching."[164] The event honored Julius and Ethel and raised money for codefendant Morton Sobell. Other protesters marked the anniversary by writing angry admonishments to the president, decrying the "miscarriage of justice."[165] The NCSJRC remained on the government's radar; in October 1954 the IRS would pursue the group for unpaid taxes, and in August 1956 HUAC would lead an investigation of the committee.[166]

Members of the NCSJRC re-tooled, creating two organizations to better represent their twin goals. The Committee to Secure Justice for Morton Sobell in the Rosenberg Case (CSJMSRC) raised money for the defense and release of Sobell. It would disband in 1969, upon Sobell's release from prison after serving nearly eighteen years; in 2008 Sobell would publicly admit he had been a spy. Activists would form the National Committee to Reopen the Rosenberg Case (NCRRC) in 1974 to campaign for martyrdom for Julius and Ethel Rosenberg and to exonerate the couple of the charge of atomic espionage.[167] The booklet *Never Losing Faith* helped the NCRRC raise money and awareness, and its efforts to reopen the case continue to this day.[168]

Prompted by the Rosenberg case, hate mail plagued liberals, especially Jews accused of taking part in Communist activities. For example, Dr. Irving Peress, a dentist for the Army, had been honorably discharged after refusing to answer questions about possible Communist affiliations before Senator McCarthy and his subcommittee. In February 1954 the dentist complained that his home in Queens, New York, had been stoned following the receipt of unsigned letters which "attacked him as a Jew, compared his family to that of Ethel and Julius Rosenberg ... and lamented that Hitler had not kill[ed] more Jews."[169] Many Americans continued to promote aggression against Communists, holding the Rosenbergs up as an example.

In furthering the government's case in the 1950s, Leslie Fiedler and Robert Warshow, both liberal anti-Communist Jewish intellectuals, wrote vicious critiques of the couple. Warshow, writing for *Commentary* magazine, soundly criticized the couple in "The 'Idealism' of Julius and Ethel Rosenberg." In particular, Warshow analyzed their letters, complaining, "In their crudity and emptiness, in their absolute and dedicated alienation from the truth and experience, these letters adequately express the Communism of 1953."[170] Fiedler, literary critic and former member of the Young Communist League, wrote "A Postscript on the Rosenberg Case" for *Encounter* magazine in October 1953, in which he explored how the Rosenbergs were able to capture "the imagination of the world" and get so many to support their case.[171] Fielder claimed he was embarrassed when Ethel referred to the Rosenbergs as "a small unoffending Jewish family" in a letter to the president; he found her style "painfully pretentious," found Julius "more devious," and found them both "unattractive and vindictive" as he questioned their Jewish faith in the face of their devout Communism.[172] Purportedly commissioned by the CIA, some claim its agents were surprised by the hostile tone of the piece.[173]

High-ranking U.S. government officials also continued to justify the prosecutions and executions. In April of 1959, former President Harry Truman gave a lecture at Columbia University entitled "On Hysteria and Witch-Hunting."[174] When a student asked about the death penalty for the Rosenbergs, Truman explained: "They had a fair trial. The jury decided on what they should have and they got it," forgetting that it was the judge who sentenced them to death. "Now I don't know how you can go behind that," he concluded. "They're already dead."[175] The students burst into laughter. Later, former Attorney General Herbert Brownell admitted that the Rosenberg case was "one of the great world controversies at the time," but recalled that the protests were primarily the product of Communist propaganda.[176] The State Department, Brownell explained, followed world reaction closely and briefed the president daily about foreign reaction to the case, but the administration knew that if Eisenhower granted clemency—if the world had seen the "government knuckling under to what we called the Communist propaganda to stop their executions," then the country would have lost a crucial battle in the global Cold War.[177] Clemency, Brownell concluded, echoing Eisenhower, "would have been interpreted as a tremendous victory of Communist propaganda over the United States government" and "a tremendous victory for Russian propaganda around the world."[178]

Not all who supported the sentence in the case remained faithful to the White House's version of events, however. Reinhold Niebuhr, the Protestant theologian whose anti-Communist writings helped justify the Rosenbergs' death, regretted his stance just months later. He observed that most Catholics around the world, with the pope in the lead, were shocked by the executions, and wondered whether it was a moral and political mistake.[179] In an article for *Look* magazine Niebuhr admitted that "the president would have been well advised to commute the sentence to life imprisonment" due to "the hysteria in Europe" over the executions.[180]

Political activists who had dedicated much time and money to freeing the Rosenbergs wrote their own explorations of the case, as uncompromising as the critiques. For example, Walter and Miriam Schneir, in *Invitation to an*

Inquest, and John Wexley, in *The Judgment of Julius and Ethel Rosenberg,* condemned the government's prosecution of the case and passionately argued for the Rosenbergs' innocence.[181] Government prosecutor Roy Cohn denounced these activists as "Rosenberg revisionists," but that did not stop their views from spreading.[182] Spurred on, activists launched commemorations in Communist countries around the world.[183]

Former Soviet premier Nikita Khrushchev would add his version of the truth when he confirmed the value of the Rosenberg spies in his lengthy memoirs. Khrushchev boasted that he was present when Stalin "mentioned the Rosenbergs with warmth" and confirmed the couple "provided very significant help in accelerating the production of our atomic bomb."[184] Some accept Khrushchev's testimony as fact, but many acknowledge the self-serving nature of his memoirs, his desire to further enshrine the Rosenbergs as martyrs, and his propensity for hyperbole.

Poets and writers struggled to express their interpretation of the executions.[185] Allen Ginsberg wrote a five-thousand-word poem, "Television Was a Baby Crawling Toward that Deathchamber," in 1961, which included sympathetic references to Julius and Ethel.[186] Sylvia Plath had the protagonist Esther Greenwood, in her 1963 novel *The Bell Jar,* obsessed with the executions.[187] In the late 1960s and early 1970s writers fictionalized the Rosenberg case in their work, using the facts selectively to tell the story in their own way.[188] Donald Freed's multimedia play *Inquest* mixed the trial transcript with several thousand visual projections and sound reenactments representing the Cold War context of the early 1950s.[189] When it first opened for a short run in Cleveland, Ohio, in 1969, Rosenberg Judge Irving Kaufman contacted the FBI, alarmed over the positive reviews of the play in the *New York Times* and Freed's sympathetic portrait of the couple. FBI agents assured Kaufman they would follow the production closely, but it closed after just three weeks on Broadway. Taking a different view, Robert Coover produced a piece of satirical fantasy fiction, *The Public Burning.*[190] Coover ridiculed everyone involved in the case and contrived to have Nixon serve as the narrator who become infatuated with Ethel. After struggles with publishers, and at more than five hundred pages, the controversial book generated conflicting responses from critics and the public alike.

Most famously, in 1971 E. L. Doctorow told the story of a troubled son and daughter after the arrest, conviction, and execution of their parents in *The Book of Daniel.*[191] The fictionalized treatment of the famous case received critical acclaim. A film adaptation titled *Daniel,* released in 1983 and starring Timothy Hutton, Mandy Patinkin, and Edward Asner, was a box office failure.[192] Doctorow closed the book with a quote from the bible: "Go thy way, Daniel; for the words are closed up and sealed until the end of time," referencing the facts about the case that could never be known.[193] But events would soon prompt the release of many sealed-up words.

In 1973, on the twentieth anniversary of their parents' execution, thirty-year-old Michael Meeropol and his twenty-six-year-old brother Robert disclosed their identity. The Rosenberg sons sued Louis Nizer, lawyer and author of *The Implosion Conspiracy*, for unauthorized use of Julius and Ethel Rosenberg's prison letters.[194] Courts dismissed accusations of defamation of character and invasion of privacy, while a remaining copyright issue was later settled out of court.[195] Years later Michael Meeropol would regain control when he edited a more accurate collection of some five hundred of his parents' letters.[196] Choosing to be in the public eye, the sons pursued additional information and worked to protect their parents' legacy.

In the political climate following the Vietnam War, Alvin H. Goldstein challenged the government's narrative and produced the first comprehensive documentary film about the couple and their codefendant Morton Sobell. In *The Rosenberg-Sobell Case Revisited* Goldstein raised many questions about the irregularities that marred the government's case, and American citizens began to demand more information and documentation.[197] In response, Attorney General Elliot Richardson—with Watergate pressures constricting the White House—ordered the government files on the Rosenbergs be made available to researchers.[198]

In late February 1974, seven months after the attorney general's order and more than twenty years after the executions, the FBI admitted it had not yet released a single page from its files.[199] The Watergate investigations had prompted Nixon to appoint Robert Bork as the new acting attorney general. Bork put limits on the files and they were caught in limbo between the Department of Justice and the FBI.[200] Two weeks later, Michael and Robert Meeropol demanded an investigation and filed Freedom of Information Act requests for the release of FBI documents concerning their parents.[201] "We want to show they are innocent," Robert explained.[202] Four years later Michael and Robert would receive a check for $195,802.50 from the federal government that went directly to their lawyers as compensation for fees incurred during their Freedom of Information Act (FOIA) lawsuit.[203]

Meanwhile, in late 1973 federal government officials had declassified the missing State Department documents, which contained the international reaction to the Rosenberg case. Without their corresponding Name Cards they could not be located, so they would go missing for another thirty-five years. As Michael and Robert Meeropol struggled to get their parents' files released officials may have pulled the State Department Name Cards, deeming these diplomatic correspondence that complicated the government's version of the Rosenberg case too problematic to be seen.[204]

Demonstrations against the FBI and calls for the release of their documents ensued. Protesters saw the sources as essential to proving what they believed, that the federal government had framed the Rosenbergs. A Jewish Socialist group protested outside FBI offices in New York City, labeling the case against the couple a "frameup" and a "Watergate-like charade."[205] Michael and Robert Meeropol appeared on popular television shows—the daytime talk show *The Mike Douglas Show* and the nighttime *60 Minutes*—to explain their efforts to reopen the case against their parents. Howard DaSilva emceed at a Rosenberg rally at Carnegie Hall, publicizing efforts to reopen case. Professional actors, including Rip Torn and Jane Alexander, read from the couple's prison letters.

Rosenberg prosecutor Roy Cohn, however, called the claim that the couple was innocent "wild, emotional and unsubstantiated."[206] Writer Daniel H. Yergin contacted Cohn and asked him to look over a piece he was writing on the Rosenberg case.[207] Cohn argued with several points concerning trial testimony and evidence, and concluded with an observation of the Rosenberg sons: "No one—least of all I—blame them for supporting their parents, but the wild, unfounded, and ill-informed nature of their emotional charges are about as persuasive as Tricia Nixon saying her father never discussed Watergate with anyone."[208]

As all involved waited for the FBI documents, emotions surrounding the meaning of the case threatened to erupt into violence. In May 1975, Judge Irving Kaufman cancelled plans to speak at the Pomona College graduation due to potential threats. "After disturbances early this year in Santa Monica" at a rally to reopen the case, Kaufman explained, "Pomona officials advised me that they feared graduation ceremonies might be disrupted if I appeared."[209] The *New York Times Magazine* printed Kaufman's speech that June; in it the judge ironically encouraged graduates to "value freedom of thought, freedom of speech, freedom of the press because they furnish vehicles for the new and provocative, and serve as barriers to tyranny."[210] Kaufman's career was long and varied—he would write a dissenting opinion as an appellate judge in the *United States v. The New York Times* in 1971, which the Supreme Court agreed with when it reversed the majority of the appellate panel and ruled that the *New York Times* could publish the Pentagon Papers. But the Rosenberg case marked him. When Kaufman died in 1992 at the age of eighty-one, a colleague claimed that "the decision plagued him to his last days."[211]

Michael and Robert Meeropol added their voices to the debate over their parents' case in 1975 with *We Are Your Sons: The Legacy of Ethel and Julius Rosenberg*.[212] They focused on holes and abnormalities in the government's case, of which there were many. As a result of the sons' effort, in July 1975 new Attorney General Edward H. Levi overruled the FBI and the U.S. Attorney in New York and ordered both to "supply files on the case" to Michael and Robert "as quickly as possible."[213] Six weeks later the FBI released the first 725 pages of its nearly 200,000-page Rosenberg files.[214] Government officials delivered the documents to historian Allen Weinstein, and to Michael and Robert, who used them in a second edition of *We Are Your Sons*. As the FBI continued to make their files public, the sons admitted that Julius and Ethel had been members of the Communist Party, but argued that their parents, particularly their mother, were innocent.[215]

Ronald Radosh and Joyce Milton drew upon the new government evidence extensively in *The Rosenberg File*, first published in 1983.[216] Their work also benefited from an arranged meeting with David and Ruth Greenglass, living under aliases.[217] In their comprehensive book Radosh and Milton admitted irregularities in the government's prosecution of the case, but argued that Julius had indeed engaged in atomic and military espionage for the Soviet Union.

As more researchers explored the trove of FBI documents, debate over the case continued. In September 1976, more than one hundred professors of law wrote to the House and Senate Judiciary Committee stating that the FBI documents they read "reveal a shocking pattern of *ex parte* contacts with the U.S. Attorney, FBI officials, and others in the Department of Justice."[218] Building on these accusations, on the anniversary of the executions in 1977 the NCRRC wrote an open letter to Judge Kaufman stating that he violated the U.S. Constitution and his oath of office by having "improper communication" with the prosecution that desecrated the role of "judge and impartial arbiter."[219] The committee insisted the judge agree to a June 1976 request from Michael and Robert Meeropol to disclose his own files on the case.[220] Kaufman refused. His papers were not made available to the public until after his death in 1992.[221]

On June 19, 1978, seven thousand people gathered in Union Square, New York—where thousands had stood twenty-five years before—for a rally commemorating the anniversary of the Rosenberg deaths. Many prominent progressives participated in the five-hour event, including actor Ossie Davis, folk singer Pete Seeger, and Vietnam War veteran and author Ron Kovic.

Artists and filmmakers in the 1980s used their craft to find meaning in the Rosenbergs' deaths, incorporating a sympathetic portrayal of the couple and the horror of their plight in their work.[222] For example, in 1988 Rob Okun and Nina Felshin curated an exhibit entitled "Unknown Secrets," under the Rosenberg Era Art Project. The art show traveled around the United States from 1988 through 1991, displaying more than sixty pieces from the 1950s and contemporary work commissioned for the project. Okun detailed the story of this "important cache of art" in a companion book.[223]

To mark the thirtieth anniversary of the executions, *The Nation* and *The New Republic* cosponsored a New York Town Hall forum entitled "Were the Rosenbergs Framed?" in June 1983. The overflow crowd of more than three thousand remained for the five-hour discussion, indicating that interest in the case had been undiminished by time.[224] Six months later, fifteen hundred people returned to Town Hall to see Ronald Radosh and Joyce Milton, authors of *The Rosenberg File*, debate Walter and Miriam Schneir, authors of *Invitation to an Inquest*.[225] The Schneirs continued to emphasize the irregularities of the case and raise reasonable doubt in the Rosenberg's conviction, while Radosh and Milton argued that government documents pointed to Julius's guilt and his participation in significant espionage work. Representing opposing interpretations of the Rosenberg case and its meaning, the debate showed that consensus remained elusive three decades later.[226]

Anniversaries continued to prompt reflection and just after the fortieth, in the summer of 1993, the Litigation Section of the American Bar Association (ABA) staged a mock retrial of the Rosenbergs in New York City.[227] Practicing lawyers represented the defense and prosecution, utilizing all the documentation then available. The ABA corrected the original trial's irregularities and used an actual federal judge, with actors standing in for witnesses and the defendants. Two separate juries of six individuals each declared the couple not guilty, convincing even more Americans that the convictions and executions had been a miscarriage of justice. More evidence, however, was on the horizon.

A new layer of Soviet documentation—the Venona transcripts—changed the narrative of the Rosenberg case. As discussed earlier, the project (code-named Venona) represented a joint intelligence gathering effort on the part of the United States and Great Britain, which cracked the Soviet diplomatic code in 1944. In 1995 the CIA and NSA released nearly three thousand translated documents concerning Soviet espionage activity in the United States. John Earl Haynes and Harvey Klehr used these cables to great effect in *Venona: Decoding Soviet Espionage in America* and concluded that Julius Rosenberg ran a large military and industrial spy ring, and that while there was no doubt that Julius was involved in atomic espionage, he was of much more value to the KGB "as a source of non-atomic technical intelligence."[228] Ethel was an accessory to her husband's work, knowledgeable but not an active agent. They argued that if Venona had been disclosed during the trial the couple's executions would have been far less likely.[229] Writers grappled with these new disclosures and their impact on the struggle for truth and remembrance.[230] How did the memory of the Rosenbergs change now that most accepted Julius had been a spy?

The new century brought shocking revelations. In 2001 Ethel's brother, David Greenglass, admitted he lied in the trial testimony that convicted his sister and resulted in her execution. *New York Times* reporter Sam Roberts revealed the admission and confirmed the government's use of Ethel as a lever to pressure Julius to confess and name other spies.[231] This convinced many observers that the government's prosecution of Ethel had been unethical and immoral.

By the fiftieth anniversary of the executions in 2003, however, NCRRC protests had tapered off considerably. When *New York Times* reporter Clyde Haberman visited the couple's grave at Wellwood Cemetery on Long Island he was surprised to see he was the only one there. When a groundskeeper noticed the reporter looking at the graves, he saw that the couple had died on the same day and asked if they had been killed in an accident.[232]

For the golden anniversary, Home Box Office presented Tony Kushner's award-winning play *Angels in America*.[233] Set in Reagan-era America, the six-hour production grapples with issues of religion and sexuality. One of the main characters is Rosenberg prosecutor Roy Cohn, who is visited by the ghost of Ethel Rosenberg while on his deathbed.[234] Ethel blames Cohn for her death; through her disgust for Cohn and delight in his demise, Kushner allows audiences to fantasize about an alternate ending to the case. That same year HBO also produced a documentary by Ivy Meeropol, Michael Meeropol's daughter, *Heir to an Execution: A Granddaughter's Story*, which wrestled with questions of guilt, legality, and legacy.

Emily Arnow Alman and David Alman, the founders and longtime managers of the NCSJRC and the NCRRC, wrote their story, *Exoneration*, which was published after Emily's death in 2004.[235] While the Almans argue for a complete pardon of the Rosenbergs that seems unsubstantiated by the evidence, this memoir offers a more personal account since the authors dedicated much of their lives to clearing the Rosenbergs' names.

In the summer of 2008 federal officials agreed for the first time to release key grand jury testimony from now deceased witnesses in the Rosenberg case.[236] The list included Ruth Greenglass, who had died that April at the age of eighty-three.[237] As many suspected, her grand jury testimony conflicted with what she subsequently stated in court during the trial. Ruth said nothing to the grand jury about Ethel typing notes about the atomic bomb, confirming that Ruth and her husband David added this to their trial testimony. David Greenglass's testimony, released in July 2015, said the same thing.[238]

Even more shocking, in the fall of 2008 Rosenberg codefendant Morton Sobell admitted for the first time that he had been a spy. Sentenced to thirty years in prison and released in 1969, Sobell consistently—and for more than fifty years—denied being involved in any espionage. Days after the release of the grand jury testimony, Sobell revealed that he and Julius had passed military secrets to the Soviet Union. Though he denied his own involvement in atomic espionage and insisted he only helped the Soviet Union as an ally during World War II, Sobell's admission caused many to re-evaluate the entire case.[239] Whatever additional evidence revealed in the future, Julius Rosenberg had engaged in espionage. Just as Julius's role became clearer, Ethel's remained controversial. After Sobell's disclosure reporter Sam Roberts released an unpublished interview with

Richard Nixon, in which the former vice president admitted Ethel Rosenberg "might have been spared the death penalty" if Eisenhower had known "that evidence against her was tainted."[240] Even Nixon was reshaping the government's 1953 narrative.

A few days later Michael and Robert Meeropol acknowledged that their father had been a spy.[241]

> Our father did, in fact, participate in passing along military information, [but the government] executed two people for stealing the secret of the atomic bomb—a crime it knew they did not commit. Those in power targeted our parents, making them the focus of the public's cold war-era fear and anger. They manufactured testimony and evidence. They arrested our mother simply as leverage to get our father to cooperate.[242]

Based on the evidence, this line of reasoning remains difficult to dispute. There are few today who do not acknowledge Julius Rosenberg engaged in espionage, but the conviction and execution of Ethel Rosenberg remains extremely problematic.

In 2009 John Earl Haynes and Harvey Klehr, with the assistance of former KGB officer Alexander Vassiliev and his notebooks, produced a comprehensive compilation of FBI, KGB, and Venona Project records.[243] The authors confirm that Julius ran perhaps one of the largest intelligence operations in the country, which peaked in early 1945 with nine agents. The documents also prove that Ethel knew of her husband's work and provided some assistance, but was not issued a codename and was not a "fully operational agent."[244] While some historians argue these sources are more suggestive than definitive, they offer a tantalizing peek into the range and character of Soviet espionage and American counterintelligence activities.[245] These documents led most scholars to conclude that Julius passed along military and industrial secrets to the Soviets, but not atomic ones; others detected atomic espionage as well; some believed the documents proved Ethel's innocence, while others concluded she was not an active agent, but an accomplice.

The disputed legacy of the Rosenbergs is reflected in many cultural references. For example, "David Greenglass" became shorthand for repugnant individuals. Filmmaker Woody Allen knew that his audience for *Crimes and Misdemeanors* (1989) would understand what he meant when his character explained to Mia Farrow's character, "I love him like a brother. David Greenglass." Other references point to the Rosenbergs as national traitors. When Lisa researches her family tree in an episode of *The Simpsons*, she becomes discouraged that they are "all horrible!" and turns to her grandfather to see if there are "a few good ancestors," vowing to not give up, "even if I have to go back to Adam and Eve." Her grandfather replies, "Oh, you mean Adam and Eve Simpson, or as you may know them, Julius and Ethel Rosenberg." Lisa groans in response.[246] The Rosenberg name lives on in popular culture.

The dramatic nature of the case also lends itself to staged representation, and resulting theatrical productions run the gamut from emotional to absurd. For example, Joan Beber's two plays, *Hunger: In Bed With Roy Cohn* and *Ethel Sings: Espionage in High C*, explore tragic-comic visions haunting Cohn and take an imaginative look at Ethel and her love of music.[247] A 2008 New York City production of *The Very Sad Story of Ethel and Julius* told the tale through marionettes, complete with a teddy bear in an electric chair.[248]

In commemoration of Woody Guthrie's one-hundredth birthday, Pete Seeger released a lost Guthrie song, "Dear Mister Eisenhower."[249] Guthrie likely wrote the lyrics while in a mental institution in 1952; in 2001 Seeger composed the music and performed it at an RFC celebration. Guthrie's lyrics, which include references to "this frame-up Rosenberg case," have a naïve veneer, harkening back to a time when a frame-up of the Rosenbergs seemed a possibility. The couple returned to the news when the U.S. government disclosed an example of twenty-first century espionage.

In June 2010 the FBI captured nearly a dozen deep-cover Russian spies, agents living as Americans but working for the SVR, the post-Cold War version of the KGB. The Russian espionage ring intended to penetrate American policy-making groups and gather nuclear weapon information, but they operated from such locations as Yonkers, New York, and Montclair, New Jersey. "They couldn't have been spies," one of their shocked neighbors remarked. "Look what she did with the hydrangeas."[250] Seven children were uprooted when their parents were returned to Russia, prompting many to reflect on the fate of the Rosenberg children.[251]

Inspired by these new spies, CNN's Rick Sanchez listed the top Russian spies in American history and placed Julius and Ethel Rosenberg at the top of the list. Sanchez embraced his own "truthiness" when he explained why: "We all know the real life Boris and Natasha. In the late 1940s, the Communist husband and wife supplied blueprints for the construction of the atom bomb to the Russians."[252] Sanchez's definitive—and on the air uncontested—statement of what "we all know" demonstrates the historical truth many Americans believed in the 1950s and choose to continue to believe. *Time* magazine echoed this faulty depiction of the Rosenbergs when they compiled a list of "history's most notorious crime duos."[253] Along with Bonnie and Clyde (#1), Butch Cassidy and the Sundance Kid (#2), and Frank and Jesse James (#3), Julius and Ethel Rosenberg earned the number seven spot, just above the Menendez Brothers (#8), the Columbine Killers (#9), and the D.C. Snipers (#10). While the magazine admitted that labeling the Rosenbergs a crime duo was still a matter of debate, the editors insisted the couple belonged on the list whether they were guilty or not, reflecting the essence of truthiness.[254] More than sixty years later the U.S. government's convincing propaganda campaign—albeit simplistic and misleading—is still successful, at least among Americans.[255]

Continuing and deep divides among activists and historians on the controversial case were on view at a June 2011 conference on the Rosenbergs and Soviet espionage hosted by George Washington University.[256] Many historians of espionage, anti-Communism, and the atomic bomb presented their research before a packed and attentive audience, and the discussion often grew heated. One historian later observed,

> Old habits clearly die hard: John Earl Haynes suggested that "radical enthusiasms" of the 1960s led to the widespread belief that the Rosenbergs were innocent. Fair enough. However, he went on to suggest that, ". . . no academics had shifted their view toward Julius' guilt", and that generally scholars did not want to "raise the ire of the Rosenberg defender lynch mob."[257]

This blanket generalization belittles the work of scholars who have attempted to untangle the complexities of the case. Many participants expressed a longing for the day when enough time has passed, enough dust has settled, and enough documents have been examined to allow for a more nuanced discussion of the meaning of the Rosenberg case.

The sixtieth anniversary of the executions in 2013 compelled voices on all sides to once again claim the right to say what happened and what it all means. Activist actors Ed Asner and Mike Farrell hosted a viewing of the film *Daniel* in Los Angeles.[258] In the discussion accompanying the screening Asner focused on anti-Semitism surrounding the trial, while Farrell used the film as a platform to speak out against the death penalty and publicize his work toward ending capital punishment. Robert Meeropol and his daughter Jenn wrote a piece for *The Guardian* discussing the Rosenberg Fund for Children (RFC), which provides support for children of jailed activists as a force for good in the face of their family's tragedy.[259] The conservative publication *FrontPage Magazine* posted an editorial touting their version of the truth: the arrest, conviction, and execution of the Rosenbergs was justified since they "were guilty—and they deserved what they got."[260] Sixty years later, individuals still spin facts and weave truths with their own agendas to craft the Rosenberg story they want told and remembered.

In the face of post-9/11 acts of espionage, many have touted the Cold War example of the Rosenbergs. The Espionage Act of 1917, passed during World War I and used to prosecute the Rosenbergs, is being used to prosecute whistleblowers Chelsea (Bradley) Manning and Edward Snowden. Manning, who leaked U.S. military information, was convicted under six Espionage Act violations and sentenced in August 2013 to thirty-five years in prison. Robert Meeropol, among others, has written about the connections between the Manning and Rosenberg cases.[261]

Former NSA contractor Edward Snowden illegally released thousands of classified documents and will likely face charges under the Espionage Act if he ever leaves Russia.[262] U.S. government officials are still considering their options in the Snowden case, but Texas Senator John Cornyn has advocated for Edward Snowden to be tried for treason. In reporting the senator's views, the Dallas News stumbled and reported that Julius and Ethel were convicted for treason, incorrectly claiming that the no one had been executed for treason since the Rosenbergs in 1953.[263] This confusion originated in the trial when Judge Kaufman claimed the couple committed treason when he sentenced them, and it continues to this day. Many American history textbooks repeat the erroneous information, and even the NSA makes the mistake in its online history.[264] Moving toward a more nuanced view of the facts of the Rosenberg case will shift the history away from myth-infused memory and truthiness and on to solid ground.

Conclusion

No one emerges from the Rosenberg story unscathed. Administration officials, prosecutors, and defendants all made decisions that undermined their own interests, and there is a plague on all their houses. This case remains emblematic of the tragic consequences that result when actions are driven by paranoia and fear.

Both Truman and Eisenhower governed within the pressure cooker that was the early Cold War. Convinced that the very future of the United States and quite possibly the world was at risk, they made national security their number one priority. Both presidents strove to avoid showing any sign of weakness, to trigger any perception of being weak on Communism. Nuclear bombs were a constant reminder that a global apocalypse was a horrifyingly real threat. Truman and Eisenhower directed their administrations to be strong and take the danger seriously, for they knew millions could die.

When the Soviet Union tested its first atomic bomb, the FBI strove to uncover espionage and punish those responsible. Pressure increased when officials—incorrectly—blamed Communist aggression in Korea on an emboldened, nuclear-armed Soviet Union.[1] Already under fire from the Republicans for his supposed softness on Communism, Truman decided he could not be gentle with the only spies they were able to indict. This included pressuring Julius with his wife's arrest and threatening to execute them both. In imposing the death penalty the administration hoped that the couple would talk, future spies would be deterred, and the world would be impressed with America's tough stand against Communism.

Eisenhower inherited the Rosenberg case. As a former military man, he understood chain of command and was not eager to use the executive branch to interfere with decisions of the judiciary. He would allow the executions to proceed. He also saw the case as an opportunity to send a signal that spies would not be tolerated.[2] He held firm, adhering to a conviction that clemency for the Rosenbergs would show weakness and threaten national security.[3] Emotional appeals concerning the Rosenberg sons did not move him; Eisenhower believed that if Julius and particularly Ethel had been good parents, they never would have put their children at risk in the first place.

When the Rosenbergs' appeals dragged on and the Korean War bogged down, many Americans clamored for a definitive victory. In Korea they had to settle for limited containment after a long and costly conflict, but as a journalist observed in 1953, Americans could score a win on the espionage front. "The U.S. could not stop the Russians from getting the bomb, sooner or later; but the Rosenbergs could be executed," he explained. "We cannot or could not end the war in Korea; but we can execute the Rosenbergs."[4] The majority of Americans embraced a cathartic electrocution to show strength, calm nuclear anxiety, and ease the pain of an inconclusive, confusing, and deadly military action thousands of miles away.

Eisenhower believed his refusal to pardon the Rosenbergs strengthened his appearance in the aftermath of his approval of an unsatisfying truce in Korea.[5] The president tolerated no sign of weakness, no letting down of the nation's collective guard in the early months of his administration. This was war—albeit a cold one—and Americans could ill afford a feeble response. In executing the couple officials proved that they were committed to defeating Communism and prevailing in the Cold War, even if it meant executing their own citizens to do so.

This fear of appearing spineless, of course, would dominate U.S. foreign policy beyond the 1950s. Indeed many American undertakings abroad—interventions in Southeast Asia, for example—can be attributed to maintaining a strong, formidable appearance. Lyndon Johnson echoed his predecessors when he explained years later that the "minute we look soft, the would-be aggressors will go wild. We'll lose all of Asia and then Europe and we'll be an island all by ourselves."[6]

Federal officials, however, could have acted differently, and plausible contingencies can be considered as a way of understanding how individuals helped shape these events.[7] FBI Director Hoover could have exposed the existence of the Venona program, or Truman could have been informed about the decryptions and made the decision to disclose the program himself.[8] If officials had somehow managed to use the secret cables in court, the jury would have concluded that Ethel played only a minor role and possibly not convicted her. Julius may still have been found guilty, but perhaps only served prison time.[9] Alternately, if the Supreme Court had allowed Justice Douglas's stay to remain in effect, the high court would have reconsidered the case in October 1953. Anti-Communist hysteria had subsided during the ensuing months, and with new Chief Justice Earl Warren the Rosenbergs might have received a reduced sentence, possibly even a new trial.[10] The case could have returned to lower courts under the Atomic Energy Act, likely resulting in a reduced sentence for Julius and freedom for Ethel.[11]

Or, during the clemency debate, Eisenhower could have listened to some advisers, spent some political capital, and reduced the death sentence to thirty years. J. Edgar Hoover wanted to reconsider Ethel's death sentence, while propaganda adviser C. D. Jackson offered numerous suggestions to encourage the couple to name names. Jackson, along with many diplomats around the world, urged reconsideration of the executions in the hopes of mitigating the negative publicity overseas and the damage it was causing to America's image and ability to lead in the Cold War. The Rosenbergs might have languished in prison, with occasional visits from their sons, perhaps eventually breaking down and naming names. The absence of an impending execution date would have kept the Rosenbergs off of front pages around the world, and the prison sentence would have clearly distinguished American justice from the suspect judicial processes involved in Soviet show trials and executions.

What if federal officials had ensured the Rosenbergs a fair trial? The irregularities and illegalities of the case were disturbingly numerous. As lawyer and scholar Robert Lichtman summarized, the "prosecutors were guilty of misconduct, the defense lawyers barely competent, Judge Kaufman's death sentence for Ethel 'a grave miscarriage of justice,' and the Supreme Court's performance patently inadequate."[12] A retrial even just a few months later may have rendered a different verdict or a less severe sentence. While the defendants were not innocent of conspiracy, problems with the trial created space for protesters to argue that they were.[13]

A stronger, judicially sound case would certainly have helped improve America's image abroad. While propaganda officials found it relatively simple to sell skittish Americans on the guilt and execution of the atomic spies, they were far less effective overseas.[14] The newly discovered documents tell the story of dissent among allies and potential allies, and Truman and Eisenhower administration bumbling. Officials assumed that protesters were Communist led and inspired, but outspoken and powerful critics—including Pope Pius XII, Chief Rabbi Herzog of Israel, artist Pablo Picasso, philosopher Jean-Paul Sartre, and French President Vincent Auriol—soon spanned the political spectrum and fanned the flames of protest in more than forty-eight countries. As the Rosenberg appeals process continued, the image of the United States became more tarnished and White House officials failed to get ahead of the spin. Propagandists wove a narrative but they could not control how it was received; what resonated in one part of the world fell flat in another. For example, what appeared reasonable in Western Europe seemed imperialistic to many Latin Americans. U.S. government officials assumed the global population would be less skeptical about their tactics, and grossly underestimated the negative reaction.

Eisenhower saw the executions as a display of strength, but friends and allies scattered across every continent perceived them as senseless violence

Map 2 World Protest Map—Cities with Documented Rosenberg Case Protest, 1952–1954. Courtesy of Ben Emerzian.

motivated by paranoid anti-Communism. Protesters around the globe decried the gap between American rhetoric and reality. They saw the persecution of the Rosenbergs not as an example of American freedom, justice, and democracy, but the exact opposite. And as historian David Caute observed: "When official America sins, she sins doubly; against her victims, and against her own traditions, ideal, and rhetoric."[15]

Put on the defensive as a result of the dissent on the Rosenberg case, Eisenhower shifted his public stance to show the world he was committed to waging peace. While he would use agencies such as the CIA to covertly continue his hardline Cold War agenda, outwardly he portrayed himself as the ultimate peaceful Cold Warrior.

Though propaganda agencies failed to convince allies and potential allies in Third World nations that the executions were necessary, it would be incorrect to deduce that officials did not care about winning hearts and minds around the world. Truman and Eisenhower created agencies—the PSB, the OCB, and the USIA—to coordinate Cold War propaganda. Eisenhower appointed C. D. Jackson as his special assistant in charge of psychological warfare and propaganda and placed him at his side in the White House. Layers of government bureaucracy and countless taxpayer dollars were dedicated to the propaganda arm of the Cold War. Both presidents were routinely updated on global reactions to U.S. policy. Administration officials cared about world opinion of the United States and strove to learn from the Rosenberg execution publicity debacle.

In the end, officials rejected any of the alternate paths in the Rosenberg case and executed the couple. Julius and Ethel took the names of other members of the military spy ring to their graves. It was in such difficult circumstances, when under political threat and in the shadow of a terrifying mushroom cloud, that the nation displayed its moral character. While the actions of the pressured Truman and Eisenhower administrations can be understood, that does not mean they should be praised.

As for the defendants, Julius and Ethel Rosenberg were two of the estimated 50,000 CPUSA members during World War II; Julius was part of the less than 1 percent of party members who engaged in espionage for the Soviet Union.[16] Issues of the Rosenbergs' guilt and innocence are neither neat nor tidy. Indeed, the label "the Rosenbergs" has evolved into a mythical creation, used and abused by all sides to represent some distortion of the truth. The Rosenbergs are alternately A-bomb spies, Communists, guilty traitors, and innocent victims. They are leads in a devastating morality play that explains more about the nature of American Cold War justice than the crimes committed.

The Rosenbergs must be examined individually to tease out something approaching the truth. Julius Rosenberg spied for the Soviet Union. As Michael Meeropol admitted in November 2014, "My father HAD been involved in stuff."[17] By all accounts Julius spied for ideological reasons. His handler, Alexander Feklisov, claimed Julius approached aiding Soviet Communism as a "religious calling."[18] Julius acted as a military intelligence Robin Hood, taking from the wealthy capitalists and giving to the poor Communists. While he primarily recruited others to the cause, he personally turned over a prototype proximity fuse to the KGB. The Soviets later used this technology to shoot down Francis Gary Powers in his U2 reconnaissance plane when they caught him spying over the Soviet Union.[19]

A committed Communist, Julius Rosenberg undoubtedly saw his efforts to help the Soviet Union as a way to fight fascism and make the world a more peaceful place for his children. Julius successfully spied for the Soviets after the Germans invaded the Soviet Union and continued following the defeat of the Nazis. Idealistic and naïve, Julius kept spying even after Soviet Union was discredited as an authoritarian regime that employed political repression, purges, and deadly show trials to silence dissent. While in prison he claimed that he was continuing to battle fascism, arguing that in American leaders he saw "a pattern of pro fascist and bellicose actions."[20] Executing Julius may have been legally possible, but proved foolish since the goal was pressuring him to name other spies.

Ethel Rosenberg had no codename and likely engaged in no active spying of her own.[21] She was, however, cognizant of her husband's espionage activities and thus in the eyes of the jury guilty of conspiracy.[22] Federal officials threatened her with the death penalty—surely a form of torture—in a desperate effort to get Julius to talk. Convincing the global community she deserved to die, however, proved nearly impossible. Years later a justice official confirmed the failure in their strategy, admitting, "She called our bluff."[23] Executing Ethel was the cruel, unjust act of a terrified nation for which the U.S. government can and should apologize.

Scholars continue to debate the value of the atomic material Julius Rosenberg forwarded to the Soviets.[24] Legally, however, it does not matter. Spies would surely prefer to transfer material of significance and worth if given the chance. If they do not, it is not for lack of trying. The debatable worth of the atomic information David Greenglass provided did make a difference in one area: it presented a propaganda challenge. The seemingly inconsequential nature of the material made it far more difficult to convince protesters overseas of the seriousness of the crime and the necessity of the sentence.

While the significance of Greenglass's contribution is questionable, other spies did speed up Soviet acquisition of nuclear technology. Without any atomic espionage, the Soviets likely would have developed the bomb by the mid-1950s instead of 1949.[25] It was not a question of if the Soviets would get the bomb, but when. There may, however, have been a benefit to speeding up nuclear parity between the United States and the Soviet Union. Perhaps the "long peace" following World War II, as historian John Lewis Gaddis has called it, remained free of global conflict precisely because the Americans and Soviets could checkmate each other with mutually assured nuclear destruction.[26]

In the years after the Rosenberg case, federal prosecutors were hesitant to threaten the death penalty to get defendants to provide more information since they had learned how badly it could backfire. Officials also did not want to declassify the secret documents or reveal the covert sources necessary to meet the threshold required for a death penalty conviction.[27] In the long run, the Rosenberg executions did not discourage espionage activity in the United States. Federal authorities would capture more spies during the Reagan administration than at any other time during the Cold War.[28]

Another legacy of the case was Korea. Though officials had blamed the Rosenbergs for starting the Korean War, their executions did not, of course, bring peace to the region. More than sixty years after the armistice, Korea remains a divided land.

In 2006 the French celebrated the one-hundredth anniversary of Captain Alfred Dreyfus's exoneration. President Jacques Chirac himself eulogized the falsely accused man, declaring unequivocally that Dreyfus had not committed treason.[29] The Jewish captain's redemption was complete and cathartic, and resulted in his commemoration on a stamp. The Dreyfus case had become a litmus test for religious tolerance and individual rights.[30]

Some also see the Rosenberg case as a litmus test, but drawing similarities between Captain Dreyfus and Julius and Ethel Rosenberg only goes so far. Protesters were doubtful the couple had engaged in espionage, especially as information dribbled out about improper irregularities in the case. But Rosenberg supporters were left waiting for a redemptive moment. The difference, of course, was that Alfred Dreyfus was innocent of all charges. Julius Rosenberg spied for the Soviet Union and Ethel knew about it. The couple did not deserve to die, and they were certainly innocent of giving "the secret" of the atomic bomb to the Soviets. But did their actions warrant a sixty-year effort to exonerate them?

As a legacy for the liberal left, the Rosenberg case was terrifically damaging. When liberal and progressive organizations joined the growing protest movement in the United States and around the world, they actively campaigned for people they believed were innocent victims of aggressive anti-Communism and likely anti-Semitism. These protesters looked naïve when claims of complete innocence could not be sustained. Historians cannot agree on the relative significance of CPUSA espionage, but they do agree that Julius Rosenberg turned over military secrets to the Soviets. In 2008, Morton Sobell publicly acknowledged this. By refusing to admit this fact, Julius and Ethel discredited the political left, both in the United States and around the world.

In her final note to Manny Bloch, dashed off in pencil before she was escorted to the death chamber, Ethel claimed she was convinced she and Julius would be "vindicated by history."[31] Earlier that day Ethel and Julius signed a letter to their sons imploring them to, "Always remember that we are innocent and could not wrong our conscience."[32] On Michael's tenth birthday Julius had explained: "We must hold fast to the truth, to the fact that we are innocent and have the courage of our convictions. Daily more and more people all over the world are coming to our support and are realizing the true nature of our case and we are confident they will help set us free."[33] Hundreds of thousands of protesters around the globe joined the cause, believing the couple was innocent or the death sentence was unjust. The American government's propaganda apparatus failed to convince the protesters they should not try. Their efforts, in turn, failed to set the Rosenbergs free.

At an event for the Rosenberg Fund for Children in 2014, an activist who grew up near the couple argued that the government might have arrested anyone in the neighborhood rather than Julius. "They could have picked on any one of them," she claimed.[34] That is unlikely. Yes, innocent activists were swept up in the hysteria of the Red Scare, where rights were violated and abuses of justice often occurred. But Julius was a spy. While he did not wrap up an atomic bomb and hand it to the Soviets, he did pass along military secrets. The government targeted him for his espionage activities, not his activism.

Officials within both the Truman and Eisenhower administrations spun their sanctioned narrative of the case. They asserted that the Rosenbergs were traitorous spies who by giving "the secret" of the atomic bomb to the Soviet Union endangered national security, prompted the Korean War, and thus deserved to die. As newly discovered documents demonstrate, that quixotic and fraudulent version of events failed to convince protesters around the world, and tarnished the image of the United States on the world stage. The same false narrative continues to distort popular and academic history to this day. Julius and Ethel Rosenberg—through their actions and deception—led liberals on a wild goose chase and tarnished the global credibility of liberalism. Cold War terror and paranoia drove the U.S. government to prosecute the couple, but in killing them federal officials truly failed. They failed to compel the couple to talk. They failed to deter future spies. And they ultimately failed to convince the world that executing the Rosenbergs was anything but a morally repugnant travesty of justice.

ABBREVIATIONS

ACLU	American Civil Liberties Union
AEA	Atomic Energy Agency
AEC	Atomic Energy Commission
AFP	Agence France Presse
AJC	American Jewish Committee
CCR	Committee for Clemency for the Rosenbergs
CDR	Committee for the Defense of the Rosenbergs
CIA	Central Intelligence Agency
CRC	Civil Rights Congress
CRR	Committee for the Rehabilitation of the Rosenbergs
CSCEJR	Committee to Secure Clemency for Ethel and Julius Rosenberg
CSJJER	Committee to Secure Justice for Julius and Ethel Rosenberg
CSJMSRC	Committee to Secure Justice for Morton Sobell in the Rosenberg Case
CSJRC	Committee to Secure Justice in the Rosenberg Case
CSR	Committee to Save the Rosenbergs
DDEL	Dwight D. Eisenhower Library
DPRK	People's Democratic Republic of Korea (North Korea)
FBI	Federal Bureau of Investigation
FOIA	Freedom of Information Act
FRUS	Foreign Relations of the United States
FSD	Foreign Service Despatch
GRU	Foreign Military Intelligence of the Soviet Union
HSTL	Harry S. Truman Library
HUAC	House Committee on Un-American Activities
KGB	Committee for State Security of the Soviet Union
NA	National Archives II, College Park, MD

NATO	North Atlantic Treaty Organization
NCRRC	National Committee to Reopen the Rosenberg Case
NCSJRC	National Committee to Secure Justice in the Rosenberg Case
NCSR	National Committee to Save the Rosenbergs
NSA	National Security Agency
NSC	National Security Council
PRC	People's Republic of China
PSB	Psychological Strategy Board
ROK	Republic of Korea (South Korea)
RFC	Rosenberg Fund for Children
SVR	Russian Foreign Intelligence Service
UN	United Nations
UNAEC	United Nations Atomic Energy Commission
USIA	United States Information Agency
VOA	Voice of America

NOTES

Preface

1. Diplomats in the 1950s communicated primarily via telegram or air-pouch memoranda. As Hannah Gurman explains, having these voices heard by those who crafted policy was challenging. "According to one estimate, there were more than 100,000 dispatches a year and 7,500,000 words a month streaming into the department after World War Two, all of which had to be processed in a timely manner." See Gurman, *The Dissent Papers*, 15.
2. Name Card Index 1950–54, Decimal File, Record Group 59, General Records of the Department of State, National Archives II at College Park, MD (hereafter cited as NA), author count June 2008, confirmed June 2009.
3. Sam Roberts, "Figure in Rosenberg Case Admits to Soviet Spying," *New York Times*, September 12, 2008; and Sam Roberts, "Father Was a Spy, Sons Conclude with Regret," *New York Times*, September 17, 2008.
4. J. Edgar Hoover, "The Crime of the Century," *Reader's Digest* 58 (May 1951): 149–168. In an interview with historian Ron Radosh, Robert Lamphere stated that FBI Agent Fern Stukenbroeker ghostwrote Hoover's article. See Radosh and Milton, *Rosenberg File*, 499.
5. No scholar has explored the impact of this reaction on the Truman and Eisenhower administrations, or detailed much beyond the United States, France, and the Soviet Union. Ron Radosh and Joyce Milton, in their comprehensive account of the Rosenberg case, only briefly mention the concerns of the propaganda arm of the White House, and include only a few State Department cables. No one put the Rosenberg case into a broader international context and used it to study the efficacy of Truman and Eisenhower propaganda efforts. In 1955, Robert B. Glynn explored the Rosenberg case as reported in the French press, but it was beyond the scope of his work to delve into the coverage in other countries. See Glynn, "L'Affaire Rosenberg in France," 498–521. David and Emily Alman received copies of some State Department documents in 1974. The Almans referenced these documents in their brief look at the clemency movement abroad in *Exoneration*. However, these copies have been held within the Alman Collection at the Howard Gotlieb Archival Research Center at Boston University, and to the best of my knowledge have not been used by any historian. I thank Andrew David for his research assistance.
6. I also searched for their sons, Michael and Robert Rosenberg, since they did not change to their adopted parents' name, Meeropol, until 1957. The index goes from "Rosenberg, Max" to "Rosenberg, Mildred Lee"; the three cards for "Rosenberg, Robert" do not refer to the younger son of the famous couple.
7. Phone conversation with David Pfeiffer, July 10, 2008. The only *Foreign Relations of the United States (FRUS)* references are three documents concerning the Rosenbergs located in the State Department's bound historical record series, United States Department of State, *Foreign Relations of the United States, 1952–1954, Volume II, Part 2* (Washington, D.C., 1984),

1640–1641, 1668–1670, 1736. The document from The Hague on page 1736 appears to have been mislabeled with 511.00/8-1853 and placed in Box 2245. This is why the editors of *FRUS* were able to locate it. I think it should have been labeled 761.5211 Rosenberg. Julius/8-1853 and filed in Box 3820.

8. Cable from Ambassador Dillon to Secretary Dulles, 2, May 16, 1953, File: R, Box 5, C. D. Jackson Records, 1953–54, Dwight D. Eisenhower Library (hereafter DDEL).

9. Ibid.

10. I contacted Michael Meeropol (the eldest Rosenberg son) asking if he had any information concerning the "missing" Name Cards, and he graciously responded that he was "quite surprised" and stated he would check the documents concerning the case he and his brother, Robert, received from their Freedom of Information Act (FOIA) request. "It would be fascinating," he wrote, "if the State Department materials were pulled sometime after 1953 to get rid of embarrassing materials like the Dillon memo—maybe the Dillon memo was not unique." July 4, 2008 email, in author's possession.

11. Email from David Pfeiffer, July 28, 2009, in author's possession. Pfeiffer later described the discovery not as luck, but rather "an intelligent guess, a very intelligent guess."

12. For example, Edward Savage, a State Department official from 1950 to 1974, declassified all Rosenberg correspondence from U.S. diplomats stationed in Europe.

Acknowledgments

1. Anthony Salvatore Scimeca, FBI File 100-432296, FOIAPA 1060894-001. Despite inactivity the FBI did not close his case until 1960.

Introduction

1. Quoted in Roberts, *Brother*, 19.

2. One reporter described the five-foot, one hundred-pound woman as "small and plump." William R. Conklin, "Pair Silent to End: Husband is First to Die—Both Composed on Going to Chair," *New York Times*, June 20, 1953, 1.

3. Bob Considine reported for the International News Service and a portion of his statement can be found in Goldstein, *Unquiet Death*, 2–3, and Philipson, *Ethel Rosenberg*, 350–351.

4. Gabe Pressman, a reporter for the *World-Telegram and Sun*, was stationed outside the prison gates. He recalled the day in "Remembering the Day of the Rosenberg Executions: Looking Back 59 Years Later," http://www.nbcnewyork.com/news/local/The-Day-of-the-Rosenberg-Execution-160065505.html.

5. Many historians label 1945–1960 the early Cold War. For a discussion of the Cold War periodization, see Dudziak, *War Time*, 76–85.

6. DDE, Annual Message to the Congress on the State of the Union, February 2, 1953, available at the American Presidency Project, http://www.presidency.ucsb.edu/ws/?pid=9829.

7. See Preston, "Monsters Everywhere," 499.

8. For a thorough discussion of issues of weakness and masculinity and their impact on early Cold War foreign policy, see Cuordileone, *Manhood*.

9. See Cuordileone, *Manhood*, vii.

10. See Dudziak, *War Time*, 83.

11. See Cuordileone, *Manhood*, 37–38.

12. According to K. A. Cuordileone, the moral decline included the "decline of traditional small-town American values, the advent of secularism, juvenile delinquency, sexual immorality, divorce, pornography, crime, apathy, welfare statism, the corrosive effects of commercialism, popular entertainment, and (for the most reactionary of conservatives) racial or ethnic integration." Cuordileone, *Manhood*, 39.

13. See Logevall, *Embers of War*, 710.

14. See Cuordileone, "The Torment of Secrecy," 619.

15. These spies likely included Treasury Assistant Secretary Harry Dexter White, senior Franklin D. Roosevelt aide Lauchin Currie, senior OSS officer Duncan Lee and assistant Maurice Halperin, some 15–20 additional agents within the OSS, and State Department officials

Laurence Duggan, Alger Hiss, and Noel Field. Duggan jumped out a sixteenth-story window after FBI agents questioned him in late 1948. See Haynes, Klehr, and Vassiliev, *Spies*, 220. Soviet espionage rings were largely dismantled after Elizabeth Bentley's defection in 1945, and "the lack of active sources crippled the KGB's activities in the United States during the first years of the Cold War." Haynes, Klehr, and Vassiliev, *Spies*, 520.

16. For simplicity I use the term KGB to refer to State Security operations of the Soviet Union, known at different times by different names. Soviet military intelligence was coordinated by GRU, also known at different times by different names.

17. See Haynes, Klehr, and Vassiliev, *Spies*; Olmsted, *Red Spy Queen*; Sibley, *Red Spies*; Usdin, *Engineering Communism*.

18. President Truman formed the NSA in 1952, though its creation was not acknowledged publicly until the 1970s.

19. For a comprehensive discussion of Venona, see Haynes and Klehr, *Venona*. Also see Moynihan, *Secrecy*, and for NSA Venona documents see www.nsa.gov/public_info/declass/venona/dated.shtml. For skepticism concerning the Venona cables, which represent a small fraction of hundreds of thousands of Soviet messages, see Cuordileone, "The Torment of Secrecy," 622, note 12.

20. The liaison was FBI agent Robert Lamphere.

21. Weisband was an American citizen born in Egypt to Russian parents. He likely tipped off the KGB after he was reactivated in February 1948. See Usdin, *Engineering Communism*, 119. For more on Weisband, see Haynes and Klehr, *Venona*. On Philby's espionage activities, see Macintyre, *A Spy Among Friends*.

22. Newspaper columnist Robert D. Novak contends that Truman was informed. See Novak, "Did Truman Know About Venona?" *History News Network*. For Haynes and Klehr's response see http://historynewsnetwork.org/article/1706.

23. The final source of espionage information came from a fleeting examination of Soviet KGB files. Between 1994 and 1996, in the aftermath of the Cold War, the Russian Foreign Intelligence Service arranged for a journalist and former Soviet operative, Alexander Vassiliev, to dip into KGB archival files. A Russian committee only allowed Vassiliev and American historian Allen Weinstein to see this information, per an agreement with—and a large sum of money earmarked for retired KGB agents from—an American publishing house. The Russians limited the files Vassiliev could see (he was not given access to Julius Rosenberg's personal file) and vetted Vassiliev's notes before Weinstein could read them. This account provides incomplete descriptions of Soviet espionage efforts in the United States from the 1930s through the early 1950s. Vassiliev was also able to smuggle out additional unvetted notes before the Russians closed the archives. Historians handle problematic sources carefully, and espionage sources are no exception. Disclosures from former spies, notebooks prepared by a former KGB agent, incomplete Venona transcripts, inaccessible documents, and potentially prejudiced FBI files all prompt caution among scholars. While some historians argue that these records cannot be the final word, they do offer a tantalizing glimpse into the range and character of Soviet espionage and American counterintelligence activities. Historians have used this imperfect raw material to paint the most comprehensive picture yet of Soviet espionage. For a thorough discussion of these KGB files, see Weinstein and Vassiliev, *Haunted Wood*; Haynes, Klehr, and Vassiliev, *Spies*; Theoharis, *Chasing Spies*; and Cuordileone, "The Torment of Secrecy." See also H-Diplo Article Roundtable Review, Volume X, No. 24 (2009), July 17, 2009, http://h-diplo.org/roundtables/PDF/Roundtable-X-24.pdf. For complete, translated transcripts of Vassiliev's notebooks, see http://digitalarchive.wilsoncenter.org/collection/86/Vassiliev-Notebooks. For the Rosenberg case see, for example, April 14, 1951—Yellow Notebook #1, 161–163 (doc p 51–53).

24. Quoted in Cuordileone, "The Torment of Secrecy," 629.

25. See Usdin, *Engineering Communism*, xii.

26. See Cuordileone, "The Torment of Secrecy," 634.

27. Sobell quoted in Ronald Radosh and Steven T. Usdin, "The Sobell Confession," Weekly Standard, March 28, 2011.

28. See Sibley, *Red Spies*, 176.

29. For the traditional view that, while crude, anti-Communism was a rational response to the threat of the CPUSA, its mission, and its spies, see works by Haynes, Klehr, and Radosh. For

the perspective that the CPUSA story should be told from the bottom up, focusing on day-to-day organizing and progressive achievements, see Schrecker, ed., *Cold War Triumphalism*.

30. By the time the Red Scare reached its zenith with a new level of aggressive and reckless anti-Communism, the threat had already passed. Senator McCarthy's witch-hunting actions grabbed headlines from 1950 to 1954, after Soviet espionage had ended.

31. Usdin, "The Rosenberg Ring Revealed," 92.

32. Barr [Scout, Meter], David Greenglass [Bumblebee, Caliber, Zinger], Ruth Greenglass [Wasp, Ida], McNutt [Fogel, Persian], Perl [Gnome, Yakov], Sarant [Hughes], Sidorovich [Lens], Sobell [Senya], and Sussman [Tuk, Nil]. See Haynes, Klehr, and Vassiliev, *Spies*, 338–340. Rosenberg and Sobell met Perl at City College. Perl, an aeronautical engineer, later denied working with Rosenberg and was convicted of perjury in 1953. Sussman and Saritsky were electrical engineers. Sarant and Barr fled to Czechoslovakia upon Rosenberg's arrest and later defected to the U.S.S.R., where they founded the Soviet Silicon Valley in Zelenograd. See Usdin, *Engineering Communism*, and Usdin, "The Rosenberg Ring Revealed." Sobell admitted to photocopying "hundreds of pages of secret Air Force documents stolen from a Columbia University [aerospace engineer] professor's safe in 1948." See Sam Roberts, "A Rosenberg Co-Conspirator Reveals More About His Role," *New York Times*, March 20, 2011; Radosh and Usdin, *Weekly Standard*, March 28, 2011.

33. All such timetables are rough estimates, based on when the Soviets began to develop the bomb, their engineering and scientific accomplishments, their ability to secure uranium, and whether the spy information they received was complete, reliable, helpful, misleading, or out-dated. It was not a question of if the Soviets would get the bomb, but when. For a thoughtful discussion of these issues see Gordin, *Red Cloud at Dawn*, 63–88.

34. See Haynes, Klehr, and Vassiliev, *Spies*, 143.

35. McNutt was never exposed and denied being a spy to his death in 2008. Haynes, Klehr, and Vassiliev, *Spies*, 39.

36. See Cuordileone, "The Torment of Secrecy," 626; Usdin, "The Rosenberg Ring Revealed," 93–94, 104–110, 140.

37. Historians continue to debate the value of the atomic information David Greenglass forwarded through Julius to the Soviets. In David Holloway's 400-page book on the Soviet Union and atomic energy from 1939–1956, he mentions the Rosenbergs once. Holloway, *Stalin and the Bomb*, 108. Peter Wyden claimed in *Day One*, "Greenglass's grasp of the secret material within his purview was laughable compared to Fuchs's extraordinary expertise and access." Wyden, *Day One*, 220. Richard Rhodes, in his 1986 landmark work *The Making of the Atomic Bomb*, does not mention David Greenglass, or the Rosenbergs, at all. Rosenberg's KGB handler, Alexander Feklisov, claimed that the material Greenglass provided in January 1945 was weak because "his theoretical and technical knowledge wasn't deep enough to allow him to comprehend the objectives of the research that was underway in New Mexico." Feklisov, *Man Behind the Rosenbergs*, 278. According to Feklisov, additional information from Greenglass—"lens drawings and explanatory notes, as well as a list of potential recruits for Soviet intelligence" from June 1945 and "a sketch of the implosion bomb and about twelve pages of descriptive material and two lists" of scientists who might be recruited from September 1945—was of "minimal" value "compared to the crucial information passed on by eminent scientists such as [Klaus] Fuchs." Feklisov, *Man Behind the Rosenbergs*, 280. Greenglass's "famous drawings of the explosive lenses," which were "certainly not technical blueprints giving the size and dimensions or even just the proportions of the objects—but rather only childish sketches," had also been described by Fuchs at "around the same period." Feklisov, *Man Behind the Rosenbergs*, 298. The youngest physicist at Los Alamos, and the only American scientist to give atomic information to Soviets was Theodore Hall [Mlad]. Motivated by fear of a U.S. atomic monopoly, Hall sought nuclear knowledge parity to make the world a safer place. Venona intercepts tipped off the FBI to Hall. Agents interviewed him but never arrested him, since they lacked evidence that could be used in court. Later Hall recalled: "You know, if it comes to that, perhaps I should give myself up and say, 'Don't pin it all on the Rosenbergs because I was more responsible than they were.'" But he did not come forward. See Albright and Kunstel, *Bombshell*, 240.

38. As discussed in Roberts, *Brother*, 406.

39. See Gordin, *Red Cloud at Dawn*, 63–88.
40. Cuordileone, "The Torment of Secrecy," 626; Feklisov, *Man Behind the Rosenbergs*, 299.
41. Feklisov, *Man Behind the Rosenbergs*, 299.
42. Haynes, Klehr, and Vassiliev, *Spies*, 136, 322.
43. Usdin, "The Rosenberg Ring Revealed," 92.
44. Haynes, Klehr, and Vassiliev, *Spies*, xix, 36–39, 104–110, 119–121, 135–142, 332–349; Weinstein and Vassiliev, *Haunted Wood*, xxiii, 172, 185, 197–198, 210, 213, 291, 332–333, 342, 364. For an interactive timeline of Rosenberg espionage based on Venona, FBI files, and the Vassiliev notebooks, see Steven T. Usdin, "The Rosenberg Archive: A Historical Timeline," Cold War International History Project, Wilson Center, www.wilsoncenter.org/publication/the-rosenberg-archive-historical-timeline.
45. Iva Toguri D'Aquino (Tokyo Rose) was convicted of treason in 1949 and sentenced to ten years. Released after six years, President Gerald Ford pardoned D'Aquino in 1977, and she died in 2006 at the age of ninety. Mildred Gillars (Axis Sally) was similarly convicted of treason in 1949 and served twelve years. She was released in 1961 and died in 1988.
46. "This crime required a degree of punishment of the theft that would deter all future thieves and sustain American superiority in the nuclear arms race." See Ferguson, *Trial in American Life*, 239.
47. Brewer, *Why America Fights*, 4; Hixson, *Parting the Curtain*, 1.
48. "The definition proposed by an army field manual in 1955 is instructive: 'Psychological warfare is the planned use of propaganda and other actions that have the primary purpose of influencing the opinions, emotions, attitudes, and behavior of enemy, neutral, or friendly groups in such a way as to support the accomplishment of national aims and objectives.' In contrast, propaganda was defined more narrowly as 'the planned dissemination of news, information, special arguments, and appeals designed to influence the beliefs, thoughts and actions of a specific group.'" Kenneth Osgood, "Words and Deeds: Race, Colonialism, and Eisenhower's Propaganda War in the Third World," in Statler and Johns, eds., *Eisenhower Administration*, 19.
49. See Preston, "Monsters Everywhere," 480.
50. Osgood, *Total Cold War*, 2.
51. Brewer, *Why America Fights*, 147, 143–144. For a detailed examination of the collaboration between broadcast news and the federal government in "selling" the Cold War to Americans, see Bernhard, *U.S. Television*.
52. Lucas, "Campaigns of Truth," 300.
53. Lears, *Fables of Abundance*, 251–255; Marchand, *Advertising the American Dream*, xxi.
54. It has been more than ten years since Thomas Bender first met with seventy foreign and American scholars in the La Pietra meetings in Florence, Italy, and grappled with the issues of internationalizing the history of the United States. Examples of this growing body of work include: Bender, *Rethinking American History*; Borgwardt, *A New Deal for the World*; McGirr, "Passion of Sacco and Vanzetti," 1085–1115; and Rodgers, *Atlantic Crossings*. Several works integrate the civil rights movement into the narrative of the Cold War. See Borstelmann, *Cold War and the Color Line*; Dudziak, *Cold War Civil Rights*; and Plummer, ed., *Window on Freedom*. Both Borstelmann and Dudziak credit international pressures with propelling, to a certain extent, the American civil rights movement. According to Borstelmann there existed "no greater weakness for the U.S. in waging the Cold War than inequality and discrimination." John Foster Dulles agreed when he told a member of Eisenhower's cabinet, "this situation [in Little Rock] is ruining our foreign policy." The world watched as mass media broadcast the mistreatment of African Americans around the globe. International pressures enhanced certain elements of civil rights reform and constricted others, as policymakers in Washington, D.C., balanced domestic political pressures with concern for the gaze of the world.
55. See Andrew L. Johns, "Hail to the Salesman in Chief," in Osgood and Frank, eds., *Selling War*.
56. Agencies in Great Britain, Canada, and Australia all implemented some version of anti-homosexual policies, mostly fearing that if they did not the United States would withhold its substantial security and intelligence network. See David K. Johnson, "America's Cold War Empire: Exporting the Lavender Scare," in Weiss and Bosia, eds., *Global Homophobia*; and Johnson, *Lavender Scare*.

57. For example see Borstelmann, *Cold War and the Color Line*; Dudziak, *Cold War Civil Rights*; and Plummer, ed., *Window on Freedom*.
58. Eisenhower quoted in Dudziak, *Cold War Civil Rights*, 133. For Dudziak's discussion of the impact of federal action on the civil rights movement, see the preface to the 2011 edition of *Cold War Civil Rights*, xviii–xix.
59. For example see Osgood, *Total Cold War*, 45; Tudda, *Truth Is Our Weapon*, 1, 15, 126–128, 162. Tudda argues that Eisenhower and Dulles failed to understand the power of their words and allowed "rhetorical diplomacy" to overwhelm their actions. According to Tudda the Eisenhower administration intensified the conflict between the United States and the Soviet Union, and strained relations between the United States and her allies.
60. See Radosh and Milton, *Rosenberg File*, 277–285.
61. Kathryn Olmsted, "Historical Treatment of the Rosenberg Case Panel, Conference on the Rosenberg Case, Soviet Espionage, and the Cold War," George Washington University, Washington, D.C., June 22, 2011. The morning session is available at www.c-span.org/video/ ?3001821-1/historical-treatment-rosenberg-case.

Chapter 1

1. See Cumings, *Korean War*, 35; Stueck, *Korean War*, 360–370.
2. Rose, *Cold War Comes to Main Street*, 33.
3. Winkler, *Life Under a Cloud*, 29.
4. Los Alamos was one of thirty-seven sites of the $2 billion Manhattan Project, which lasted for three years and employed about 127,000 people.
5. Quoted in Rhodes, *Making of the Atomic Bomb*, 761.
6. John Hersey, "Hiroshima," *New Yorker*, August 31, 1946. The piece became a best-selling book with Knopf publishers later in 1946. For more on Hersey's report and its reception, see Boyer, *By the Bomb's Early Light*, 204–210.
7. Quoted in Boyer, *By the Bomb's Early Light*, 208. While the vast majority of letters and telegrams the *New Yorker* received approved of the piece, not all were sensitive to its meaning. One reader responded: "I read Hersey's report. It was marvelous. Now let us drop a handful on Moscow." Quoted in Boyer, *By the Bomb's Early Light*, 334.
8. Quoted in Boyer, *By the Bomb's Early Light*, 209.
9. George Orwell, "You and the Atomic Bomb," *The Tribune*, October 19, 1945, http://orwell. ru/library/articles/ABomb/english/e_abomb. For a discussion of how the cold war became the Cold War, see Hajimu, *Cold War Crucible*.
10. Rose, *Cold War Comes to Main Street*, 33.
11. Cuordileone, *Manhood*, 3.
12. Preston, *Sword of the Spirit*, 429.
13. Quoted in Preston, *Sword of the Spirit*, 413. For a discussion of Truman and his religiously inspired foreign policy, see Preston, *Sword of the Spirit*, 412–439; Smith, *Religion in the Oval Office*, 228–259.
14. Not all Protestants approved of working with the Vatican. See Preston, *Sword of the Spirit*, 414, 465–495.
15. Quoted in Preston, *Sword of the Spirit*, 413.
16. Acheson quoted in Gaddis, *Cold War*, 33.
17. See Schrecker, *Many Are the Crimes*.
18. Herbert F. York, quoted in Rhodes, *Making of the Atomic Bomb*, 327.
19. York quoted in Rhodes, *Making of the Atomic Bomb*, 760.
20. Quoted in Winkler, *Life Under a Cloud*, 67.
21. Truman, "Statement by the President Announcing the Use of the A-Bomb on Hiroshima," August 6, 1945, available at the American Presidency Project, http://www.presidency.ucsb. edu/ws/?pid=12169.
22. Quoted in Halberstam, *Fifties*, 36.
23. The Smyth Report bore the official title *Atomic Energy for Military Purposes*. Holloway, *Stalin and the Bomb*, 173. See also Gordin, *Red Cloud at Dawn*, 93–104.

24. The Smyth Report represented the "faded echo of Niels Bohr's appeal for openness." Rhodes, *Making of the Atomic Bomb*, 750.

25. For a discussion of the failure of the United States, the Soviet Union, and Great Britain to champion international control and pre-empt a nuclear arms race see Bundy, *Danger and Survival*, 130–196; Winkler, *Life Under a Cloud*, 34–56. It is worth remembering that the Manhattan Project was not a solely American effort; British, Canadian, and German émigré scientists were crucial to the bomb's development. Similarly, the Soviet project included Russians, Ukrainians, Georgians, and Germans. See Gordin, *Red Cloud at Dawn*, 19–21. Years later Einstein admitted to chemist Linus Pauling: "I made one great mistake in my life—when I signed the letter to President Roosevelt recommending that an atomic bomb be made." Quoted in Wyden, *Day One*, 342.

26. Winkler, *Life Under a Cloud*, 45–46.

27. The UNAEC was operational from January 1946 to mid-1948, and supported an American plan to create an international agency that would own processed uranium and set penalties for violations with no Security Council veto power. Having not tested their own bomb yet, the Soviets could not support this and abstained from the vote that "ended any real hope of acceptance." Winkler, *Life Under a Cloud*, 53. The disclosure of spies in the British team in Los Alamos halted cooperation between the United States and Great Britain, until the British announced their own successful nuclear test in October 1952. See Bundy, *Danger and Survival*, 470.

28. See Holloway, *Stalin and the Bomb*, 173–189; Rhodes, *Making of the Atomic Bomb*, 750–751; Smyth Report, http://www.atomicarchive.com/Docs/SmythReport/.

29. *Iowa Democrat & Leader*, September 23, 1949.

30. Boyer, *By the Bomb's Early Light*, 69; Rose, *Cold War Comes to Main Street*, 313.

31. Target cities included New York, Los Angeles, Chicago, Detroit, Milwaukee, Fort Worth, San Francisco, and Philadelphia. Rose, *Cold War Comes to Main Street*, 311–313.

32. The *Bulletin* has changed the clock every few years responding to changing conditions, with the most optimistic in 1991, 17 minutes before midnight coinciding with the end of the Cold War in 1991. Scientists moved it to 3 minutes before midnight in January 2015: http://thebulletin. org/clock/2015. See Winkler, *Life Under a Cloud*, 39–40, and Rose, *Cold War Comes to Main Street*, 99.

33. Neville, *Press*, ix. There appeared to be no end to the things to be afraid of in the late 1940s. Polio would soon reach an epidemic level, randomly afflicting young children from coast to coast and causing fever, paralysis, a life sentence in an iron lung, and sometimes death. See Oshinsky, *Polio*.

34. Leo Cherne, "How to Spot a Communist," *Look* 11, no. 5, March 4, 1947, 21–25.

35. Ibid.

36. Hearst columnist Westbrook Pegler, "U.S. Should Execute Communists as Its Foes," *New York Journal-American*, June 29, 1950, 3. Quoted in Neville, *Press*, 14–15.

37. See White, *Alger Hiss's Looking-Glass Wars*; Jacoby, *Alger Hiss and the Battle for History*.

38. Quoted in Halberstam, *Coldest Winter*, 191.

39. Cuordileone, *Manhood*, 45.

40. Cuordileone, *Manhood*, 45.

41. "Watching and Waiting for Peace," *Newsweek*, February 20, 1950, 17.

42. Whitfield, *Culture of the Cold War*, 30–31. For a discussion of McCarthy's tactics see Cuordileone, *Manhood*, 91.

43. Another spy who provided atomic information to the Soviets was George Koval. In 2007, Russian President Vladimir Putin posthumously awarded Koval its highest civilian honor, Hero of the Russian Federation, for transmitting information from the Manhattan Project from roughly 1940 to 1948. See William J. Broad, "A Spy's Path: Iowa to A-Bomb to Kremlin Honor," *New York Times*, November 12, 2007, A1. In their preface to *Spies*, Haynes and Klehr contend that Russian military intelligence may have been exaggerating Koval's role in atomic espionage to bolster their image. See *Spies*, ix.

44. The crucial information Fuchs provided is described as "unparalleled," of "great value," and likely saved the Soviets years in the development of their atomic technology. See Holloway,

Stalin and the Bomb, 107–108; Rhodes, *Making of the Atomic Bomb*, 770; Sibley, *Red Spies*, 163–166.

45. The Soviets made a mistake when they allowed Gold to be courier for both Fuchs and Greenglass.

46. Fuchs died in Dresden in 1988.

47. *New York Times*, February 1, 1950, 1.

48. Ibid.; Rhodes, *Making of the Atomic Bomb*, 770. Bundy argues that Fuchs's confession, four days before the president's announcement, "came too late to influence Truman's action, but it would have had a quite different weight if the president had been leaning the other way," *Danger and Survival*, 217.

49. Oppenheimer participated in the State Department Panel of Consultants on Disarmament in recommending a moratorium on hydrogen bomb testing in October 1952. See Bird and Sherwin, *American Prometheus*, 450.

50. Thanks to *Washington Post* political cartoonist Herbert Block who coined the term in March of 1950, critics now had a name for this particularly virulent form of anti-Communism—"McCarthyism."

51. Quoted in Cuordileone, *Manhood*, 46.

52. Ibid.

53. "A Report to the National Security Council by the Executive Secretary on U.S. Objectives and Programs for National Security—NSC-68," April 14, 1950, President's Secretary's File, HSTL, www.trumanlibrary.org/whistlestop/study_collections/coldwar/documents/sectioned.php, 60 (declassified by the authority of Henry Kissinger in February 1975). For religious crusade elements in NSC-68, see Preston, *Sword of the Spirit*, 429.

54. NSC-68, 60.

55. Ibid.

56. NSC-68, 56.

57. NSC-68, 63.

58. Dudziak, *War Time*, 89.

59. North Korea launched five raids at the same time that day. For detailed descriptions of early maneuvers in Korea and Washington, D.C., see Millett, *War for Korea*.

60. See Halberstam, *Coldest Winter*, 201.

61. Cumings, *Korean War*, 139.

62. Millett, *War for Korea*, 46.

63. Cumings, *Korean War*, 142–143. According to Bruce Cumings: "Anyone who thinks they know exactly what happened in June 1950 is insufficiently well read in the documentation; there is still much more to be learned from Soviet, Chinese, and North and South Korean archives—and from the U.S. National Security Agency, which still has not declassified crucial signals intelligence on the Korean War." Cumings, *Korean War*, 260, FN 47.

64. Kathryn Weathersby, "Soviet Aims in Korea and the Origins of the Korean War, 1945–1950: New Evidence from Russian Archives," Working Paper No. 8, Cold War International History Project, November 1993, 36.

65. Stalin rejected Kim in March 1949 and September 1949. The Soviet Politburo told Kim that the September 1949 request was "ill-timed" and "impermissible." See Hunt and Levine, *Arc of Empire*, 134; Stueck, *Rethinking the Korean War*, 70–72.

66. Stalin quoted in Stueck, *Rethinking the Korean War*, 73.

67. Stalin quoted in Hunt and Levine, *Arc of Empire*, 134.

68. Ibid.

69. Acheson contended this phrase was taken out of context. Dean Acheson, "Speech on the Far East," National Press Club, January 12, 1950, http://www.foia.cia.gov/sites/default/files/document_conversions/44/1950-01-12.pdf.

70. See Holloway, *Stalin and the Bomb*, 276–278. Many historians still agree with what Truman believed in 1950, in spite of contradictory evidence. On page 143 of *Spies*, Haynes, Klehr, and Vassiliev argue: "Confident that his possession of atomic weapons neutralized America's strategic advantage, Stalin was emboldened to unleash war in Korea in 1950." On page 631 of "The Torment of Secrecy: Reckoning with American Communism and Anticommunism after

Venona," *Diplomatic History* 35, no. 4 (September 2011), K. A. Cuordileone explains: "That Soviet possession of the bomb also had the effect of emboldening North Korea to invade South Korea is also accepted by many historians." On page 160 of Schrecker, ed., *Cold War Triumphalism*, Maurice Isserman and Ellen Schrecker claim the bomb "may well have contributed to Stalin's decision to give Kim Il Sung a green light to invade South Korea." While Truman believed the bomb influenced the June 1950 invasion, and it certainly influenced the president's actions, historians are ill advised to continue to cite it as fact.

71. Preston, *Sword of the Spirit*, 479.
72. Quoted in Beisner, *Dean Acheson*, 396.
73. See Millett, *War for Korea*, 50; Cumings, *Korean War*, 6.
74. Papers of George Elsey, June 26, 1950, HSTL, quoted in Halberstam, *Coldest Winter*, 92–93.
75. Resolution 82 demanded North Korea end its invasion and Resolution 84 called on UN member nations to provide military assistance to South Korea.
76. In addition to the United States, the following countries provided troops to assist Republic of Korea forces: Great Britain, Canada, Australia, Belgium, the Netherlands, Colombia, Ethiopia, South Africa, New Zealand, Turkey, Greece, Thailand, the Philippines, and Luxembourg.
77. See Millett, *War for Korea*, 86.
78. See Casey, *Selling the Korean War*, 367; Cumings, *Korean War*, 243.
79. For the impact of the Korean conflict on U.S. intervention in Vietnam, see Logevall, *Embers of War*, 256–259.
80. Truman Press Conference, June 29, 1950, available at the American Presidency Project, http://www.presidency.ucsb.edu/ws/index.php?pid=13544.
81. Truman's July 19, 1950 radio address. See Casey, *Selling the Korean War*, 69.
82. Neville, *Press*, 11. Neville claims that the mainstream American press covered the case in line with the federal government's "anti-Communist story," 107.
83. Stueck, *Korean War*, 357. For government propaganda efforts within the United States during the Korean War see Marilyn Young, "Hard Sell: The Korean War," in Osgood and Frank, eds., *Selling War In a Media Age*, and Casey, *Selling the Korean War*.
84. The Rosenbergs lived at 10 Monroe Street, apartment GE-11. Knickerbocker Village, located in lower Manhattan between the Manhattan and Brooklyn Bridges, was the first apartment development to receive federal funding to be built in the early 1930s. This building was an improvement for the Rosenbergs since for the first time they had an elevator and hot running water. For biographic information on the Rosenbergs, see Radosh and Milton, *Rosenberg File*; Philipson, *Ethel Rosenberg*; Roberts, *Brother*; and Meeropol, *Execution in the Family*.
85. Roberts, *Brother*, 43. The Great Depression contributed to a rise in CPUSA membership. Harvey Klehr, citing Communist Party USA (CPUSA) leader Earl Browder's figures, states approximately 40,000 members upon CPUSA's creation in late 1919. Membership declined in the 1920s, dropping to 7,545 in 1930. The Depression prompted a rise in 1931 (9,219) and 1932 (18,119), but membership dropped again to 14,937 in 1933. Klehr, *Heyday of American Communism*, 91. According to the State Department, CPUSA membership in 1949 "reached 54,174 but has steadily declined since that time." American Embassy Moscow to State Department, June 22, 1973, File POL 13-10 US, Box 2681, General Records of the Department of State—Record Group 59 (RG 59), Subject Numeric Files, 1970-73, Political & Defense, NA. Whitfield cites some 43,000 members of the Communist Party in 1950 and 32,000 in 1951, or .0287% of the 150 million Americans, *Culture of the Cold War*, 4. Oshinsky argues that by 1950 the Communist Party "was no longer a force in American life"; *Conspiracy So Immense*, 102.
86. See Roberts, *Brother*, 47.
87. Feklisov, *Man Behind the Rosenbergs*, 107, 120. For David Greenglass's recollection of Julius's early spy activities, see Roberts, *Brother*, 52–53.
88. See Feklisov, *Man Behind the Rosenbergs*, 125–128. General George Patton claimed the proximity fuse was significant in the Battle of the Bulge victory. See Usdin, *Engineering Communism*, 116; Usdin, "The Rosenberg Ring Revealed," 114–115.
89. Haynes, Klehr, and Vassiliev, *Spies*, 105. For a detailed look at Julius and David's activities, see Schneir and Schneir, *Final Verdict*.

90. Feklisov later claimed, "The fact is, I never did meet Ethel"; *Man Behind the Rosenbergs*, 113.
91. For a thorough discussion of security at Los Alamos, and how David Greenglass, an active Communist, received his clearance, see Roberts, *Brother*, 70–87, 97, 107. Only Greenglass and Fuchs were ever prosecuted for their roles in atomic espionage, but some working in Los Alamos argued that security was so lax in the machine shops "anyone who had wanted to could have given away secrets." Roberts, *Brother*, 78.
92. Roberts, *Brother*, 104–105.
93. Quoted from the Vassiliev notebooks in Usdin, "The Rosenberg Ring Revealed," 112.
94. Roberts, *Brother*, 152, 193. Greenglass would later state that he shifted away from Communism in response to Stalin's aggressive tactics in Berlin in 1948. Roberts, *Brother*, 177.
95. Olmsted, *Red Spy Queen*, 89.
96. See Olmsted, *Red Spy Queen*, 37. For the story of Harry Gold, see Hornblum, *The Invisible Harry Gold*.
97. David later recalled this conversation from June 7, 1950, quoted in Roberts, *Brother*, 227.
98. Greenglass confessed at 9:25 p.m. on Thursday, June 15, 1950. See Roberts, *Brother*, 240.
99. Quoted in Roberts, *Brother*, 248.
100. Roberts, *Brother*, 268.
101. Officials released David Greenglass's August 3, 1950 grand jury testimony in July 2015. See www.archives.gov/research/court-records/rosenberg-jury.html, 30.
102. O. John Rogge memo quoted in Fineberg, *Rosenberg Case*, 92.
103. FBI File, New York File, Julius Rosenberg, Section 2, Serials 68–80, https://vault.fbi.gov/rosenberg-case.
104. Three-year-old Robert was already asleep; Michael had been listening to *The Lone Ranger* on the radio. Meeropol, *An Execution in the Family*, 6; Ivy Meeropol, *Heir to an Execution*, HBO Documentary Film, 2004.
105. FBI Memo from A. H. Belmont to D. M. Ladd, July 17, 1950, FBI File, Julius Rosenberg Et Al. Bureau File, 65-58236, Section 26, https://vault.fbi.gov/rosenberg-case/julius-and-ethel-rosenberg.
106. Pretrial interrogation of David Greenglass:

    Assistant U.S. Attorney Myles J. Lane: Was Ethel present in any of these occasions? David Greenglass: Never. Lane: Did Ethel talk to you about it? Greenglass: Never spoke about it to me . . . that's a fact.

    Recounted in Radosh and Milton, *Rosenberg File*, 164–165. Greenglass's grand jury testimony, released July 2015, confirmed these responses.
107. Philipson, *Ethel Rosenberg*, 245.
108. See Olmsted, "Blond Queens, Red Spiders," 78–91.
109. FBI Memo from A. H. Belmont to D. M. Ladd, July 17, 1950, FBI File, Julius Rosenberg Et Al. Bureau File, 65-58236, Section 26, https://vault.fbi.gov/rosenberg-case/julius-and-ethel-rosenberg.
110. Ibid.
111. Memo, redacted address, July 17, 1950, FBI File, New York File, Julius Rosenberg, 65-15348, Section 3, https://vault.fbi.gov/rosenberg-case.
112. FBI Memo from J. Edgar Hoover to Attorney General McGrath, July 19, 1950, FBI File, Julius Rosenberg Et Al. Bureau File, 65-58236, Section 26, https://vault.fbi.gov/rosenberg-case/julius-and-ethel-rosenberg.
113. Lindesay Parrott, "U.S. Line Yields in Korea Center," *New York Times*, July 28, 1950, 1; Walter Sullivan, "North Koreans' Losses Estimated at 31,000 Men, 270 of 300 Tanks," *New York Times*, July 30, 1950, 1.
114. "Atom Bomb Hits New York City," Chesley Bonestell's illustration for "Hiroshima, U.S.A.," *Collier's*, August 5, 1950, cover illustration, https://www.nyhistory.org/exhibit/atom-bomb-hits-new-york-city-illustration-hiroshima-usa-colliers-5-august-1950-cover.
115. Quoted in "Plot to Have G. I. Give Bomb Data to Soviet is Laid to His Sister Here," *New York Times*, August 12, 1950, 1, 30.
116. Ibid.

117. Sibley details pre- and early Cold War Soviet military-industrial espionage. These suc-
cesses, she argues, replicated the Soviet Union's spy effort overall, with its focus on
industrial and military intelligence. Sibley, *Red Spies in America*, 98–104, 195. As
explained, those same Venona transcripts speak to Ethel's work merely as an accessory, a coconspirator for the conspiracy charge, but not active enough to justify her
execution. Haynes, Klehr, and Vassiliev, *Spies*, xix, 36–39, 104–110, 119–121, 135–
142, 332–349; Weinstein and Vassiliev, *Haunted Wood*, xxiii, 172, 185, 197–198, 210,
213, 291, 332–333, 342, 364. See Usdin, "The Rosenberg Ring Revealed." For an interactive timeline of Rosenberg espionage based on Venona, FBI files, and the Vassiliev
notebooks, see Steven T. Usdin, "The Rosenberg Archive: A Historical Timeline," Cold
War International History Project, Wilson Center, www.wilsoncenter.org/publication/
the-rosenberg-archive-historical-timeline.
118. Letter from Lane to McGrath, April 23, 1951, File LAM 120, Box 104, Papers of J. Howard
McGrath, Attorney General Records, HSTL.
119. Per Supreme Court case, *Rosenberg v. United States*, 346 U.S. 273, 310 (1953), https://
supreme.justia.com/cases/federal/us/346/273/case.html. If the Soviet Union had been a
declared enemy during the time of the Rosenbergs' suspected spying, the couple could have
been charged with treason. Treason would have been more difficult to prove, requiring two
eyewitnesses, according to Article III, Section 3 of the U.S. Constitution. Truman administration officials, for their part, would have appreciated the flexibility in sentencing, since
perpetrators guilty of treason could be sentenced to life in prison.
120. The Espionage Act of 1917 (Section 32, Title 50 of the U.S. Code) was also used to prosecute whistleblower Daniel Ellsberg (Pentagon Papers, 1973).
121. Rosenberg Trial Transcript, http://law2.umkc.edu/faculty/projects/ftrials/Rosenberg/
RosenbergTrial.pdf, 2337.
122. Officials would continue to have a problem explaining to the global community why, for the
crime of conspiracy to commit espionage, the Rosenbergs could get either thirty years or
death, but did not have the option of a life sentence.
123. As discussed in Roberts, *Brother*, 406.
124. Rhodes does not mention Greenglass in *The Making of the Atomic Bomb*.
125. Rosenberg Trial Transcript, http://law2.umkc.edu/faculty/projects/ftrials/Rosenberg/
RosenbergTrial.pdf, 2339. Proving a conspiracy in a court of law can be challenging. It
is such a vague legal concept that Supreme Court Justice Robert Jackson, in *Krulewitch
v. United States* 336 U.S. 440 (1949), stated, "The modern crime of conspiracy is so vague
that it almost defies definition," and complained about "the long evolution of that elastic,
sprawling and pervasive offense." See https://supreme.justia.com/cases/federal/us/336/
440/case.html.
126. U.S. Attorney Irving Saypol (the lead prosecutor) expressed concern that, in Deputy
Attorney General Peyton Ford's words: "The state's intention of the [Justice] Department
to seek the death penalty for defendant Julius Rosenberg might be prejudicial and subject
for condemnation by the courts." Ford replied to Saypol: "The Department regards this case
as the most serious one of its kind thus far prepared for prosecution and one which warrants the Government's recommendation that the death sentence be imposed in the event
of conviction. For this reason and because it was necessary to impress upon the Atomic
Energy Commission, as well as the Joint Congressional Committee on Atomic Energy, the
seriousness and importance of this prosecution, I authorized the statement that [Julius]
Rosenberg's acts are considered by the Department to constitute a capital offense. There is,
of course, no question of a 'commitment' to anyone and I don't understand how the position of the Department could possibly be prejudicial or subject to condemnation by the
court. It is, therefore, unnecessary for you to make any 'advance commitment.'" Letter from
Ford to Saypol, February 28, 1951, File: Rosenberg, Box 123, Papers of J. Howard McGrath,
Attorney General Records, HSTL.
127. Gordon Dean statement, quoted in Gentry, *J. Edgar Hoover*, 421.
128. Kaufman stated he was "prepared to impose" the death penalty "if the evidence warrants."
Quoted in Roberts, *Brother*, 286; see also "Judge Irving Kaufman, of Rosenberg Spy Trial
and Free-Press Rulings, Dies at 81," *New York Times*, February 3, 1992; and Meeropol and

Meeropol, *We Are Your Sons*, 366–373. Kaufman had served as the judge for the Brothman-Moscowitz trial four months before, which many saw as a dry run of the Rosenberg case. See Zoe Schlanger, "Miriam Moscowitz, 98, Fights to Clear Her Name of McCarthy-Era Charges," *Newsweek*, August 26, 2014; Tina Susman, "64 Years Later, A Battle to Erase a McCarthy-Era Conviction," *Los Angeles Times*, November 25, 2014.

129. Zion, *Autobiography of Roy Cohn*, 65.
130. Zion, *Autobiography of Roy Cohn*, 77.
131. For the surprised reaction to Ethel's death sentence, see Radosh and Milton, *Rosenberg File*, 284–286.
132. Kaufman also consulted with Justice Department and FBI officials. *Time* magazine labeled Saypol "the nation's number one legal hunter of top Communists" since he had supervised the second Hiss trial and the prosecution of the CPUSA leaders under the Smith Act. See Caute, *Great Fear*, 63. Roy Cohn later described Saypol as having "bottomless vanity." See Roberts, *Brother*, 379–380; Radosh and Milton, *Rosenberg File*, 277–285; Zion, *Autobiography of Roy Cohn*, 68–69.
133. "Week's Casualties of U.S. in Korea Put at 1,977," *New York Times*, September 7, 1950, 7. According to Senator Styles Bridges (R-NH), the casualty figures were "being concealed" and the nation would be stunned if the Pentagon disclosed "the whole truth" about Americans killed and wounded in Korea. See "Unproved Casualties Handed to Congress," *New York Times*, August 12, 1950, 3.
134. Quoted in Cumings, *Korean War*, 14.
135. Cumings, *Korean War*, 22.
136. Quoted in Halberstam, *Fifties*, 85.
137. According to Bruce Cumings, this had less to do with defending the Chinese-Korean border and more to do with "coming to their aid because of the sacrifice of so many Koreans in the Chinese revolution, the anti-Japanese resistance, and the Chinese civil war." Cumings, *Korean War*, 25. For a thorough discussion of Mao's decision to enter the Korean War and its impact, see Millett, *War for Korea*, 291–320.
138. Millett, *War for Korea*, 297.
139. Casey, *Selling the Korean War*, 103.
140. Letters from the Korean War theater were not subject to censor, as World War II letters had been, because commanders believed soldiers could not relay any vital information in a timely manner. This unfettered flow of information had a negative impact on morale at home. See Casey, *Selling the Korean War*, 223.
141. Cuordileone, *Manhood*, 45.
142. See Oshinsky, *Conspiracy So Immense*, 177.
143. Radosh and Milton, *Rosenberg File*, 292–318.
144. The witness was the commercial photographer who took passport photos of the Rosenbergs prior to David Greenglass's arrest.
145. Roberts, *Brother*, 92–93.
146. Radosh and Milton, *Rosenberg File*, 163–164.
147. Assistant federal prosecutor James Kilsheimer, quoted in Roberts, *Brother*, 236.
148. In an interview in 2001 with *60 Minutes II*, David Greenglass admitted that prosecuting attorney Roy Cohn encouraged him to embellish his story about his sister Ethel. He no longer recalled Ethel typing any reports. See "Cold War, Colder Brother," *60 Minutes II*, CBS News, February 11, 2009, www.cbsnews.com/stories/2001/12/05/60II/main320135.shtml.
149. For Rosenberg Grand Jury Testimony see www.archives.gov/research/court-records/rosenberg-jury.html. That Ruth Greenglass avoided all punishment, while her brother-in-law and sister-in-law faced execution, would prove a bone of contention for those who protested the handling of the case. Attorney Staughton Lynd called it "monstrously disproportionate," in Lynd, "Is There Anything More to Say?," 45.
150. Sam Roberts asserts that David's handwriting was actually quite neat. See Roberts, *Brother*, 295–298.
151. Quoted in Roberts, *Brother*, 483–484.
152. Rosenberg Trial Transcript, http://law2.umkc.edu/faculty/projects/ftrials/Rosenberg/RosenbergTrial.pdf, 2291.

153. Max Lerner, "Vultures and Victims," *New York Post*, June 19, 1952, 22.
154. That same month Estes Kefauver held crime committee hearings in the Foley Square court-house. It was also the site, just weeks before, of the highly publicized Smith Act trials of the leaders of the CPUSA, creating a link between the two trials in the minds of many. In 2003 it was named the Thurgood Marshall U.S. Courthouse.
155. For a discussion of the challenges the defendants faced in securing good quality counsel in the shadow of the *Dennis* trial, especially since their lawyers served up to six months in prison, see Falk, "Saga of the Rosenbergs," 285.
156. For complete trial transcripts see *United States of America vs. Julius Rosenberg, Ethel Rosenberg, Anatoli A. Yakovlev, also known as "John," David Greenglass, and Morton Sobell*, http://law2. umkc.edu/faculty/projects/ftrials/Rosenberg/RosenbergTrial.pdf.
     At the start of the trial, Saypol asked for and received permission to sever Anatoli A. Yakovlev from the case. Yakovlev ("John," Anatoly Yatskov, Soviet vice-consul in New York City and agent in charge of Soviet atomic bomb espionage) had left the United States in late 1946.
157. The term "implosion" was, however, declassified in 1951 for the Rosenberg trial. See Alex Wellerstein, "Tale of Openness and Secrecy," 47–53.
158. Memo from Scottsmiller, November 25, 1952, FBI File, New York File, Julius Rosenberg, 65-15348, Section 47, https://vault.fbi.gov/rosenberg-case.
159. Zion, *Autobiography of Roy Cohn*, 75–76.
160. "South Korean Casualties 169,000," *New York Times*, March 7, 1951, 3.
161. Rosenberg Trial Transcript, http://law2.umkc.edu/faculty/projects/ftrials/Rosenberg/RosenbergTrial.pdf, 2078.
162. Witnesses for the defense were Julius, Ethel, the *Herald Tribune* employee who identified a photo of Harry Gold, and an attorney for Macy's who did not have a receipt for a table the Rosenbergs said they had bought there.
163. Rosenberg Trial Transcript, http://law2.umkc.edu/faculty/projects/ftrials/Rosenberg/RosenbergTrial.pdf, 2167.
164. Ibid., 2350.
165. Ibid., 2399.
166. All jurors agreed on their guilt, but one held out for hours, uncomfortable with the idea of possibly sending a woman to her death. Ted Morgan, "The Rosenberg Jury," 105. The jury consisted of ten white men, one African American male, and one female.
167. Rosenberg Trial Transcript, http://law2.umkc.edu/faculty/projects/ftrials/Rosenberg/RosenbergTrial.pdf, 2398.
168. FBI Memo, Roy J. Barloga, April 3, 1951, FBI File, New York File, Julius Rosenberg, 65-15348, Section 38, https://vault.fbi.gov/rosenberg-case.
169. By most accounts the Greenglasses were shocked by the severity of the sentence. See Roberts, *Brother*, 385.
170. Kaufman's sentencing of Sobell, Rosenberg Trial Transcript, http://law2.umkc.edu/faculty/projects/ftrials/Rosenberg/RosenbergTrial.pdf, 2462.
171. Sam Roberts, "57 Years Later, Figure in Rosenberg Case Says He Spied for Soviets," *New York Times*, September 12, 2008, A1, A14.
172. FBI Memo, Edward Scheidt, April 4, 1951, FBI File, New York File, Julius Rosenberg, 65-15348, Section 38, https://vault.fbi.gov/rosenberg-case.
173. Kaufman's sentencing of Sobell, Rosenberg Trial Transcript, http://law2.umkc.edu/faculty/projects/ftrials/Rosenberg/RosenbergTrial.pdf, 2447.
174. Ibid.
175. Kaufman was so concerned about Soviet espionage during the Cold War that he took time during the sentencing of the Rosenbergs to urge Congress "to reexamine the penal provisions of the espionage statute" to address passing atomic secrets to the Soviets in that year (1951). Kaufman, "Sentencing of Julius and Ethel Rosenberg," Rosenberg Trial Transcript, http://law2.umkc.edu/faculty/projects/ftrials/Rosenberg/RosenbergTrial.pdf, 2447–2455.
176. Ibid.
177. Ibid.
178. Ibid.

179. Ibid.

180. Ibid.

181. The "nefarious" comment is from the sentencing of David Greenglass, quoted in Ben Bradlee's analysis of the case, December 20, 1952, 3819, 11, 345, File 761.5211, RG 59, NA.

182. Kaufman, "Sentencing of Julius and Ethel Rosenberg," Rosenberg Trial Transcript, http://law2.umkc.edu/faculty/projects/ftrials/Rosenberg/RosenbergTrial.pdf, 2451–2454.

183. "U.S. Casualty Toll in Korea Now 58,550," *New York Times*, April 5, 1951, 2.

184. Brewer, *Why America Fights*, 144.

185. Halberstam, *Coldest Winter*, 149.

186. See Radosh and Milton, *Rosenberg File*, 330.

187. For example, see Goldstein, *The Unquiet Death of Julius and Ethel Rosenberg*.

188. Quoted in Roberts, *Brother*, 10.

189. Quoted in "Judge Irving Kaufman, of Rosenberg Spy Trial and Free-Press Rulings, Dies at 81," *New York Times*, February 3, 1992.

190. Zion, *Autobiography of Roy Cohn*, 76–77.

191. Ibid.

192. Ibid. Yet Roy Cohn searched for more justification. In May of 1951 he requested information on "How many women were executed during the Purge Trials in Moscow?" The reply: "No women were executed in the purge trials as very few were involved." Memo, May 9, 1951, FBI File, New York File, Julius Rosenberg, 65-15348, Section 40, https://vault.fbi.gov/rosenberg-case.

193. Casey, *Selling the Korean War*, 230–231.

194. For the political climate concerning MacArthur's sacking, see ibid., 233–244.

195. After losing the first primary in New Hampshire in the spring of 1952, Truman announced he would not run for re-election in 1952.

196. Casey, *Selling the Korean War*, 258.

197. Millett, *War for Korea*, 425; Cumings, *Korean War*, 156–157.

198. Cumings concluded: "It is now clear that Truman did not remove MacArthur simply because of his repeated insubordination, but also because he wanted a reliable commander on the scene should Washington decide to use nuclear weapons: that is, Truman traded MacArthur for his atomic policies." Cumings, *Korean War*, 156–157.

199. See Casey, *Selling the Korean War*, 358–362.

200. Approximately 4,000 Americans were executed in the electric chair between 1890 and 2008. See the database Death Penalty Information Center, www.deathpenaltyinfo.org. "Institutional Records: Sing Sing Correctional Facility," New York State Archives, http://nysa32.nysed.gov/a/research/res_topics_gen_guide_prison.shtml. In 1901, President McKinley assassin Leon Czolgosz expressed "surprise and dismay" to learn he would not be electrocuted at Sing Sing, but rather near the site of the murder in Buffalo, New York. See Rauchway, *Murdering McKinley*, 86.

201. It was this protracted appeals process which went on for more than two years that became a bone of contention. While U.S. officials saw courts weighing in on the case as a sign of a strong commitment to justice, many in the global community would criticize the years languishing on death row as a form of torture. In addition, in the time the sentences were pending, a protest movement was able to gather steam.

202. Ferguson, *Trial in American Life*, 239.

203. Letter from McGrath to Cohn, April 18, 1951, File CO 40, Box 82, Papers of J. Howard McGrath, Attorney General Records, HSTL. McGrath also sent thank you notes to Irving Saypol, Judge Irving Kaufman, and Myles J. Lane.

204. Letter from J. Edgar Hoover to Irving H. Saypol (prosecutor), March 30, 1951, FBI File, New York File, Julius Rosenberg, 65-15348, Section 38, https://vault.fbi.gov/rosenberg-case.

205. Gordon Gray was the first PSB director; Henry Kissinger was an early consultant. For more on the PSB see Hixson, *Parting the Curtain*; Lucas, "Campaigns of Truth"; Osgood, *Total Cold War*; Belmonte, *Selling the American Way*.

206. Rosenberg attorney Manny Bloch had suggested the series. See Deery, "'Never Losing Faith,'" 165. Critics viewed the *National Guardian* as a front for the Communist Party. For a discussion of the role of the KGB and the Communist Party USA in the campaign for the Rosenbergs within the United States see Radosh, "A Tale of Two Trials," 83.

207. Reuben reached out to Albert Einstein, asking him to issue a statement explaining that David Greenglass was not qualified to forward atomic bomb secrets of any value. Einstein replied that he could not issue such a statement since Greenglass's testimony was not publicly available and he could not make that judgment call about his abilities. Einstein would later join the protesters. Einstein's reply to Reuben is quoted in Roberts, *Brother*, 405.

208. Radosh and Milton, *Rosenberg File*, 322–330. In the summer of 1951 lawyers took eight-year-old Michael and four-year-old Robert on the first of what would be a dozen prison trips to visit their parents. They had not seen their parents since their arrests a year before. The sons spent time under the care of their paternal grandmother until her health issues prompted their move to the home of friends of their parents in New Jersey. Meeropol and Meeropol, *We Are Your Sons*, 98–136. That Julius and Ethel could communicate with each other and enjoy visits from their sons might surprise Americans accustomed to more severe treatment of those convicted of federal crimes. Government officials likely hoped that bringing the boys to visit would help convince Julius and Ethel to talk.

209. Julius and Ethel knew their letters would not be private; government and prison officials would read them and they would be published. For a discussion of the correspondence, see David Thorburn, "The Rosenberg Letters," in Garber and Walkowitz, ed., *Secret Agents*, 171–182. For a discussion of the criticism that the letters did not humanize the couple, see Cuordileone, *Manhood*, 112–115. For Michael's interpretation of his parents' letters, and that perhaps subconsciously, they were intended as "preparation for the possibility that he [Julius] would not live to see us grow old enough to understand," see Meeropol, ed., *Rosenberg Letters*, 629.

210. According to Radosh and Milton, the CPUSA did not support the Committee, ignored its existence, and harbored hostility toward the group, perhaps going so far as to believe the Rosenbergs were expendable. The Committee also published Julius and Ethel's letters, which garnered national and international attention. See *Rosenberg File*, 327–328.

211. Deery, "'Never Losing Faith,'" 183.

212. Ibid., 168–169, 183.

213. Ibid., 171, 182.

214. For example, see ibid., 163–191, and Deery's discussion of Australian pro-Rosenberg clemency campaigns, "Securing Justice?," 3–17.

215. "Korea Casualties of U.S. Now 73,604," *New York Times*, June 21, 1951, 3.

216. In the first fifteen months of WWII there were 80,620 casualties with 6,860 killed; during same period in Korea there were 85,469 casualties with 14,280 killed. "Newsgram," *U.S. News and World Report*, October 5, 1951, 9.

217. "Casualties Rise—No End to Conflict in Sight," *U.S. News and World Report*, October 5, 1951, 21.

218. "Newsgram," *U.S. News and World Report*, October 5, 1951, 9.

219. Quoted in Halberstam, *Fifties*, 62.

220. Cumings, *Korean War*, 157.

221. J. Robert Oppenheimer traveled to Korea to observe these tests. Cumings, *Korean War*, 156–158.

222. Cumings, *Korean War*, 157.

223. For a thorough discussion of negotiations, see Stueck, *Rethinking the Korean War*, 143–181.

224. "U.S. Casualties in Korea Up 890 to 120,269," *New York Times*, October 9, 1952, 3. The British launched their first successful nuclear bomb that same week; nearly 38,000 servicemen from the United Kingdom would die in the Korean War.

225. "Couple Calm Over Decision," *New York Times*, October 14, 1952, 18.

226. Justices Black, Frankfurter, and Burton voted to grant the petition. If Justice Douglas had supported the Rosenbergs, as he would in June 1953, he would have been the fourth vote, and the high court would have heard the case. See Lichtman, *Supreme Court and McCarthy-Era Repression*, 58.

227. *Daily Worker*, October 28, 1952, FBI File, New York File, Rosenbergs, Batch #43, https://vault.fbi.gov/rosenberg-case/julius-and-ethel-rosenberg.

228. According to the CPUSA paper, countries with protest movements included: Scotland, Ireland, England, France, China, Mexico, Canada, Australia, and New Zealand. "Rosenberg Case is Front Page News from Scotland to China," *Daily Worker*, August 7, 1952, FBI File, New York File, Julius Rosenberg, 65-15348, Section Sub E (1), https://vault.fbi.gov/rosenberg-case.

229. FSD from Winfree, AmLegation Bern to State, October 22, 1952, Box 3819, Section 10, Document 285, Central Decimal File, 1950-54, Department of State, Record Group 59 (hereafter RG 59), National Archives II at College Park, College Park, MD (hereafter NA). While the Box number is a National Archive designation, Section 10 and Document 285 refer to the author's personal cataloging method. Each of the two boxes of new material, 3820 and 3819, was divided into roughly fifty document sections. The boxes were delivered 3820, then 3819, thus 3820 contains Sections 1–10, and 3819 contains Sections 10–18. These documents are all State Department designation 761.5211 Rosenberg, Julius.

230. Bern to State, October 22, 1952, 3819,10, 285, 761.5211, RG 59, NA.

231. For a discussion comparing two twentieth century "left-wing causes célèbres"—Sacco and Vanzetti and the Rosenbergs—see Temkin, *Sacco-Vanzetti Affair*, 216, 302, n. 91. Temkin argues that Sacco and Vanzetti were executed in part *because* of the international campaign to save them. See also McGirr, "The Passion of Sacco and Vanzetti," 1085–1115. Communist and author Howard Fast also saw the connection between the cases when he wrote a novel that he published with his press for blacklisted writers. See Fast, *Passion of Sacco and Vanzetti*.

232. Another cause célèbre in 1951 was that of African American handyman Willie McGee, arrested in late 1945 for raping a white woman in Mississippi. Bella Abzug, in what she called her first civil rights case, argued that the death penalty was only being used because the defendant was black and challenged the fact that there were no African Americans on the jury. The Ku Klux Klan subsequently threatened Abzug. Protest within the United States and outside (in Paris, China, and Moscow) continued (Paul Robeson, Albert Einstein, William Faulkner, and Josephine Baker pleaded for clemency) until his execution by "traveling electric chair" in May 1951. Julius Rosenberg, in a letter to Ethel, explained they were similar to McGee because they were also political prisoners.

See "Willie McGee and the Traveling Electric Chair" on NPR, www.npr.org/templates/transcript/transcript.php?storyId=126539134. In December 1952, Deputy Assistant Secretary of State for Public Affairs (Phillips) mentioned that the State Department had received more than two thousand protests concerning the Willie McGee case. United States Department of State, *Foreign Relations of the United States, 1952–54, Volume II, Part 2* (Washington, D.C.: Government Printing Office, 1984), 1640.

233. Haynes, Klehr, and Vassiliev, *Spies*. For complete, translated transcripts of Vassiliev's notebooks, see http://digitalarchive.wilsoncenter.org/collection/86/Vassiliev-Notebooks. For Rosenberg case see April 14, 1951—Yellow Notebook #1, 161–163 (doc p 51–53).

234. KGB documents rarely mentioned Ethel other than to say she was cognizant of her husband's activities.

235. See http://digitalarchive.wilsoncenter.org/document/112856, doc p 51–53.

236. Ibid.

237. Ibid.

238. Phillip Deery contends, "This April 1951 cable was wrongly used [by Ronald Radosh in "A Tale of Two Trials," 4] as confirmation that the clemency campaign 'had been created directly in Moscow from the very start.'" Deery, "Securing Justice?," 38, n. 1: 14.

239. For an alternate interpretation of the propaganda role of the KGB and an analysis of the Rosenberg case and the Slansky trial see Radosh, "A Tale of Two Trials," 80–87; Deery, "Securing Justice?," 5–6; Deery, "'Never Losing Faith,'" 176–178.

240. Deery, "Securing Justice?," 6; "'Never Losing Faith,'" 176.

241. Quoted in Glynn, "L'Affaire Rosenberg in France," 509.

242. For a contemporary examination that links anti-Communism and anti-Semitism, see Dawidowicz, "Anti-Semitism and the Rosenberg Case," 41–45.

243. Telegram from Gifford, London to State, November 28, 1952, 3819, 10, 296, 761.5211, RG 59, NA. See also Gifford to State, December 9, 1952, 3819, 11, 307–308, 761.5211, RG 59, NA.

244. CIA Memorandum, December 29, 1952, Rosenbergs, http://www.foia.cia.gov/collection/atomic-spies-ethel-and-julius-rosenberg.

245. Telegram from Dunn, Paris to State, October 15, 1952, 3819, 10, 283, 761.5211, RG 59, NA; Telegram from Gifford, London to State, November 21, 1952, 3819, 10, 293, 761.5211, RG 59, NA; Telegram from Gifford, London to State November 28, 1952, 3819, 10, 296, 761.5211, RG 59, NA.

246. Telegram from Bunker, Rome to State, October 21, 1952, 3819, 10, 284, 761.5211, RG 59, NA; FSD from Donovan, AmEmbassy, The Hague to State, October 30, 1952, 3819, 10, 286–287, 761.5211, RG 59, NA.

247. The embassy assumed the protest letters from the Netherlands Women's Movement (Nederlandse Vrouwen Beweging) claiming to represent "tens of thousands of Netherlands women" were Communist generated; Telegram from Bunker, Rome to State, October 21, 1952, 3819, 10, 284, 761.5211, RG 59, NA; FSD from Donovan, AmEmbassy, The Hague to State, October 30, 1952, 3819, 10, 286–287, 761.5211, RG 59, NA.

248. *Daily Worker*, November 3, 1952 and November 21, 1952, FBI File, New York File, Julius Rosenberg, 65-15348, Section Sub E (1), https://vault.fbi.gov/rosenberg-case/julius-rosenberg.

249. CIA Memorandum, December 29, 1952, Rosenbergs, http://www.foia.cia.gov/collection/atomic-spies-ethel-and-julius-rosenberg. Telegram from Gifford, London to State, November 10, 1952, 3819, 10, 290, 761.5211, RG 59, NA; Telegram from Gifford, London to State, November 21, 1952, 3819, 10, 293, 761.5211, RG 59, NA; Telegram from Gifford, London to State, November 28, 1952, 3819, 10, 296, 761.5211, RG 59, NA; Telegram from Bruce, State to AmEmbassy, London, November 29, 1952, 3819, 10, 297, 761.5211, RG 59, NA.

250. Telegram from Gifford, London to State, December 9, 1952, 3819, 11, 307–308, 761.5211, RG 59, NA; Telegram from Acheson to London, December 11, 1952, 3819, 11, 311, 761.5211, RG 59, NA.

251. Telegram from Gifford, London to State, December 9, 1952, 3819, 11, 307–308, 761.5211, RG 59, NA; Telegram from Acheson to London, December 11, 1952, 3819, 11, 311, 761.5211, RG 59, NA; Document AGAM Dec 10 Acheson referred to could not be located.

252. Emphasis in original, Telegram from Gifford, London to State, November 21, 1952, 3819, 10, 293, 761.5211, RG 59, NA.

253. Memo, December 11, 1952, FBI File, New York File, Julius Rosenberg, 65-15348, Section 48, https://vault.fbi.gov/rosenberg-case/julius-rosenberg.

254. Airmail from Vest, Ottawa to State, December 22, 1952, 3819, 12, 352, 761.5211, RG 59, NA.

255. Canadian Communists were limited in Quebec because "all police organizations are on the alert to hamper communist activities of whatever nature." FSD from Butrick, Montreal to State, December 13, 1952, 3819, 11, 318–319, 761.5211, RG 59, NA.

256. Letter from Greenwell to Truman, November 8, 1952, Box 2673, The Rosenbergs, G-L, DDE White House Central Alpha File, DDEL.

257. *Daily Worker*, November 24, 1952, FBI File, New York File, Julius Rosenberg, 65-15348, Section: Sub E (1), https://vault.fbi.gov/rosenberg-case/julius-rosenberg.

258. James Clement Dunn had succeeded David K.E. Bruce, moving from Rome to Paris, when Bruce was appointed Under Secretary of State in February 1952. "Mr. Dunn to Paris," *New York Times*, February 21, 1952; Telegram from Dunn, Paris to State, copy to London, Moscow, Rome, Bonn, Berlin, and UNN for EAD, October 15, 1952, 3819, 10, 283, 761.5211, RG 59, NA.

259. Telegram from Dunn, Paris to State, copy to London, Moscow, Rome, Bonn, Berlin, and UNN for EAD, October 15, 1952, 3819, 10, 283, 761.5211, RG 59, NA.

260. Telegram from Dunn, Paris to State, October 15, 1952, 3819, 10, 283, 761.5211, RG 59, NA.

261. Memo from Edward Scheidt, June 3, 1952 and June 6, 1952, FBI File, New York File, Julius Rosenberg, 65-15348, Section 46, https://vault.fbi.gov/rosenberg-case/julius-rosenberg.

262. Ibid.
263. Memo, December 10, 1952, FBI File, New York File, Julius Rosenberg, 65-15348, Section 48, https://vault.fbi.gov/rosenberg-case/julius-rosenberg. Kaufman likely had protection when he met with Julius Rosenberg's family in December 1952, where the judge was able to offer the family little comfort. See Roberts, *Brother*, 413.

Chapter 2

1. May, *Homeward Bound*, 107; Rhodes, *Making of the Atomic Bomb*, 778.
2. In terms of TNT, the bomb dropped on Hiroshima was equivalent to 12,500 tons of TNT, Nagasaki was 22,000, and this H-bomb test was 10.4 million tons of TNT. See Rhodes, *Making of the Atomic Bomb*, 777; Bird and Sherwin, *American Prometheus*, 450.
3. Quoted in Winkler, *Life Under a Cloud*, 77.
4. Quoted in Boyer, *By the Bomb's Early Light*, 307.
5. For a discussion of anti-intellectualism in the 1952 election see Cuordileone, *Manhood*, 89–91.
6. In early July 1952 McCarthy gave his "One Communist Too Many" speech.
7. Quoted in Halberstam, *Fifties*, 54.
8. United Press reporter George Reedy quoted in Halberstam, *Fifties*, 55.
9. Quoted in Oshinsky, *Conspiracy So Immense*, 197. Marshall had been U.S. Army Chief of Staff (September 1939–November 1945), Secretary of State (January 1947–January 1949) and Secretary of Defense (September 1950–September 1951).
10. See Oshinsky, *Conspiracy So Immense*, 199–200, 235–246.
11. Quoted in Cuordileone, *Manhood*, 89.
12. Cuordileone, *Manhood*, 90.
13. American casualties were listed at 124,659. "Week's Korea Toll of U.S. Up By 1,174," *New York Times*, November 6, 1952, 3.
14. See Casey, *Selling the Korean War*, 336–339.
15. *New York Times*, November 19, 1952, 1, 18.
16. See Charles S. Murphy, Special Counsel to the President, Oral History Interview, HSTL, https://www.trumanlibrary.org/oralhist/murphy.htm, 423.
17. Truman made this offer to Eisenhower and Democratic candidate Adlai Stevenson. See Newton, *Eisenhower*, 68. Newton describes relations between Truman and Eisenhower as "frosty," 91.
18. Truman press conference, December 11, 1952, available at the American Presidency Project, http://www.presidency.ucsb.edu/ws/index.php?pid=14356.
19. Quoted in "The Story of Two Spies," *U.S. News & World Report*, January 9, 1953, 43.
20. Kaufman statement, January 2, 1953, FBI File, Julius Rosenberg Et Al. Bureau File, 65-58236, Section 63, https://vault.fbi.gov/rosenberg-case/rosenberg-referrals, 5.
21. Ibid., 9.
22. Ibid., 6.
23. Irving R. Kaufman, "Reviewing the Crime and Sentence," January 2, 1953, reprinted in the *Washington Evening Star*, June 20, 1953, clipping in Box 14, Oveta Culp Hobby (Sec of Health, Education & Welfare) Papers, 1952–1955, DDEL.
24. Radosh and Milton, *Rosenberg File*, 344.
25. Radosh and Milton, *Rosenberg File*, 335; Murphy, *Wild Bill*, 315–316.
26. See Simon and Blaskovich, *Comparative Analysis of Capital Punishment*, 78–79.
27. CIA Memorandum, December 29, 1952, Rosenbergs, http://www.foia.cia.gov/collection/atomic-spies-ethel-and-julius-rosenberg.
28. FSD from Bowman, Rome, December 1, 1952, 3819, 10, 298–299, 761.5211, RG 59, NA.
29. Ibid.
30. Telegram from Acheson to AmEmbassy, Rome, January 12, 1953, 3819, 10, 301, 761.5211, RG 59, NA.
31. Nenni would succeed in steering Italy to the right by forming a coalition government with moderates by the end of the 1950s, but his open support of the Rosenbergs in 1952 helped keep his voice from being heard in Washington.

32. Telegram from Bunker, Rome to Acheson, December 16, 1952, 3819, 11, 324, 761.5211, RG 59, NA.
33. Telegram from Steere, Warsaw to Acheson, December 9, 1952, 3819, 11, 310, 761.5211, RG 59, NA.
34. Telegram from Bonn to Acheson, December 22, 1952, 3819, 11, 350, 12, 351, 761.5211, RG 59, NA.
35. Krugler, *Voice of America*, 1, 221; Osgood, *Total Cold War*, 31, 37, 96.
36. Memorandum of Conversation from meeting with C. E. Nicholson, John N. Wilkins, and J. A. Cronin, all from Department of Justice, and Merritt N. Cootes, WE/P and Louis Atlas, IPS/E, December 12, 1952, 3819, 11, 315–317, 761.5211, RG 59, NA.
37. Merritt N. Cootes quoted in Memorandum of Conversation from meeting with C. E. Nicholson, John N. Wilkins, and J. A. Cronin, all from Department of Justice, and Merritt N. Cootes, WE/P and Louis Atlas, IPS/E, December 12, 1952, 3819, 11, 315–317, 761.5211, RG 59, NA.
38. Memorandum of Conversation from meeting with C. E. Nicholson, John N. Wilkins, and J. A. Cronin, all from Department of Justice, and Merritt N. Cootes, WE/P and Louis Atlas, IPS/E, December 12, 1952, 3819, 11, 315–317, 761.5211, RG 59, NA.
39. Ibid.
40. Telegram from State to Paris, December 13, 1952, 3819, 11, 320–322, 761.5211, RG 59, NA; Telegram from State to Rome, Paris, Moscow, Brussels, Bonn, December 18, 1952, 3819, 11, 325–326, 761.5211, RG 59, NA; Telegram from State to Rome, December 18, 1952, 3819, 11, 327, 761.5211, RG 59, NA.
41. Telegram from State to Paris and London, December 15, 1952, 3819, 11, 323, 761.5211, RG 59, NA.
42. Fast, "The Rosenberg Case," *L'Humanité*, November 14, 1952, translated and sent from Paris to J. Edgar Hoover, Howard Fast FBI file; in Rosenberg file, per Radosh and Milton, *Rosenberg File*, 350. Fast was one of the few Communists to speak out in support of the Rosenbergs. See Deery, " 'Never Losing Faith,' " 180.
43. Quoted in Neville, *Press*, 82. Bradlee later admitted in an October 1995 *Booknotes* interview with Brian Lamb that he was "a disastrous diplomat." Bradlee would famously serve as executive editor of the *Washington Post*.
44. Quoted in Neville, *Press*, 122. The Rosenberg case overlaps a period of disunity between the United States and France. Similar to disagreements over policy in Southeast Asia, relations between the United States and France were strained as government officials failed to develop clear goals and policies between 1950 and 1954, and suspicions marred relations between these two important allies. The Rosenberg case added to this disunity. For a discussion of the complicated relations between the United States and France, particularly concerning Indochina, see Statler, *Replacing France*, and Logevall, *Embers of War*, 311–316.
45. Bradlee, *Good Life*, 137.
46. Telegram from Dunn, Paris, December 4, 1952 (#3276 & 3284), 3819, 11, 305–306, 761.5211, RG 59, NA.
47. Ibid.
48. Ibid.
49. Ibid. For example, the Communist campaign used "American witch-hunting" to explain the government's refusal to readmit actor and director Charlie Chaplin into the country, and Dunn feared it would be similarly successful with the Rosenberg case. Chaplin had retained his British citizenship but lived in the United States consistently from 1914 until 1952. When Chaplin left the United States in September 1952 the U.S. government barred him from re-entry into the country for twenty years. Truman Attorney General James McGranery charged Chaplin with "moral turpitude" and having Communist Party affiliations.
50. Telegram from Dunn, Paris, December 4, 1952 (#3276 & 3284), 3819, 11, 305–306, 761.5211, RG 59, NA.
51. Ibid.
52. Ibid.
53. Some American lawyers also raised these issues. On December 19 a group of prominent Chicago lawyers wrote to attorneys throughout Illinois, asking for their support in a detailed

petition to the president urging executive clemency. Their major concerns reiterated the complaints raised in Paris. Open letter from Chicago Attorneys Love, Curtis, Kenoe, and Grant, December 19, 1952, forwarded to DDE by Attorney Stanislaus E. Basinsky, December 21, 1952, File: The Rosenbergs (1), Box 2672, Alpha File, White House Central, DDEL.

54. Bradlee sent half a dozen cables to the State department requesting information that went unanswered. Neville, *Press*, 80.

55. Robert Thayer, the CIA station chief in Paris and an old friend of Bradlee's family, financed the press attaché's trip. Bradlee met with Myles J. Lane, district attorney for New York's Southern District. Neville, *Press*, 82, 87; Bradlee, *Good Life*, 138–139.

56. Radosh and Milton, *Rosenberg File*, 374.

57. Bradlee, *Good Life*, 138.

58. Dunn, AmEmbassy, Paris to Acheson, December 20, 1952, 3819, 11, 328–347, 761.5211, RG 59, NA.

59. European cities: Belgrade, Bonn, Brussels, Copenhagen, The Hague, Helsinki, Lisbon, London, Madrid, Oslo, Rome, Stockholm, and Trieste; French colonial cities: Algiers, Casablanca, Saigon, and Tunis. Dunn, AmEmbassy, Paris, December 20, 1952, 3819, 11, 328–347, 761.5211, RG 59, NA.

60. Bradlee's 18-page report has rarely been directly quoted. The CIA would also distribute it in late January 1953 (see Chapter 3). Despite priority pouch, the Department of State did not receive Bradlee's analysis until January 8, 1953. Dunn, AmEmbassy, Paris, December 20, 1952, 3819, 11, 328–347, 761.5211, RG 59, NA.

61. Dunn, AmEmbassy, Paris, December 20, 1952, 3819, 11, 346–347, 761.5211, RG 59, NA.

62. Memo to Hoover, FBI from Lyman B. Kirkpatrick, Assistant Director CIA, August 4, 1952, Rosenbergs, http://www.foia.cia.gov/collection/atomic-spies-ethel-and-julius-rosenberg. For NCSJRC accusations of anti-Semitism, see Deery, " 'Never Losing Faith,' " 178.

63. Bradlee's analysis, AmEmbassy, Paris, December 20, 1952, 3819, 11, 346–347, 761.5211, RG 59, NA.

64. For example, see Marcus, *American Jew*, 300.

65. Ibid.

66. See Ginsberg, *Fatal Embrace*, 121; Hertzberg, *Jews in America*, 295. "An unmistakable message was being conveyed, the Jewish community was not to be identified with the Rosenbergs." Hertzberg, *Jews in America*, 360.

67. Navasky, *Naming Names*, 114. The AJC would further prove their separation in 1953 when they published S. Andhil Fineberg's *The Rosenberg Case: Fact and Fiction*, in which Fineberg reaffirmed the couple's guilt and insisted that anti-Semitism played no role in the verdict or sentence.

68. Navasky, *Naming Names*, 114.

69. In 1950 the total number of Jews in the United States was estimated at 4,500,000–5,000,000. See Marcus, *American Jew*, 385. The link between Jews and Communists reflected a long-standing fear that aviator, isolationist, and America First activist Charles Lindbergh had exploited most recently in the lead up to World War II. Andrew Preston asserts that "most Americans did not lump communism and Judaism together," *Sword of the Spirit*, 471. For anti-Rosenberg graffiti, see Deery, " 'Never Losing Faith,' " 172.

70. Sociologist Ilene Philipson argues that Americans who supported the death penalty often embraced the popular stereotype that all spies were part of a worldwide Jewish Communist conspiracy. See Philipson, *Ethel Rosenberg*, 69. See also Garber and Walkowitz, ed., *Secret Agents*, particularly essays by Morton J. Horwitz, Blanche Wiesen Cook, Alice Jardine, David Suchoff, and Karl E. Klare; Neville, *Press*; and Radosh and Milton, *Rosenberg File*.

71. Horowitz in Garber and Walkowitz, eds., *Secret Agents*, 260.

72. The ACLU board vote was 18–4. Walker, *In Defense of American Liberties*, 206; Ginsberg, *Fatal Embrace*, 121–122.

73. Vincent Lebonitte quoted in Ted Morgan, "The Rosenberg Jury," *Esquire* (May 1975): 124.

74. Ibid. Sam Roberts confirms that the jury included no Jews, "while nearly one in three residents of New York City at the time was Jewish . . . Moreover, it is debatable whether the presence of one or more Jews on the jury would have made any difference. Prosecutors said

later they were seeking to exclude only two groups categorically: Unpredictable oddballs and also housewives." Roberts, *Brother*, 302.

75. Editorial in *Toronto Daily Hebrew Journal*, November 24, 1952, quoted in Toronto flier for January 4, 1953 rally, 3819, 14, 128, 761.5211, RG 59, NA.

76. Memorandum from Simmons, Chief of Protocol, Tripoli, Libya to Stephens, January 21, 1953; translation of letter from Nahum to American Legation at Tripoli, December 31, 1953, The Rosenbergs, N-Q, Alpha File Box 2673, White House Central Files, DDEL.

77. Memorandum from Simmons, Chief of Protocol, Tripoli, Libya to Stephens, January 21, 1953; translation of letter from Nahum to American Legation at Tripoli, December 31, 1953, The Rosenbergs, N-Q, Alpha File Box 2673, White House Central Files, DDEL.

78. FSD from Davis, AmEmbassy, Tel Aviv, December 9, 1952, 3819, 11, 313–314, 13, 080, 761.5211, RG 59, NA.

79. FSD from Chase, AmConsulate Haifa, November 14, 1952, 3819, 10, 291–292, 761.5211, RG 59, NA.

80. Ibid.

81. Telegram from Bonn, December 22, 1952, 3819, 11, 350, 12, 351, 761.5211, RG 59, NA.

82. Ibid.

83. Telegram from Acheson, State to Bonn, December 23, 1952, 3819, 12, 353, 761.5211, RG 59, NA.

84. Telegram from Dunn, Paris, December 23, 1952, 3819, 12, 354, 761.5211, RG 59, NA.

85. Ibid.

86. Telegram from Acheson to Paris, December 24, 1952, 3819, 12, 357, 761.5211, RG 59, NA.

87. Telegram from Achilles, Paris, December 29, 1952, 3819, 13, 059–060, 761.5211, RG 59, NA.

88. Telegram from Achilles, Paris, January 5, 1953, 3819, 13, 072, 761.5211, RG 59, NA; Telegram from Acheson to Paris, January 6, 1953, 3819, 13, 079, 761.5211, RG 59, NA.

89. Telegram from Acheson to Paris, January 6, 1953, 3819, 13, 079, 761.5211, RG 59, NA.

90. Telegram from Paris, page two missing, January 6, 1953, 3819, 13, 080, 761.5211, RG 59, NA.

91. Underlined by hand in original. Telegram from Paris, page two missing, January 6, 1953, 3819, 13, 080, 761.5211, RG 59, NA.

92. Ibid.

93. Telegram from Achilles, Paris, January 8, 1953, 3819, 14, 110, 761.5211, RG 59, NA; Telegram from Achilles, Paris, January 9, 1953, 3819, 14, 134–146, 761.5211, RG 59, NA.

94. Communist coverage could be seen in the Communist paper *Ce Soir*, which focused on the horrors of death by execution. Telegram from Achilles, Paris, January 8, 1953, 3819, 14, 110, 761.5211, RG 59, NA; Telegram from Achilles, Paris, January 9, 1953, 3819, 14, 134–146, 761.5211, RG 59, NA.

95. Telegram from Achilles, Paris, January 9, 1953, 3819, 14, 134–146, 761.5211, RG 59, NA.

96. Ibid.

97. Ibid.

98. FSD from The Hague, December 23, 1952, 3819, 12, 355–356, 761.5211, RG 59, NA.

99. FSD from Chalker, AmConGen, Duesseldorf, Germany, January 2, 1953, 3819, 13, 065, 761.5211, RG 59, NA; FSD from Timberlake, AmConGen, Hamburg, January 9, 1953, 3819, 14, 131–133, 761.5211, RG 59, NA.

100. FSD from Timberlake, AmConGen, Hamburg, January 9, 1953, 3819, 14, 131–133, 761.5211, RG 59, NA.

101. FSD from AmConGen, Amsterdam, January 8, 1953, 3819, 14, 106–108, 761.5211, RG 59, NA.

102. Ibid.

103. Ibid.

104. The Norwegian Communist paper *Friheten* gave the case prominent front-page treatment, declared the Rosenbergs were not Communists, and urged readers to write a "storm of protests to save them." The fact that very little coverage was found in the Oslo non-Communist press seemed to American officials to confirm Communist control of the protest. Telegram from Bay, Oslo, January 8, 1953, 3819, 14, 109, 761.5211, RG 59, NA. The legation in

Budapest, Hungary, received a telegram concerning the Rosenberg case from a group of workers and students at the local Technical Teachers College, demanding freedom for the "innocent peace-fighter couple." Press coverage in Budapest continued "half-heartedly" with an article in *Szabad Nép,* which questioned the procedures followed in the trial and featured an "anti-Semitic angle." Telegram from Budapest, January 9, 1953, 3819, 14, 130, 761.5211, RG 59, NA.

105. Telegram from Cowen, Brussels, January 7, 1953, 3819, 14, 105, 761.5211, RG 59, NA; Telegram from Cowen, Brussels, January 27, 1953, 3819, 17, 276, 761.5211, RG 59, NA.

106. FSD from Miller, AmEmbassy, Brussels, January 15, 1953, 3819, 15, 187–188, 761.5211, RG 59, NA.

107. Ibid.

108. Telegram from Cowen, Brussels, January 11, 1953, 3819, 14, 139, 761.5211, RG 59, NA.

109. Ibid.

110. Telegram from Acheson to Brussles, January 13, 1953, 3819, 14, 137, 761.5211, RG 59, NA.

111. Telegram from Bunker, Rome, January 12, 1953, 3819, 14, 148, 761.5211, RG 59, NA.

112. Ibid.

113. Ibid.

114. FSD from Hudson, Milan, December 24, 1952, 3819, 12, 358–360, 761.5211, RG 9, NA.

115. Ibid.

116. Ibid. For example, for Communist-led protests in Israel, see FSD from Tyler, AmConGen, Jerusalem, June 24, 1953, 3820, 6, 052, 761.5211, RG 59, NA.

117. Lord Chorley, F. Elwyn Jones, MP, and Gerald Gardiner; Telegram from Gifford, London, January 6, 1953, 3819, 13, 078, 761.5211, RG 59, NA.

118. A statement Ambassador Walter Sherman Gifford vehemently disagreed with. Ibid.

119. Their placards read: "Remember Sacco and Vanzetti!" "Toronto's Citizens Urge: Commute the Death Sentence!" "'I am amazed, outraged'—Dr. H. C. Urey—Nobel Prize Winner—Famed Atomic Scientist!" "'Rosenberg Verdict Hysterical'—C. E. Raven, Chaplain to Queen Elizabeth II." FSD from Haering, Consulate General, Toronto, Canada, January 2, 1953, 3819, 13, 066–068, 761.5211, RG 59, NA.

120. A "fairly impressive" crowd turned out to hear Alfred E. Kahn, a "vehement" speaker and author who emphasized the questionable quality of the witnesses in the case, the lack of objectivity of the judge (was he a "real Jew"?), and the "emotion-laden" atmosphere in which the case was tried. Kahn highlighted the Cold War tension, "war-profiteering, anti-Semitism, and anti-peace psychology," going so far as to charge that "civil defense A-bomb drills were designed by the government to induce war tension and make high taxes more palatable to the people," a provocative reference to the then-classified NSC-68. On January 12 the Toronto Consulate General forwarded *The Canadian Tribune* (Communist press) coverage of Alfred E. Kahn's rally speech on January 4. Air Pouch from Vest, AmEmbassy, Ottawa, January 5, 1953, 3819, 13, 073–076, 761.5211, RG 59, NA; FSD from Colquitt, Consulate General, Toronto, Canada, January 9, 1953, 3819, 14, 121–129, 761.5211, RG 59, NA.

121. FSD from Colquitt, Consulate General, Toronto, Canada, January 9, 1953, 3819, 14, 121–129, 761.5211, RG 59, NA.

122. The petition stated: "It may not be said that the great people of the United States, borne upon a wave of hysteria, put to death a man and his wife for a crime no greater . . . than those which earned for many proven traitors during the last war sentences of imprisonment. Let it not be said of American justice in the Rosenberg case what has been said of the Sacco-Vanzetti case." Air Pouch from Vest, AmEmbassy, Ottawa, January 5, 1953, 3819, 13, 073–076, 761.5211, RG 59, NA.

123. Letter from Vest, US Embassy, Ottawa, January 7, 1953, 3819, 13, 084–086, 761.5211, RG 59, NA.

124. Radosh and Milton, *Rosenberg File,* 347.

125. Neville, *Press,* 98.

126. *New York World-Telegram & Sun,* January 10, 1953, 2, quoted in Neville, *Press,* 99.

127. "The Story of Two Spies," *U.S. News & World Report*, January 9, 1953, 42.
128. "Espionage: Still Defiant," *Time*, January 12, 1953, 21.
129. *New York Herald Tribune*, January 7, 1953, 3.
130. *New York Times*, January 7, 1953, 3.
131. Ethel Rosenberg to Manny Bloch, December 18, 1952, quoted in Neville, *Press*, 87.
132. December 25, 1952 letter in Meeropol, ed., *Rosenberg Letters*, 528. The Rosenbergs celebrated Chanukah but also embraced a secular Christmas. See Meeropol and Meeropol, *We Are Your Sons*, 122, 171.
133. The CRC also produced a booklet claiming there was a frame-up against the Rosenbergs. See Deery, " 'Never Losing Faith,' " 180; Neville, *Press*, 88–89.
134. Sorin, *Howard Fast*, 255; "Pickets Keep Up Rosenberg Plea," *New York Times*, December 29, 1952, 8.
135. Canadian National Committee to Save the Rosenbergs flier, January 1953, 3819, 13, 075, 761.5211, RG 59, NA.
136. Ibid.
137. See Okun, ed., *Rosenbergs*. Pablo Picasso urged all Frenchmen to appeal in writing to Truman on behalf of the Rosenbergs. He also produced portraits of Julius and Ethel Rosenberg that were widely copied to draw attention to the couple. Picasso gave the originals to the Rosenberg sons; Schneir, *Invitation to an Inquest*, 180. Letters were often read at protest rallies. For example, a letter from Bertold Brecht to Ernest Hemingway was read to a German crowd; "Rally in East Berlin," *New York Times*, January 7, 1953, 3.
138. Quoted in January 8, 1953, 3819, 16, 242, 761.5211, RG 59, NA.
139. Ibid.
140. "Cry of 'Save Rosenbergs' Sweeps World Art, Science, Literary Circles," *Daily Worker*, January 14, 1953, FBI File, New York File, Julius Rosenberg, 65-15348, Section Sub E (3), https://vault.fbi.gov/rosenberg-case/julius-rosenberg.
141. Memorandum from Wilber, State Department, January 5, 1953, 3819, 13, 069, 761.5211, RG 59, NA; Statement to State Department, January 5, 1953, 3819, 13, 070–071, 761.5211, RG 59, NA.
142. Ibid.
143. Ibid.
144. Ibid.
145. Ibid.
146. Alpha File, Box 2673, The Rosenbergs, Files: F, G-L, M, N-Q, White House Central Files, DDEL; January 7, 1953, Official File, Box 1761, File: 3480, Papers of HST, HSTL.
147. Ibid.
148. Truman quoted in Preston, *Sword of the Spirit*, 413. See also Smith, *Religion in the Oval Office*, 243–247.
149. Alpha File, Box 2673, The Rosenbergs, Files: F, G-L, M, N-Q, White House Central Files, DDEL; January 7, 1953, Official File, Box 1761, File: 3480, Papers of HST, HSTL.
150. For example, the Communist paper *Hoy* in Havana, Cuba reported that Minister Angel Campa promised to intercede personally on behalf of the Rosenbergs, and transmit a petition for clemency from the Democratic Federation of Cuban Women. Telegram from Beaulac, Habana, Cuba, January 7, 1953, 3813, 13, 081, 761.5211, RG 59, NA. The Cuban Communist Party urged its members to flood the American Embassy in Havana with telegrams protesting "the legalized murder of the Rosenbergs." CIA Memorandum, January 31, 1953, Rosenbergs, http://www.foia.cia.gov/collection/atomic-spies-ethel-and-julius-rosenberg. The same day the Textile Industry Labor Union of Guatemala, in the name of women textile workers, wrote to Truman requesting clemency for the Rosenbergs. Translator's Summary of Correspondence from Guatemala to Truman, January 7, 1953, OF-3480, Box 1761, Official File 3477-3480, Papers of HST, HSTL. In Chile, multiple groups that the CIA labeled Communist-front organizations conducted rallies and letter writing campaigns to save the Rosenbergs. Pamphlets supporting the candidacy of Salvador Allende and the People's National Front (Frente del Pueblo) in his unsuccessful run for president in the fall of 1952 included reasons to protest the execution of the Rosenbergs, and the PNF continued to distribute them even after Allende's early career defeat. Ultimately elected in

1970, Allende served until the Pinochet coup on September 11, 1973. "A pamphlet titled *Programa del Frente del Pueblo* (FRENAP) it outlined the Frente del Pueblo program"; CIA Memorandum, February 3, 1953, Rosenbergs, http://www.foia.cia.gov/collection/atomic-spies-ethel-and-julius-rosenberg. The embassy in Guatemala reported that "a significant number" of the fifty-eight deputies in the Guatemalan Congress (part of the left-leaning Arbenz government) had signed a petition demanding pardons for the Rosenbergs based on what they saw as the questionable legality of their trial. Twenty-two of fifty-eight deputies signed petition. While a few signers represented the Communist Party, the majority did not. The petition appeared to be part of a "minor propaganda campaign," but both the Communist press and the pro-government paper also carried similar articles condemning the Rosenberg death sentence. FSD from AmEmbassy, Guatemala, December 20, 1952, 3819, 11, 348–349, 761.5211, RG 59, NA.

151. FSD from Walmsley, AmEmbassy, Rio de Janeiro, January 15, 1953, 3819, 15, 189–191, 761.5211, RG 59, NA.
152. FSD from Walmsley, AmEmbassy, Rio de Janeiro, January 15, 1953, 3819, 15, 191, 761.5211, RG 59, NA.
153. *Daily Worker*, January 11, 1953, FBI File, New York File, Julius Rosenberg, 65-15348, Section Sub E (3) https://vault.fbi.gov/rosenberg-case/julius-rosenberg; FSD from Hill, Am Consulate General, Marseille, France, January 12, 1953, 3819, 14, 150, 15, 151, 761.5211, RG 59, NA.
154. FSD from Hill, Am Consulate General, Marseille, France, January 12, 1953, 3819, 14, 150, 15, 151, 761.5211, RG 59, NA.
155. Ibid.
156. "Einstein Supports Rosenberg Appeal," *New York Times*, January 13, 1953, 15.
157. Ibid.
158. Telegram from Dunn, Paris, January 14, 1953, 3819, 15, 166, 761.5211, RG 59, NA.
159. FSD from Sacksteder, American Consulate, Lyon, France, January 14, 1953, 3819, 15, 164–165, 761.5211, RG 59, NA.
160. Ibid.
161. FSD from Free, AmEmbassy, Rome, January 19, 1953, 3819, 16, 219–220, 761.5211, RG 59, NA.
162. FSD from Chalker, AmConGen, Duesseldorf, January 15, 1953, 3819, 15, 181–182, 761.5211, RG 59, NA.
163. FSD from West, Bonn, December 2, 1952, 3819, 10, 302, 11, 303–304, 761.5211, RG 59, NA.
164. FSD from West, Bonn, December 2, 1952, 3819, 10, 302, 11, 303–304, 761.5211, RG 59, NA.
165. Ibid.
166. "Rally in East Berlin," *New York Times*, January 7, 1953, 3..
167. FSD from Beerner, HiCoG, Bonn, February 4, 1953, 3819, 17, 300, 761.5211, RG 59, NA.
168. Telegram from Acheson to Paris, January 8, 1953, 3819, 14, 111, 761.5211, RG 59, NA.
169. FSD from Cunningham, US ConGen, Winnipeg, Canada, January 12, 1953, 3819, 14, 140–147, 761.5211, RG 59, NA; FSD from US Consulate General, Winnipeg, Canada, January 14, 1953, 3819, 15, 158–159, 761.5211, RG 59, NA.
170. Air Mail from Clattenburg, ConGen, Montreal, Canada, January 15, 1953, 3819, 15, 192–193, 761.5211, RG 59, NA.
171. Ibid.
172. Ibid.
173. Press coverage of the demonstrations was limited to the Communist Party weekly paper, *Tribune*. The Toronto Consul General wondered if "silence of the Toronto press on this subject has been due in part to the influence of certain authorities who are friendly to the United States and the Consulate General" and not actually a representation of the concerns of Toronto Canadians. FSD from Haering, ConGen, Toronto, Canada, January 16, 1953, 3819, 15, 194–197, 761.5211, RG 59, NA; FSD from Cavanaugh, AmConsulate, Windsor, January 19, 1953, 3819, 16, 215–218, 761.5211, RG 59, NA.

174. FSD from Cavanaugh, AmConsulate, Windsor, January 19, 1953, 3819, 16, 217, 761.5211, RG 59, NA.

175. Officials of the 10th Canadian District of International Fur and Leather Workers Union presented a petition, explaining that members had varying opinions concerning the guilt or innocence of the couple, but agreed on the excessiveness of the death sentence "on purely humanitarian grounds" and concern the executions would do "much evil both at home and abroad" to the "American democratic tradition." Memo from Vest, U.S. Embassy, Ottawa, Ontario, Canada, January 9, 1953, 3819, 14, 118, 120, 761.5211, RG 59, NA. In response, the Ottawa Embassy sent a propaganda update to all Canadian consular offices, emphasizing the role of the Communist Party in organizing mass meetings, picketing, pamphlets, and petitions in Ottawa, Montreal, Toronto, Regina, Winnipeg, and Vancouver. The embassy recommended all consulates allow picketing, receive protesters "politely and without comment," and avoid "counter-measures or counter propaganda." Memo from Ottawa to all consular offices, January 9, 1953, 3819, 14, 119, 761.5211, RG 59, NA.

176. Air Pouch from Vest, Am Embassy Ottawa, January 14, 1953, 3819, 15, 167–180, 761.5211, RG 59, NA.

177. Ibid.

178. Ibid.

179. Conservative papers highlighted the role of the Communist propaganda campaign in the clemency efforts, and explained this case was "a far cry, both in time and character, from Sacco and Vanzetti." Air Pouch from Vest, Am Embassy Ottawa, January 14, 1953, 3819, 15, 167–180, 761.5211, RG 59, NA.

180. The secretary of the Privy Council, Jack Pickersgill was one. Air Pouch from Vest, AmEmbassy, Ottawa, January 14, 1953, 3819, 15, 167–169, 761.5211, RG 59, NA.

181. Air Pouch from Vest, Am Embassy Ottawa, January 14, 1953, 3819, 15, 167–180, 761.5211, RG 59, NA.

182. Telegram from Mills, New Delhi, India, January 6, 1953, 3819, 13, 077, 761.5211, RG 59, NA.

183. Ibid.

184. Telegram from Mills, New Delhi, India, January 6, 1953, 3819, 13, 077, 761.5211, RG 59, NA; Telegram from Mills, New Delhi, January 10, 1953, 3819, 14, 138, 761.5211, RG 59, NA.

185. FSD from AmConGen, Tunis, January 13, 1953, 3819, 15, 152–153, 761.5211, RG 59, NA.

186. Telegram from Sydney, January 9, 1953, 3819, 14, 116, 761.5211, RG 59, NA.

187. Petition for Clemency, January 9, 1953, 3819, 18, 307–344, 761.5211, RG 59, NA; January 15, 1953, News Conference, HSTL.

188. Special Paper #9, January 14, 1953, RG 306, USIA, Coordinator for Psychological Intelligence, Special Papers, Box 1, File: The Rosenberg Case, State Department Papers, NA; copy in PSB Central File Series, Box 26, File: PSB 383.4, White House Office, National Security Staff Papers, 53–61, DDEL (declassified 1991).

189. Ibid.

190. Ibid.

191. Telegram from Steere, Warsaw, December 9, 1952, 3819, 11, 310, 761.5211, RG 59, NA.

192. Special Paper #9, 1, January 14, 1953, RG 306, USIA, Coordinator for Psychological Intelligence, Special Papers, Box 1, File: The Rosenberg Case, State Department Papers, 761.5211, RG 59, NA; copy in PSB Central File Series, Box 26, File: PSB 383.4, White House Office, National Security Staff Papers, 53–61, DDEL (declassified 1991).

193. Ibid.

194. Memorandum from Bonbright to Bruce, January 15, 1953, File: PSB 383.4, Box 26, PSB Central File Series, National Security Staff Papers, 53–61, White House Office, DDEL.

195. Letter from Murphy to Kirk, December 23, 1952, Box 1761, Official File, HSTL.

196. Memo from O'Connor to Kirk, December 30, 1953, File 383.4 Rosenberg Case, Box 32, PSB Files, HSTL; Memo from Sergeant to Bruce, December 29, 1952, 3819, 13, 064, 761.5211, RG 59, NA; PSB Draft of Presidential Statement on Rosenberg Case, December 30, 1952, File: Rosenberg Case Statement , Box 32, Administration Series, Ann Whitman File, 1953–1961, DDE Papers, DDEL.

197. Memo from Sergeant to Bruce, December 29, 1952, 3819, 13, 064, 761.5211, RG 59, NA.
198. Eisenhower would use similar language in his denial of clemency two months later. PSB Draft of Presidential Statement on Rosenberg Case, December 30, 1952, File: Rosenberg Case Statement, Box 32, Administration Series, Ann Whitman File, 1953–1961, DDE Papers, DDEL; and File: 383.4 Rosenberg, Box 32, Psychological Strategy Board Files, HSTL.
199. PSB Draft of Presidential Statement on Rosenberg Case, December 30, 1952, File: Rosenberg Case Statement, Box 32, Administration Series, Ann Whitman File, 1953–1961, DDE Papers, DDEL; and File: 383.4 Rosenberg, Box 32, Psychological Strategy Board Files, HSTL.
200. Memorandum from O'Connor to Kirk, PSB, January 7, 1953, File: PSB 383.4, Box 26, PSB Central Files Series, National Security Staff: Papers, 1953–1961, White House Office, DDEL.
201. Ibid.
202. Memo from Arthur M. Cox, January 15, 1953, PSB Central File Series, Box 26, File: PSB 383.4, Psychological Strategy Board, National Security Council Staff: Papers, 1953–1961, White House Files, DDEL (declassified 1999).
203. Ibid.
204. Ibid.
205. The PSB staff resorted to issuing weak statements explaining the need to improve security. In a classic case of closing the barn door after the horse has left, more than a year after the Rosenberg convictions the PSB advised the FBI to begin clearing military personnel to prevent Soviet spies. In the fall of 1952, the PSB devoted an entire staff meeting to security and espionage. Guest speakers highlighted issues based on specific spy cases. From the Rosenberg case they learned that there was no "typical Soviet spy" but that careful selection of personnel, such as clearing names with the FBI (which, amazingly, was not done in the case of David Greenglass), and "increased attention to security," they dryly noted, would be of tremendous benefit. General Staff Meeting Minutes, September 26, 1952, File: 337 Staff Meetings, 1952–1/53, Box 27, PSB Files, HSTL.
206. Letter from Myles J. Lane, U.S. Attorney (written by James B. Kilsheimer, III, Assistant U.S. Attorney) to Daniel M. Lyons, Pardon Attorney, Department of Justice, January 14, 1953, FBI File JR Et al, File HQ, 65-58236, volume 28, part 64, https://vault.fbi.gov/rosenberg-case/rosenberg-referrals, 90–99.
207. Ibid.
208. Ibid.
209. See Zion, *Autobiography of Roy Cohn*, 78.
210. According to the Gallup Poll, 73% of Americans agreed that the punishment for treason should be death, January 11–16, 1953. The answer could have been different if Americans had been asked about the appropriate penalty for conspiracy to commit espionage, or asked specifically about Ethel Rosenberg, but it is not likely; many Americans assumed the Rosenbergs had committed treason. And 54% saw Korea as the most important problem facing the nation with every other problem rating 8% or less. Gallup, *Gallup Poll*, 1117, 1118.
211. Many Americans also agreed that Communist propaganda fueled discontent overseas; a professor of history and political science at the University of Tennessee used the Rosenbergs in her International Relations class to study "the use Communists are making of this case in their propaganda." Professor Stephens requested materials on the case, which the State Department provided four months later. Letter from Ruth Stephens to the State Department, January 16, 1953, 3819, 15, 198, 761.5211, RG 59, NA.
212. Telegram from Carpenter to Truman, January 19, 1953, Box 1761, Official File, HSTL.
213. Truman News Conference, January 15, 1953, available at the American Presidency Project, http://www.presidency.ucsb.edu/ws/index.php?pid=14391.
214. See Brewer, *Why America Fights*, 169.

Chapter 3

1. "By some estimates 68% of the television sets in the country were tuned to the show." See Halberstam, *Fifties*, 200.
2. Lucille Ball and Desi Arnaz Jr., "Lucy's $50,000,000 Baby," *TV Guide* 1, no.1, April 3, 1953.

3. Ball may have held party meetings at her home, but she testified that she only joined the party to placate her socialist grandfather. Within days of her testimony, HUAC took the unprecedented action of calling a press conference and announcing that there was "no shred of evidence" linking Ball to the Communist Party. Pressure from CBS and *I Love Lucy* sponsors, particularly Philip Morris, likely prompted HUAC's action. Far from being blacklisted, in November 1953 Ball performed in front of Eisenhower on the CBS television special *Dinner with the President*. See Doherty, *Cold War, Cool Medium*, 49–59. Ball's husband, Desi Arnaz, famously quipped, "the only thing that is red about this kid is her hair—and even that is not legitimately red." Quoted in Doherty, *Cold War, Cool Medium*, 53.

4. Quoted in Doherty, *Cold War, Cool Medium*, 59.

5. Gallup, *Gallup Poll*, 1116. More Americans had watched *I Love Lucy* the night before. "The fertile Ricardos easily out-Nielsened the menopausal Eisenhowers." Doherty, *Cold War, Cool Medium*, 52. Truman's inaugural in January 1949 had been the first televised, but there were less than 200,000 sets in the country at the time.

6. Eisenhower Inaugural Address in Washington, D.C., January 20, 1953, available at the American Presidency Project, http://www.presidency.ucsb.edu/ws/?pid=9600. For a discussion of the religious themes in this address, see Kruse, *One Nation Under God*, ix–xii; Preston, *Sword of the Spirit*, 447–448.

7. This should not imply, however, that relations between Eisenhower and Truman had warmed. Their frosty presidential transition period concluded in the car on inaugural morning when, as Jim Newton describes, "the only warmth . . . came when Eisenhower asked who had ordered John Eisenhower home from Korea for the ceremony. 'I did,' Truman replied. Eisenhower thanked him, then resumed his silence for the balance of the ride." Newton, *Eisenhower*, 91.

8. "Battle Toll in Korea of U.S. Up to 128,971," *New York Times*, January 22, 1953, 2.

9. For a description of Eisenhower and McCarthy's relationship, see Oshinsky, *Conspiracy So Immense*, 234–238.

10. Petition for Clemency, January 9, 1953, 3819, 18, 307–344, 761.5211, RG 59, NA. During his administration Eisenhower would receive 4,100 petitions and pardon 1,110, while issuing commutation to 47. This is a rate similar to that of his predecessor; Harry Truman, who received 5,030 petitions, pardoned 1,913 and commuted 118. See www.justice.gov/pardon/statistics.htm.

11. Neville, *Press*, 141.

12. Even before Eisenhower launched his political career, he spoke publicly about the need for improved U.S. propaganda efforts, for example in Denver in 1950. See "A Crusade to Win Men's Minds," *Los Angeles Times*, September 6, 1950; Hixson, *Parting the Curtain*, 22.

13. Osgood, *Total Cold War*, 367.

14. Eisenhower quoted in Osgood, "Words and Deeds: Race, Colonialism, and Eisenhower's Propaganda War in the Third World," in Statler and Johns, eds., *Eisenhower Administration*, 3.

15. Statler and Johns, eds., *Eisenhower Administration*, viii.

16. Eisenhower's S.F. campaign speech, October 8, 1952, File: Robert Cutler, Box 2, C. D. Jackson Records, 1953–1954, DDEL.

17. Jamieson, *Packaging the Presidency*, 42, 85–86.

18. Eisenhower was baptized on February 1, 1953. See Inboden, *Religion and American Foreign Policy*, 257, 264–265.

19. When the president forgot to start one cabinet meeting this way, he reportedly proclaimed, "Oh, goddammit, we forgot the silent prayer." Eisenhower quoted in Preston, *Sword of the Spirit*, 442. See also Lodge, *As It Was*, 62; Inboden, *Religion and American Foreign Policy*, 266.

20. Preston, *Sword of the Spirit*, 448.

21. Eisenhower heard Reverend George M. Docherty preach about adding the phrase to the Pledge of Allegiance to distinguish it from "a similar pledge to their hammer-and-sickle flag in Moscow." Quoted in Whitfield, *Culture of the Cold War*, 89. Nearly 70% of Americans polled approved this addition. See Gallup, *Gallup Poll*, 1140.

22. Inboden, *Religion and American Foreign Policy*, 257.

23. Reagan spoke in June 1952 in Fulton, Missouri, where Churchill had given his "Iron Curtain" speech in 1946.

24. Reagan, "America the Beautiful," in Houck and Kiewe, eds., *Actor, Ideologue, Politician*, 6.

25. Quoted in Cuordileone, *Manhood*, 82, and Whitfield, *Culture of the Cold War*, 81.
26. Quoted in Whitfield, *Culture of the Cold War*, 87.
27. Ibid.
28. Inboden, *Religion and American Foreign Policy*, 258.
29. Ibid.
30. Ibid., 260. See also Whitfield, *Culture of the Cold War*, 77–100.
31. Eisenhower would succeed in restoring positive relations with the pope in 1954. See Inboden, *Religion and American Foreign Policy*, 263.
32. Dulles's grandfather was former Secretary of State John Watson Foster, who served in Benjamin Harrison's administration, and his uncle was Robert Lansing, Woodrow Wilson's Secretary of State.
33. Dulles was part of Bernard Baruch's Reparations Commission and Economic Counsel in 1919.
34. According to Jim Newton, "They occasionally disagreed. Ike watched his secretary closely at the outset and would forcefully overrule him in their later years together, but he never lost his admiration for Dulles's devotion or intellect. Eisenhower understood that Dulles brought depth and intelligence to the administration. Their relationship would form the core partnership of Eisenhower's administration." Newton, *Eisenhower*, 86. Stephen Kinzer writes, "On some days, Foster spoke personally or by telephone with Eisenhower as many as ten times. At dusk he often visited the White House for a chat over drinks." Kinzer, *Brothers*, 131.
35. Using spiritual Cold War rhetoric, Dulles criticized George Kennan's containment doctrine, stating that allowing the "Kremlin to continue to rule its 800 million captives" represented an example of "non-moral diplomacy." Yet in actual policy he stayed fairly close to containment. Dulles quoted in Inboden, *Religion and American Foreign Policy*, 231, 227.
36. Dulles confirmation hearing testimony, Senate Foreign Relations Committee, quoted in Kinzer, *Brothers*, 106. For a discussion of Eisenhower and Dulles and their approach to "spiritual diplomacy," see Preston, *Sword of the Spirit*, 442–464.
37. Telegram from Dulles to Athens, Bern, Brussels, Copenhagen, Habana, Helsinki, London, Mexico, Montivideo [*sic*], Moscow, Oslo, Ottawa, Panama, Paris, Rio de Janeiro, Rome, Santiago, Stockholm, The Hague, Wellington, Algiers, Johannesburg, Sydney, Trieste, and Bonn, January 22, 1953, 3819, 16, 226, 761.5211, RG 59, NA.
38. The State Department initially forwarded all incoming and outgoing telegrams to the president for his perusal. Just days after his inauguration Eisenhower felt inundated, and asked Dulles to stop "the flood of cables" and discuss with the president any particular problems. Telephone Conversation, DDE and JFD, January 21, 1953, File: White House Telephone Conversation January to April 1953, Box 10, Telephone Call Series, John Foster Dulles Papers, DDEL.
39. Telegram from Johnson, Sao Paulo, February 13, 1953, 3819, 18, 346, 761.5211, RG 59, NA. FSD from Stuart, First Secretary of Embassy, Montevideo, February 23, 1953, 3819, 12, 025, 761.5211, RG 59, NA; FSD from Ambassador Schoenfeld, Guatemala, February 20, 1953, 3819, 12, 021–022, 761.5211, RG 59, NA; FSD from Waynick, AmEmbassy, Bogota, February 24, 1953, 3819, 12, 026, 761.5211, RG 59, NA; FSD from Stuart, First Secretary of Embassy, Montevideo, March 20, 1953, 3820, 1, 021–022, 761.5211, RG 59, NA; FSD from Siracusa, Second Secretary of Embassy, Buenos Aires, March 25, 1953, 3820, 1, 024, 761.5211, RG 59, NA; FSD from Martindale, First Secretary of Embassy, Buenos Aires, April 7, 1953, 3820, 1, 040, 761.5211, RG 59, NA.
40. Dispatch from Aitken, Assistant Press Attaché, American Embassy, Buenos Aires, January 21, 1953, 3819, 16, 225, 761.5211, RG 59, NA; dispatch from Aitken, Assistant Press Attaché, American Embassy, Buenos Aires, January 29, 1953, 3819, 17, 298, 761.5211, RG 59, NA.
41. Operations Memorandum from American Embassy, Buenos Aires, February 4, 1953, 3819, 17, 301, 761.5211, RG 59, NA.
42. Dispatch from Johnson, First Secretary of Embassy, Ciudad Trujillo (Santo Domingo), Dominican Republic, March 9, 1953, 3820, 1, 010, 761.5211, RG 59, NA.
43. Ibid.

44. Ibid.

45. Trujillo was just one example of a dictator the Eisenhower administration supported to combat Communism in Latin America.

46. Dulles also wanted to preserve these relationships. "Do nothing to offend the dictators," he implored, "they are the only people we can depend on." Dulles quoted in diplomat Adolf A. Berle's diary, Berle and Jacobs, eds., *Navigating the Rapids*, 654.

47. For an explanation of coalition-building struggles, particularly the "great schism" between religious liberals and conservatives, see Preston, *Sword of the Spirit*, 465–495.

48. Preston, *Sword of the Spirit*, 414. HUAC investigated Oxnam after accusing him of Communist sympathies in July 1953.

49. Letter from Oxnam to Dulles, March 3, 1953 (reply March 9, 1953), 3819, 13, 050–054, 761.5211, RG 59, NA.

50. An official noted: "I think the Secretary . . . will probably wish to mention it to the President personally," but someone else wrote on the memo "acknowledge only," indicating official word never got to Eisenhower. Letter from Oxnam to Dulles, March 3, 1953 (reply March 9, 1953), 3819, 13, 050–054, 761.5211, RG 59, NA.

51. Letters to Dulles and DDE from A. J. Muste, January 22, 1953, 3819, 16, 227–236, 761.5211, RG 59, NA.

52. Ibid.

53. Ibid.

54. FSD from Pasquet, American Consul, Tananarive, Madagascar, January 24, 1953, 3819, 17, 254–255, 761.5211, RG 59, NA. The author thanks Angelique Duvet-Tovar for her translation.

55. Ibid.

56. Telegram from Bunker, Rome, January 12, 1953, 3819, 14, 148, 761.5211, RG 59, NA.

57. Ibid. Italian Communist protest continued as well, particularly when a delegation headed by Communist senators called on the American Embassy in Rome with petitions containing 3,500 signatures requesting clemency. This was the fourth such delegation over the previous four months in Rome. As with the others, it elicited no response. FSD from Freers, First Secretary of Embassy, Rome, February 2, 1953, 3819, 17, 299, 761.5211, RG 59, NA.

58. CIA Memorandum on Rosenberg Case, January 22, 1953, transcribed from the original, Rosenberg Fund for Children, http://www.rfc.org/supportingmaterial. Blanche Weisen Cook states in *Declassified Eisenhower*, 162–163, that new CIA director Allen Dulles originally made this proposal. Radosh and Milton, in *Rosenberg File*, 562, correctly disagree with Cook, stating that "the memo did not originate from Dulles, but he merely passed on the memorandum 'solely for the Bureau's information,' and he emphasized that 'no psychological warfare projects concerning the Rosenbergs should be promoted without first consulting with the FBI.' Attached to B.P. Keay to A.H. Belmont, 2/2/53, made available to Liaison Agent Keay by Allen Dulles." Julius Rosenberg Papers, FBI Headquarters Case No., HQ-65-58236-1489, https://vault.fbi.gov/rosenberg-case/julius-rosenberg.

59. CIA Memorandum on Rosenberg Case, January 22, 1953, transcribed from original, The Rosenberg Fund for Children, http://www.rfc.org/supportingmaterial.

60. Ibid.

61. Ibid.

62. February 5, 1953 letter, FBI File, New York File, Julius Rosenberg, File: 65-15348, Sub E (3), https://vault.fbi.gov/rosenberg-case/julius-rosenberg.

63. CIA Memorandum, May 15, 1953, Rosenbergs, http://www.foia.cia.gov/collection/atomic-spies-ethel-and-julius-rosenberg. After Stalin's death, relations between the U.S.S.R. and Israel resumed under Prime Minister Malenkov.

64. Ibid.

65. Evidence indicates that the Executive Council of Australian Jewry may have supported the Rosenbergs more out of sympathy for Communist causes than anti-Semitic concerns. See Mendes, "The Melbourne Jewish Left," 512–515.

66. Embassy officials noted that the ASIO, Australia's secret service, had learned of the delegation through its own investigation. The clemency appeal was signed by Dr. Michael Bialoguski, who would later play a central role in the defection of Vladimir Petrov. For a discussion of Petrov, and the links between the ASIO and American diplomats stationed in Australia, see Phillip Deery, "Securing Justice?," 7–8. FSD from Byrd, Counselor of Embassy, Canberra, January 27, 1953, 3819, 17, 277–283, 761.5211, RG 59, NA.

67. "File—W[hite] H[ouse] advised orally . . . unable to forward cc to WH prior to President's denial for clemency." Had the embassy sent a telegram it would have been received in a few hours. According the State Department Office of the Historian, in some cases sending an air pouch instead of a telegram may have been an error on the part of the diplomats. At other embassies the State Department had regulations about what should be telegraphed, instructions not to overburden telegraph facilities, and rules to only send cables under exceptional circumstances.

68. Miller had won a Pulitzer Prize for *Death of a Salesman* in 1949, but his outspoken political views attracted government attention. In 1954, the State Department withheld his passport and kept him from traveling to Brussels for a French-language premiere of *The Crucible*; he had no passport for five years. Miller was called before HUAC in 1956 and agreed to speak about himself, but not implicate others. Subsequently, he was cited for contempt of Congress, receiving a thirty-day suspended sentence and a $500 fine. Courts overturned his conviction in 1958. See Bigsby, *Arthur Miller*, 471–475; Murphy, *Congressional Theatre*, 68–69; Navasky, *Naming Names*, 61.

69. Murphy, *Congressional Theatre*, 2.

70. Several of *The Crucible* actors themselves were later blacklisted. Murphy, *Congressional Theatre*, 2, 106. Elia Kazan probably would have directed the play, as he had done for many of Miller's plays in the past, if not for a falling out over Kazan's naming-names HUAC testimony. See Bigsby, *Arthur Miller*, 438.

71. Murphy, *Congressional Theatre*, 156. According to the *Daily Worker*, on at least one occasion the play ended with a dozen curtain calls and a plea at final curtain from an audience member to "save the Rosenbergs from death." June 8, 1953, *Daily Worker*, in FBI File, New York File, Julius Rosenberg, File: 65-15348, Sub E (4), https://vault.fbi.gov/rosenberg-case/julius-rosenberg. According to Brooks Atkinson, "Neither Mr. Miller nor his audiences are unaware of certain similarities between the perversions of justice then and today." See "At the Theater," *New York Times*, January 23, 1953, 15. Historians agree with the political overtones, arguing that "at the premiere, in a gesture not purely theatrical, a wildly enthusiastic crowd called the cast back for nineteen curtain calls." See Thomas Doherty, *Cold War, Cool Medium*, 131.

72. Miller, *Crucible*, 58. Also, John Proctor's admonition to his wife—"Give them no tear. Show them a heart of stone and sink them with it"—could have been lifted straight from a letter written by Julius to Ethel Rosenberg in 1953. Miller, *Crucible*, 90. "Darling, we've got to be strong," Julius wrote, "because there is a storm of fear sweeping our land." March 13, 1952 letter in Meeropol, ed., *Rosenberg Letters*, 322.

73. Miller, *Crucible*, 80–81.

74. Arthur Miller, "*The Crucible* and the Execution: A Memoir," in Okun, *Rosenbergs*, 85–88; Miller, *Timebends*, 347; interview with author in 2003 in Bigsby, *Arthur Miller*, 411.

75. CIA Memorandum, January 30, 1953, Rosenbergs, http://www.foia.cia.gov/collection/atomic-spies-ethel-and-julius-rosenberg.

76. Ibid.

77. This relationship was strained after Eisenhower effectively demoted Smith to undersecretary of state. Smith had left the directorship of the CIA, hoping the new president would appoint him secretary of state. Eisenhower passed over Smith, appointing John Foster Dulles instead. According to Jim Newton, Smith was "invaluable to Ike, not just as an adviser, but as a counterpoint to the capable John Foster and the less reliable Allen." Newton, *Eisenhower*, 90.

78. Letter from Bloch to Smith (State), February 9, 1953, 3819, 18, 306, 761.5211, RG 59, NA.

79. Letter from Phleger (State) to Bloch, February 11, 1953, 3819, 18, 305, 761.5211, RG 59, NA.

80. FBI File, New York File, Julius Rosenberg, File: 65-15348, Sub E (3), https://vault.fbi.gov/rosenberg-case/julius-rosenberg.

81. One United Kingdom resident agreed with her and petitioned the United Nations urging its Human Rights division to conduct a formal, publicized investigation of the "judicial murders." The UN took no action. See U.S. Mission to the UN, July 16, 1953, 3820, 9, 225–256, 761.5211, RG 59, NA.

82. Other articles include the right "to a fair hearing by an independent and impartial tribunal," "the right to be presumed innocent until proved guilty," and the sanctity of the family as a "natural and fundamental group unit of society . . . entitled to protection by society and the state." See "Universal Declaration of Human Rights," http://www.un.org/en/universal-declaration-human-rights/. While critics viewed it as "unenforceable," others admitted it was "widely used as a yardstick to measure achievement." Borgwardt, *New Deal for the World*, 264.

83. For conservatives, "Eleanor Roosevelt had long served as the archetypical do-gooding, fellow-traveling, liberal bleeding-heart—'momism' politicized." Cuordileone, *Manhood*, 39.

84. The executive was from Prentice Hall Publishing Company. Memo to File from SAC, NYC, January 28, 1953, FBI File, New York File, Julius Rosenberg, et al., File: 65-15348-2156, https://vault.fbi.gov/rosenberg-case/rosenberg-referrals.

85. Memo to File from SAC, NYC, January 28, 1953, FBI File, New York File, Julius Rosenberg, et al., File: 65-15348-2156, https://vault.fbi.gov/rosenberg-case/rosenberg-referrals.

86. Ibid.

87. Ibid.

88. FSD from Smith, Second Secretary of Embassy, Brussels, January 27, 1953, 3819, 17, 284–286, 761.5211, RG 59, NA. It is unclear whether other embassies were similarly asked. The original request from Acheson (Telegram 910 of January 14) could not be located, but was referenced in the Brussels correspondence.

89. FSD from Smith, Second Secretary of Embassy, Brussels, January 27, 1953, 3819, 17, 284–286, 761.5211, RG 59, NA.

90. Ibid.

91. Ibid.

92. Ibid

93. Ibid.

94. Ibid. Chemist Harold C. Urey had belittled the significance of the Rosenbergs' actions from a scientific perspective.

95. Ibid.

96. Ibid. The White House similarly received a larger number of telegrams from Belgium in late January. Convinced they "must yield to the evidence," fifty-five Socialists urged Eisenhower to consider clemency—even though they admitted feeling "repugnance" at associating with Communist protests. FBI File, New York File, Julius Rosenberg, File: 65-15348, Sub E (3), https://vault.fbi.gov/rosenberg-case/julius-rosenberg.

97. PSB Draft of Presidential Statement on Rosenberg Case, December 30, 1952, Administration Series, Box 32, File: Rosenberg Case Statement, DDE Papers, Ann Whitman File, 1953–1961, DDEL.

98. Memo from Arthur M. Cox, January 15, 1953, PSB Central File Series, Box 26, File: PSB 383.4, PSB, National Security Council Staff: Papers, 1953–1961, White House Files, DDEL (declassified 1999).

99. In September 1953 the Operations Coordinating Board replaced the PSB. Bradley H. Patterson, "Eisenhower's Innovations in White House Staff Structure and Operations," in Warshaw, ed., *Reexamining the Eisenhower Presidency*, 37. See also Osgood, *Total Cold War*; Belmonte, *Selling the American Way*.

100. Jackson Committee Report, June 30, 1953, United States Department of State, *FRUS, 1952–54, Volume II*, 1795–1875. Committee members included Robert Cutler, Gordon Gray, C. D. Jackson, and several businessmen.

101. Osgood, "Words and Deeds," 5–6.

102. That same month Eisenhower endorsed aggressive anti-Communism and issued an executive order to address questions of loyalty among federal employees. Superseding Truman's March 1947 order establishing the Federal Employee Loyalty Program, Eisenhower's order

placed each federal department or agency head in charge of ensuring all employees were unwaveringly loyal to the U.S. government and did not pose a threat to national security.

103. PSB Draft of Presidential Statement on Rosenberg Case, December 30, 1952, Administration Series, Box 32, File: Rosenberg Case Statement, DDE Papers, Ann Whitman File, 1953–1961, DDEL. This draft is identical to Eisenhower's press release of February 11, 1953, located in the same file.

Memo from Arthur M. Cox, January 15, 1953, PSB Central File Series, Box 26, File: PSB 383.4, Psychological Strategy Board, National Security Council Staff: Papers, 1953–1961, White House Files, DDEL (declassified 1999).

104. There were 129,819 American casualties; "Korean Battle Toll of U.S. Up 395 in Week," *New York Times*, February 12, 1953, 2. Nearly two million Chinese and North Koreans were also dead; "Estimate of Enemy Casualties," *New York Times*, February 14, 1953, 2.

105. Rosenberg Trial Transcript, http://law2.umkc.edu/faculty/projects/ftrials/Rosenberg/RosenbergTrial.pdf, 2431.

106. "In Central Files is a copy of the Attorney General's letter, dated February 9, 1953, reviewing the Rosenberg case and recommending that the petition be denied. Mr. Brownell presented it personally to the President at the White House on the afternoon of February 11, at which time the President denied the petition and affixed his signature to the document." Cabinet Meeting Minutes, L. Arthur Minnich Series, File: Miscellaneous—R, January 53–June 58, Box 1, White House Office of the Staff Secretary: Records, 52–61, DDEL.

107. See Radosh and Milton, *Rosenberg File*, 344–345.

108. See ibid., 428–429.

109. Ibid.

110. On April 11 seven of the justices ruled that accusations of misconduct by the prosecution did not warrant review by the high court. Justices Black and Frankfurter dissented. See Lichtman, *Supreme Court and McCarthy-Era Repression*, 58.

111. Memorandum from Hopkins to Stephens, February 12, 1953, File: 101-R Rosenbergs (1), Box 411, Official File, White House Central Files, DDEL.

112. File: 101-R Rosenbergs (1), Box 411, Official File, White House Central Files, DDEL. Ultimately the White House received thirty large boxes of letters, wires, and petitions, but only a selection were saved. July 21, 1953, Alpha File Box 2673, The Rosenbergs, U-W, White House Central Files, DDEL.

113. FBI File, New York File, Julius Rosenberg, File: 65-15348, Sub E (3), https://vault.fbi.gov/rosenberg-case/julius-rosenberg.

114. Ibid.

115. Ibid.

116. Signs: "Uruguay Parliament Wires for Mercy" and "Do Not Hurt U.S. Prestige Abroad," in protest footage from Ivy Meeropol, *Heir to an Execution*, HBO Documentary Film, 2004.

117. Per Meeropol, ed., in *Rosenberg Letters*, 542.

118. Annette Rubinstein quoted in Duberman, *Paul Robeson*, 390.

119. Duberman, *Paul Robeson*, 390.

120. Harry Belafonte, "I put my hand through a car window in February 1953, the night the Supreme Court turned down the Rosenberg appeal." Belafonte probably meant Eisenhower's clemency denial in February since the Supreme Court acted in April and June. Navasky, *Naming Names*, 193. In England, the "Let Robeson Sing" campaign—organized in 1954 to restore Paul Robeson's passport when the State Department withheld it for political reasons—grew out of a committee originally created to try to save the Rosenbergs. Duberman, *Paul Robeson*, 424.

121. The CRC championed a broad range of civil rights issues and in doing so endured accusations of harboring Communist sympathies. FBI memo from Cleveland to Laughlin, February 16, 1953, FBI File, New York File, Julius Rosenberg, et al., Section 67, HQ File: 65-58236, Serials = June mail, https://vault.fbi.gov/rosenberg-case/rosenberg-referrals . Far more Americans paid attention to the 25th Academy Awards, the first televised from New York and Los Angeles, on March 19, 1953. FBI File, New York File, Julius Rosenberg, File: 65-15348, Sub E (3), https://vault.fbi.gov/rosenberg-case/julius-rosenberg.

122. CBS televised *Your Are There* from 1953 to 1958.

123. Doherty, *Cold War, Cool Medium*, 131.
124. Cronkite quoted in ibid.
125. FBI File, New York File, Julius Rosenberg, File: 65-15348, Sub E (4), https://vault.fbi.gov/rosenberg-case/julius-rosenberg.
126. Ibid. See also Deery, " 'Never Losing Faith,' " 182.
127. Quoted in Roberts, *Brother*, 398.
128. Ibid.
129. Quoted in ibid., 399.
130. Eisenhower also received a visit from J. Robert Oppenheimer on May 22. They met for half an hour and while there are no notes from that meeting, Oppenheimer likely urged limiting atomic bomb tests, and they may have discussed the Rosenbergs.
131. Rally Flier, File: Rosenberg Case Statement, Box 32, Ann Whitman File, 1953–1961, Administration Series, DDE Papers, DDEL.
132. March 8, 1953 letter in Meeropol, ed., *Rosenberg Letters*, 629.
133. February 1–5, 1953, Question #1a, and February 22–27, 1953, Question #2a, Gallup, *Gallup Poll*, 1123, 1129. An April 21 survey of two hundred American housewives showed just over 50% approved the death sentence specifically for Julius and Ethel Rosenberg. These results demonstrate a bit of hesitation when the death penalty was applied to specific persons rather than unnamed guilty spies. Memo to Governor Adams, April 21, 1953, File: 101-R, Rosenbergs (1), Box 411, Official File, White House Central Files, DDEL.
134. See Neville, *Press*, 142.
135. Bernhard, *U.S. Television News*, 2–4.
136. Ibid.
137. Neville, *Press*, 11.
138. By the end of May 1953 the *Washington Post* would join the *Chicago Daily News* in supporting clemency for the Rosenbergs. See Neville, *Press*, 103–104.
139. Cabinet Meeting Minutes, February 12, 1953, p. 13, Box 1, File: C-2 (1), Office of the Staff Secretary: Records, 1952–1961, Cabinet Series, White House Office Files, DDEL; and Box 1, File: Miscellaneous—R, January 1953–June 1958, L. Arthur Minnich Series, DDEL.
140. Cabinet Meeting Minutes, February 12, 1953, p. 13, Box 1, File: C-2 (1), Office of the Staff Secretary: Records, 1952–1961, Cabinet Series, White House Office Files, DDEL.
141. Ibid.
142. Ibid.
143. Ibid. This conflicts with Stephen Ambrose's record of events. In Chapter 13 of *Ike's Spies*, Ambrose explains in two footnotes that he based his section on the Rosenberg case on his interviews with Eisenhower and Attorney General Herbert Brownell, and Eisenhower's memoir of White House years 1953–1956, *Mandate for Change*. On page 182 of *Ike's Spies* Ambrose writes: "Some of Ike's most trusted advisers told him he would have to grant a stay of execution because the nation simply could not put to death the mother of small children. Many in the Cabinet recommended clemency." I do not believe any part of these statements to be true. While we cannot know what Eisenhower or Brownell told Ambrose when interviewed, in *Mandate for Change* Eisenhower makes no mention of advisers urging clemency because Ethel was a mother, or for any other reason. For cabinet recommendations, I attempted to corroborate Ambrose's account with cabinet meeting minutes. However, minutes from the two meetings where the cabinet discussed the Rosenberg case (February 12, 1953, and June 19, 1953, the day of the executions) contradict Ambrose's assertions. According to the cabinet minutes of Staff Secretary L. Arthur Minnich, no one expressed support for clemency when asked at the February meeting. During the June meeting, UN Ambassador Henry Cabot Lodge and presidential advisor C. D. Jackson suggested the need for an additional presidential statement on the case, but no one recommended clemency. According to Attorney General Herbert Brownell's oral history housed at the Eisenhower Library (interview by Ed Edwin, May 5, 1967, OH-157, 3 of 5, 189–196), Brownell stated (page 193–194): "I cannot recall that any Cabinet member voiced such a position [support for pardon] at the Cabinet meetings . . . I can't remember any Cabinet member ever dissenting from that viewpoint [that the Rosenbergs were guilty]". Brownell continued on page 196 that Eisenhower "would have subordinated his views about the world-wide effect

on the Russian government's propaganda campaign" and offered clemency if the president doubted the Rosenbergs' guilt, which Brownell asserted he did not. While it is theoretically possible that Brownell, in a subsequent (undated) interview with Ambrose, contradicted his earlier insistence that Eisenhower allow the executions to proceed, this does not hold up to the preponderance of evidence. Indeed, as discussed, while international opinion ran hot for clemency, the majority of Americans appeared to support the executions and had little problem putting "to death the mother of small children." See also Newton, *Eisenhower*, 97, 377.

144. Telephone Conversation between Dulles and James Hagerty, February 13, 1953, John Foster Dulles Papers, JFD Chronological Series, Box 1, Chronological-JFD February 1953, DDEL.

145. Ibid.

146. February 13, 1953 Press and Radio Conference, 10:35 a.m., 4:02 p.m., Box 1, Series 1, Kevin McCann: Collection of Press and Radio Conferences and Press Releases, 1952–1961, DDEL.

147. Eisenhower would also head down to Georgia and play Augusta National on February 27, 28, and March 1. During his eight years in office greater than one-third of his days included at least one round of golf (more than 1,000 days of his 2,920 days in office, or 34%). See *Golf Digest*'s chart, "Ike's 1,000-Plus Days of Golf in Office," April 2008, http://www.golfdigest.com/story/ike-2008-04.

148. Comment in a letter to his grandson David Eisenhower, November 17, 1965, Box 13, Secretary's Series, Post Presidential Papers, DDEL.

149. The putting green was installed in 1954. Intermittently since 1877 the South Lawn has been the sight of the annual Easter Egg Roll, http://www.whitehousemuseum.org/grounds/putting-green.htm.

150. See Gallup, *Gallup Poll*, 1151. Though some Americans questioned his faith when he played on Sundays in lieu of attending church. See Preston, *Sword of the Spirit*, 442.

151. "Sons at a Prison," *Life*, March 2, 1953.

152. FSD from Cushing, Information Officer, AmEmbassy, Habana, February 19, 1953, 3819, 12, 018, 761.5211, RG 59, NA.

153. February 13, 1953 letter in Meeropol, ed., *Rosenberg Letters*, 602.

154. Ibid.

155. February 13, 1953 letter in Meeropol, ed., *Rosenberg Letters*, 604. Julius also wrote to Ethel "the Attorney General brought over the file to the Presidents [*sic*] Office at 4:00 P.M. and at 5:07 PM the prepared statement was read." February 12 letter, Julius to Ethel, in Meeropol, ed., *Rosenberg Letters*, 595.

156. February 14, 1953 letter in Meeropol, ed., *Rosenberg Letters*, 606.

157. Carnegie, *How to Help Your Husband*. According to Mrs. Carnegie, Ethel's job was to "help your husband get ahead," "participate in his long-range plans," "never betray a confidence," "be prepared for emergencies," and "be a believer" when things go wrong. See Carnegie, *How to Help Your Husband*, 19, 46, 68, 88, 123, 161, 57. Adlai Stevenson would echo these themes of "women's special duty to restore her husband's sense of self" in his commencement address to an all-female graduating class of 1955. See Cuordileone, *Manhood*, 121–123.

158. Per Mike Meeropol, October 2015, email in author's possession. Even the cosmopolitan Ricardos of television's *I Love Lucy* moved from New York City to Westport, Connecticut, in the 1956–1957 season. William J. Levitt, developer of the early suburbs of Levittown, once famously claimed, "No man who owns his own house and lot can be a Communist. He has too much to do." Quoted in Jackson, *Crabgrass Frontier*, 231; May, *Homeward Bound*, 143. See Halberstam, *Fifties*, 145; Jackson, *Crabgrass Frontier*, 231–251.

159. According to attorney Alan M. Dershowitz, Julius Rosenberg's family initially asked Ernst to join the defense team. Ernst explained to the FBI that he could use this position to get the Rosenbergs to confess. The FBI did not support this, but did use his profile. See Dershowitz, *America on Trial*, 325–326.

160. Ernst and Loth, *Report on the American Communist*, 180; Radosh and Milton, *Rosenberg File*, 358; Ginsberg, *Fatal Embrace*, 122; Cuordileone, *Manhood*, 77–78.

161. The first edition of the *Diagnostic and Statistical Manual of Mental Disorders* was published in 1952. For a discussion of psychological research methods as they related to the defense of

President William McKinley assassin, Leon Czolgosz, see Rauchway, *Murdering McKinley*, 205–206.

162. Radosh and Milton, *Rosenberg File*, 358.

163. Michael Grossberg, "Liberation and Caretaking: Fighting Over Children's Rights in Postwar America," in Fass and Grossberg, eds., *Reinventing Childhood*, 30.

164. For the role of gender in the Rosenberg case see Olmsted, "Blond Queens, Red Spiders"; Garber and Walkowitz, *Secret Agents*; Gentry, *J. Edgar Hoover*; Neville, *The Press*; Philipson, *Ethel Rosenberg*; and Radosh and Milton, *Rosenberg File*. For a discussion of twentieth-century Communist Party women, see Slutsky, *Gendering Radicalism*.

165. See Olmsted, "Blond Queens, Red Spiders," 80; Cuordileone, *Manhood*, 78–79.

166. James Daniel, "Mrs. Rosenberg Was Like a Red Spider," *New York World-Telegram and Sun*, January 15, 1953, quoted in Olmsted, "Blond Queens, Red Spiders," 83. Some critics even labeled the immensely popular Lucille Ball a domineering wife in her role in *I Love Lucy*. This characterization of women proved funny in entertainment, but fearful in espionage.

167. See Robert Meeropol in Garber and Walkowitz, eds., *Secret Agents*, 245.

168. Radosh and Milton, *Rosenberg File*, 281.

169. See this in Eisenhower's letter to his son, DDE to Major John S.D. Eisenhower, June 16, 1953, Box 3, File: December 1952–July 1953 (1), Ann Whitman File, 1953–1961, DDE Diary Series, DDE Papers, DDEL; and his correspondence with a friend, Professor Clyde Miller to DDE, June 8, 1953, Box 32, File: Rosenberg Case Statement, Ann Whitman File, 1953–1961, Administration Series, DDE Papers, DDEL. For more on depictions of Ethel as a "bad mother" see Marie Ashe in Garber and Walkowitz, eds., *Secret Agents*, 217–218.

170. Olmsted, "Blond Queens, Red Spiders," 82.

171. Hoover and his assistant D. M. Ladd, quoted in Radosh and Milton, *Rosenberg File*, 280.

172. Radosh and Milton, *Rosenberg File*, 280–281. Radosh and Milton argue that Hoover changed his view of Ethel's sentence after he learned that she "was not a good mother after all," presumably when she refused to unmask spies to save her life. Gentry contends that Hoover used Ethel as a lever believing "that no mother would willingly desert her two children." Gentry, *J. Edgar Hoover*, 427.

173. Radosh and Milton, *Rosenberg File*, 280–281; Gentry, *J. Edgar Hoover*, 428.

174. Hoover to Dulles, February 17, 1953, 3819, 12, 032, 761.5211, RG 59, NA.

175. Dulles to Hoover, February 20, 1953, 3819, 12, 033, 761.5211, RG 59, NA.

176. Hoover to Dulles, February 25, 1953, 3819, 12, 031, 761.5211, RG 59, NA.

177. February 23, 1953, File: Brownell, Herbert, Box 2, C. D. Jackson Records, 1953–1954, DDEL.

178. Ibid.

179. Ethel's psychiatrist was Dr. Saul Miller. Her psychologist, and Michael's, was Dr. Elizabeth Phillips. Roberts, *Brother*, 12; Philipson, *Ethel Rosenberg*, 190–195, 323.

180. Dulles, Circular Telegram 862, Infoguide Bulletin 260, February 11, 1953, 7:45pm. This telegram is not located in the two boxes of newly located Rosenberg documents in the National Archives in College Park. It is one of the three Rosenberg documents included in the *FRUS, 1952–54, Volume II, Part 1*, 1668–1670. I believe the reason it is not with the other Rosenberg documents (and how it was found and included in *FRUS*) is that it was mislabeled with 512.00, when all the previously missing Rosenberg documents are stamped 761.5211 Rosenberg, Julius. *FRUS* does not list the specific posts to which this bulletin was sent.

181. Dulles, Circular Telegram 862, Infoguide Bulletin 260, February 11, 1953, 7:45pm, *FRUS, 1952–54, Volume II, Part 1*, 1668–1670.

182. Ibid.

183. Ibid.

184. Ibid.

185. Ibid.

186. Alpha File, Box 2673, The Rosenbergs, Files: F, G-L, M, N-Q, White House Central Files, DDEL; January 7, 1953, Official File, Box 1761, File: 3480, Papers of HST, HSTL; Papal Message as printed in February 16, 1953 *Daily Worker*, FBI File, New York File, Julius Rosenberg, File: 65-15348, Sub E (3), https://vault.fbi.gov/rosenberg-case/julius-rosenberg.

187. Letter from Senator Lyndon B. Johnson to State Department, March 3, 1953, reply March 13, 1953, 3819, 13, 055–057, 761.5211, RG 59, NA.
188. Ibid.
189. Ibid.
190. Telegram from Holmes, London Embassy, February 16, 1953, 3819, 18, 350, 761.5211, RG 59, NA.
191. Sidney Silverman, Labor MP; FBI File, New York File, Julius Rosenberg, File: 65-15348, Sub E (3), https://vault.fbi.gov/rosenberg-case/julius-rosenberg.
192. FBI File, New York File, Julius Rosenberg, File: 65-15348, Sub E (3), https://vault.fbi.gov/rosenberg-case/julius-rosenberg. Even Winston Churchill had to admit that there were "current differences of view" between the United States and Great Britain, particularly concerning ending the conflict in Korea, where more than a thousand British soldiers had given their lives. Winston Churchill quoted in Clifton Daniel, "Churchill Opposes Seeing Eisenhower; Minimizes Discord," *New York Times*, May 21, 1953, 1.
193. Telegram from Paris, February 12, 1953, 3819, 18, 345 (missing page two), 761.5211, RG 59, NA.
194. Telegram from Paris, February 13, 1953, 3819, 18, 348 (also missing page two), 761.5211, RG 59, NA.
195. Ibid.
196. Telegram from Dunn, Paris, February 14, 1953, 3819, 18, 349, 761.5211, RG 59, NA. Telegram from Dunn, Paris, February 18, 1953, 3819, 12, 012, 761.5211, RG 59, NA.
197. Telegram from Dunn, Paris, February 18, 1953, 3819, 12, 012, 761.5211, RG 59, NA.
198. "Top Issue in France," *New York Times*, February 22, 1953, E4.
199. FBI File, New York File, Julius Rosenberg, File: 65-15348, Sub E (3), https://vault.fbi.gov/rosenberg-case/julius-rosenberg.
200. Louis Mittelberg later sculpted the bronze statue of Capt. Alfred Dreyfus, located in Tuileries Gardens in Paris.
201. Diplomats also explained to Washington derisively: "The fact that he [one Viet Tha] can comment on the case knowing as little as he does about it shows the shallowness of Saigon journalism." Memorandum from Wellborn, Counselor of Saigon Embassy to Simpson, Press Officer, USIS, March 4, 1953, 3820, 1, 008–009, 761.5211, RG 59, NA. According to Mike Meeropol the writer was likely Ho Chi Minh. While in Cuba in 1978 at a meeting "where a number of people were talking about organizing" the World Youth Festival, "a Vietnamese member of the meeting said that in the early 1950s Ho Chi Minh had written 'several' articles about the case (under assumed names) in Vietnam—that fact coupled with the writer's statement that he had been in Paris in 1927 fits Ho Chi Minh's biography." October 2015 email in author's possession.
202. *The Winnipeg Tribune* reported the dozen protesters represented some "400 Winnipeggers who passed a resolution which was forwarded to the American Consulate." Placards read: "Clemency for the Rosenbergs," "Vigil for Clemency," "Commute the Death Sentence," "Queen's Chaplain Asks for Clemency," and "Einstein Asks for Clemency." FSD from Cunningham, ConGen, Winnipeg, Canada, January 23, 1953, 3819, 17, 253, 761.5211, RG 59, NA. FSD from Kuykendall, US Consul General, Winnipeg, January 28, 1953, 3819, 17, 287, 761.5211, RG 59, NA. The American Consul General in Hamilton reported half a dozen picketers, several of whom "were obviously Semitic in appearance and most of them had a foreign look." Their placards read: "Pressure President Truman to Reprieve Rosenbergs," "Remember Sacco & Vanzetti—They Were Innocent Too," "Help Save the Rosenbergs," "Truman to Give Rosenbergs Another Hearing." The Ottawa Embassy ordered the consulates to use Paris press attaché Ben Bradlee's analysis of the case, and the embassy was pleased that it was "used to great advantage" in pro-U.S. editorials. The consulate in Hamilton asked to "have more of this kind of ammunition" [like Bradlee's report], "to use in furthering anti-Communist activities at Hamilton." FSD from Jester, American Consul General, Hamilton, Canada, January 29, 1953, 3819, 17, 290–297, 761.5211, RG 59, NA; FSD from Hawthorne, Edmonton, Alberta, January 19, 1953, 3819, 16, 221–224, 761.5211, RG 59, NA.
203. They also sold taped copies to raise funds for the Canadian Save the Rosenbergs campaign. FSD from Haering, Consulate General, Toronto, January 26, 1953, 3819, 17, 256–273, 761.5211, RG 59, NA.

204. FSD from Haering, Consulate General, Toronto, January 26, 1953, 3819, 17, 256–273, 761.5211, RG 59, NA.

205. Ibid. Since the broadcast violated no Canadian law, and consulate officials did not want to "meddle in Canadian internal affairs and rights of free speech," they considered pressuring the station owner not to air it by threatening to charge the station with broadcast pirating.

206. Ibid.

207. Ibid.

208. Lester Pearson served as Secretary of State for External Affairs from 1948–1957, and received the 1957 Nobel Peace Prize. He was later Prime Minister from 1963–1968. FSD from Vest, AmEmbassy, Ottawa, February 16, 1953, 3819, 18, 363–365, 761.5211, RG 59, NA; Memorandum of Conversation between Ignatieff and Raynor, February 20, 1953, 3819, 12, 023–024, 761.5211, RG 59, NA.

209. FSD from Vest, AmEmbassy, Ottawa, February 16, 1953, 3819, 18, 363–365, 761.5211, RG 59, NA. Memorandum of Conversation between Ignatieff and Raynor, February 20, 1953, 3819, 12, 023–024, 761.5211, RG 59, NA.

210. Memorandum of Conversation between Ignatieff and Raynor, February 20, 1953, 3819, 12, 023–024, 761.5211, RG 59, NA. Many other Canadians, for their part, did support President Eisenhower. Toronto was still dealing with the fallout of the January broadcast of the "Communist-inspired" Rosenberg program, when the radio station's program director admitted being inundated with "adverse public reaction" in response to the "dramatized appeal on behalf of atom spies Julius and Ethel Rosenberg." The station replied to this swell of protest by banning "all between-election broadcasts by Communists or fellow-travelers." FSD from Haering, Consul General, Toronto, February 17, 1953, 3819, 12, 005–006, 761.5211, RG 59, NA.

211. Telegram from Bunker, Rome, January 12, 1953, 3819, 14, 148, 761.5211, RG 59, NA. Telegram from Bunker, Rome, February 13, 1953, 3819, 18, 347, 761.5211, RG 59, NA.

212. Telegram from Bunker, Rome, February 13, 1953, 3819, 18, 347, 761.5211, RG 59, NA.

213. FSD from Free, Counselor for Public Affairs, Rome, February 19, 1953, 3819, 12, 013–014, 761.5211, RG 59, NA.

214. CIA agents paid particular attention to protest in the contested Free Territory of Trieste. After World War II the United Nations was set to govern the region, but both Italy and Yugoslavia fought over the occupied land. Concerned about the Communist Party possibly making inroads, agents maintained solid infiltration and routinely cabled about the activities of the Trieste Communist Party and the Committee for Defense of the Rosenbergs. In January 1953, the Communist Party of Trieste insisted its members should "be less lethargic toward the Rosenberg case," concluding that "if everyone does not do his best to save the Rosenbergs, he will be somewhat responsible for their death." The party organized protests and lectures, and routinely urged all members to discuss this matter "in every factory and enterprise," and send petitions and telegrams to "American authorities in Trieste, Rome, and Washington." CIA Memorandum, February 20, 1953; CIA Memorandum, March 4, 1953; CIA Memorandum, March 27, 1953; CIA Memorandum, May 7, 1953, Rosenbergs, http://www.foia.cia.gov/collection/atomic-spies-ethel-and-julius-rosenberg.

215. FSD from Childs, Consul General, Antwerp, February 16, 1953, 3819, 18, 351–362, 761.5211, RG 59, NA; FSD from Childs, Consul General, Antwerp, February 18, 1953, 3819, 12, 007, 761.5211, RG 59, NA; FSD from Childs, Consul General, Antwerp, February 20, 1953, 3819, 12, 019, 761.5211, RG 59, NA; FSD from Childs, Antwerp, February 25, 1953, 3819, 12, 030, 761.5211, RG 59, NA; FSD from Childs, Consul General, Antwerp, March 31, 1953, 3820, 1, 035–038, 761.5211, RG 59, NA.

216. FSD from Donovan, Second Secretary of Embassy, The Hague, March 20, 1953, 3820, 1, 020, 761.5211, RG 59, NA. In nearby Rotterdam, a minor Communist demonstration at the consulate resulted in an increased presence of police guards, a deployment the consulate decided to continue indefinitely to deal with growing anti-American tensions. FSD from Lancaster, American Consul, Rotterdam, February 19, 1953, 3819, 12, 015–017, 761.5211, RG 59, NA.

217. Telegram from Lyon, Berlin, February 16, 1953, 3819, 12, 001, 761.5211, RG 59, NA. The chairman of the Council of the Evangelical Church in Berlin also wrote, protesting the death sentences. FSD from Barnes, Berlin, February 25, 1953, 3819, 12, 034–036, 761.5211, RG 59, NA.

218. Telegram from Rice, Stuttgart, Germany, February 16, 1953, 3819, 18, 366–367, 761.5211, RG 59, NA; Telegram from Rice, Stuttgart, February 17, 1953, 3819, 12, 002, 761.5211, RG 59, NA; FSD from Rice, Consul General, Stuttgart, Germany, February 26, 1953, 3819, 12, 042–046; 13, 047–049, 761.5211, RG 59, NA; FSD from Duffield, Consul General, Frankfurt, February 18, 1953, 3819, 12, 008–011, 761.5211, RG 59, NA; Telegram from Pearson, Munich Consulate, March 25, 1953, 3820, 1, 023, 761.5211, RG 59, NA; Telegram from Thayer, Munich, January 23, 1953, 3819, 17, 252, 761.5211, RG 59, NA; FSD from Beerner, Director, Office of Public Affairs, ConGen, Bonn, February 4, 1953, 3819, 17, 300, 761.5211, RG 59, NA.
219. FSD from Timberlake, Consul General, Hamburg, March 30, 1953, 3820, 1, 025–026, 761.5211, RG 59, NA.
220. FSD from Timberlake, American Consul General, Hamburg, January 28, 1953, 3819, 17, 288–289, 761.5211, RG 59, NA.
221. Ibid.
222. FSD from Green, First Secretary of Embassy, Stockholm, March 11, 1953, 3820, 1, 012–014, 761.5211, RG 59, NA.
223. FSD from Green, First Secretary of Embassy, Stockholm, March 17, 1953, 3820, 1, 017, 761.5211, RG 59, NA.
224. FSD from Green, First Secretary of Embassy, Stockholm, March 11, 1953, 3820, 1, 012–014, 761.5211, RG 59, NA. FSD from Green, First Secretary of Embassy, Stockholm, March 17, 1953, 3820, 1, 017, 761.5211, RG 59, NA.
225. FSD from Styles, Consul General, Göteborg, March 17, 1953, 3820, 1, 018–019, 761.5211, RG 59, NA; FSD from Styles, Consul General, Göteborg, March 31, 1953, 3820, 1, 039, 761.5211, RG 59, NA.
226. FSD from Wells, First Secretary of Legation, Helsinki, March 6, 1953, 3820, 1, 006–007, 761.5211, RG 59, NA.
227. Ibid.
228. FSD from Byrd, Counselor of Embassy, Canberra, March 5, 1953, 3820, 1, 005, 761.5211, RG 59, NA; FSD from Ingraham, Vice Consul, Perth, Australia, March 30, 1953, 3820, 1, 027–034, 761.5211, RG 59, NA. See also Deery, "Securing Justice?," 8–9.
229. FSD from Prince, Second Secretary of Embassy, Wellington, New Zealand, February 5, 1953, 3819, 17, 302; 18, 303, 761.5211, RG 59, NA.
230. FSD from Scotten, Wellington, February 26, 1953, 3819, 12, 037–041, 761.5211, RG 59, NA.
231. Ibid.
232. FSD from Prince, Second Secretary of Embassy, Wellington, New Zealand, February 5, 1953, 3819, 17, 302; 18, 303, 761.5211, RG 59, NA.
233. FSD from Payne, Public Affairs Officer, AmEmbassy, Cairo, February 6, 1953, 3819, 18, 304, 761.5211, RG 59, NA.
234. FSD from Lawson, AmLegation, Reykjavik, January 22, 1953, 3819, 16, 238–250; 17, 251 761.5211, RG 59, NA.
235. Ibid.
236. CIA Memorandum, April 2, 1953, Rosenbergs, http://www.foia.cia.gov/collection/atomic-spies-ethel-and-julius-rosenberg.
237. CIA Memorandum, February 20, 1953, Rosenbergs, http://www.foia.cia.gov/collection/atomic-spies-ethel-and-julius-rosenberg.
238. Telegram from Flack, Warsaw, February 17, 1953, 3819, 12, 003, 761.5211, RG 59, NA.
239. FSD from Abbott, Counselor of Legation, AmLegation, Budapest, February 25, 1953, 3819, 12, 027–029, 761.5211, RG 59, NA.
240. Ibid.
241. Hughes, *Ordeal of Power*, 100.
242. Jackson quoted in Osgood, *Total Cold War*, 58.
243. See Osgood, *Total Cold War*, 59–60.
244. Cabinet Meeting Minutes, March 6, 1953, Box 1, File: C-2, Office of the Staff Secretary: Records: 1952–1961, Cabinet Series, White House Office Files, DDEL. Dulles, however, tried to get diplomatic posts on board to "capitalize on emotions" within the "Soviet orbit"

and "exacerbate their confusion" to "weaken [the] regime." See Dulles telegram to eleven posts, March 5, 1953, *FRUS, 1952–54, Volume II, Part 1*, 1681–1684.

245. Mitrovich, *Undermining the Kremlin*, 126.
246. See Osgood, *Total Cold War*, 56.
247. Osgood, "Words and Deeds," 7.
248. For a thorough discussion of the "The Chance for Peace" speech, see Osgood, *Total Cold War*, 57–67. After three days of golf at Augusta National, Eisenhower traveled to Washington to deliver the speech before the American Society of Newspaper Editors and officially open the baseball season at Griffith Stadium. He then returned to Augusta for another four days of golf. Noting his apparent illness, reporters close enough to the president during the speech commented on how Ike persevered through abdominal pain. Newton, *Eisenhower*, 130. It was televised on all networks and rebroadcast in many languages around the world.
249. Eisenhower, "The Chance for Peace," April 16, 1953, available at the American Presidency Project, http://www.presidency.ucsb.edu/ws/?pid=9819.
250. Ibid.
251. Ibid. Hughes, *Ordeal of Power*, 102, 113.
252. Eisenhower, "The Chance for Peace," April 16, 1953, available at the American Presidency Project, http://www.presidency.ucsb.edu/ws/?pid=9819.
253. W. H. Lawrence, "5-Point Plan Given," *New York Times*, April 17, 1953, 1.
254. Eisenhower, "The Chance for Peace," April 16, 1953, available at the American Presidency Project, http://www.presidency.ucsb.edu/ws/?pid=9819.
255. Ibid.
256. Osgood, *Total Cold War*, 67; Eisenhower, *Mandate for Change*, 143–146; Hughes, *Ordeal of Power*, 101–115.
257. Radosh and Milton, *Rosenberg File*, 361–366.
258. Ibid., 371.
259. Quoted in ibid., 366.
260. "Rosenberg Rally Hears New Story," *New York Times*, May 4, 1953, 4; Radosh and Milton, *Rosenberg File*, 366–367.
261. Ibid.
262. Memorandum of Telephone Conversation between Merritt N. Cootes, State Department and Mr. Kilsheimer, Assistant U.S. Attorney, NY, May 4, 1953, 3820, 2, 063, 761.5211, RG 59, NA; Radosh and Milton, *Rosenberg File*, 361; Dulles, State Department Circular, Control 724, May 6, 1963, 3820, 2, 064, 761.5211, RG 59, NA. Greenglass quoted in telegram from Dillon, Paris, April 20, 1953, 3820, 1, 052; 2, 053, 761.5211, RG 59, NA.
263. Other authors whose work was pulled included Albert Einstein, Howard Fast, Ernest Hemingway, Arthur Miller, Thomas Paine, Jean-Paul Sartre, Upton Sinclair, and Henry David Thoreau. See Osgood, *Total Cold War*, 295–296; Schrecker, *Many Are the Crimes*, 256–257.
264. Oshinsky, *Conspiracy So Immense*, 279; Telegram from Dillon to Dulles, sent 1pm May 16, 1953, File: R, Box 5, C. D. Jackson Records, 1953–54, DDEL, also 3820, 2, 069–070, 761.5211, RG 59, NA; Bradlee, *Good Life*, 140.
265. *Eugene Register-Guard*, December 25, 1985, 8D.
266. "McCarthyism: Myth and Menace," *Time*, June 29, 1953, http://content.time.com/time/magazine/article/0,9171,889710,00.html.
267. Stebbins, *United States in World Affairs, 1953*, 39–40.
268. Telegram from Dillon to Dulles, sent 1pm May 16, 1953, File: R, Box 5, C. D. Jackson Records, 1953–54, DDEL, also 3820, 2, 069–070, 761.5211, RG 59, NA.
269. "McCarthyism: Myth & Menace," *Time*, June 29, 1953, http://content.time.com/time/magazine/article/0,9171,889710,00.html.
270. Dulles airgram to Paris, London, Rome, Brussels, Amsterdam, Copenhagen, Vienna, and The Hague, May 6, 1953, 3820, 2, 064–066, 761.5211, RG 59, NA.
271. Ibid.
272. Ibid.
273. Ibid.

274. FSD from Mein, First Secretary of Embassy, Oslo, April 29, 1953, 3820, 2, 057–059, 761.5211, RG 59, NA.
275. Harold B. Minor was the first American ambassador to Beirut, after it moved from legation to embassy status in 1952. Minor was surprised because, as he explained, "press and other comment emphasized that their conviction was justified and that it should prove to Americans that Jewish elements are untrustworthy." According to Minor, some in Beirut believed— incorrectly—that Atomic Energy Commission reported that the material Greenglass passed "did not enable the Soviets to construct an atomic bomb owing to the unimportance of this information." While many scientists had made this argument, no public AEC document did. See FSD from Minor, Am Embassy, Beirut, Lebanon, April 30, 1953, 3820, 2, 060–062, 761.5211, RG 59, NA; Radosh and Milton, *The Rosenberg File*, 432–449.
276. FSD from The Hague, May 13, 1953, 3820, 2, 067, 761.5211, RG 59, NA; FBI File, New York File, Julius Rosenberg, File: 65-15348, Sub E (4), https://vault.fbi.gov/rosenberg-case/ julius-rosenberg.
277. FSD from AmConsulate, Strasbourg, France, May 28, 1953, 3820, 2, 088–092, 761.5211, RG 59, NA.
278. Ibid.
279. Ibid. Greenglass's testimony was not "auxiliary" but essential for a conspiracy to commit espionage conviction.
280. Ibid.
281. Eisenhower, Mayer, Secretary Dulles, U.S. Ambassador Dillon, and French Ambassador Bonnet attended these talks on March 26 and 27. See Statler, *Replacing France*, 61.
282. Statler, *Replacing France*, 63.
283. Telegram from Dillon, Paris, April 20, 1953, 3820, 1, 052; 2, 053, 761.5211, RG 59, NA.
284. Dillon later served as Secretary of Treasury in the Kennedy administration. See Eric Pace, "Douglas Dillon Dies at 93," *New York Times*, January 12, 2003; Statler, *Replacing France*, 69.
285. Telegram from Dillon, Paris, April 20, 1953, 3820, 1, 052; 2, 053, 761.5211, RG 59, NA.
286. Telegram from Dulles to Dillon, April 20, 1953, 3820, 2, 054, 761.5211, RG 59, NA.
287. Bradlee's oral history with Radosh, 1982, in Radosh and Milton, *Rosenberg File*, 374. Rosenberg support in France included four French nobles, including Andre Mornet, the Chief Government Attorney of France, FBI File, New York File, Julius Rosenberg, File: 65- 15348, Sub E (3), https://vault.fbi.gov/rosenberg-case/julius-rosenberg.
288. Telegram from Dillon to Dulles, May 16, 1953, File: R, Box 5, C. D. Jackson Records, 1953– 54, DDEL; also 3820, 2, 069–070, 761.5211, RG 59, NA.
289. Telegram from Dillon to Dulles, May 16, 1953, File: R, Box 5, C. D. Jackson Records, 1953– 54, DDEL.
290. Ibid. He referred particularly to Klaus Fuchs, who by all accounts provided more valuable material to the Soviets than Rosenberg. Fuchs was sentenced in Great Britain to fourteen years and served nine.
291. Ibid.
292. Ibid.
293. Ibid.
294. Eyes Only Distribution, 3820, 2, 073, 761.5211, RG 59, NA. Memo from W. J. McWilliams to General Smith, May 18, 1953, 3820, 3, 104, 761.5211, RG 59, NA. Memo from W. J. McWilliams to General Smith, May 21, 1953, 3820, 3, 103; memo from W. J. McWilliams to General Smith, May 30, 1953, 3820, 3, 102, 761.5211, RG 59, NA. Memo from Leffas to Scott, May 31, 1953, 3820, 2, 099; note from J. S. Earman, Executive Assistant to the Director of CIA to Mr. Scott, June 4, 1953, 3820, 3, 101, 761.5211, RG 59, NA.
295. Memo from Merchant to Smith, May 19, 1953, 3820, 2, 079, 761.5211, RG 59, NA.
296. Telegram from Smith to Dillon, May 19, 1953, 3820, 2, 080, 761.5211, RG 59, NA.
297. Memorandum from Smith to Eisenhower, May 20, 1953, 3820, 2, 075, 761.5211, RG 59, NA; memo from W. J. McWilliams, Director, Executive Secretariat to Mrs. Whitman, May 21, 1953, 3820, 2, 081, 761.5211, RG 59, NA.
298. He was enjoying the middle of a great run of golf. He played on Saturday April 25, Tuesday April 28, Saturday May 2 (with Bob Hope), Wednesday May 6, Wednesday May 13,

Saturday May 16, Sunday May 17, Wednesday May 20, Tuesday May 26, Thursday May 28, and Saturday May 30.

299. Dillon's May 16 dispatch "aroused the ire" of J. Edgar Hoover; Radosh and Milton, *Rosenberg File*, 375.

300. One Foreign Service Officer was William Avery Crawford, and he had also been the subject of a loyalty investigation in 1951. The 1953 report is moderately redacted, but it indicates that Crawford had acquaintances that may have been Communists, but that Crawford himself was considered "eligible in loyalty." FBI Memo from Ladd to Hoover, May 22, 1953, Julius Rosenberg Papers, FBI Headquarters Case No., HQ-65-58236, Section 68 Referrals, Main File, https://vault.fbi.gov/rosenberg-case/rosenberg-referrals.

301. Ibid.

302. It is unlikely the attorney general acted on this information, though he did enjoy a cordial working relationship with the FBI director. Responding to a positive cover story by *Time* magazine in May 1957, Hoover told Brownell "it has been a real personal privilege to serve as a member of your team." Brownell replied congratulating the director on his 33rd anniversary with the Bureau, thanking him "for the assistance you have given us these past four years in maintaining vigorous, yet equitable, enforcement of federal laws." May 8, 1957, May 10, 1957, File: FBI (1), Box 38, Herbert Brownell Papers, 1877–1988, DDEL.

303. May 14, 1953 letter in Meeropol, ed., *Rosenberg Letters*, 660–661.

304. Ibid.

305. The announcement of the Court's April action was delayed as Justice Frankfurter debated whether to write a dissent. See Lichtman, *Supreme Court and McCarthy-Era Repression*, 58–59; Parrish, "Cold War Justice," 822–825.

306. Among other liberal voters Douglas had cast a dissenting vote in *Dennis v. U.S.*, arguing that the CPUSA was a failed political movement and not a threat to the United States.

307. Quoted in Murphy, *Wild Bill*, 315–318.

308. Ibid.

309. See ibid.; Lichtman, *Supreme Court and McCarthy-Era Repression*, 59; Parrish, "Cold War Justice," 824–826.

310. Quoted in Parrish, "Cold War Justice," 825.

311. Memo for File, Conversation with Brownell, May 27, 1953, Box 5, File: R, C. D. Jackson Records, 1953–1954, DDEL.

312. Ibid.

313. "Justice and Propaganda," *Washington Post*, May 28, 1953, 26.

314. Ibid.

315. Ibid.

316. Ibid.

317. See Stueck, *Rethinking the Korean War*, 171–181. Bruce Cumings argues that the Joint Chiefs urged Eisenhower to order a nuclear attack against China in May as a form of "atomic blackmail" to force an armistice but that "there is little evidence that Ike's nuclear threats made any difference in the Communist decision to end the war," Cumings, *Korean War*, 34.

318. Seven KIA, 1 MIA, 4 POW, 4 injured, "Casualties in Korea," *New York Times*, June 1, 1953, 2.

319. FBI File, New York File, Julius Rosenberg, File: 65-15348, Sub E (6), https://vault.fbi.gov/rosenberg-case/julius-rosenberg.

320. See Begley, *Why the Dreyfus Affair Matters*.

321. Steven Erlanger, "French Ministry Posts Online Full File on 'Dreyfus Affair,'" *New York Times*, March 7, 2013, A9.

322. Glynn, "L'Affaire Rosenberg in France," 509. The *National Guardian* titled an August 1951 article on the Rosenbergs, "Is this the Dreyfus Case of Cold War America?"

323. In May 1953, 74% of Americans polled stated that during the previous three months Eisenhower had not done or said anything they disapproved of. See Gallup, *Gallup Poll*, 1145.

Chapter 4

1. According to Julius Rosenberg, Bennett met for an hour with Julius, for a half hour with Ethel, and then an additional half hour with the couple with the warden present. Meeropol, ed., *Rosenberg Letters*, 675. See also Memorandum from James Bennett to Herbert Brownell, June 5, 1953, File B (3), Box 75, Herbert Brownell Papers, 1877–1988, DDEL. The Dulles brothers had agreed they were "disposed to do something about her" and reached out to Attorney General Brownell to find a way to get Ethel to talk. Telephone Conversation with Allen W. Dulles, June 5, 1953, File: Telephone Memoranda May–June 1953 (2), Box 1, Telephone Call Series, John Foster Dulles Papers, DDEL.
2. Julius's letter to Ethel, June 4, 1953, Meeropol, ed., *Rosenberg Letters*, 675.
3. Memorandum from James Bennett to Herbert Brownell, June 5, 1953, File B (3), Box 75, Herbert Brownell Papers, 1877–1988, DDEL.
4. Rosenbergs' statement, June 7, 1953, in Meeropol, ed., *Rosenberg Letters*, 673–674.
5. Ibid.
6. Ibid.
7. Ibid.
8. Julius's letter to Ethel, June 4, 1953, Meeropol, ed., *Rosenberg Letters*, 675.
9. Ibid.
10. June 4, 1953, File: Log 1953(2), Box 68, C. D. Jackson Papers, 1931–89, DDEL. According to an interview by Sam Roberts with FBI Supervisor Robert Lamphere, Hoover entertained the idea of letting Ethel live since he was moved by "the small amount of evidence" against her. Roberts, *Brother*, 432, 519.
11. Attorney General Brownell insisted in a 1967 oral history that Eisenhower (and members of an early version of the USIA) received daily briefs on the case and global reaction to it from the State Department. These updates may have prompted Ike's second thoughts. Herbert Brownell Oral History with Ed Edwin, May 5, 1967, OH-157, #3 of 5, 191, Columbia University Oral History Project, DDEL.
12. DDE letter to Professor Clyde Miller, Columbia University, June 10, 1953, Ann Whitman File, 1953–1961, Administration Series, Box 32, File: Rosenberg Case Statement, DDE Papers, DDEL.
13. Ibid.
14. Ibid.
15. Ibid. See also Lucas, *Freedom's War*, 167 and Radosh and Milton, *Rosenberg File*, 358.
16. Ernst and Loth, *Report on the American Communist*, 180.
17. Americans who believed no agreement was possible rose from 54% in April to 74% in May. Between 52% and 58% believed the war not worth fighting. "Public Opinion on the Korean War, 1953, Memorandum on Recent Polls, June 2, 1953", C. D. Jackson Records, DDEL, www.eisenhower.archives.gov/research/online_documents/korean_war.html. See also Casey, *Selling the Korean War*, 358–361.
18. Cumings, *Korean War*, 33.
19. Memo from Charles H. Taquey, May 29, 1953, PSB Central File Series, Box 17, File: PSB 092. (1), PSB, National Security Council Staff: Papers, 1953–1961, White House Files, DDEL (declassified 1994).
20. Ibid.
21. Ibid.
22. Ibid.
23. As discussed in Chapter 3, four days into his first term Eisenhower created a committee to review the PSB, and in September 1953 he approved the formation of the Operations Coordinating Board to replace it.
24. FSD from U.S. ConGen, Montreal, May 28, 1953, 3820, 2, 083, 085–086, 761.5211, RG 59, NA.
25. Ibid.
26. FSD from U.S. ConGen, Montreal, June 10, 1953, 3820, 3, 141–142, 761.5211, RG 59, NA.
27. Ibid.
28. FSD from U.S. Consulate General, Toronto, Canada, May 29, 1953, 3820, 2, 094–095, 761.5211, RG 59, NA; FSD from Con General, Toronto, June 8, 1953, 3820, 3, 111, 761.5211, RG 59, NA.

29. FSD from AmEmbassy, Montevideo, June 15, 1953, 3820, 4, 190, 761.5211, RG 59, NA; telegram from Walmsley, Rio de Janeiro, June 13, 1953, 3820, 6, 077 (3820, 4, 187), 761.5211, RG 59, NA.

30. FSD from American Embassy, Guatemala, June 18, 1953, 3820, 8, 157–158, 160–161, 761.5211, RG 59, NA. According to the embassy, the "leading signers were Sr. Francisco Fernandez Foncea, Secretary General of the leading Government party, *Partido Acción Revolucionaria* (PAR) and Julio Estrada de la Hoz, former President of Congress."

31. FSD from American Embassy, Guatemala, June 18, 1953, 3820, 8, 157–158, 160–161, 761.5211, RG 59, NA.

32. Ibid.

33. Ibid.

34. Rabe, *Killing Zone*, 19.

35. For explorations of anti-Americanism and accusations of U.S. imperialism in Latin America see McPherson, *Yankee No!*; McPherson, ed., *Anti-Americanism*; and Rabe, *Killing Zone*.

36. FSD from AmConsul, Surabaya, Indonesia, June 9, 1953, 3820, 3, 130–131, 761.5211, RG 59, NA.

37. FSD from AmEmbassy, Djakarta, Indonesia, June 27, 1953, 3820, 6, 097–098, 761.5211, RG 59, NA.

38. FSD from AmConsul, Sydney, Australia, June 8, 1953, 3820, 3, 113–117, 761.5211, RG 59, NA.

39. Ibid.

40. Memo from Merchant to Smith, June 4, 1953, 3820, 2, 097-98, 761.5211, RG 59, NA; Memorandum of Conversation, Kahn (Wiley's office) and Cootes (State), June 5, 1953, 3820, 3, 106, 761.5211, RG 59, NA; Memo from Merchant to Scott, June 9, 1953, 3820, 3, 124, 761.5211, RG 59, NA; Memo from W. K. S. to Smith, June 16, 1953, 3820, 3, 125, 761.5211, RG 59, NA.

41. Neville, *Press*, 80; Glynn, "L'Affaire Rosenberg in France," 507, 514; Telegram from Dillon, June 9, 1953, 3820, 3, 128–129, 761.5211, RG 59, NA. *Le Monde* argued that the Rosenbergs' "guilt has never been concretely established" and doubts remain in many people's minds, "especially in [the] case of Mrs. Rosenberg." Joseph Brainin, National Committee to Secure Justice in the Rosenberg Case telegram to Secretary Dulles which quoted extensively from the June 5 editorial in *Le Monde*, June 9, 1953, 3820, 3, 132–133, 761.5211, RG 59, NA.

42. FBI File, New York File, Julius Rosenberg, File: 65-15348, Sub E (4), https://vault.fbi.gov/rosenberg-case/julius-rosenberg.

43. Telegram from Dillon, June 9, 1953, 3820, 3, 128–129, 761.5211, RG 59, NA.

44. Ibid.

45. Ibid.

46. Dillon explained that most activity stemmed from petitions (7,598 petitions since 1951, some with as many as 2,000 signatures) and public appeals (3,289 appeals since March and 2,653 just in the previous two weeks). Telegram from Dillon, June 12, 1953, 3820, 4, 155, 761.5211, RG 59, NA.

47. Ibid.

48. In Lyon, the consulate received five to ten petitions every day and nervously awaited an advertised "mass meeting" scheduled for June 12. A consul official expressed alarm at the "surprising number of fellow travelers in this area," admitting that this propaganda had "aroused considerable feeling on the subject among sections of the population usually well removed from Communist influence," including Catholic faculty members, the Archbishop of Lyon, and the editors of the "strongly rightist and Catholic daily" *Echo Liberté*. FSD from Am Consulate, Lyon, France, June 12, 1953, 3820, 4, 157–158, 761.5211, RG 59, NA.

49. Ibid.

50. G. Edward Reynolds, the American Vice Consul complained, "the job was done so effectively that it drew attention of passersby and will take two men two days to remove." FSD from AmConsulate, Strasbourg, France, June 12, 1953, 3820, 4, 161, 761.5211, RG 59, NA.

51. George C. Marshall, retired Secretary of State and Defense, represented the United States at the coronation. Radosh and Milton, *Rosenberg File*, 377.

52. FBI File, New York File, Julius Rosenberg, File: 65-15348, Sub E (4), https://vault.fbi.gov/rosenberg-case/julius-rosenberg.

53. Ibid.

54. FSD from London, June 8, 1953, 3820, 3, 107–110, 761.5211, RG 59, NA.

55. Ibid.

56. Telegram from U.S. Embassy Brussels, June 8, 1953, 3820, 3, 123 (duplicated as part of alphabetized Department summary, 3820, 6, 070), 761.5211, RG 59, NA.

57. Ibid.

58. Ibid.

59. *Le Matin* was part of the liberal press, *Het Handelsblad* part of the conservative. Telegram from Childs, Antwerp, Belgium, June 11, 1853, 3820, 3, 143–144, 761.5211, RG 59, NA.

60. Telegram from Childs, Antwerp, Belgium, June 11, 1853, 3820, 3, 148, 761.5211, RG 59, NA.

61. Ibid.

62. Telegram from U.S. Embassy Brussels, June 8, 1953, 3820, 3, 123 (duplicated as part of alphabetized Department summary, 3820, 6, 070), 761.5211, RG 59, NA; FSD from AmEmbassy, Brussels, June 19, 1953, 3820, 5, 003–005, 761.5211, RG 59, NA.

63. The leader of the group of lawyers, Bâtonnier Henri Botson, and two former ministers of justice who agreed to sign on, Marcel Grégoire and Paul Tschoffen, "are not tainted" and represent "Belgium's outstanding legal minds." Telegram from U.S. Embassy Brussels, June 8, 1953, 3820, 3, 123 (duplicated as part of alphabetized Department summary, 3820, 6, 070), 761.5211, RG 59, NA; FSD from AmEmbassy, Brussels, June 19, 1953, 3820, 5, 003–005, 761.5211, RG 59, NA.

64. Telegram from U.S. Embassy Brussels, June 8, 1953, 3820, 3, 123 (duplicated as part of alphabetized Department summary, 3820, 6, 070), 761.5211, RG 59, NA; FSD from AmEmbassy, Brussels, June 19, 1953, 3820, 5, 003-005, 761.5211, RG 59, NA.

65. FSD from AmEmbassy, Brussels, June 19, 1953, 3820, 5, 003–005, 761.5211, RG 59, NA. Protest accelerated in nearby Netherlands as well, and The Hague Embassy continued to receive "several dozen letters of protest" each week. Netherlands Prime Minister Drees refused to agree to the request of two Communist members of the Second Chamber that he intercede "as Prime Minister or as a private person with the United States authorities on the Rosenbergs' behalf." FSD from The Hague, June 8, 1953, 3820, 3, 112, 761.5211, RG 59, NA; telegram from U.S. Embassy Brussels, June 8, 1953, 3820, 3, 123 (duplicated as part of alphabetized Department summary, 3820, 6, 070), 761.5211, RG 59, NA.

66. See Parrish, "Cold War Justice," 828–831.

67. Letter from Julius to Ethel, June 10–11, 1953, in Meeropol and Meeropol, *We Are Your Sons*, 221.

68. Telegram from Millard, Brussels, June 14, 1953, 3820, 4, 187 (duplicate 3820, 6, 079), 761.5211, RG 59, NA.

69. Ibid.

70. Ibid. Emphasis in original.

71. Ibid.

72. The senators were Henri Rolin, Social-Christian Senator Etienne de la Vallée-Poussin, and Socialist Deputy Edmond Leburton. FSD from Smith, AmEmbassy, Brussels, June 15, 1953, 3820, 7, 106–107, 761.5211, RG 59, NA.

73. Telegram from Childs, Antwerp, Belgium, June 11, 1953, 3820, 3, 143–144, 761.5211, RG 59, NA.

74. Ibid.

75. Ibid.

76. Ibid.

77. Telegram from Dillon, June 10, 1953, 3820, 3, 134, 136, 761.5211, RG 59, NA. A handwritten note on an attached distribution list indicates that the European copy of this cable was "burned 1/25/55."

78. Ibid.

79. FSD from John B. Ketcham, Luxembourg, June 19, 1953, 3820, 5, 001–002, 761.5211, RG 59, NA.

80. Ibid.

81. On June 12, thirty women and children demonstrated with banners before the Stuttgart consulate, and later that day more than a hundred women joined them, chanting slogans and submitting letters to the consulate. FSD from AmConGen, Stuttgart, June 17, 1953, 3820, 7, 137–141, 761.5211, RG 59, NA. An increase in female protesters in Duesseldorf heightened security concerns; the consul general requested police to be ready "in next few days" should things "threaten to get out of hand." FSD from Am ConGen, Duesseldorf, June 12, 1953, 3820, 4, 185, 761.5211, RG 59, NA.

82. FSD from Am ConGen, Duesseldorf, June 12, 1953, 3820, 4, 185, 761.5211, RG 59, NA. The council issued an appeal to use negotiation to ease international stress. Stebbins, *United States in World Affairs*, 487.

83. Telegram from Budapest to Secretary of State, June 1, 1953, 3820, 2, 096, 761.5211, RG 59, NA; Telegram from Ravndal, Budapest, June 9, 1953, 3820, 3, 127, 761.5211, RG 59, NA.

84. Ibid.

85. Ibid.

86. FSD from AmLegation, Budapest, June 12, 1953, 3820, 4, 162–184, 761.5211, RG 59, NA.

87. FSD from U.S. ConGen, Montreal, June 10, 1953, 3820, 3, 137–40, 149, 761.5211, RG 59, NA. An eyewitness claimed two officers of the Czechoslovak Consulate General sat in a coffee shop across the street and observed the entire demonstration.

88. FSD from U.S. ConGen, Montreal, June 10, 1953, 3820, 3, 137–140, 149, 761.5211, RG 59, NA. Two days later dozens of protesters submitted petitions that questioned whether the United States would become known only for "the harsh and unprecedented executions." FSD from U.S. ConGen, Montreal, June 11, 1953, 3820, 3, 149–150, 761.5211, RG 59, NA; FSD from U.S. ConGen, Montreal, June 12, 1953, 3820, 3, 151–152, 761.5211, RG 59, NA.

89. FSD from U.S. ConGen, Montreal, June 10, 1953, 3820, 3, 137–140, 149, 761.5211, RG 59, NA.

90. FSD from AmConsulate, Windsor, Ontario, June 12, 1953, 3820, 4, 156, 761.5211, RG 59, NA; FSD from U.S. ConGen, Toronto, Canada, June 12, 1953, 3820, 4, 159–160, 761.5211, RG 59, NA. In Union Square, New York City, the National Committee to Secure Justice in the Rosenberg Case also held a clemency rally at 5 p.m. on June 11. Rally Flier, June 11, 1953, File: Rosenberg Case Statement, Box 32, DDE Papers, Ann Whitman Files, 1953–61, Administration Series, DDEL.

91. June 12, 1953, Telephone Calls Series, Box 1, File: Telephone Memoranda, May–June 1953 (2), Papers of John Foster Dulles, DDEL.

92. June 11, 1953, Box 5, File R, C. D. Jackson Records, 1953–1954, DDEL. CIA Director Allen Dulles also raised the issue with his brother, Secretary of State John Foster. Director Dulles was worried about the "considerable concern in European churches" that he anticipated regarding the executions. Secretary Dulles forwarded a copy of the memo to the attorney general two days later, and filed the original with no evidence of action. See Memo to Secretary Dulles from CIA Director Dulles, June 16, 1953, 3820, 7, 108, 761.5211, RG 59, NA.

93. "The President often asked for my evaluation of the state of public opinion." Lodge, *As It Was*, 119. See also Greenstein, *Hidden-Hand Presidency*, 60.

94. Memo from Henry Cabot Lodge Jr. to C. D. Jackson, June 12, 1953, Box 5, File R, C. D. Jackson Records, 1953–54, DDEL.

95. Telegrams from Pierre Marie Cardinal Gerlier Archbishop of Lyon and Cardinal Maurice Feltin, Archbishop of Paris, 8 a.m., June 12, 1953, Box 5, File R, C. D. Jackson Records, 1953–54, DDEL. The author thanks Angelique Duvet-Tovar for her translation.

96. Telegram from Urey, June 12, 1953, *New York Times* coverage of telegram, White House Memorandum concerning Urey's visit, File: 101-R Rosenbergs (1), Box 411, Official File, White House Central Files, DDEL.

97. Ibid.

98. Ibid.

99. Letter from Miller to DDE, June 6, 1953, Alpha File, Box 2673, The Rosenbergs, M, White House Central Files, DDEL.

100. Ibid.

101. Lichtman, *Supreme Court and McCarthy-Era Repression*, 59; Parrish, "Cold War Justice," 831–832.

102. Murphy, *Wild Bill*, 319.

103. Dulles sent it to IBS/NY, USUN/NY, Berlin, Bonn, Brussels, Cairo (*Addis Ababa, Amman, Jidda,* Tripoli), Canberra (Wellington), Frankfort (Ankara, Athens, Copenhagen, Helsinki, Moscow, Oslo, Stockholm, Warsaw), London (Baghdad, Beirut, *Damascus,* Dublin), *Manila* (Djakarta, *Hong Kong, Rangoon,* Saigon, *Singapore, Taipei*), Mexico City, Montevideo, New Delhi (Bangkok, Colombo, *Kabul, Karachi*), Paris (*Belgrade,* Bern, Geneva, Lisbon, Luxembourg, Madrid, *Praha,* Strasbourg), *Pretoria,* Rio de Janeiro, Rome, Santiago Chile, Tehran, Tel Aviv, The Hague, Tokyo (Pusan), Trieste, Vienna (Bucharest, Budapest) and pouched it to Algiers, *Asuncion,* Bogota, Buenos Aires, Caracas, Casablanca, Ciudad Trujillo, Guatemala City, Habana, *La Paz, Lima,* Managua, Ottawa, Panama City, *Port-Au-Prince, Quito,* Reykjavik, San Jose, San Salvador, *Tegucigalpa,* and Tunis. For the emphasized posts there is no State Department documentary evidence concerning the Rosenberg case. Infoguide Bulletin 378 from Dulles, June 13, 1953, 3820, 6, 083–086, 761.5211, RG 59, NA.

104. Ibid.

105. Ibid.

106. Ibid.

107. Ibid.

108. Deery, " 'Never Losing Faith,' " 186.

109. "7,000 in Capital March for Spies," *New York Times,* June 15, 1953, 44; Memorandum for the Files, June 14, 1953, letter from Michael Rosenberg to DDE, The Rosenbergs R, Alpha File Box 2673, White House Central, DDEL. Michael's previous letter, dated May 1953, is discussed in Chapter 3.

110. Justices Black and Frankfurter dissented. See Lichtman, *Supreme Court and McCarthy-Era Repression,* 59–60; and Snyder, "Taking Great Cases."

111. John H. Finerty, who joined Rosenberg attorney Manny Bloch, was not much more successful in arguing for a writ of habeas corpus for the Rosenbergs than he was some twenty-five years earlier, when he had attempted to persuade the court to overturn the Sacco and Vanzetti convictions. Murphy, *Wild Bill,* 320; Radosh and Milton, *Rosenberg File,* 397–399; Parrish, "Cold War Justice," 833–834.

112. FSD from Vest, AmEmbassy, Ottawa, June 16, 1953, received June 20, 3820, 7, 114–116, Infoguide Bulletin 378 from Dulles, June 13, 1953, 3820, 6, 083–086, 761.5211, RG 59, NA. The protest emphasized numerous individuals who had spoken out in favor of the Rosenbergs, including Eleanor Roosevelt.

113. FSD from Smith, AmEmbassy, Brussels, June 15, 1953, received June 20, 3820, 7, 106–107, 761.5211, RG 59, NA. Embassy officials admitted that in spite of their best efforts—including providing mimeographed handouts of Bradlee's analysis of the case—the "general sentiment in opposition to execution is very great."

114. Telegram from Ambassador Chapin, The Hague, June 15, 1953, noon, rec'd 2:25pm (corrected copy), 3820, 6, 101–102; Infoguide Bulletin 378 from Dulles, June 13, 1953, 3820, 6, 083–086, 761.5211, RG 59, NA.

115. Opposition to the death sentence was partly the result of "longstanding disapproval [of] capital punishment, which was abolished in the Netherlands in 1872." Telegram from Ambassador Chapin, The Hague, June 15, 1953, noon, received 2:25pm (corrected copy), 3820, 6, 101–102; Infoguide Bulletin 378 from Dulles, June 13, 1953, 3820, 6, 083–086, 761.5211, RG 59, NA.

116. FSD from Ward, AmConGen, Geneva, June 16, 1953, received June 19, 7, 111, 761.5211, RG 59, NA.

117. FSD from AmEmbassy, Lisbon, Portugal, June 26, 1953, received June 30, 3820, 6, 093; Infoguide Bulletin 378 from Dulles, June 13, 1953, 3820, 6, 083–086, 761.5211, RG 59, NA.

118. CIA Memorandum, Polish Government Offer of Sanctuary, June 16, 1953, http://www.foia. cia.gov/collection/atomic-spies-ethel-and-julius-rosenberg; Telegram from Ambassador Flack, Warsaw, June 16, 1953, noon, 3820, 7, 110, 761.5211, RG 59, NA; Telegram from Ambassador Joseph Flack, Warsaw, June 15, 1953, 5 p.m., 3820, 4, 189 (in Polish, 3820, 6, 099–100), 761.5211, RG 59, NA; Telegram from Ambassador Joseph Flack, Warsaw, June 17, 1953, noon, 3820, 7, 145, 761.5211, RG 59, NA. Katherine Sibley notes that when

Morton Sobell was arrested in Mexico and brought back to the United States for trial with the Rosenbergs, he had "airline and steamship brochures in his apartment, with information about Poland-bound ships." Sibley, *Red Spies*, 199.

119. CIA Memorandum, Polish Government Offer of Sanctuary, June 16, 1953, http://www.foia. cia.gov/collection/atomic-spies-ethel-and-julius-rosenberg; Telegram from Ambassador Flack, Warsaw, June 16, 1953, noon, 3820, 7, 110, 761.5211, RG 59, NA; telegram from Ambassador Joseph Flack, Warsaw, June 15, 1953, 5 p.m., 3820, 4, 189 (in Polish, 3820, 6, 099–100), 761.5211, RG 59, NA; telegram from Ambassador Joseph Flack, Warsaw, June 17, 1953, noon, 3820, 7, 145, 761.5211, RG 59, NA.

120. FBI File, New York File, Julius Rosenberg, File: 65-15348, Sub E (6), https://vault.fbi.gov/ rosenberg-case/julius-rosenberg.

121. CIA Memorandum, Polish Government Offer of Sanctuary, June 16, 1953, http://www. foia.cia.gov/collection/atomic-spies-ethel-and-julius-rosenberg.

122. Telegram from Dillon, Paris, June 15, 1953, sent 10 p.m., received 8:31 p.m., 3820, 7, 103, 761.5211, RG 59, NA; FSD from Dillon, American Embassy, Paris, June 16, 1953, air pouch, received June 19, 3820, 7, 112, 761.5211, RG 59, NA.

123. Telegram from Dillon, Paris, June 15, 1953, sent 10 p.m., received 8:31 p.m., 3820, 7, 103, 761.5211, RG 59, NA; FSD from Dillon, American Embassy, Paris, June 16, 1953, air pouch, received June 19, 3820, 7, 112, 761.5211, RG 59, NA. The embassy also received an appeal from the Bishop of Orleans, who asked that "in the name of Christ and therefore outside any partisan opinion" Eisenhower should reprieve the Rosenbergs. Bishop quoted in "Slim Hope for Rosenbergs," *The Guardian*, June 15, 1953.

124. Defense attorneys had tentatively raised the issue of the Atomic Energy Act and the death penalty in the January 1953 Petition for Executive Clemency, 3819, 18, 334, 761.5211, RG 59, NA. New lawyers included Fyke Farmer and Daniel G. Marshall. For a clear summary of the numerous issues Rosenberg lawyers raised questioning the trial and the sentence, see Parrish, "Cold War Justice," 812–814.

125. Parrish, "Cold War Justice," 834.

126. Douglas, *Court Years*, 80–81.

127. Ibid.

128. Ibid.

129. Memo Scott to Dulles, June 16, 1953, Box 73, Entry A1 1587-M, File: IPO-P, MacKnight, Rosenberg Case (1952–53), Subject Files of the Policy Plans & Guidance Staff, 1946–62, Bureau of Public Affairs, RG 59, NA; and 3820, 6, 063–087, 761.5211, RG 59, NA; Memo Scott to Brownell, June 16, 1953, 3829, 7, 128, 761.5211, RG 59, NA.

130. Memo Scott to Brownell, June 16, 1953, 3829, 7, 128, 761.5211, RG 59, NA.

131. Telephone conversation with Dulles and Brownell, 11:07 a.m., June 16, 1953, John Foster Dulles Papers, Telephone Conversation Series, Box 1, Telephone Memo May–June 1953 (1), DDEL.

132. Ibid. Dulles also explained it was unfortunate that the possible stay in the Rosenberg case coincided with the court's recent overturning of a Communist Party member's perjury conviction case (Harry Bridges), which he feared some might see as a judicial weakness for Communism.

133. Ethel Rosenberg to DDE, June 16, 1953, File: 101-R Rosenbergs(1), Box 411, Official File, White House Central Files, DDEL. The *New York Times* printed this letter on June 19, 1953. See also Meeropol, ed., *Rosenberg Letters*, 697–699.

134. Ethel Rosenberg to DDE, June 16, 1953, File: 101-R Rosenbergs(1), Box 411, Official File, White House Central Files, DDEL.

135. Ibid.

136. Ibid.

137. Meeropol, ed., *Rosenberg Letters*, 699–700.

138. Ibid.

139. DDE letter to Major John S. D. Eisenhower, June 16, 1953, Box 3, File: December 1952–July 1953 (1), Ann Whitman File, 1953-1961, DDE Diary Series, DDE Papers, DDEL.

140. Ibid.

141. Ibid.

142. Ibid. Eisenhower also believed there were "the out and out cranks," who wrote "threatening letters," requiring the president to order increased security for his grandchildren.
143. Letter from Professor Clyde Miller to DDE, June 8, 1953, File: Rosenberg Case Statement Box 32, Administration Series, Ann Whitman File, 1953–1961, DDE Papers, DDEL.
144. Telegram to Mrs. Eisenhower from Mrs. Sophie Rosenberg, June 15, 1953, DDE White House Central Alpha File, Box 2672, File: The Rosenbergs (J&E) (1), DDEL.
145. Ibid.
146. "Ike Won't Spare Spies, Clergy Says," *Milwaukee Sentinel*, June 17, 1953, 1, 6. Ignoring the gravity of the situation, the paper chose to run a regular feature "Today's Chuckle," adjacent to the article.
147. Niebuhr, *Christian Realism*, 34.
148. This was essentially the same essay he published in *The New Leader* on June 8, 1953. The piece was also used as a radio broadcast, airing ten days after the Rosenbergs were executed. Fox, *Reinhold Niebuhr*, 255.
149. Quoted in Fox, *Reinhold Niebuhr*, 255.
150. FSD from Haering, U.S. ConGen, Toronto, Canada, June 19, 1953, 3820, 8, 192, 761.5211, RG 59, NA.
151. Papers included the *London Daily Worker, New Statesman and Nation,* the *Manchester Guardian,* and the *London Times.* Telegram from London Embassy, June 16, 1953, 8 p.m., rec'd 5:14 p.m., 3820, 7, 109, 761.5211, RG 59, NA; *Manchester Guardian,* June 17, 1953, quoted in Glynn, "L'Affaire Rosenberg in France," 498, 502.
152. "Slim Hope for Rosenbergs," *The Guardian,* June 15, 1953; Telegram from London, June 16, 1953, 8 p.m., rec'd 5:14 p.m., 3820, 7, 109, 761.5211, RG 59, NA.
153. FSD from McClelland and Hulley, London, July 7, 1953, 3820, 9, 209, 761.5211, RG 59, NA.
154. Telegram from Nufer, Buenos Aires, June 16, 1953, 6 p.m., received 6:03 p.m., 3820, 7, 129, 761.5211, RG 59, NA.
155. FSD from Hoard, AmConsul, Porto Alegre, Brazil, June 16, 1953, received June 20, 2:15 p.m., 3820, 7, 130, 761.5211, RG 59, NA; Telegram from Caracas, June 16, 1953, 3 p.m., received 6:42 p.m., 3820, 7, 131, 761.5211, RG 59, NA.
156. FSD from American Embassy, Guatemala, June 18, 1953, 3820, 8, 159, 761.5211, RG 59, NA.
157. FSD from AmEmbassy, Mexico, D.P., June 16, 1953, received June 18, 1:37 p.m., 3820, 7, 132–133, 761.5211, RG 59, NA.
158. Embassy officials initially dismissed the event as a failure because the majority of protesters were women and the elderly. FSD from Smith, AmEmbassy, Brussels, June 17, 1953, 3820, 7, 142–144, 761.5211, RG 59, NA.
159. Officials also reminded Washington that an international panel of lawyers from Brussels and throughout Europe, organized earlier in June, was working on the case. "It would be a very useful thing," they explained, "from the standpoint of American prestige, if this 'tribunal' arrived at the same conclusion reached by the New York Federal jury," though they feared this was unlikely in the current European "emotional climate." The panel would not reach a verdict until after the executions. FSD from Smith, AmEmbassy, Brussels, June 17, 1953, 3820, 7, 142–144, 761.5211, RG 59, NA.
160. Telegram from Copenhagen Embassy, June 16, 1953, 3820, 7, 121–122, 761.5211, RG 59, NA.
161. Airgram from Dulles to AmEmbassy, Copenhagen, July 7, 1953, 3820, 7, 120, 761.5211, RG 59, NA.
162. Telegram from Elisabeth, Duchess of Bavaria to President Eisenhower, June 15, 1953, 3820, 6, 062, 761.5211, RG 59, NA.
163. Memo from Sherman Adams to Mr. Simmons, State Department, June 16, 1953, 3820, 6, 061, 761.5211, RG 59, NA.
164. Across the Iron Curtain, a massive labor strike in East Berlin and throughout East Germany—nearly 400,000 workers and growing—forced the Eisenhower administration to consider a course of action. The CIA had played a role in spreading the uprising, and administration officials had spoken of moving beyond containment and liberating those

in the Soviet bloc, but the White House ultimately chose not to intervene. The president and secretary of state feared that openly supporting the protesters in East Berlin could provoke a nuclear confrontation with the Soviet Union. Better, they decided, to demonstrate American power with continued covert support and public displays of strength. The Cold Warriors likely saw executing two atomic spies as a great way to display such strength. The instability in Eastern Europe would encourage the administration to embrace the findings of Project Solarium, resulting in the Fall 1953 NSC 162 series, which re-evaluated the world post-Stalin, questioned the rollback of global Communism, and called for a possible negotiated settlement of the Cold War. See Kinzer, *Brothers*, 140–142; Mitrovich, *Undermining the Kremlin*, 132–151.

165. Brogi, "Ambassador Clare Boothe Luce," 269–294.

166. Telegram from Luce, Rome, June 16, 1953, 3820, 7, 124, 761.5211, RG 59, NA.

167. Memo for files sent to Bernard Shanley, Presidential Adviser, June 17, 1953, Alpha File Box 2673, File: The Rosenbergs (B), White House Central Files, DDEL.

168. Telegram from Dillon, Paris, June 16, 1953, 1 p.m., received 9:37 a.m., 3820, 7, 117–118, 761.5211, RG 59, NA [second page missing in file].

169. Ibid.

170. Ibid.

171. Ibid.

172. Ibid.

173. Telegram from Dillon, Paris, June 16, 1953, 9 p.m., received 8:49 p.m., 3820, 7, 119, 761.5211, RG 59, NA.

174. Ibid.

175. Ibid.; Memorandum from O'Connor, State Department to Hagerty, White House, June 17, 1953, 3820, 8, 153, 761.5211, RG 59, NA.

176. Murphy, *Wild Bill*, 323; A. H. Belmont to D. M. Ladd, June 17, 1953, copy in File: John V. Lindsay Correspondence, 1989–95, Box 18, Herbert Brownell Jr.: Additional Papers, 1897–1996, DDEL. This collection of papers explores the accusation of *ex parte* communication between Brownell and Vinson. See Sharlitt, *Fatal Error*, 66–74; Radosh and Milton, *Rosenberg File*, 403; Parrish, "Cold War Justice," 835.

177. The 136 American casualties included 19 killed, 101 wounded, 10 prisoners, and 6 injured; "Casualties in Korea," *New York Times*, June 17, 1953, 2.

178. Secretary Dulles "disclosed yesterday that eleven books in the State Department libraries actually had been burned in recent weeks." See Anthony Leviero, "Eisenhower Backed on Book Ban Talk," *New York Times*, June 17, 1953, 1. The speech endorsed "free thought," but the State Department ordered that it not be broadcast around the world on Voice of America.

179. Press Conference, June 17, 1953, Press Conference Series, Box 1, File: Press Conference, Ann Whitman File, DDE Papers, DDEL.

180. Murphy, *Wild Bill*, 324; Douglas, *Court Years*, 80–81; Radosh and Milton, *Rosenberg File*, 402. Douglas was particularly concerned "whether this death sentence may be imposed for this offense except and unless a jury recommends it." Quoted in Lichtman, *Supreme Court and McCarthy-Era Repression*, 60.

181. Murphy, *Wild Bill*, 324; Douglas, *Court Years*, 80–81; Radosh and Milton, *Rosenberg File*, 402.

182. Telephone Conversation with Dulles and Allen Dulles, 11:40 a.m., June 17, 1953, John Foster Dulles Papers, Telephone Conversation Series, Box 1, Telephone Memo May–June 1953 (1), DDEL. Some have argued that if the stay had remained in effect and the case was brought before the high court under new Chief Justice Earl Warren in October, hysteria likely would have subsided during the ensuing months and the Rosenbergs may have received a reduced sentence and possibly a new trial. See Radosh and Milton, *Rosenberg File*, 409; Meeropol and Meeropol, *We Are Your Sons*, 231; Parrish, "Cold War Justice," 840.

183. Hundreds of protesters petitioned in Le Havre; Memorandum from American Consulate, Le Havre, France, June 16, 1953, 3820, 7, 125–126, 761.5211, RG 59, NA; Memorandum from American Consulate, Le Havre, France, June 17, 1953, 3820, 7, 146–147, 761.5211, RG 59, NA.

184. FBI File, New York File, Julius Rosenberg, File: 65-15348, Sub E (6), https://vault.fbi. gov/rosenberg-case/julius-rosenberg. Consulate officials told the delegation their petition would receive "appropriate consideration," but the diplomats believed the women's group was a Communist front and forwarded the petition via air pouch where it did not reach Washington, D.C. until June 25, nearly a week after the executions. FSD from Anderson, AmConsulate General, Belfast, June 18, 1953, received June 25, 3820, 8, 171, 761.5211, RG 59, NA.

185. Telegram from Bay, Oslo Embassy, June 17, 1953, received 2:02 p.m., 3820, 8, 151, 761.5211, RG 59, NA.

186. Telegram from Chapin, The Hague Embassy, June 17, 1953, 3 p.m., received 2:10 p.m., 3820, 8, 152, 761.5211, RG 59, NA.

187. Ibid.

188. Ibid.

189. FSD from Vest, Embassy, Ottawa, June 19, 1953, received June 22, 3820, 8, 181–191, 761.5211, RG 59, NA (duplicated 3820, 5, 006–008).

190. According to embassy officials, stories concerning the Rosenberg case were often based on the daily cables of the Agence France Presse (AFP). FSD from AmEmbassy, Montevideo, Uruguay, June 17, 1953, received June 20, 3820, 8, 154, 761.5211, RG 59, NA.

191. FSD from AmEmbassy, Montevideo, Uruguay, June 17, 1953, received June 20, 3820, 8, 154, 761.5211, RG 59, NA. Communist protest also occurred on the afternoon of the fifteenth; the Embassy in Montevideo, Uruguay, reported "a last-minute flurry of clemency requests" from Communists "on behalf of the Rosenberg couple." Protests came in the form of eighteen telegrams; a letter from the Union de Obreros y Empleados de Almacenes, Cafés, y Bars (a Communist-controlled labor union); a petition presented by two adults and some thirty school children on behalf of the Israelite Central School; and an announcement in *Justicia*, the Communist newspaper, of a petition presented to the Embassy by Union Feminina. According to Embassy officials, all protests originated from pro-Communist sources. FSD from Devine, AmEmbassy, Montevideo, Uruguay, June 15, 1953, received June 18, 3820, 4, 190, 761.5211, RG 59, NA.

192. FSD from Aragon, AmEmbassy, San Jose, Costa Rica, June 18, 1953, received June 22, 3820, 8, 164–165, 761.5211, RG 59, NA.

193. The Costa Rican Red Cross received word from the Polish Red Cross asking them to support Rosenberg clemency, which they promptly declined. FSD from Aragon, AmEmbassy, San Jose, Costa Rica, June 18, 1953, received June 22, 3820, 8, 164–165, 761.5211, RG 59, NA.

194. Telegram from Jones, Tel Aviv Embassy, June 17, 1953, 3 p.m., received June 18, 12:01 p.m., 3820, 7, 135, 761.5211, RG 59, NA.

195. Ibid.

196. Brownell/Dulles Telephone Conversation, June 17, 1953, 4 p.m., File: Telephone Memoranda May–June 1953(1), Box 1, Telephone Call Series, John Foster Dulles Papers, DDEL.

197. Douglas believed that Vinson "had no authority to convene a Special Term of Court," which needed a vote of five justices. Vinson "was in a towering rage at the suggestion" and Douglas let it go. Douglas was also upset that the court would have met without him since Vinson "never tried to reach me, as he easily could have by alerting the state police of Pennsylvania." Douglas, *The Court Years*, 80–81, 237; Murphy, *Wild Bill*, 324; Brownell/Dulles Telephone Conversation, June 17, 1953, 4 p.m., File: Telephone Memoranda May–June 1953(1), Box 1, Telephone Call Series, John Foster Dulles Papers, DDEL.

198. Quoted in Radosh and Milton, *Rosenberg File*, 417; Philipson, *Ethel Rosenberg*, 355.

199. DDE letter to Mr. C. C. Burlingham, June 17, 1953, Box 411, File: 101R, Rosenbergs (2), Official File, White House Central Files, DDE Papers, DDEL.

200. "East Berlin Riots—Julius and Ethel Rosenberg—June 17, 1953," *See It Now*, June 17, 1953, audio file at 11:33, http://pastdaily.com/2014/06/17/east-berlin-riots-julius-ethel-rosenberg-june-17-1953/.

201. See William Whelan to New York, June 15, 1953, FBI File, New York File, Julius Rosenberg, File: 65-15348-2398, Sub E (6), https://vault.fbi.gov/rosenberg-case/julius-rosenberg.

202. FBI File, New York File, Julius Rosenberg, File: 65-15348-2398, Sub E (4), https://vault.fbi.gov/rosenberg-case/julius-rosenberg.
203. Meeropol and Meeropol, *We Are Your Sons*, 236.
204. Bob Considine, "Keep Phone Lines Open for Rosenbergs to 'Sing,'" *Milwaukee Sentinel*, June 17, 1953, 1, 6.
205. William Whelan to New York, 15 June 1953, FBI File, New York File, Julius Rosenberg, File: 65-15348-2398, Sub E (6), https://vault.fbi.gov/rosenberg-case/julius-rosenberg; Thomas McAndrews to New York, June 15, 1953, File: 65-15348-2400, Sub E (6), https://vault.fbi.gov/rosenberg-case/julius-rosenberg.
206. Thomas McAndrews to New York, June 15, 1953, File: 65-15348-2400, Sub E (6), https://vault.fbi.gov/rosenberg-case/julius-rosenberg.
207. William Whelan to New York, June 15, 1953, FBI File, New York File, Julius Rosenberg, File: 65-15348-2398, Sub E (6), https://vault.fbi.gov/rosenberg-case/julius-rosenberg.
208. FSD from Aragon, AmEmbassy, San Jose, Costa Rica, June 18, 1953, received June 22, 3820, 8, 164–166, 761.5211, RG 59, NA. In Cuba, the stay of execution was front-page news. *Hoy*, the Communist daily in Havana, Cuba, used the headline "Partial Victory of the World Peace Movement" in coverage that emphasized "the 'railroading' of the Rosenbergs." *Hoy* also claimed that Justice Douglas's decision was "the product of the intense and growing mobilization of the masses in the whole world" and was supported by all but those in the "imperialistic circles" within the United States. The Havana Embassy also received about twenty telegrams, six letters, and some fifty signatures petitioning for clemency. FSD from Crain, AmEmbassy, Habana, Cuba, June 18, 1953, received June 19, 3820, 8, 155–156, 761.5211, RG 59, NA.
209. FSD from Vest, Embassy, Ottawa, June 19, 1953, received June 22, 3820, 8, 181–191, 761.5211, RG 59, NA.
210. Consulate officials claimed they could tell that the "violently anti-American" protesters were Communists and most were Jewish. FSD from US ConGen Toronto to State, June 22, 1953, 3820, 5, 010–011, 761.5211, RG 59, NA.
211. FSD from Vest, Embassy, Ottawa, June 19, 1953, received June 22, 3820, 8, 181–191, 761.5211, RG 59, NA; FSD from Johnson, AmConsulate, Regina, Saskatchewan, Canada, June 19, 1953, 3820, 8, 178–180, 761.5211, RG 59, NA.
212. FSD from AmConsul, Calcutta, India to State, June 22, 1953, 3820, 5, 012–016, 761.5211, RG 59, NA.
213. Telegram from Dillon, Paris, June 18, 1953, 6 p.m., received 4:10 p.m., 3820, 8, 170, 761.5211, RG 59, NA.
214. Ibid.
215. Telegram from Dillon, Paris, June 19, 1953, noon, received 8:03 a.m., 3820, 8, 172–174, 761.5211, RG 59, NA.
216. Ibid. Friendly is misspelled "firendly" in original.
217. Ibid.
218. Court of Appeals Judge Jerome Frank (who wrote to sustain the convictions in 1952) later stated that if Douglas's stay had not been vacated, "there is no doubt that the Court of Appeals would have held that the imposition of the death sentence was improper." Douglas, *Court Years*, 79.
219. Douglas, *Court Years*, 81.
220. Ibid. See also Parrish, "Cold War Justice," 835–836.
221. FBI File, New York File, Julius Rosenberg, File: 65-15348-2422E, https://vault.fbi.gov/rosenberg-case/julius-rosenberg.
222. Murphy, *Wild Bill*, 325. The final vote to vacate was 6–3, with Black, Frankfurter, and Douglas dissenting. Chief Justice Vinson died after a heart attack in September 1953, and Earl Warren succeeded him in October.
223. Bruce Allen Murphy argues that the Rosenbergs died in part because "on a frayed Supreme Court, Felix Frankfurter and Robert Jackson were motivated to prevent Douglas from taking the moral high ground." See Murphy, *Wild Bill*, 324–326; Douglas, *Court Years*, 39, 81, 83. For a different view of Frankfurter's role see Parrish, "Cold War Justice," 836–837. Jill Lepore states Frankfurter "may have been the most divisive Justice ever to serve on the Court." For a

discussion of Frankfurter and his missing court papers, see Lepore, "The Great Paper Caper," *New Yorker*, December 1, 2014, 33.

224. Representative Frank L. Chelf quoted in Lichtman, *Supreme Court and McCarthy-Era Repression*, 62.

225. Cabinet Meeting Minutes, June 19, 1953, 71–76, Cabinet Series, Box 1, File: C-5 (2), Office of the Staff Secretary: Records, 1952–1961, White House Office, DDE Papers, DDEL.

226. Reported by L. Arthur Minnich, Cabinet Minutes, June 19, 1953, p. 3, Box 2, Cabinet Series, DDEL; Cabinet Meeting Notes, June 19, 1953, File C-5 (2), Box 1, Cabinet Series, White House Office, Office of the Staff Secretary: Records, 52–61, DDEL.

227. Emphasis in original. Cabinet Meeting Minutes, June 19, 1953, 71–76, Cabinet Series, Box 1, File: C-5 (2), Office of the Staff Secretary: Records, 1952–1961, White House Office, DDE Papers, DDEL. C. D. Jackson suggested they prepare a "White Book" on the case to clear up "confusion even in well-meaning minds." June 19, 1953 Log, File: Log 1953 (2), Box 68, C. D. Jackson Papers, 1931–89, DDEL.

228. Cabinet Meeting Minutes, June 19, 1953, 71–76, Cabinet Series, Box 1, File: C-5 (2), Office of the Staff Secretary: Records, 1952–1961, White House Office, DDE Papers, DDEL. Stephen Ambrose discusses the Rosenberg case in *Eisenhower: The President*. On page 84 Ambrose writes that on the day of the executions Eisenhower "said he could not remember a time in his life when he felt more in need of help from someone more powerful than he," which I believe to be an incorrect statement. Ambrose's footnote cites Hughes, *Ordeal of Power*, 80; and Minnich, Cabinet, Reported by L. Arthur Minnich, Cabinet Minutes, June 19, 1953, p. 3, Box 2, Cabinet Series, DDEL, and neither source makes mention of Eisenhower's "need of help." This sentiment is not in any of the versions of the June 19 Cabinet meeting agendas or minutes.

229. June 17, 1953, 1–2, Box 411, File: 101-R Rosenbergs (2), Official File, White House Central Files, DDEL.

230. June 19, 1953 Log, File: Log 1953 (2), Box 68, C. D. Jackson Papers, 1931-89, DDEL.

231. Press Release, June 19, 1953, Alpha File Box 2673, The Rosenbergs, U-W, White House Central Files, DDEL. C. D. Jackson prepared the draft, which Eisenhower and Hagerty approved nearly in its entirety. One line that did not make it into the final statement: "Democracy does not use the firing squad without due process of law." June 19, 1953, memo and draft from Jackson to Hagerty, File R, Box 5, C. D. Jackson Records, 1953-54, DDEL.

232. Author Stephen Kinzer argues that Ike's refusal to pardon the Rosenbergs "toughened his image" in the aftermath of his approval of the truce in Korea, "but it was not enough." Kinzer links CIA action in Iran in 1953 to the administration needing a "quick success." *Brothers*, 129–130.

233. May 9–14, 1953, Question #1, and July 4–9, 1953, Question #1a, Gallup, *Gallup Poll*, 1142, 1157.

234. William Whelan to New York, June 19, 1953, FBI File, New York File, Julius Rosenberg, File: 65-15348-2422C, https://vault.fbi.gov/rosenberg-case/julius-rosenberg.

235. Tradition dictates that Shabbat begins with the lighting of candles eighteen minutes before sunset on Friday night and continues until Saturday evening.

236. Roberts, *Brother*, 11.

237. Ibid.

238. Radosh and Milton, *Rosenberg File*, 414–415.

239. Ibid.

240. John Foster Dulles telephone conversation with Attorney General Brownell, June 19, 1953, 5:50pm, File: Telephone Memoranda, May–June 1953 (1), Telephone Call Series, Box 1, John Foster Dulles Papers, DDEL. The Senators lost to the Cleveland Indians that evening. "1953 Washington Senators Schedule," Baseball Almanac, http://www.baseball-almanac.com/teamstats/schedule.php?y=1953&t=WS1.

241. Arthur Krock, "Case of the Rosenbergs Will Long Be Debated," *New York Times*, June 21, 1953.

242. Quoted in Neville, *Press*, 134.

243. Telegram from Chapin, The Hague, June 22, 1953, 6 p.m., received 2:37 p.m., 3820, 5, 028, 761.5211, RG 59, NA.
244. FSD from AmLegation, Bern, June 19, 1953, received June 25, 3820, 8, 175–177, 761.5211, RG 59, NA.
245. As president of Columbia University, Eisenhower had listened to Churchill and taken up painting to relieve stress. As president of the United States, Eisenhower would agree with Churchill and orchestrate a U.S.-led coup in Iran to overthrow the Mossadegh government in the summer of 1953. Newton, *Eisenhower*, 104.
246. "Execution of the Rosenbergs," *The Guardian*, June 20, 1953, http://www.theguardian.com/world/1953/jun/20/usa.fromthearchive.
247. See www.rosenbergtrial.org.
248. Some accounts stated that the man shot later died. FBI File: Julius and Ethel Rosenberg, Part 2, p. 108, www.foia.fbi.gov/foiaindex/roberg.htm.
249. "The Rosenbergs' Appeal for Stay of Execution is Unsuccessful," The Camel News Caravan, New York: NBC Universal, June 19, 1953, http://bcps.nbclearn.com/portal/site/k-12/flatview?cuecard=1787.
250. Deputy Director D. M. Ladd to Director J. Edgar Hoover memo, June 15, 1953, quoted in Radosh and Milton, *Rosenberg File*, 416, n. 576. According to Radosh and Milton, the warden "had strenuously objected to the possibility of giving the Rosenbergs a chance to talk after they entered the execution chamber, noting that this was a violation of the prison's strict policy against allowing the condemned to deliver any 'last words.'"
251. Confirmed in October 2015 email from Mike Meeropol in author's possession. See also Meeropol and Meeropol, *We Are Your Sons*, 137, 232–238. In a nod to anti-Communism in April 1953 the Cincinnati Reds changed their name to Redlegs. They reverted back in 1959: "If the communists don't like it, let them change their name. We were Reds before they were." Greg Rhodes, Cincinnati Reds team historian, quoted in Bob Greene, "When the Reds Showed Their Legs," May 29, 2011, http://www.cnn.com/2011/OPINION/05/29/greene.redlegs/.
252. Dodgers 8–11, 7–1; Yankees lost 3–2; http://www.baseball-reference.com/boxes/CHN/CHN195306191.shtml.
253. Six-year-old Robert, just completing kindergarten, recalled playing "a lot of Monopoly" that summer, which he later claimed was "quite a life lesson for the child of Communists." Meeropol, *Execution in the Family*, 1–2.
254. Quoted in Roberts, *Brother*, 14.
255. Meeropol and Meeropol, *We Are Your Sons*, 237; Meeropol, ed., *Rosenberg Letters*, 704; Roberts, *Brother*, 14.
256. Luther A. Huston, "Six Justices Agree, President Says Couple Increased 'Chances of Atomic War,'" June 20, 1953, *New York Times* 1, 8.
257. According to the rabbi's wife in Ivy Meeropol's documentary, *Heir to an Execution*, Rabbi Koslowe himself chose Julius to go first.
258. Gentry, *J. Edgar Hoover*, 427.
259. An electrician and an executioner, Francel worked for $150 per prisoner, and had been killing for the state for fourteen years. He resigned after the execution of the Rosenbergs, saying he was tired of inquisitive reporters and anonymous threats. One such threat came from Madrid, Spain, on August 29, 1953, FBI File, New York File, Julius Rosenberg, File: 65-15348-2505, Sub E (6), https://vault.fbi.gov/rosenberg-case/julius-rosenberg. For more on Francel, see Roberts, *Brother*, 13, 16.
260. Quoted in Roberts, *Brother*, 18; see also Gentry, *J. Edgar Hoover*, 427.
261. Roberts, *Brother*, 15.
262. William R. Conklin, "Pair Silent to End: Husband is First to Die—Both Composed on Going to Chair," *New York Times*, June 20, 1953, 1.
263. Roberts, *Brother*, 16.
264. Conklin, "Pair Silent To End," 1, 6; Bob Considine (International News Service), Relman Morin (Associated Press), and Jack Woliston (United Press) were the three.
265. Quoted in Roberts, *Brother*, 19.

266. A total of 614 prisoners, eight of them women, were executed by electrocution at Sing Sing Prison between 1891 and 1963. Ethel Rosenberg's execution is considered "botched"; see Sarat, *Gruesome Spectacles*, 61–89. The sun set at 8:30 p.m.; Shabbat had begun at 8:12 p.m.
267. FBI Supervisor and Venona cryptanalyst Robert Lamphere, in Roberts, *The Brother*, 432, 519N; Gentry, *J. Edgar Hoover*, 428; Douglas Martin, "Robert J. Lamphere, 83, Spy Chaser for the F.B.I., Dies," *New York Times*, February 11, 2002.
268. The Rosenbergs remain the only Americans and only civilians to be executed for crimes related to espionage. The FBI learned, as Katherine Sibley later wryly noted: "Dead spies don't talk"; *Red Spies*, 235.
269. Quoted in Roberts, *Brother*, 432.
270. Telegrams 6, 095–096; 5, 046; 7, 104–107; 5, 012–016; 9, 209; 5, 006–008; 5, 043–044; 8, 178–180; 5, 038–040; 5, 049; 5, 028; 5, 010–011, 6, 055–056; 761.5211, RG 59, NA.
271. Writer John Wexley attended the Union Square meeting and recalls people "packed into the street running from Union Square to Fifth Avenue. You couldn't move between people, the street was so packed." Wexley went on to write about the Rosenberg case, and was interviewed for McGilligan and Buhle, eds., *Tender Comrades*, 719.
272. On June 19 Central Park's high temperature was eighty-nine degrees and moderately humid; the following day Central Park's high was ninety-seven degrees and humid.
273. *New York Times*, June 20, 1953, 1, 6; Roberts, *Brother*, 15.
274. Kaufman had married Helen Rosenberg (no relation to Julius or Ethel) in June 1936. See Roberts, *Brother*, 21.
275. Max Lerner, "The Long Last Day," *New York Post*, June 21, 1953, 8-M.
276. "Curiosity," episode 38 of the first season of *The Adventures of Ozzie and Harriet*, aired on June 19, 1953. See http://www.tv.com/shows/the-adventures-of-ozzie-and-harriet/curiosity-19411/.
277. Miller, *Timebends*, 347.
278. Meeropol and Meeropol, *We Are Your Sons*, 235; Meeropol, ed., *Rosenberg Letters*, 703.

Chapter 5

1. John Fitzpatrick, "Ike Likes Golf . . . and it Booms!," *Golf Digest* 4, July 1953. Per *Golf Digest*, 1953: April (6 days of golf), May (8), June (5), July (5), August (9), September (8). See http://www.golfdigest.com/story/ike-2008-04.
2. June 19, 1953 Log, File: Log 1953 (2), Box 68, C. D. Jackson Papers, 1931-89, DDEL.
3. *Le Monde* editorial, quoted in FSD from Dillon, Paris, June 22, 1953, in FBI File, Julius Rosenberg, File: 65-58236 (HQ), Section: 68 Referrals, Main File, https://vault.fbi.gov/rosenberg-case/rosenberg-referrals.
4. According to the Gallup Poll, more than 63% of Americans approved the use of the death penalty in November 1953. Considine used the phrase "meet their maker" in reporting the Rosenberg executions.
5. Sylvia Plath, diary entry, June 19, 1953, quoted in Okun, ed., *Rosenbergs*, 22.
6. According to Mike Meeropol, Julius's sister, Ethel Rosenberg Goldberg, also attended but "in effect incognito." October 2015 email in author's possession. Brooklyn hit a record for June 21 of 93.7 degrees. I. J. Morris Funeral Chapel at Church Avenue and Rockaway Parkway in Brooklyn, New York. Roberts, *Brother*, 22.
7. Excerpt from W. E. B. DuBois, "The Rosenbergs: Ethel and Michael, Robert and Julius," in Okun, ed., *Rosenbergs*, 140.
8. Quoted in "Bloch, Attorney for Spies, is Dead," *New York Times*, January 31, 1954.
9. For Bloch's eulogy see "Milestones," *Time*, February 8, 1954; "Bloch, Attorney for Spies, is Dead," *New York Times*, January 31, 1954; "Counsel for Spies Faces Bar Inquiry" and "McCarthy Discusses Lawyers," *New York Times*, June 25, 1953.
10. H.R. 290. The only prior Supreme Court impeachment was Samuel Chase in 1804, which ended in an acquittal; Douglas, *Court Years*, 86–87, 330; "Justice Douglas Accused in House," *New York Times*, June 30, 1953, 13.
11. See Lichtman, *Supreme Court and McCarthy-Era Repression*, 62.

12. "House Move to Impeach Douglas Bogs Down; Sponsor Is Told He Fails to Prove His Case," *New York Times*, July 1, 1953, 18.

13. *Washington Post*, July 2, 1953.

14. Douglas, *Court Years*, 86–87, 330. Many members of Congress refrained from openly expressing their opinion on the case. For example, neither Lyndon Johnson nor John F. Kennedy discussed the Rosenbergs publicly, perhaps reflecting the careful line they both walked in criticizing the actions of fellow senator, Joseph McCarthy. Johnson enjoyed considerable influence as the leader of the Democratic Party and set the Senate's agenda, which finally acted on the censorship of McCarthy in 1954. Kennedy tried to avoid controversy while in office, not wanting to alienate anyone as he set his sights on the White House. John Shaw argues that Kennedy "acted cautiously" and perhaps used back-surgery recovery to avoid the Senate vote to censure McCarthy in December 1954 (he was the only Democrat to not vote for condemnation). Shaw, *JFK in the Senate*, 64, 86. Just five days after the Rosenbergs were executed, JFK announced his engagement to Jacqueline Bouvier. Kennedy also stayed away from McCarthy because he was a friend of his father's and his brother Robert's former boss. Other than attacking Manny Bloch, Senator McCarthy kept his views on the Rosenbergs to himself. For a possible explanation, see Alman and Alman, *Exoneration*, 281–284.

15. Justice Felix Frankfurter dissent to *Rosenberg v. United States*, 346 U.S. 273, 310, https://supreme.justia.com/cases/federal/us/346/273/case.html.

16. Justice Hugo Black dissent to *Rosenberg v. United States*, 346 U.S. 273, 301, https://supreme.justia.com/cases/federal/us/346/273/case.html.

17. Quoted in Stuart Taylor Jr., "Opposition to Rehnquist Nomination Hardens as 2 New Witnesses Emerge," *New York Times*, July 27, 1986, 18. In 1986 President Ronald Reagan nominated Associate Justice William Rehnquist for the post of Chief Justice, and Senate hearings prompted the release and examination of many of the judge's writings.

18. Infoguide Bulletin 382, Rosenbergs, Circular from Dulles to NY, copy to Berlin, Bern, Bonn, Brussels, Copenhagen, Dublin, London, Ottawa, New Delhi, Oslo, Paris, Rome, Stockholm, Tel Aviv, The Hague, and Vienna, June 19, 1953, 511.00/6-1953, Box 2248 (511.00/5-153—511.00/9-3053), RG 59, NA. For a look at the close relationship between John Foster Dulles, Allen Dulles, and American media, see Kinzer, *Brothers*, 125–126.

19. Infoguide Bulletin 382, Rosenbergs, Circular from Dulles to NY, copy to Berlin, Bern, Bonn, Brussels, Copenhagen, Dublin, London, Ottawa, New Delhi, Oslo, Paris, Rome, Stockholm, Tel Aviv, The Hague, and Vienna, June 19, 1953, 511.00/6-1953, Box 2248 (511.00/5-153—511.00/9-3053), RG 59, NA.

20. "Rosenbergs Are Put to Death," *Life* 34, no. 25, June 22, 1953, 45–46.

21. Ibid.

22. The reporter was Eddie Ranzell, memorandum from SAC, NY, to file, June 23, 1953, FBI File, New York File, Julius Rosenberg, File: 65-15348-2426, Sub E (6), https://vault.fbi.gov/rosenberg-case/julius-rosenberg.

23. Memorandum from SAC, NY, to file, June 23, 1953, FBI File, New York File, Julius Rosenberg, File: 65-15348-2426, Sub E (6), https://vault.fbi.gov/rosenberg-case/julius-rosenberg.

24. Ibid.

25. Neville, *Press*, 139–141. Neville detected a "patriotic bias and political prejudice" in the fourteen U.S. daily papers he analyzed.

26. Infoguide Bulletin 382, Rosenbergs, Circular from Dulles to NY, copy to Berlin, Bern, Bonn, Brussels, Copenhagen, Dublin, London, Ottawa, New Delhi, Oslo, Paris, Rome, Stockholm, Tel Aviv, The Hague, and Vienna, June 19, 1953, 511.00/6-1953, Box 2248 (511.00/5-153—511.00/9-3053), RG 59, NA.

27. FSD from Colquitt, ConGen, Toronto, June 22, 1953, 3820, 5, 010–011, 761.5211, RG 59, NA.

28. Ibid.

29. Memorandum from ConGen, Toronto, June 30, 1953, 3820, 8, 194, 761.5211, RG 59, NA.

30. CIA Memorandum, Cuba Information Report, June 23, 1953, http://www.foia.cia.gov/collection/atomic-spies-ethel-and-julius-rosenberg.

31. FSD from Crain, Havana, Cuba, June 25, 1953, 3820, 6, 091–092, 761.5211, RG 59, NA.

32. CIA Memorandum, Uruguay Information Report, August 24, 1953; CIA Memorandum, Panama Information Report, August 3, 1953; Panama Information Report, August 20, 1953; CIA Memorandum, Information Report—Ecuador, August 28, 1953, Rosenbergs, http://www.foia.cia.gov/collection/atomic-spies-ethel-and-julius-rosenberg.

33. CIA Memorandum, Panama Information Report, August 3, 1953; CIA Memorandum, Information Report—Ecuador, August 28, 1953, Rosenbergs, http://www.foia.cia.gov/collection/atomic-spies-ethel-and-julius-rosenberg.

34. FSD from Siracusa, Buenos Aires, June 23, 1953, 3820, 5, 046, 761.5211, RG 59, NA; FSD from Hanna, Asunción, Paraguay, June 23, 1953, 3820, 5, 045, 761.5211, RG 59, NA.

35. Letter from Rollan Welch, First Secretary of Embassy, Managua, Nicaragua, to C. D. Jackson, June 29, 1953, reply from Jackson to Welch, July 9, 1953, File: 101-R Rosenbergs (1), Box 411, Official File, White House Central Files, DDEL.

36. FSD from Lockett, ConGen, Algiers, June 26, 1953, 3820, 6, 095–096, 761.5211, RG 59, NA.

37. Ibid.

38. Telegram from Lebreton, Tunis, Tunisia, June 22, 1953, 3820, 5, 024, 761.5211, RG 59, NA.

39. FSD from Merris, ConGen, Cape Town, South Africa, June 22, 1953, 3820, 5, 017–022, 761.5211, RG 59, NA.

40. Ibid.

41. Ibid.

42. FSD from Minnigerode, Port Elizabeth, South Africa, June 22, 1953, 3820, 5, 025–027, 761.5211, RG 59, NA.

43. American diplomats in Tangier, however, chose to dedicate their three-page report to Washington on one pro-execution editorial in the newspaper, *España*, which they argued represented "the valiant attempt to understand and present the American position . . . in a favorable light." This was likely due to Francisco Franco's control over the press. Increasing opposition to Spanish control would lead to independence for Morocco in 1956. FSD from Witman, AmLegation, Tangier, Spain, June 25, 1953, 3820, 6, 058–060, 761.5211, RG 59, NA.

44. Telegram from Russell, Tel Aviv, June 23, 1953, 3820, 5, 049, 761.5211, RG 59, NA.

45. Ibid.; FSD from Tyler, ConGen, Jerusalem, June 24, 1953, 3820, 6, 052, 761.5211, RG 59, NA.

46. FSD from Tyler, ConGen, Jerusalem, June 24, 1953, 3820, 6, 052, 761.5211, RG 59, NA.

47. FSD from Berry, Baghdad, Iraq, July 15, 1953, 3820, 9, 224, 761.5211, RG 59, NA.

48. FSD from Wilson, Consul General, Calcutta, India, June 22, 1953, 3820, 5, 012–016, 761.5211, RG 59, NA.

49. FSD from Curtis, Embassy, Djakarta, June 27, 1953, 3820, 6, 097–098, 761.5211, RG 59, NA.

50. Ibid.

51. Ibid.

52. FSD from Green, Stockholm, Sweden, June 23, 1953, 3820, 5, 047–048, 761.5211, RG 59, NA. Famous anti-Communist Swedes who had joined the appeal for clemency included: Archbishop Yngve Brilioth, the head of Sweden's state church; Professor Arne Tiselius of Uppsala University, a Nobel Prize winner; Einar Norrman, vice-president of Sweden's Confederation of Trade Unions; and Karl Gerhard, a prominent producer.

53. FSD from Green, Stockholm, Sweden, June 23, 1953, 3820, 5, 047–048, 761.5211, RG 59, NA.

54. Ibid.

55. FSD from Styles, Göteborg Consulate, June 25, 1953, 3820, 6, 089–090, 761.5211, RG 59, NA.

56. Ibid.

57. Ibid.

58. FSD from Wells, Legation, Helsinki, June 22, 1953, 3820, 5, 029–035, 761.5211, RG 59, NA.

59. Ibid.

60. Telegram from Bohlen, Moscow, June 21, 1953, 3820, 10, 266, 761.5211, RG 59, NA.

61. Ibid.

62. Ibid.

63. CIA Memorandum, U.S.S.R. Information Report, April 8, 1954, http://www.foia.cia.gov/collection/atomic-spies-ethel-and-julius-rosenberg.

64. Telegram from Flack, Warsaw, June 22, 1953, 3820, 5, 023, 761.5211, RG 59, NA.

65. Ibid. The political cartoons came to my attention from the Reference Department of the Jagiellonian Library in Krakow, via Jan Adamczyk of the Slavic Reference Service at the University of Illinois at Urbana-Champaign.

66. A crowd of two hundred Londoners positioned themselves outside the *Manchester Guardian* offices at one o'clock in the morning. Forty-five minutes later an official announced that the Rosenbergs were dead, and the crowd reacted in shock and disgust, and then dispersed. "Execution of the Rosenbergs," *The Guardian*, June 20, 1953. FSD from Am ConGen, Geneva, June 22, 1953, 3820, 5, 041, 761.5211, RG 59, NA; FSD from Williamson, AmEmbassy, Rome, June 22, 1953, 3820, 5, 038–040, 761.5211, RG 59, NA. In The Hague, about a hundred people participated in a silent vigil at the time of executions. Telegram from Chapin, The Hague, June 22, 1953, 3820, 5, 028, 761.5211, RG 59, NA.

67. FSD from Roberts, AmEmbassy, Dublin, Ireland, June 25, 1953, 3820, 6, 087–088, 761.5211, RG 59, NA.

68. FSD from Am ConGen, Geneva, June 22, 1953, 3820, 5, 041, 761.5211, RG 59, NA; FSD from Oakley, AmConGen, Geneva, Switzerland, June 24, 1953, 3820, 6, 054, 761.5211, RG 59, NA. Three days after the executions the Executive Secretary of the Red Cross Societies complained to the Consulate General of Geneva, Switzerland, that his organization "has willy-nilly been brought into the Rosenberg case." Seventy countries had been asked by Polish Red Cross to intervene on behalf of Rosenbergs. The League of Red Cross Societies informed the Polish Red Cross "the subject was an internal matter of the United States and completely outside the competence of the League."

69. FSD from Williamson, AmEmbassy, Rome, June 22, 1953, 3820, 5, 038–040, 761.5211, RG 59, NA.

70. FSD from Watrous, AmEmbassy, Lisbon, Portugal, June 26, 1953, 3820, 6, 093–094, 761.5211, RG 59, NA; FSD from Jova, Am Consulate, Oporto, Portugal, June 23, 1953, 3820, 5, 042, 761.5211, RG 59, NA.

71. Telegram from Chapin, The Hague, June 22, 1953, 3820, 5, 028, 761.5211, RG 59, NA.

72. FSD from Roberts, AmEmbassy, Dublin, Ireland, June 25, 1953, 3820, 6, 087–088, 761.5211, RG 59, NA.

73. Ibid. The *Irish Press* focused its editorial disapproval on the role David Greenglass played, since his testimony prompted many in Ireland "to believe that a man so devoid of family affection must also be a perjurer."

74. FSD from Williamson, AmEmbassy, Rome, June 22, 1953, 3820, 5, 038–040, 761.5211, RG 59, NA; CIA Memorandum, Italy Information Report, June 30, 1953, http://www.foia.cia.gov/collection/atomic-spies-ethel-and-julius-rosenberg.

75. FSD from Williamson, AmEmbassy, Rome, June 22, 1953, 3820, 5, 038–040, 761.5211, RG 59, NA.

76. Ibid.

77. Ibid.

78. June 23, 1953, Box 1, File: White House Correspondence, 1953(3), White House Memoranda Series, Papers of John Foster Dulles, DDEL (draft declassified 1984); June 25, 1953, Box 33, File: Italy (9), Ann Whitman File, International Series, DDE Papers, DDEL (final telegram declassified 1989).

79. Ibid.

80. CIA Memorandum, France Information Report July 30, 1953, http://www.foia.cia.gov/collection/atomic-spies-ethel-and-julius-rosenberg.

81. Ibid.

82. Bradlee, *Good Life*, 139.

83. FSD from Dillon, Paris, June 22, 1953, in FBI File, Julius Rosenberg, File: 65-58236 (HQ), Section: 68 Referrals, Main File, https://vault.fbi.gov/rosenberg-case/rosenberg-referrals.

84. Ibid.

85. Ibid.

86. Ibid.

87. Ibid.

88. Sartre quoted in Fineberg, *Rosenberg Case*, viii.

89. Sartre quoted in *Daily Worker*, July 12, 1953, the *National Guardian*, July 6, 1953, and FSD from Dillon, Paris, June 22, 1953, in FBI File, Julius Rosenberg, File: 65-58236 (HQ), Section: 68 Referrals, Main File, https://vault.fbi.gov/rosenberg-case/rosenberg-referrals.

90. Sartre quoted in *Daily Worker*, July 12, 1953, the *National Guardian*, July 6, 1953.

91. Robert Barrat, "From France: The Rosenberg Case," *The Commonweal*, August 14, 1953, 464–466, in Rosenberg Vertical File, HSTL; Radosh and Milton, *Rosenberg File*, 355, 560–561.

92. Telephone Conversation with the president, 5 p.m., June 23, 1953, File: White House Tel Conv., May–Dec 31, 1953 (2), Box 10, Telephone Calls Series, John Foster Dulles Papers, DDEL.

93. Ibid.

94. Ibid.

95. Telegram from Dillon, Paris, June 23, 1953, 3820, 5, 043–044, 761.5211, RG 59, NA.

96. Ibid.

97. Ibid.

98. Memorandum from Paris to FBI, July 23, 1953, in FBI File, Julius Rosenberg, File: 65-58236 (HQ), Section: 68 Referrals, Main File, https://vault.fbi.gov/rosenberg-case/rosenberg-referrals.

99. Ibid.; Memorandum from Achilles, Paris, July 10, 1953, in FBI File, Julius Rosenberg, File: 65-58236 (HQ), Section: 68 Referrals, Main File, https://vault.fbi.gov/rosenberg-case/rosenberg-referrals. Paris Embassy officials sent copies of the summary report to Moscow, London, Rome, Bonn, and Brussels, and every American consulate in France. There was an inquiry by a Mr. Yarmolinsky (a lawyer connected to the French government) who contacted George Jaeger, analyst with State Department, Department of Public Affairs. Yarmolinsky was writing a piece on Rosenbergs for a newsletter *France Actual* and "it was his understanding that one of the difficulties underlying the critical reception of the Rosenberg case in France was the lack of adequate background materials available to the American Embassy in Paris." Jaeger: "I was rather surprised to hear that the American Embassy in Paris had not received background information on the Rosenberg case since it was my understanding that a good deal of factual background material had been distributed to our posts abroad." Jaeger denied any problems and sent Yarmolinsky to the press office. See Memorandum for the Files, George Jaeger, June 24, 1953, 3820, 6, 053, 761.5211, RG 59, NA.

100. Memo from Blum to Jackson, June 22, 1953, memo from Jackson to Blum, July 3, 1953, with *Le Monde* from June 21, 1953, File: 101-R Rosenbergs (1), Box 411, Official File, White House Central Files, DDEL.

101. Ibid.

102. Fineberg, *Rosenberg Case*. See also Radosh and Milton, *Rosenberg File*, 355, 560–561.

103. Memorandum from MacKnight to Craig, November 20, 1953, File: Rosenberg Case, Box 62, Subject Series, White House Central Files, DDEL; Radosh and Milton, *Rosenberg File*, 355, 560–561.

104. Memo from C. D. Jackson to Jesse M. MacKnight, January 6, 1954, File IPO-P, MacKnight, Rosenberg Case (1952–53), Box 73, Subject Files of the Policy Plans & Guidance Staff, 1946–62, Bureau of Public Affairs, RG 59, NA.

105. Memo from Sherman Adams to Attorney General of the State of New Hampshire, July 21, 1953, Alpha File Box 2673, The Rosenbergs, U-W, DDE White House Central Files, DDEL.

106. CIA officials forwarded these lists even though they admitted, "due to the questionable legibility of some of the signatures, the names and addresses herein may be slightly inaccurate." See CIA Memorandum, redacted to/from, September 1, 1954, http://www.foia.cia.gov/collection/atomic-spies-ethel-and-julius-rosenberg.

107. CIA Memorandum, to/from redacted, Julius and Ethel Rosenberg, Letters Concerning, March 16, 1954, http://www.foia.cia.gov/collection/atomic-spies-ethel-and-julius-rosenberg. A heavily redacted CIA Memorandum concerning Sweden and dated February 12, 1954, asked for the names and address of letters sent to the White House concerning the Rosenbergs and originating in Sweden, explaining that the material had been "funneled through" the FBI and then was "handled and retained by the White House detail of the Secret

Service," http://www.foia.cia.gov/collection/atomic-spies-ethel-and-julius-rosenberg. See also CIA Memorandum regarding pro-Rosenberg campaign in Cuba, June 17, 1955, http://www.foia.cia.gov/collection/atomic-spies-ethel-and-julius-rosenberg.

108. Memorandum from Achilles, Paris, July 10, 1953, in 3820, 8, 218–219, 761.5211, RG 59, NA.

109. Ibid.

110. Ibid.

111. The family was the Bachs. No immediate family members would agree to take the boys. Julius's brother David changed his last name to Roberts to distance himself from the stigma of the Rosenberg name. See Ivy Meeropol, *Heir to an Execution.*

112. Letter from Roberts to Washburn, October 16, 1953, and attached memo to C. D. Jackson, File: Rosenberg Case, Box 62, Subject Series, White House Central Files, DDEL.

113. Ibid.

114. "Bloch, Attorney for Spies, is Dead," *New York Times,* January 31, 1954.

115. See Meeropol and Meeropol, *We Are Your Sons,* 246–255.

116. Several French telegrams, a Berlin telegram, a British letter, a South African letter, and a report of an editorial in Volksdagblad, Voor Nederland were gathered by the White House, February/March 1954, File: Rosenberg Children, Box 2672, Alpha File, White House Central Files, DDEL.

117. Described in Radosh and Milton, *Rosenberg File,* 423.

118. Dean Johnson was also affiliated with Columbia University and "a personal friend of Eisenhower" with "impeccable establishment credentials." Radosh and Milton, *Rosenberg File,* 424.

119. Michael and Robert used these words to describe their adoptive father in a letter to the editor, *New York Times,* July 23, 1986, A22. The sons had first met the Meeropols Christmas Eve 1953 at the home of W. E. B. DuBois. See Meeropol and Meeropol, *We Are Your Sons,* 243; Meeropol, *Execution in the Family,* 16–17.

120. Joan Cook, "Abel Meeropol, 83, A Songwriter, Dies," *New York Times,* October 31, 1986, A20.

121. "Toll of Korea Foe Hits 10,000 in Week," *New York Times,* June 23, 1953, 2.

122. See Casey, *Selling the Korean War,* 284–289, 348–349, 353; Stueck, *Rethinking the Korean War,* 176–179.

123. Representatives from the United States, North Korea, and China signed the armistice. The government of South Korea refused to sign. See Cumings, *Korean War,* 34–35; Stueck, *Rethinking the Korean War,* 179–181.

124. Stueck, *Rethinking the Korean War,* 179.

125. Eisenhower, "Radio and Television Address to the American People Announcing the Signing of the Korean Armistice," July 26, 1953, 10 p.m., available at the American Presidency Project, http://www.presidency.ucsb.edu/ws/?pid=9653.

126. Figures from Cumings, *Korean War,* 35.

127. Casey, *Selling the Korean War,* 365.

128. Eisenhower quoted in Osgood, *Total Cold War,* 71.

129. See Kinzer, *Brothers,* 129–130.

130. Halberstam, *Fifties,* 360.

131. Introduction, "Report on the Covert Activities of the Central Intelligence Agency" (Doolittle Report), September 30, 1954, 5–7, http://www.foia.cia.gov/collection/atomic-spies-ethel-and-julius-rosenberg.

132. Ibid.

133. For a discussion of Soviet thermonuclear technology and its nonreliance on American design, see Holloway, *Stalin and the Bomb,* 303–309.

134. *Bulleting of the Atomic Scientists,* www.thebulletin.org/.

135. Bird and Sherwin, *American Prometheus,* 469.

136. Ibid.

137. Ibid., 550.

138. The act passed the Senate 79–0 and the House 265–2, while the amendment making CP membership a criminal offense was not included in the final version of S 3706/Public Law 637; *Congressional Quarterly Almanac, 83rd Congress, 2nd Session, 1954, Volume X,* 334–347.

139. Richard H. Rovere, "Letter from Bermuda," *New Yorker*, December 19, 1953, 116.

140. Memorandum of Conversation, Bermuda Meeting, December 4, 1953, International Meetings Series, Bermuda State Department Report, Box 1, DDE Papers, DDEL.

141. Osgood, *Total Cold War*, 154. For a complete discussion of the psychological impact of the Atoms for Peace speech and the public information campaign it came out of, see Osgood, *Total Cold War*, 153–180.

142. Press Release, "Atoms for Peace" Speech, December 8, 1953, UN Speech, Box 5, Speech Series, DDE Papers, DDEL.

143. Ibid.

144. Osgood, *Total Cold War*, 159.

145. See Osgood, *Total Cold War*, 179.

146. Quoted in Holloway, *Stalin and the Bomb*, 336.

147. March 12, 1954 statement quoted in Bird and Sherwin, *American Prometheus*, 452. Days later in a NSC meeting, Eisenhower seemed to agree when he replied to a question about post-World War III alliances: "An ensuing general war would be so utterly terrible that . . . all government would be totalitarian and dictatorship to gain survival, and it was entirely too speculative to think of what kind of post war organization should be created with 'friendly allies.'" "US Objectives in the Event of General War with the USSR," March 25, 1954, File: War Objectives, Box 8, Special Staff File Series, Staff Paper, 1953-61, White House Office: National Security Council, DDEL.

148. Quoted in Bird and Sherwin, *American Prometheus*, 453.

149. See Holloway, *Stalin and the Bomb*, 338.

150. "Atomic Secrecy Deemed Overdone," *New York Times*, March 17, 1954, 5.

151. Ibid.

152. Ibid.

153. Quoted in Carmichael, *Framing History*, 88.

154. Ibid.

155. Some members of Eisenhower's own party complained he was too peaceful. In early 1954, Eisenhower was annoyed when some conservative members of the Republican Party described the Eisenhower Administration as "too New Deal-ish." See Walter Trohan, "G.O.P. Aids Go Home to Whip Up 2D Crusade," *Chicago Daily Tribune*, February 8, 1954, 1, 6.

156. According to the May 9 Gallup Poll, 69% of Americans were in favor of adding "under God" to the Oath of Allegiance. See Gallup, *Gallup Poll*, 1140.

157. Colbert discussed truthiness as The Word in the pilot episode of *The Colbert Report*, which aired on October 17, 2005. See Adam Sternbergh, "Stephen Colbert Has America by the Ballots," *New York Magazine*, October 16, 2006, http://nymag.com/news/politics/22322/.

158. "Sometimes," as historian Ari Kelman argues, "stories complement one another; sometimes they clash. Sometimes they intersect; sometimes they diverge." Kelman, *Misplaced Massacre*, 279.

159. The holiday had taken on "major significance" in the postwar years, as fatherhood became a "badge of masculinity and meaning." May, *Homeward Bound*, 129.

160. Jay Maeder, "Last Mile of the Julius and Ethel Rosenberg Show," *New York Daily News*, November 24, 2000.

161. Quoted in ibid.

162. Emphasis in original, letter from Wellwood Cemetery Assn., Inc., Long Island to New York FBI, June 16, 1953, FBI File, New York File, Julius Rosenberg, File: 65-15348-2688, Sub E (6), https://vault.fbi.gov/rosenberg-case/julius-rosenberg. Ivy Meeropol, in *Heir to an Execution*, asserts that the NCSJRC had to lie to secure the burial plots because no cemetery would accept them.

163. "350 at SF Rosenberg Memorial Aid Sobell," *Daily People's World*, July 1954, 6.

164. Ibid.

165. Telegram to DDE from six mothers in London, June 19, 1954, Alpha File, Box 2672, File: The Rosenbergs (Julius & Ethel) (4), DDE White House Central File, DDEL.

166. Deery, "'Never Losing Faith,'" 190.

167. "Committee Remembers the Rosenbergs, Launches New Initiative," *New Jersey Jewish Standard*, June 11, 2010, www.jstandard.com/index.php/content/print/13797/.

168. See National Committee to Reopen the Rosenberg Case at http://ncrrc.org/1169-2/; Deery, " 'Never Losing Faith,' " 191.

169. "Peress Says Hoodlums Stoned His Home; Blames Incident on 'McCarthy Terrorism,' " *New York Times*, March 1, 1954.

170. Essay in R. Warshow, *Immediate Experience*, 51.

171. The essay is identical to "Afterthoughts on the Rosenbergs," in Fiedler, *New Fiedler Reader*, 44–64, quoted from 46. See Cuordileone, *Manhood*, 113–115.

172. Fielder, *New Fiedler Reader*, 52, 58.

173. Bigsby, *Arthur Miller*, 421.

174. Truman, *Truman Speaks*, 117.

175. Ibid. Truman was not the only American former president in favor of the Rosenbergs' execution. Herbert Hoover supported more aggressive conspiracy and treason legislation to target Communists and other subversives, and had been openly supportive of Congressman Richard Nixon's work with HUAC and Senator Joseph McCarthy's investigations. Best, *Herbert Hoover*, 335, 338.

176. Herbert Brownell Oral History with Ed Edwin, May 5, 1967, OH-157, #3 of 5, Columbia University Oral History Project, DDEL, 189–196.

177. Ibid.

178. Ibid.

179. Fox, *Reinhold Niebuhr*, 254. In addition, on November 9, 1953, Secretary Dulles wrote to Bishop G. Bromley Oxnam, a prominent Washington, D.C., Methodist and open critic of McCarthyism. "Surely, the problems are, as you say," the secretary explained, "complex and baffling. I try to meet them in the light of Christian principles, but sometimes these principles seem to get in each other's way." Dulles was reflecting on his first ten months in office and he may have included the Rosenberg case. Quoted in Inboden, *Religion and American Foreign Policy*, 241.

180. However, life imprisonment was never an option for conspiracy to commit espionage. Reinhold Niebuhr, "To Suspect Innocent Ones of Guilt Does Not Make Guilty Men Innocent," *Look* 17, no. 23, November 17, 1953, 37.

181. Schneir and Schneir, *Invitation to an Inquest*; Wexley, *Judgment of Julius and Ethel Rosenberg*.

182. Zion, *Autobiography of Roy Cohn*, 93.

183. In 1958, supporters placed a Theo Balden wooden sculpture of Ethel in the Museum der Stadt Gustrow in the former German Democratic Republic, see Okun, ed., *Rosenbergs*, 98. In Hungary, the Communist government renamed the street behind the American Embassy, *Rosenber házaspár utca* ("Rosenberg couple street"); in the early 1990s it was renamed Hold *utca* ("Moon street"); see Falk, "The Saga of the Rosenbergs," 284. In June 1964, the *New York Daily News* reported that the Cuban Communists had added Julius and Ethel Rosenberg to their list of political heroes. Clipping from *New York Daily News*, June 26, 1964, FBI File, New York File, Julius Rosenberg, File: 65-15348-2962, Sub E (6), https://vault.fbi.gov/ rosenberg-case/julius-rosenberg.

184. Khrushchev, *Khrushchev Remembers*, 193–194.

185. The *National Police Gazette* put its own unique tabloid spin on the case when it published an expose on "How Reds Use Rosenberg's Ghost to Collect Millions." *National Police Gazette*, June 1956.

186. Allen Ginzberg, "Television Was a Baby Crawling Toward that Deathchamber," excerpted in Okun, ed., *The Rosenbergs*, 107. In his 1955 work *Howl*, Ginzberg explained that the line on page six, "Moloch, heavy Judger of men," was a reference to Julius and Ethel Rosenberg; see Carmichael, *Framing History*, 206.

187. Plath quoted in Marie Ashe, "*The Bell Jar* and the Ghost of Ethel Rosenberg," in Garber and Walkowitz, eds., *Secret Agents*, 215–231. Plath's use of electroshock therapy, a savior for Esther Greenwood but deadly for Ethel Rosenberg, speaks to the complicated legacy of electroshock treatment for mental illness. Plagued with depression, Plath herself committed suicide later that year.

188. The Rosenbergs even showed up in unexpected places. For example, in *Fear of Flying*, the popular erotic novel of 1973, Erica Jong referred to the couple "in their damp cells . . . anticipating what it would be like to be electrocuted . . . in the name of civilization." See *Fear of Flying* (New York: Holt, Rinehart & Winston, 1973), 83, 280.

189. For an excerpt of *Inquest*, see Okun, ed., *Rosenbergs*, 100–105. For a discussion of the work and its reception, see Carmichael, *Framing History*, 202–206. Newspaper clipping, 1970, FBI File, New York File, Julius Rosenberg, File: 65-15348-3012, Sub E (6), https://vault. fbi.gov/rosenberg-case/julius-rosenberg.

190. Coover, *Public Burning*.

191. For a discussion of Doctorow's *Book of Daniel*, see Carmichael, *Framing History*, 131–155.

192. In October 2011, Michael and Robert Meeropol made a rare joint public appearance at a screening of *Daniel*, Jacob Silverman, "Rosenberg Boys Appear at 'Daniel' Screening," *Tablet*, October 17, 2011, http://www.tabletmag.com/scroll/80910/rosenberg-boys-appear-at-%E2%80%98daniel%E2%80%99-screening. In 1969, Filmmaker Otto Preminger announced he would begin work in June 1970 on a film about the trial of Julius and Ethel Rosenberg, entitled "Open Question." Preminger died in 1986 having never progressed on the film.

193. Doctorow, *Book of Daniel*, 303.

194. Gerry Nadel, "And the Rosenberg Kids," *Esquire*, May 1975, 107.

195. "Louis Nizer, Lawyer to the Famous, Dies at 92," *New York Times*, November 11, 1994.

196. Meeropol, ed., *Rosenberg Letters*.

197. Alvin H. Goldstein, *The Unquiet Death of Julius and Ethel Rosenberg/The Rosenberg-Sobell Case Revisited* (PBS, 1974, 2010) and companion book, Goldstein, *The Unquiet Death of Julius and Ethel Rosenberg*.

198. Documentary filmmaker Alvin H. Goldstein and historian Allen Weinstein demanded the files. "Rosenberg Files Retained by FBI," *New York Times*, February 25, 1974, 52.

199. Ibid.

200. Ibid.

201. "2 Rosenberg Sons Try to Vindicate Executed Parents," *New York Times*, March 10, 1974, 1. The sons requested files from the Department of Army on February 20, 1975, FBI File, Julius Rosenberg, File: 65-58236 (HQ), Section: 68 Referrals, Main File, https://vault.fbi. gov/rosenberg-case/rosenberg-referrals.

202. "2 Rosenberg Sons Try to Vindicate Executed Parents," *New York Times*, March 10, 1974, 1.

203. Robert Meeropol, *Execution in the Family*, 149–151. Confirmed with Mike Meeropol, October 2015 email in author's possession.

204. Emily Alman, Rosenberg activist and sociology professor at Rutgers University, requested copies of State Department documents in 1973. She received numerous documents in 1974. It is likely Alman's request prompted the review and release of these documents, but she likely did not know that without the Name Cards to track them no one else could see or use them. The collection at Boston University has only recently been made available to researchers. See Alman and Alman, *Exoneration*, 389–431, and the Alman Collection at the Howard Gotlieb Archival Research Center at Boston University.

205. Demonstration flier, April 24, 1974, FBI File, New York File, Julius Rosenberg, File: 65-15348-3043, Sub E (6), https://vault.fbi.gov/rosenberg-case/julius-rosenberg.

206. "2 Rosenberg Sons Try to Vindicate Executed Parents," *New York Times*, March 10, 1974, 1.

207. David Yergin, "Victims of a Desperate Age," *New Times Magazine*, May 16, 1975 (a biweekly magazine from 1973–1979).

208. Roy M. Cohn to Dan Yergin, November 13, 1974, FBI File, New York File, Julius Rosenberg, File: 65-15348-3065, Sub E (6), https://vault.fbi.gov/rosenberg-case/julius-rosenberg.

209. Irving R. Kaufman, "From an Absent Guest: A Free Speech for the Class of '75," *New York Times Magazine*, June 8, 1975. According to Mike Meeropol this was a tear gas grenade attack on the NCRRC. Email in author's possession.

210. Ibid.

211. "Judge Irving Kaufman, of Rosenberg Spy Trial and Free-Press Rulings, Dies at 81," *New York Times*, February 3, 1992.

212. Robert and Michael Meeropol, *We Are Your Sons*.

213. "Rosenbergs' Sons Will Be Given Access to Files on Their Parents," *New York Times*, July 11, 1975, 8.

214. "Rosenberg Data Released by FBI," *New York Times*, August 30, 1975, 13. The FBI initially estimated it to be 48,000 pages.

215. Meeropol and Meeropol, *We Are Your Sons*.
216. Radosh and Milton, *Rosenberg File*. The second edition in 1997 also included released Venona references.
217. See Radosh and Milton, *Rosenberg File*, 473.
218. Quoted in "An Open Letter to Judge Irving R. Kaufman," *New York Times*, June 19, 1977, 18E.
219. Ibid.
220. Ibid.
221. Irving R. Kaufman Papers, Manuscript Division, Library of Congress, Washington, D.C. The Meeropol brothers received government documents concerning Judge Kaufman in late 1975 and made them public in June 1976. See Robert Meeropol, *Execution in the Family*, 139.
222. The 1982 documentary *The Atomic Cafe* brought many images of the early Cold War to life for a generation too young to remember. While the "Duck and Cover" footage had a macabre humor, the detailed reporting of the deaths of Julius and Ethel Rosenberg was a chilling reminder of the reality of the executions as they unfolded. Jayne Loader, Kevin Rafferty, and Pierce Rafferty, *The Atomic Cafe*, The Archives Project, 1982. In the mid-1980s, political artist Dennis Adams replaced product-pushing advertisements on bus shelters with large Cold War photos; he installed the Rosenbergs' arrest photo from 1950 on a bus stop at 14th Street and 3rd Avenue in New York City. For two years Adams forced bus patrons to consider the image and its meaning, or at least wonder who the people in the photos were.
223. Okun, ed., *Rosenbergs*, 14. Okun, along with Daniel Keller and Charles Light, also produced a half-hour documentary about the exhibit, *Unknown Secrets: Art and the Rosenberg Era*. For a discussion of the compilation and reception of the exhibit, see Carmichael, *Framing History*, 206–208.
224. Okun, ed., *Rosenbergs*, 15.
225. This was a follow-up to their fall 1983 letter exchange in the *New York Review of Books*. Walter and Miriam Schneir, *Invitation to an Inquest*; Radosh and Milton, *Rosenberg File*.
226. Bob Dylan commemorated the thirtieth anniversary with his own composition, "Julius and Ethel," which was unambiguously sympathetic to the couple. Bob Dylan, "Julius and Ethel," transcribed by Manfred Helfert, April 27, 1983, New York, New York, www.folkarchive.de/julius.html.
227. For a complete discussion of the retrial, see the introduction in Meeropol, *Rosenberg Letters*, xxxiv–xxxix. For a different interpretation, see Ronald Radosh, "The ABA Acquits the Rosenbergs with Poor History and PC," *Wall Street Journal*, August 18, 1993.
228. Haynes and Klehr, *Venona*, 295.
229. Haynes and Klehr, *Venona*, 16. Little new information was added in 2001 by Julius Rosenberg's Soviet contact, Alexander Feklisov. In his own account of the case, *The Man Behind the Rosenbergs*, he provided details of Julius's spy activities and described the miniscule role Ethel played. Feklisov emphasized Julius as a "linchpin" of a major spy network, and one who was "convinced he was doing nothing wrong" in giving military information to America's World War II ally, the Soviet Union. Feklisov, *Man Behind the Rosenbergs*, 110, 115–116.
230. For example see Jacob Weisberg, "Cold War Without End," *New York Times Magazine*, November 28, 1999.
231. See Roberts, *Brother*.
232. See Jacob Silverman, "Rosenberg Boys Appear at 'Daniel' Screening," *Tablet Magazine*, October 17, 2011, http://www.tabletmag.com/scroll/80910/rosenberg-boys-appear-at-%E2%80%98daniel%E2%80%99-screening.
233. The HBO miniseries won five Golden Globes and eleven Emmy Awards. An operatic version of the work premiered in Paris in 2004. In the fall of 2010, the Signature Theater in New York City hosted a revival of *Angels in America*. In describing the process of writing about the case for the DVD release, Kushner admitted: "You have to approach it as something sacred that will require the best of you to decode it, and on some level you will fail."
234. Diagnosed with AIDS in 1984, Cohn died of the disease in 1986, just days after New York State disbarred him for unethical behavior in several legal matters. Albin Krebs, "Roy Cohn, Aide to McCarthy and Fiery Lawyer, Dies at 59," *New York Times*, August 3, 1986. Alan

M. Dershowitz, a lawyer involved in numerous prominent court cases of the 1970s–1990s, later claimed that Roy Cohn "proudly told me shortly before his death that the government had 'manufactured' evidence against the Rosenbergs, because they knew Julius was the head of a spy ring. In the process," Cohn explained, "they also made up evidence against Ethel Rosenberg." Writing in 2004, Dershowitz concluded: "It is fair to characterize the execution of Ethel Rosenberg as a case of judicial homicide far more criminal than anything she may have done." Dershowitz, "The Trial of the Rosenbergs," in *America on Trial*, 323.

235. Alman and Alman, *Exoneration*.
236. The National Security Archive, and several historians including R. Bruce Craig, petitioned for release of the grand jury testimony.
237. Dennis Hevesi, "Ruth Greenglass, Key Witness in Trial of Rosenbergs, Dies at 83," *New York Times*, July 9, 2008.
238. David Greenglass's death in 2014 left the door open for the publication of his grand jury testimony. Officials released it on July 15, 2015.
239. Sam Roberts, "57 Years Later, Figure in Rosenberg Case Says He Spied for Soviets," *New York Times*, September 12, 2008, A1, A14; Morton Sobell, Letter to the Editor, *New York Times*, September 19, 2008, A18.
240. Sam Roberts, "Nixon Cited Missed Clues in Defense of a Rosenberg," *New York Times*, September 13, 2008.
241. Sam Roberts, "Father Was a Spy, Sons Conclude with Regret," *New York Times*, September 17, 2008.
242. Michael Meeropol and Robert Meeropol, "The Essential Lessons of the Rosenberg Case," *Los Angeles Times*, October 5, 2008.
243. Haynes, Klehr, and Vassiliev, *Spies*.
244. Haynes, Klehr, and Vassiliev, *Spies*, xix, 322, 333, 339, 341, 349.
245. Kathy Olmsted argues that scholars "are understandably frustrated by their dependence on Vassiliev's notebooks" since they "are forced to use as their research assistant a former KGB agent with a clear ideological agenda and a somewhat mixed record on disclosure." Combined with "self-serving accounts of defectors, the often-biased FBI case files, and the incomplete Venona cables," this raw material leaves "plenty of room for scholarly disagreement." See Olmsted, "The Truth about Spies," 140. G. Edward White acknowledged, "all we can do is . . . treat the Vassiliev notebooks as a plausible surrogate for some KGB archives [for] we are not likely to get any better access to the archives in the foreseeable future." White quoted in Thomas Maddux and Diane Labrosse, ed., "Soviet Espionage in the United States During the Stalin Era," H-Diplo Article Roundtable Review, Volume X, No. 24 (2009), July 17, 2009, http://h-diplo.org/roundtables/PDF/Roundtable-X-24.pdf.
246. "The Color Yellow," Episode 13, Season 21, *The Simpsons*, original airdate February 21, 2010. Others used the case as a liberal litmus test. In the 1998 movie *You've Got Mail*, Patricia Eden (Parker Posey) emphasizes the liberal street cred of Frank Navasky (Greg Kinnear), claiming, "This man is the greatest living expert on Julius and Ethel Rosenberg." Posey's character continued, "You know what always fascinated me about Julius and Ethel Rosenberg is how old they looked. When they were really just our age. You know?" To provide historical context, and remind viewers that Don Draper lives in the New York suburb of Ossining in the 1950s, in season two of *Mad Men* a character remarked: "Whenever it's this hot I think about that summer they executed the Rosenbergs. It was always about to rain." "Maidenform," Episode 6, Season 2, *Mad Men*, original airdate August 31, 2008. Historian Doris Kearns Goodwin recalled in her baseball memoir *Wait Till Next Year* that she "became absorbed by the story of Julius and Ethel Rosenberg" since she was the same age as their son Michael and because "the short, plump Mrs. Rosenberg looked more like one of my friends' mothers than an international spy." Goodwin, *Wait Till Next Year*, 170.
247. Beber's attorney father had tried to help the Rosenbergs. "Hunger: In Bed With Roy Cohn Plays Odyssey Theater," *Broadway World*, http://www.broadwayworld.com/los-angeles/article/HUNGER-IN-BED-WITH-ROY-COHN-Plays-Odyssey-Theater-20120120; "Ethel Sings: Espionage in High C Opens June 28 at Walker Space," *Broadway World*, http://www.broadwayworld.com/article/ETHEL-SINGS-Espionage-in-High-C-Opens-June-28-at-Walker-Space-20130615.

248. Anita Gates, "An Unsettling Execution, Told Through Teddy Bears," *New York Times*, December 3, 2008. Filmmaker John Sayles has also announced that he is working on a Rosenberg project. The Rosenberg Fund for Children website asks, "Who do you see playing Julius and Ethel?"

249. YouTube clip, © Rosenberg Fund for Children, https://www.youtube.com/watch?v=J4QpKxCtfUI. Lyrics © Woody Guthrie Publications, Inc./ Woody Guthrie Archives. Guthrie's lyrics to "Dear Mister Eisenhower" had been found in his archives in New York City in 2000. The author thanks Dan Cady for his assistance.

250. "In Ordinary Lives, U.S. Sees the Work of Russian Agents," *New York Times*, June 28, 2010; Scott Shane and Charlie Savage, "10 People Arrested Inside U.S. as Deep-Cover Russian Agents," *New York Times*, June 29, 2010, A1, A3. The hydrangeas harkened back to disbelief over the threat Ethel Rosenberg posed: could "someone who chose to wear hats with six-inch high flowers sticking straight out of them" really "represent the international Communist menace?" Philipson, *Ethel Rosenberg*, 4.

251. Fernanda Santos, "Spies? Perhaps. Bad Parent? The Evidence Says No," *New York Times*, July 1, 2010, A3.

252. "Rick's List," Rick Sanchez, CNN, June 29, 2010, http://edition.cnn.com/TRANSCRIPTS/1006/29/rlst.02.html.

253. "Top 10 Crime Duos," *Time*, www.time.com/time/specials/packages/completelist (linked to History News Network).

254. In another example of a distorted legacy, in a larger discussion of patriotism and loyalty, an editorial writer for the *Washington Post* wrote: "New rule: The only U.S. citizens anyone should be able to call 'anti-American' are those who have sworn allegiance to a foreign terrorist group, or Julius and Ethel Rosenberg. Anything else is just name-calling." Stephen Stromberg, https://www.washingtonpost.com/blogs/post-partisan/post/demint-most-americans-are-anti-american/2011/08/11/gIQA5XLK9I_blog.html.

255. The reaction to Walter and Miriam Schneir's 2010 *Final Verdict* speaks to the strength of the U.S. government's narrative on the case. A postscript to their *Invitation to an Inquest*, the Schneir's still believe the convictions were unjust. While researching the case, they themselves were investigated by the FBI. Harvey Klehr and John Earl Haynes dismiss the Schneirs as apologists, and label their work pro-Soviet distortion. Klehr and Haynes, "A Very Cold War: The Dying Gasps of the Rosenberg Apologists," *The Weekly Standard* 16, No. 23, February 28, 2011, http://www.weeklystandard.com/article/very-cold-war/550401.

256. "The Rosenberg Case, Soviet Espionage, and the Cold War," Elliot School of International Affairs, George Washington University, June 22, 2011. The morning session of the all-day event can be seen on C-SPAN, www.c-span.org/video/?300182-1/historical-treatment-rosenberg-case.

257. Falk, "The Saga of the Rosenbergs," 288.

258. Chris Elliott, "Legendary Hollywood Activists Mark Rosenberg Executions' 60th Anniversary," *Peoples World*, June 24, 2013, http://peoplesworld.org/legendary-hollywood-activists-mark-rosenberg-executions-60th-anniversary/.

259. Robert Meeropol and Jenn Meeropol, "Out of the Horror of the Rosenbergs' Executions, a Force for Good," *The Guardian*, June 15, 2013, http://www.theguardian.com/commentisfree/2013/jun/15/horror-rosenbergs-executions-force-good. See also "The Rosenberg Fund for Children's 'Constructive Revenge,'" *Huff Post New York*, June 12, 2013, http://www.huffingtonpost.com/sam-roberts/the-rosenberg-fund-for-ch_b_3428117.html?utm_hp_ref=new-york. Robert Meeropol also wrote several pieces in early 2012, marking the sixtieth anniversary of the U.S. Appeals Court's confirmation of the Rosenberg conviction. He focused on his personal memories, few since he was only six when they died, and interpretations. Robert also emphasized the work his organization, the Rosenberg Fund for Children (RFC), does, providing "for the educational and emotional need of children of jailed U.S. activists." John O'Connor, "First Person: Robert Meeropol," *Financial Times*, May 26, 2012, http://www.ft.com/cms/s/2/5b06eb90-a46d-11e1-a701-00144feabdc0.html. See also Robert Meeropol, "60 Years Too Late to Save the Rosenbergs," *Peoples World*, February 27, 2012, http://www.peoplesworld.org/60-years-too-late-to-save-the-rosenbergs. Jenn Meeropol took over the fund in 2013.

260. Matthew Vadum, "The Rosenberg Traitors: 60 Years Later," *FrontPage Magazine* June 21, 2013, http://www.frontpagemag.com/fpm/193927/rosenberg-traitors- 60-years-later-matthew-vadum.

261. Robert Meeropol has urged Americans to "scream bloody murder" and demand Manning's release; "Ethel Rosenberg's Orphaned Son Says, 'Scream Bloody Murder' for Bradley Manning," *The Vancouver Observer*, March 7, 2013, http://www.vancouverobserver. com/world/united-states/scream-bloody-murder-bradley-manning-rosenbergs-son. "The Rosenberg case," Meeropol argues, "resonates from the inmates of Guantanamo to Private Bradley Manning to the Oval Office of the White House." Quoted in Chris Elliott, "Legendary Hollywood Activists Mark Rosenberg Executions' 60th Anniversary," *Peoples World*, June 24, 2013, http://peoplesworld.org/legendary-hollywood-activists-mark-rosenberg-executions-60th-anniversary/.

262. A panel discussion on the Snowden case and its links to the Rosenbergs in 2014 concluded, "the execution of Julius and Ethel Rosenberg was an egregious act of desperation on behalf of the United States to appear strong against what was suspected of being a communist threat." See Allison Kaufman, "Panel Explores Rosenberg, Snowden, Espionage in America," *The Daily Free Press*, October 8, 2014, http://dailyfreepress.com/2014/10/08/rosenberg-panel/. The panel consisted of Michael and Robert Meeropol, Boston University professors Joseph Wippl and Igor Lukes, *New York Times* journalist Stephen Kinzer, and *Newsweek* reporter Jonathan Alter. The event marked the opening of an exhibit at the Howard Gotlieb Archival Research Center at Boston University, and the launch of a corresponding website "Love-Conscience-Conviction: The Rosenberg Case," which includes new Rosenberg letters and artifacts.

263. "Try NSA Leaker Edward Snowden for Treason, Says Sen. John Cornyn," *Dallas News*, June 12, 2013, http://trailblazersblog.dallasnews.com/2013/06/try-nsa-leaker-edward-snowden-for-treason-says-sen-john-cornyn.html/.

264. NSA, *60 Years of Defending Our Nation*, 2012, https://www.nsa.gov/public_info/press_ room/2012/nsa_60.shtml. Many history textbooks, for example, continue to repeat the error, stating the crime as treason instead of the correct charge of conspiracy to commit espionage, while others confuse the crime or fail to mention the couple at all. For example, see Howard Zinn, *A People's History of the United States* (New York: Harper Perennial, 2005); William Chafe, *The Unfinished Journey: America Since World War II* (New York: Oxford University Press, 2014).

Conclusion

1. As discussed in Chapter 1, Truman blamed the Rosenbergs for giving the bomb to the Soviets and empowering them to order North Korea to invade South Korea. Historians of the Korean War argue that the reality was far more complex. But the reality did not matter; what federal officials believed dictated policy.

2. See Radosh and Milton, *Rosenberg File*, 380.

3. Broadwater, *Eisenhower and the Anti-Communist Crusade*, 80.

4. H. W. Benson, "Hysteria, Panic and Fear in the Rosenberg Execution," *Labor Action* (Independent Socialist Weekly), June 29, 1953, 8.

5. Stephen Kinzer argues that the Rosenberg executions were "not enough," and connects CIA action in Iran to the administration's need for a "quick success." See Kinzer, *Brothers*, 129–130.

6. Johnson in 1968, quoted in Andrew Preston, "Monsters Everywhere," 478.

7. Fredrik Logevall is a proponent of the value of cautiously considered counterfactuals to enhance historical understanding. As he explains in his treatment of the United States and the French Indochina War, the story "is a contingent one, full of alternate political choices, major and minor, considered and taken, reconsidered and altered . . . it's a reminder to us that to the decision makers of the past, the future was merely a set of possibilities." *Embers of War*, xvii.

8. The wisdom of keeping Truman in the dark on Venona and allowing FBI and Army officials to make such important decisions, particularly considering the ramifications of secrecy, can certainly be debated. Many scholars have discussed whether officials could have made the decryptions public once the Soviets were aware of the breach of security. Per K. A. Cuordileone: "If

knowledge of Venona had been less restricted. . .could the effort to cleanse the government of any lingering Soviet agents have proceeded in a less reckless and more rational, targeted, focused manner?" Cuordileone, "The Torment of Secrecy," 636. Senator Daniel Patrick Moynihan contends that disclosure of Venona would have cut the legs out from under Senator Joseph McCarthy. Moynihan, *Secrecy*, 98. John Earl Haynes and Harvey Klehr explain that "even after it sank in at the NSA, sometime in the 1950s, that Venona had been exposed . . . the agency still had reasons for keeping the project highly secret. It did not want Moscow to learn of its subsequent success with GRU, Naval GRU, and the earlier KGB traffic. Nor did it want Moscow to find out which messages had been read and which remained opaque. American interests, at least in the short run, were served by Moscow's uncertainty over how much the United States had really learned." Haynes and Klehr, *Venona*, 56. For a thoughtful discussion of the long-term corrosive impact of government secrets in a democracy, see Olmsted, *Real Enemies*.

9. Haynes and Klehr, *Venona*, 16. Steven Usdin cites a February 1956 FBI memo that "outlined obstacles to using Venona decryptions in court," including that the defense would challenge their use based on hearsay evidence, codenames, and incomplete messages, and the defense could claim other messages might have cleared their clients. See Usdin, *Engineering Communism*, 306–307, N27.

10. See Radosh and Milton, *Rosenberg File*, 409; Meeropol and Meeropol, *We Are Your Sons*, 231.

11. Meeropol and Meeropol, *We Are Your Sons*, 231.

12. Lichtman, *Supreme Court and McCarthy-Era Repression*, 63.

13. It remains contested whether knowledge of the spy ring was enough to convict Ethel, or if she needed to engage in an overt act—and if recruiting her brother was such an act—to participate in the conspiracy.

14. These tactics mirrored the propaganda campaign to sell the Korean War to the American people. See Casey, *Selling the Korean War*, 358–363.

15. Caute, *Great Fear*, 18. Other historians make similar observations. Elizabeth Borgwardt explains: "The paradox of America in the world has been the way the United States simultaneously led the world and dragged its feet in the area of human rights." Borgwardt, *New Deal for the World*, 291–292. Lisa McGirr could have been referring to the Rosenbergs rather than the case of Sacco and Vanzetti when she concludes: "A country claiming global influence—partly based on universal values of democracy and freedom—is the rightful subject of international criticism when free institutions and democratic values appear to fail." McGirr, "The Passion of Sacco and Vanzetti," 1115. Laura Belmonte argues that "Selling 'America' will never work if we do not close the gap between how we define ourselves—and how we actually act at home and abroad." Belmonte, *Selling the American Way*, 184. Image issues continue to plague the United States. A 2015 piece about the nation's history of racism observes, "not only American authority but also American contradictions play out on the world stage." Jelani Cobb, "A President and a King," *New Yorker*, January 26, 2015, 21.

16. Per Isserman and Shrecker, "of the approximately 50,000 party members in World War II, 49,700 were uninvolved in espionage, even taking the highest estimate of communist participation in the KGB's network." Isserman and Schrecker in Schrecker, ed., *Cold War Triumphalism*, 159. Communist Party membership dropped to approximately 43,000 in 1950 and 32,000 in 1951.

17. Emphasis in original. Quoted in Allen Abel, "Postcard from Washington: Echoes of Pain for America's Nuclear Family," November 28, 2014, http://o.canada.com/news/world/postcard-from-washington-echoes-of-pain-for-americas-nuclear-family.

18. Feklisov, *Man Behind the Rosenbergs*, 120.

19. Ibid., 125–128.

20. Julius letter to Ethel, May 14, 1953 letter in Meeropol, ed., *Rosenberg Letters*, 660.

21. For a time the International Spy Museum in Washington, D.C., claimed that Ethel was an active spy, and that her codename was "Ethel." See Wiener, *How We Forgot the Cold War*, 143–144.

22. Conspiracy is such a vague term that in 1949 Supreme Court Justice Robert Jackson complained that it "almost defies definition." See *Krulewitch v. U.S.* 336 U.S. 440 (1949), https://supreme.justia.com/cases/federal/us/336/440/case.html.

23. Deputy Attorney General William Rogers in a 2008 interview, quoted in Roberts, *Brother*, 432.
24. For example, when David Greenglass's death in July 2014 was announced that October, controversy erupted over the *New York Times* obituary (see Robert D. McFadden, "David Greenglass, Who Helped Seal the Rosenbergs' Doom, Dies at 92," *New York Times*, October 15, 2014, A1). McFadden claimed that there was "consensus among historians" that "the Greenglass-Rosenberg atomic bomb details were of little value to the Soviets, except to corroborate what they already knew, and that Ethel Rosenberg had played no active role in the conspiracy." Five historians of Soviet espionage challenged the assertion, writing that they could not "fathom how that statement can be supported" (see Allen M. Hornblum, Harvey Klehr, John Earl Haynes, Ronald Radosh, and Steven Usdin, "The *New York Times* Gets Greenglass Wrong," *Weekly Standard*, October 17, 2014). "Julius Rosenberg's spy ring," they explained, "provided an extraordinary trove of nonnuclear espionage on radar, sonar, and jet propulsion engines to the Soviet Union, but the Rosenbergs' contributions to the Soviet nuclear weapons program were also important. The information from David Greenglass and from a second nuclear spy recruited by Julius Rosenberg, Russell McNutt, was welcomed by the KGB as valuable and practical *confirmation of data* it was receiving from Klaus Fuchs and Ted Hall, the two major Soviet nuclear spies in the Manhattan Project" [my emphasis]. Setting aside that fact that McNutt was an engineer at Oak Ridge, and likely able to deliver higher quality material than a mechanic at Los Alamos, since Rosenberg recruited both McNutt and Greenglass and they both confirmed data, how does this differ from the *New York Times'* assertion that the "Greenglass-Rosenberg atomic bomb details were of little value to the Soviets, except to corroborate what they already knew?" The historians claim that "it is long past time that the *New York Times* stops abetting the continuing efforts by the Rosenberg sons and others who have spent decades misrepresenting the espionage activities of Julius and Ethel Rosenberg," but distortion can be found on all sides. While these historians argue Greenglass gave the Soviets "highly valuable" intelligence about the bomb, not all agree. Even Usdin, one of the five historians, wrote in 2009 that Greenglass's "information was not, however, remotely as damaging as the secrets leaked by other Manhattan Project spies, such as Theodore Hall, who never faced any charges, or Fuchs, who was imprisoned but then freed in a Cold War spy swap" (see Usdin, "The Rosenberg Ring Revealed," 113). Barring additional information pouring out of Russian archives—which seems unlikely anytime soon—there will continue to be disagreement over the value of the atomic information that David Greenglass provided. On the subject of Ethel Rosenberg and her role in the conspiracy, this dispute gets to the heart of the contested evidence. Ethel may have hid money and the table used for photographing documents. She may have been at meetings and served as a signal to Feklisov. She likely helped recruit her brother, David. But she had no codename and the Soviets admitted she engaged in no active espionage. It is clear she was aware of her husband's activities, and thus by definition participated in the conspiracy. Stating she was a functioning spy is stretching the credibility of available evidence. Implying she deserved the death penalty is unnecessarily inflammatory. Only a nuanced examination can provide clarity and move away from the truthiness both conservatives and liberals embrace. To my reading, the *New York Times* may have downplayed the significance of the Rosenberg ring, which Feklisov boasted, perhaps self-servingly, as "one of the best Soviet intelligence networks," particularly in providing nonnuclear, military information (Feklisov, *Man Behind the Rosenbergs*, 283). But the obituary was for Greenglass, who was by all accounts solely involved in atomic intelligence. The obituary also implies that Ruth Greenglass's role was minimal, which is incorrect since she had a codename and passed along espionage information. The page one *New York Times* obituary of Greenglass highlights the importance of the case and the subsequent dispute demonstrates how the facts are still contested more than sixty years later.
25. As previously discussed, KGB spies had infiltrated the Manhattan Project, allowing the Soviets to test an atomic bomb an estimated one to five years earlier than they otherwise would have done. All such timetables are rough estimates, based on when the Soviets began to develop the bomb, their engineering and scientific accomplishments, their ability to secure uranium, and whether the spy information they received was complete, reliable, helpful, misleading, or outdated. For a thoughtful discussion of these issues see Gordin, *Red Cloud at Dawn*, 63–88.

26. See Parrish, "Review Essay," 116; Lynd, "Is There Anything More to Say About the Rosenberg Case?," 49.
27. See Sibley, *Red Spies*, 235.
28. Sibley attributes this to several new espionage laws passed during the Carter administration. See *Red Spies*, 11. The Rosenberg deaths led the Soviet government to reconsider its approach to espionage. Daunted after the executions, the Soviets "focused increasingly on cultivating American spies overseas, especially men in uniform." See Sibley, *Red Spies*, 222. In 2008, 88% of criminologists stated they did not see the death penalty as an effective deterrent to crime. See the Death Penalty Information Center at www.deathpenaltyinfo.org.
29. Quoted in Begley, *Why the Dreyfus Affair Matters*, 183.
30. The Alger Hiss case was similarly a litmus test for anti-Communist liberals. While left-wing Democrats were busy debating Hiss's guilt, right-wing Republicans took the opportunity to seize the offensive against Communism. Democrats, pushed back on their heels, propelled forward to prove their Cold War mettle by aggressively prosecuting the Rosenbergs. See Cuordileone, *Manhood*, 40–45.
31. Ethel Rosenberg letter to Manny Bloch, June 19, 1953, Meeropol, ed., *Rosenberg Letters*, 704.
32. Julius and Ethel Rosenberg letter to Michael and Robert, June 19, 1953, Meeropol, ed., *Rosenberg Letters*, 703.
33. Julius Rosenberg letter to Michael, March 8, 1953, Meeropol, ed., *Rosenberg Letters*, 629.
34. Lee Ross quoted in Bill Soren and Michael McIntee, " 'Constructive Revenge': When the U.S. Government Executes Your Grandparents," *The Uptake*, November 17, 2014, http://theuptake. org/2014/11/17/constructive-revenge-when-the-u-s-govt-executes-your-grandparents.

BIBLIOGRAPHY

Archives

Dwight D. Eisenhower Presidential Library, Abilene, Kansas (DDEL)

Herbert Brownell Oral History
Herbert Brownell Papers
John Foster Dulles Papers
Dwight D. Eisenhower Papers/Ann Whitman File
C. D. Jackson Records
Arthur Minnich Series
National Security Staff Papers
White House Central Files

Harry S. Truman Library, Independence, Missouri (HSTL)

Official File
Papers of J. Howard McGrath
Papers of Harry S. Truman
Psychological Strategy Board (PSB) Files

National Archives II at College Park, Maryland (NA)

Record Group (RG) 59—General Records of the Department of State
Record Group (RG) 306—Records of the U.S. Information Agency (USIA)

United States Department of State. *Foreign Relations of the United States, 1952–54, Volume II.*
(*FRUS*) Washington, D.C.: Government Printing Office, 1984.

Congressional Records

Congressional Quarterly Almanac. Washington, D.C.: Congressional Quarterly, Inc.

FBI Files

Rosenberg Case (summary): https://vault.fbi.gov/rosenberg-case/rosenberg-case-summary/
rosenberg-case-summary-part-01-of-01/view
Julius and Ethel Rosenberg (complete files): http://vault.fbi.gov/rosenberg-case

Presidential Public Papers

American Presidency Project: www.presidency.ucsb.edu

Rosenberg Grand Jury Testimony

National Security Archive: www.gwu.edu/~nsarchiv/news/20080911/index.htm
Rosenberg Trial Transcript, *United States of America v. Julius Rosenberg, Ethel Rosenberg, Anatoli A. Yakovlev, also known as "John," David Greenglass, and Morton Sobell.* University of Missouri—Kansas City School of Law, http://law2.umkc.edu/faculty/projects/ftrials/Rosenberg/RosenbergTrial.pdf

Vassiliev Notebooks

Complete, translated transcripts: http://digitalarchive.wilsoncenter.org/collection/86/vassiliev-notebooks

Venona Documents

National Security Agency: www.nsa.gov/public_info/declass/venona/dated.shtml

Films

Goldstein, Alvin H. *The Unquiet Death of Julius and Ethel Rosenberg/The Rosenberg-Sobell Case Revisited.* PBS, 1974, 2010.
Meeropol, Ivy. *Heir to an Execution: A Granddaughter's Story.* Home Box Office, Inc., 2004.

Television

"Cold War, Colder Brother," *60 Minutes II*, CBS News, February 11, 2009, www.cbsnews.com/stories/2001/12/05/60II/main320135.shtml.

Newspapers and Magazines

Chicago Daily Tribune
Daily Worker
Esquire
Eugene Register-Guard
Golf Digest
Iowa Democrat & Leader
Labor Action
Life
Look
Los Angeles Times
Milwaukee Sentinel
The Nation
National Guardian
The New Republic
New Yorker
New York Post
New York Times
Time
U.S. News and World Report
Wall Street Journal
Washington Post
Weekly Standard

Books and Articles

Albright, Joseph, and Marcia Kunstel. *Bombshell: The Secret Story of America's Unknown Atomic Spy Conspiracy*. New York: Times Books, 1997.

Alman, Emily Arnow, and David Alman. *Exoneration: The Trial of Julius & Ethel Rosenberg and Morton Sobell—Prosecutorial Deceptions, Suborned Perjuries, Anti-Semitism, and Precedent for Today's Unconstitutional Trials*. Seattle: Green Elms Press, 2010.

Ambrose, Stephen E. *Eisenhower: The President, Volume Two*. New York: Simon & Schuster, 1984.

Ambrose, Stephen E. *Ike's Spies: Eisenhower and the Espionage Establishment*. New York: Doubleday, 1981.

Barnhisel, Greg, and Catherine Turner. *Pressing the Fight: Print, Propaganda, and the Cold War*. Amherst: University of Massachusetts Press, 2010.

Begley, Louis. *Why the Dreyfus Affair Matters*. New Haven, CT: Yale University Press, 2009.

Beisner, Robert L. *Dean Acheson: A Life in the Cold War*. New York: Oxford University Press, 2006.

Belmonte, Laura A. *Selling the American Way: U.S. Propaganda and the Cold War*. Philadelphia: University of Pennsylvania Press, 2008.

Bender, Thomas. *Rethinking American History in a Global Age*. Berkeley: University of California Press, 2002.

Berle, Beatrice Bishop, and Travis Beal Jacobs, eds. *Navigating the Rapids, 1918–1971: From the Papers of Adolf A. Berle*. New York: Harcourt Brace Jovanovich, 1973.

Bernhard, Nancy E. *U.S. Television News and Cold War Propaganda, 1947–1960*. Cambridge: Cambridge University Press, 1999.

Best, Gary Dean. *Herbert Hoover: The Postpresidential Years, 1933–1964*. Stanford, CA: Hoover Institution Press, 1983.

Bigsby, Christopher. *Arthur Miller: 1915–1962*. Cambridge, MA: Harvard University Press, 2010.

Bird, Kai, and Martin J. Sherwin. *American Prometheus: The Triumph and Tragedy of J. Robert Oppenheimer*. New York: Knopf, 2005.

Borgwardt, Elizabeth. *A New Deal for the World*. Cambridge, MA: Harvard University Press, 2005.

Borstelmann, Thomas. *The Cold War and the Color Line: American Race Relations in the Global Arena*. Cambridge, MA: Harvard University Press, 2001.

Boyer, Paul. *By the Bomb's Early Light: American Thought and Culture at the Dawn of the Atomic Age*. Chapel Hill: University of North Carolina Press, 1985, 1994.

Bradlee, Ben. *A Good Life: Newspapering and Other Adventures*. New York: Simon & Schuster, 1995.

Brewer, Susan A. *Why America Fights: Patriotism and War Propaganda from the Philippines to Iraq*. New York: Oxford University Press, 2009.

Broadwater, Jeff. *Eisenhower and the Anti-Communist Crusade*. Chapel Hill: University of North Carolina Press, 1992.

Brogi, Alessandro. "Ambassador Clare Boothe Luce and the Evolution of Psychological Warfare in Italy." *Cold War History* 12, no. 2 (May 2012): 269–294.

Bundy, McGeorge. *Danger and Survival: Choices About the Bomb in the First Fifty Years*. New York: Random House, 1988.

Carmichael, Virginia. *Framing History: The Rosenberg Story and the Cold War*. Minneapolis: University of Minnesota Press, 1993.

Carnegie, Mrs. Dale. *How To Help Your Husband Get Ahead in His Social and Business Life*. New York: Greystone Press, 1953.

Casey, Steven. *Selling the Korean War: Propaganda, Politics, and Public Opinion in the United States, 1950–1953*. New York: Oxford University Press, 2008.

Caute, David. *The Great Fear: The Anti-Communist Purge Under Truman and Eisenhower*. New York: Simon & Schuster, 1978.

Considine, Bob. *It's All News to Me: A Reporter's Deposition*. New York: Meredith Press, 1967.

Cook, Blanche Wiesen. *The Declassified Eisenhower: A Startling Reappraisal of the Eisenhower Presidency*. New York: Penguin, 1984.

Cooney, Terry A. "Trials Without End: Some Comments and Reviews on the Sacco-Vanzetti, Rosenberg, and Hiss Cases." *Michigan Law Review* 77, no. 3 (January–March 1979): 834–859.

Coover, Robert. *The Public Burning*. New York: Viking Press, 1977.

Cumings, Bruce. *The Korean War: A History*. New York: Random House, 2010.

Cuordileone, K. A. *Manhood and American Political Culture in the Cold War*. New York: Routledge/ Taylor & Francis, 2005.

Cuordileone, K. A. "The Torment of Secrecy: Reckoning with American Communism and Anticommunism after Venona." *Diplomatic History* 35, no. 4 (September 2011): 615–642.

Dawidowicz, Lucy S. "Anti-Semitism and the Rosenberg Case." *Commentary* 14 (July 1952): 41–45.

Deery, Phillip. "'Never Losing Faith': An Analysis of the National Committee to Secure Justice in the Rosenberg Case, 1951–1953." *American Communist History* 12, no. 3 (December 2013): 163–191.

Deery, Phillip. "Securing Justice? The Australian Campaign to Save the Rosenbergs." *Journal of Australian Studies* 38, no. 1 (October 2013): 3–17. http://dx.doi.org/10.1080/14443058.2013.849279.

Dershowitz, Alan M. *America on Trial: Inside the Legal Battles That Transformed Our Nation*. New York: Warner, 2004.

Doctorow, E. L. *The Book of Daniel*. New York: Random House, 1971, 1999, 2007.

Doherty, Thomas. *Cold War, Cool Medium: Television, McCarthyism, and American Culture*. New York: Columbia University Press, 2003.

Douglas, William O. *The Court Years, 1939–1975*. New York: Random House, 1980.

Duberman, Martin. *Paul Robeson*. New York: Knopf, 1988, 1989. Reprint, New York: The New Press, 2005.

Dudziak, Mary L. *Cold War Civil Rights: Race and the Image of American Democracy*. Princeton, NJ: Princeton University Press, 2000, 2011.

Dudziak, Mary L. *War Time: An Idea, Its History, Its Consequences*. New York: Oxford University Press, 2012.

Eisenhower, Dwight D. *Mandate for Change, 1953–1956: The White House Years, A Personal Account*. New York: Doubleday, 1963.

Ernst, Morris L., and David Loth. *Report on the American Communist*. New York: Holt & Co., 1952.

Ewald, William Bragg Jr. *Who Killed Joe McCarthy?* New York: Simon & Schuster, 1984.

Falk, Barbara J. "The Saga of the Rosenbergs: The Trial That Keeps on Giving." *American Communist History* 12, no. 3 (2013): 283–298.

Fass, Paula S., and Michael Grossberg, eds. *Reinventing Childhood After World War II*. Philadelphia: University of Pennsylvania Press, 2012.

Fast, Howard. *The Passion of Sacco and Vanzetti: A New England Legend*. New York: Blue Heron Press, 1953.

Feklisov, Alexander. *The Man Behind the Rosenbergs*. New York: Enigma Books, 2001.

Ferguson, Robert A. *The Trial in American Life*. Chicago: University of Chicago Press, 2007.

Fiedler, Leslie. *A New Fiedler Reader*. Amherst, NY: Prometheus Books, 1999.

Fineberg, S. Andhil. *The Rosenberg Case: Fact and Fiction*. New York: Oceana Publications, 1953.

Foglesong, David S. "Roots of 'Liberation': American Images of the Future of Russia in the Early Cold War, 1948–1953." *The International History Review* 21, no. 1 (March 1999): 57–79.

Fox, Richard. *Reinhold Niebuhr: A Biography*. San Francisco: Harper & Row, 1985.

Freeland, Richard M. *The Truman Doctrine and the Origins of McCarthyism: Foreign Policy, Domestic Politics, and Internal Security, 1946–1948*. New York: Knopf, 1972.

Gaddis, John Lewis. *The Cold War: A New History*. New York: Penguin, 2005.

Gaddis, John Lewis. *We Now Know: Rethinking Cold War History*. New York: Oxford University Press, 1998.

Gallup, George. *The Gallup Poll: Public Opinion, 1935–1971*. Volume 1. New York: Random House, 1972.

Garber, Marjorie, and Rebecca L. Walkowitz, eds. *Secret Agents: The Rosenberg Case, McCarthyism and Fifties America*. New York: Routledge, 1995.

Gentry, Curt. *J. Edgar Hoover: The Man and the Secrets*. New York: Norton, 1991.

Ginsberg, Benjamin. *The Fatal Embrace: Jews and the State, The Politics of Anti-Semitism in the United States*. Chicago: University of Chicago Press, 1993, 1999.

Glynn, Robert B. "L'Affaire Rosenberg in France." *Political Science Quarterly* 70, no. 4 (December 1955): 498–521.

Goldstein, Alvin H. *The Unquiet Death of Julius and Ethel Rosenberg*. New York: Lawrence Hill & Co., 1975.

Goodwin, Doris Kearns. *Wait Till Next Year: A Memoir*. New York: Simon & Schuster, 1998.

Gordin, Michael D. *Five Days in August: How World War II Became a Nuclear War*. Princeton, NJ: Princeton University Press, 2007.

Gordin, Michael D. *Red Cloud at Dawn: Truman, Stalin, and the End of the Atomic Monopoly*. New York: FSG, 2009.

Greenstein, Fred I. *The Hidden-Hand Presidency: Eisenhower as Leader*. New York: Basic Books, 1982.

Griffith, Robert. *The Politics of Fear: Joseph R. McCarthy and the Senate*. Amherst: University of Massachusetts Press, 1970.

Gurman, Hannah. *The Dissent Papers: The Voices of Diplomats in the Cold War and Beyond*. New York: Columbia University Press, 2012.

Hajimu, Masuda. *Cold War Crucible: The Korean Conflict and the Postwar World*. Cambridge, MA: Harvard University Press, 2015.

Halberstam, David. *The Coldest Winter: America and the Korean War*. New York: Hyperion, 2007.

Halberstam, David. *The Fifties*. New York: Ballantine Books, 1993.

Haynes, John Earl. "The Cold War Debate Continues: A Traditionalist View of Historical Writing on Domestic Communism and Anti-Communism." *Journal of Cold War Studies* 2, no. 1 (Winter 2000): 76–115.

Haynes, John Earl, and Harvey Klehr. *In Denial: Historians, Communism and Espionage*. San Francisco: Encounter Books, 2003.

Haynes, John Earl, and Harvey Klehr. *Venona: Decoding Soviet Espionage in America*. New Haven, CT: Yale University Press, 1999.

Haynes, John Earl, Harvey Klehr, and Alexander Vassiliev. *Spies: The Rise and Fall of the KGB in America*. New Haven, CT: Yale University Press, 2009.

Heil Jr., Alan L. *Voice of America: A History*. New York: Columbia University Press, 2003.

Herman, Arthur. *Joseph McCarthy: Reexamining the Life and Legacy of America's Most Hated Senator*. New York: Free Press, 2000.

Hertzberg, Arthur. *The Jews in America, Four Centuries of an Uneasy Encounter: A History*. New York: Simon & Schuster, 1989.

Hixson, Walter L. *Parting the Curtain: Propaganda, Culture, and the Cold War, 1945–1961*. New York: St. Martin's, 1997.

Hofstadter, Richard. *The Paranoid Style in American Politics and Other Essays*. New York: Knopf, 1965.

Holloway, David. *Stalin and the Bomb: The Soviet Union and Atomic Energy, 1939–1956*. New Haven, CT: Yale University Press, 1994.

Hoover, J. Edgar. "The Crime of the Century." *Reader's Digest* 58 (May 1951): 149–168.

Hornblum, Allen M. *The Invisible Harry Gold: The Man Who Gave the Soviets the Atom Bomb*. New Haven, CT: Yale University Press, 2010.

Houck, Davis W., and Amos Kiewe, eds., *Actor, Ideologue, Politician: The Public Speeches of Ronald Reagan*. Westport, CT: Greenwood Press, 1993.

Hughes, Emmet John. *The Ordeal of Power: A Political Memoir of the Eisenhower Years*. New York: Atheneum, 1963.

Hunt, Michael H., and Stephen I. Levine. *Arc of Empire: America's Wars in Asia from the Philippines to Vietnam*. Chapel Hill: University of North Carolina Press, 2012.

Inboden, William. *Religion and American Foreign Policy, 1945–1960: The Soul of Containment*. New York: Cambridge University Press, 2008.

Jackson, Kenneth T. *Crabgrass Frontier: The Suburbanization of the United States*. New York: Oxford University Press, 1985.

Jacoby, Susan. *Alger Hiss and the Battle for History*. New Haven, CT: Yale University Press, 2009.

Jamieson, Kathleen Hall. *Packaging the Presidency: A History and Criticism of Presidential Campaign Advertising*. 3rd ed. New York: Oxford University Press, 1996.

Jong-yil, Ra. "Special Relationship at War: The Anglo-American Relationship during the Korean War." *The Journal of Strategic Studies* 7, no. 3 (September 1984): 301–317.

Johnson, David K. "America's Cold War Empire: Exporting the Lavender Scare." In Meredith L. Weiss and Michael J. Bosia, eds., *Global Homophobia: States, Movements, and the Politics of Oppression*. Urbana: University of Illinois Press, 2013, 55–74.

Johnson, David K. *The Lavender Scare: Cold War Prosecution of Gays and Lesbians in the Federal Government*. Chicago: University of Chicago Press, 2014.

Jones, Charles O. *The Presidency in a Separated System*. Washington, DC: The Brookings Institution, 1994.

Kelman, Ari. *A Misplaced Massacre: Struggling Over the Memory of Sand Creek*. Cambridge, MA: Harvard University Press, 2013.

Khrushchev, Nikita. *Khrushchev Remembers: The Glasnost Tapes*. Translated and edited by Jerrold L. Schecter and Vyacheclav V. Luchkov. Boston: Little, Brown & Company, 1990.

Kinzer, Stephen. *The Brothers: John Foster Dulles, Allen Dulles, and Their Secret World War*. New York: Times Books, 2013.

Klehr, Harvey. *The Heyday of American Communism: The Depression Decade*. New York: Basic Books, 1984.

Korda, Michael. *Ike: An American Hero*. New York: HarperCollins, 2007.

Krugler, David F. *The Voice of America and the Domestic Propaganda Battles, 1945–1953*. Columbia: University of Missouri Press, 2000.

Kruse, Kevin M. *One Nation Under God: How Corporate America Invented Christian America*. New York: Basic Books, 2015.

Lears, Jackson. *Fables of Abundance: A Cultural History of Advertising in America*. New York: Basic Books, 1994.

Lichtman, Robert M. *The Supreme Court and McCarthy-Era Repression: One Hundred Decisions*. Urbana: University of Illinois Press, 2012.

Lodge, Henry Cabot. *As It Was: An Inside View of Politics and Power in the 50s and 60s*. New York: Norton, 1976.

Logevall, Fredrik. *Embers of War: The Fall of an Empire and the Making of America's Vietnam*. New York: Random House, 2012.

Lucas, Scott. "Campaigns of Truth: The Psychological Strategy Board and American Ideology, 1951–1953." *The International History Review* 18, no. 2 (May 1996): 279–302.

Lucas, Scott. *Freedom's War: The American Crusade Against the Soviet Union*. New York: New York University Press, 1999.

Lynd, Staughton. "Is There Anything More to Say About the Rosenberg Case?" *Monthly Review: An Independent Socialist Magazine* 62, no. 9 (February 2011): 43–53.

Macintyre, Ben. *A Spy Among Friends: Kim Philby and the Great Betrayal*. New York: Crown, 2014.

Marchand, Roland. *Advertising the American Dream: Making Way for Modernity, 1920–1940*. Berkeley: University of California Press, 1985.

Marcus, Jacob R. *The American Jew, 1585–1990: A History*. Brooklyn: Carlson Publishing Inc., 1995.

Matray, James I. *The Reluctant Crusade: American Foreign Policy in Korea, 1941–1950*. Honolulu: University of Hawaii Press, 1985.

May, Elaine Tyler. *Homeward Bound: American Families in the Cold War Era*. New York: Basic Books, 1988, 2008.

McGilligan, Patrick, and Paul Buhle, eds. *Tender Comrades: A Backstory of the Hollywood Blacklist*. New York: St. Martin's, 1997; Minneapolis: University of Minnesota Press edition, 2012.

McGirr, Lisa. "The Passion of Sacco and Vanzetti: A Global History." *The Journal of American History* 93, no. 64 (March 2006): 1085–1115.

McMahon, Robert J. *Dean Acheson and the Creation of an American World Order*. Washington, DC: Potomac Books, 2008.

McPherson, Alan, ed. *Anti-Americanism in Latin America and the Caribbean*. New York: Berghahn Books, 2006.

McPherson, Alan. *Yankee No! Anti-Americanism in U.S.-Latin American Relations*. Cambridge, MA: Harvard University Press, 2006.

Mead, Rebecca. "Setting It Straight: 'Phantom Spies, Phantom Justice,'" *New Yorker*, November 29, 2010.

Meeropol, Robert. *An Execution in the Family: One Son's Journey*. New York: St. Martin's, 2003.

Meeropol, Robert, and Michael Meeropol. *We Are Your Sons: The Legacy of Ethel and Julius Rosenberg*. Urbana: University of Illinois Press, 1975, 1986.

Meeropol, Michael, ed. *The Rosenberg Letters: A Complete Edition of the Prison Correspondence of Julius and Ethel Rosenberg*. New York: Routledge/Taylor & Francis, 1994.

Mendes, Philip. "The Melbourne Jewish Left, Communism and the Cold War. Responses to Stalinist Anti-Semitism and the Rosenberg Spy Trial." *Australian Journal of Politics and History* 49, no. 4 (2003): 501–516.

Miller, Arthur. *The Crucible*. New York: Dramatists Play Service, 1952, 1982.

Miller, Arthur. *Timebends: A Life*. New York: Grove Press, 1987, Penguin, 1995.

Millett, Allan R. *The War for Korea, 1950–1951: They Came from the North*. Lawrence: University Press of Kansas, 2010.

Mitrovich, Gregory. *Undermining the Kremlin: America's Strategy to Subvert the Soviet Bloc, 1947–1956*. Ithaca, NY: Cornell University Press, 2000.

Morgan, Ted. *Reds: McCarthyism in Twentieth Century America*. New York: Random House, 2004.

Morgan, Ted. "The Rosenberg Jury." *Esquire* 83, no. 5 (May 1975): 104–132.

Moynihan, Daniel P. *Secrecy: The American Experience*. New Haven, CT: Yale University Press, 1998.

Murphy, Brenda. *Congressional Theatre: Dramatizing McCarthyism on Stage, Film, and Television*. New York: Cambridge University Press, 1999.

Murphy, Bruce Allen. *Wild Bill: The Legend and Life of William O. Douglas*. New York: Random House, 2003.

Nadel, Gerry. ". . . And the Rosenberg Kids." *Esquire* 83, no. 5 (May 1975): 106–107.

Navasky, Victor S. *Naming Names*. New York: Viking/Penguin, 1980.

Neustadt, Richard E. *Presidential Power and the Modern Presidents: The Politics of Leadership from Roosevelt to Reagan*. New York: Free Press, 1980.

Neville, John F. *The Press, the Rosenbergs and the Cold War*. Westport, CT: Praeger, 1995.

Newton, Jim. *Eisenhower: The White House Years*. New York: Doubleday, 2011.

Niebuhr, Reinhold. *Christian Realism and Political Problems*. New York: Scribner, 1953.

Niebuhr, Reinhold. "Communism and the Protestant Clergy." *Look* 17, no. 23 (November 17, 1953): 37.

Okun, Rob A., ed. *The Rosenbergs: Collected Visions of Artists and Writers*. 2nd ed. Montague, MA: Cultural Forecast, 1988, 1993.

Olmsted, Kathryn S. *Red Spy Queen: A Biography of Elizabeth Bentley*. Chapel Hill: The University of North Carolina Press, 2002.

Olmsted, Kathryn S. "Blond Queens, Red Spiders, and Neurotic Old Maids." *Intelligence and National Security* 19, no. 1 (Spring 2004): 78–91.

Olmsted, Kathryn S. *Real Enemies: Conspiracy Theories and American Democracy, World War I to 9/11*. New York: Oxford University Press, 2009.

Olmsted, Kathryn S. "The Truth About Spies." *Diplomatic History* 35, no. 1 (January 2011): 137–142.

Oshinsky, David M. *A Conspiracy So Immense: The World of Joe McCarthy*. New York: Free Press, 1983, Oxford University Press, 2005.

Oshinsky, David M. *Polio, An American Story: The Crusade That Mobilized the Nation Against the 20th Century's Most Feared Disease*. New York: Oxford University Press, 2005.

Osgood, Kenneth. *Total Cold War: Eisenhower's Secret Propaganda Battle at Home and Abroad.* Lawrence: University Press of Kansas, 2006.

Osgood, Kenneth, and Andrew K. Frank, eds. *Selling War in Media Age: The Presidency and Public Opinion in the American Century.* Gainesville: University Press of Florida, 2010.

Painter, David S. *The Cold War: An International History.* London: Routledge, 1999.

Parrish, Michael E. "Cold War Justice: The Supreme Court and the Rosenbergs." *American Historical Review* 82, no. 4 (October 1977): 805–842.

Parrish, Michael E. "Review Essay: Soviet Espionage and the Cold War." *Diplomatic History* 25, no. 1 (Winter 2001): 105–120.

Parry-Giles, Shawn J. *The Rhetorical Presidency, Propaganda, and the Cold War, 1945–1955.* Westport: Praeger, 2002.

Philipson, Ilene. *Ethel Rosenberg: Beyond the Myth.* New York: Franklin Watts, 1988.

Plummer, Brenda Gayle. *Rising Wind: Black Americans and U.S. Foreign Affairs, 1935–1960.* Chapel Hill: University of North Carolina Press, 1996.

Plummer, Brenda Gayle, ed. *Window on Freedom: Race, Civil Rights, and Foreign Affairs, 1945–1988.* Chapel Hill: University of North Carolina Press, 2003.

Preston, Andrew. "Monsters Everywhere: A Genealogy of National Security." *Diplomatic History* 38, no. 3 (June 2014): 477–500.

Preston, Andrew. *Sword of the Spirit, Shield of Faith: Religion in American War and Diplomacy.* New York: Knopf, 2012.

Rabe, Stephen G. *The Killing Zone: The United States Wages Cold War in Latin America.* New York: Oxford University Press, 2011.

Radosh, Ronald. "A Tale of Two Trials." *World Affairs Journal* (May/June 2012): 80–87.

Radosh, Ronald, and Joyce Milton. *The Rosenberg File.* New Haven, CT: Yale University Press, 1983, 1997.

Rauchway, Eric. *Murdering McKinley: The Making of Theodore Roosevelt's America.* New York: Hill and Wang, 2003.

Reeves, Thomas C. *The Life and Times of Joe McCarthy.* New York: Stein and Day, 1982; Lanham, MD: Madison Books, 1997.

Redish, Martin H. *The Logic of Persecution: Free Expression and the McCarthy Era.* Redwood City, CA: Stanford University Press, 2005.

Rhodes, Richard. *The Making of the Atomic Bomb.* New York: Simon & Schuster, 1986.

Roberts, Sam. *The Brother: The Untold Story of the Rosenberg Case.* New York: Random House, 2001, 2003.

Robeson, Paul. *Here I Stand.* Boston: Beacon Press, 1958, 1988.

Rodgers, Daniel T. *Atlantic Crossings: Social Politics in a Progressive Age.* Cambridge, MA: Harvard University Press, 1998.

Rorabaugh, W. J. *Kennedy and the Promise of the Sixties.* Cambridge: Cambridge University Press, 2002.

Rose, Lisle A. *The Cold War Comes to Main Street: America in 1950.* Lawrence: University Press of Kansas, 1999.

Rose, Richard. *The Postmodern President.* 2nd ed. Chatham, NJ: Chatham House, 1991.

Rovere, Richard. *Senator Joe McCarthy.* New York: Harcourt Brace, 1959.

Sarat, Austin. *Gruesome Spectacles: Botched Executions and America's Death Penalty.* Redwood City, CA: Stanford University Press, 2014.

Schlanger, Zoe, "Miriam Moscowitz, 98, Fights to Clear Her Name of McCarthy-Era Charges." *Newsweek*, August 26, 2014.

Schneir, Walter, and Miriam Schneir. *Invitation to an Inquest.* New York: Pantheon, 1965, 1983; Penguin, 1974.

Schneir, Walter, and Miriam Schneir. *Final Verdict: What Really Happened in the Rosenberg Case.* Brooklyn: Melville House, 2010.

Schrecker, Ellen, ed. *Cold War Triumphalism: The Misuse of History after the Fall of Communism.* New York: Free Press, 2004.

Schrecker, Ellen. *Many Are the Crimes: McCarthyism in America.* New York: Little Brown, 1998.

Schrecker, Ellen. *No Ivory Tower: McCarthyism and the Universities.* New York: Oxford University Press, 1986.

Sharlitt, James. *Fatal Error: The Miscarriage of Justice That Sealed the Rosenbergs' Fate.* New York: Scribner, 1989.

Shaw, John T. *JFK in the Senate: Pathway to the Presidency.* New York: St. Martin's, 2013.

Sibley, Katherine A. S. *Red Spies in America: Stolen Secrets and the Dawn of the Cold War.* Lawrence: University Press of Kansas, 2004.

Simon, Rita J., and Dagny A. Blaskovich. *A Comparative Analysis of Capital Punishment: Statutes, Policies, Frequencies, and Public Attitudes the World Over.* New York: Lexington Books, 2002.

Skowronek, Stephen. *The Politics Presidents Make: Leadership from John Adams to George Bush.* Cambridge, MA: Belknap Press/Harvard University Press, 1993.

Slutsky, Beth. *Gendering Radicalism: Women and Communism in Twentieth-Century California.* Lincoln: University of Nebraska Press, 2015.

Smith, Gary Scott. *Religion in the Oval Office: The Religious Lives of American Presidents.* New York: Oxford University Press, 2015.

Snyder, Brad. "Taking Great Cases: Lessons from the Rosenberg Case." *Vanderbilt Law Review* 63, no. 4 (May 2010): 885–956.

Sorin, Gerald. *Howard Fast: Life and Literature in the Left Lane.* Bloomington: Indiana University Press, 2012.

Statler, Kathryn C., and Andrew L. Johns, eds. *The Eisenhower Administration, the Third World, and the Globalization of the Cold War.* Lanham, MD: Rowman & Littlefield, 2006.

Statler, Kathryn C. *Replacing France: The Origins of American Intervention in Vietnam.* Lexington: The University Press of Kentucky, 2007.

Stebbins, Richard P. *The United States in World Affairs, 1953.* New York: Council on Foreign Relations/Harper & Brothers, 1955.

Stueck, William. *Rethinking the Korean War: A New Diplomatic and Strategic History.* Princeton, NJ: Princeton University Press, 2002.

Stueck, William. *The Korean War: An International History.* Princeton, NJ: Princeton University Press, 1995.

Temkin, Moshik. *The Sacco-Vanzetti Affair: America on Trial.* New Haven, CT: Yale University Press, 2009.

Theoharis, Athan, and John Stuart Cox. *The Boss: J. Edgar Hoover and the Great American Inquisition.* Philadelphia: Temple University Press, 1988.

Theoharis, Athan. *Chasing Spies: How the FBI Failed in Counterintelligence But Promoted the Politics of McCarthyism in the Cold War Years.* Chicago: Ivan R. Dee, 2002.

Theoharis, Athan, ed. *The FBI: A Comprehensive Reference Guide.* Phoenix: The Oryx Press, 1999.

Truman, Harry S. *Truman Speaks: The Principal Speeches and Addresses of President Harry S. Truman.* Whitefish, MT: Literary Licensing, 2011.

Tudda, Chris. *The Truth Is Our Weapon: The Rhetorical Diplomacy of Dwight D. Eisenhower and John Foster Dulles.* Baton Rouge: Louisiana State University Press, 2006.

Usdin, Steven T. "The Rosenberg Ring Revealed: Industrial-Scale Conventional and Nuclear Espionage." *Journal of Cold War Studies* 11, no. 3 (Summer 2009): 91–143.

Usdin, Steven T. *Engineering Communism: How Two Americans Spied for Stalin and Founded the Soviet Silicon Valley.* New Haven, CT: Yale University Press, 2005.

Von Eschen, Penny M. *Race Against Empire: Black Americans and Anticolonialism, 1937–1957.* Ithaca, NY: Cornell University Press, 1997.

Walker, Samuel. *In Defense of American Liberties: A History of the ACLU.* New York: Oxford University Press, 1990.

Warshaw, Shirley Anne, ed. *Reexamining the Eisenhower Presidency.* Westport, CT: Greenwood Press, 1993.

Warshow, Robert. *The Immediate Experience: Movies, Comics, Theatre and Other Aspects of Popular Culture.* New York: Doubleday, 1962; Cambridge, MA: Harvard University Press, 2001.

Weales, Gerald, ed. *Arthur Miller: Death of a Salesman, Text and Criticism*. New York: Penguin, Viking, 1949, 1967.

Weathersby, Kathryn. "Soviet Aims in Korea and the Origins of the Korean War, 1945–1950: New Evidence from Russian Archives." Working Paper No. 8. Cold War International History Project, Woodrow Wilson International Center for Scholars (November 1993): 5–37.

Weinstein, Allen, and Alexander Vassiliev. *The Haunted Wood: Soviet Espionage in America—The Stalin Era*. New York: Random House, 1999.

Wellerstein, Alex. "A Tale of Openness and Secrecy: The Philadelphia Story." *Physics Today* (May 2012): 47–53.

Wexley, John. *The Judgment of Julius and Ethel Rosenberg*. New York: Cameron & Kahn, 1955. Reprint, New York: Ballantine Books, 1977.

White, G. Edward. *Alger Hiss's Looking-Glass Wars: The Covert Life of a Soviet Spy*. New York: Oxford University Press, 2004.

Whitfield, Stephen J. *The Culture of the Cold War*. 2nd ed. Baltimore: Johns Hopkins University Press, 1991, 1996.

Wiener, Jon. *How We Forgot the Cold War: A Historical Journey Across America*. Berkeley: University of California Press, 2012.

Winkler, Allan M. *Life Under a Cloud: American Anxiety About the Atom*. New York: Oxford University Press, 1993.

Wyden Peter. *Day One: Before Hiroshima and After*. New York: Simon & Schuster, 1984.

Zion, Sidney. *The Autobiography of Roy Cohn*. Secaucus, NJ: Lyle Stuart, 1988.

INDEX